This excellent *Handbook* provides an exceptio the Jewish roots of Jesus and Christianity. It is with effective and concise discussions of a bro presented by a team of outstanding scholars... in particular strength is the fact that a good number of contributors are Jewish believers in Jesus who have a special sensitivity to the continuities between Jewish and Christian worlds. The *Handbook* is positive in its orientation and, given the variety of contributors, amazingly coherent. Readers will come away with a richer understanding of the whole Bible and the history of salvation.

Donald A. Hagner
George Eldon Ladd Professor Emeritus of New Testament
Fuller Theological Seminary

So just how Jewish is the Christian teaching about Jesus? The answer is quite a lot. So much so that it is just about everywhere. That is what *A Handbook on the Jewish Roots of the Christian Faith* shows so admirably. A reading of this book will demonstrate just how rooted the Christian faith is in Jewish hope.

Darrell L. Bock, Executive Director for Cultural Engagement and Senior
Research Professor of New Testament Studies
Dallas Theological Seminary

This helpful and well-informed work edited by Evans and Mishkin rightly highlights the Jewish identity and context of Jesus and his earliest followers.

Craig S. Keener, F. M. and Ada Thompson Professor of Biblical Studies
Asbury Theological Seminary

An exciting volume by a diverse range of scholars on the Jewish origins of the early church and the New Testament. Readers interested in biblical backgrounds, ancient history, Jewish institutions and festivals, how the Old Testament relates to the New Testament, how Jesus and the apostles related to other Jews, or simply pining for a deeper knowledge of the Bible will benefit immensely from this book. It is useful too with its account of how Messianic Jews and Christian Arabs can worship together in Israel.

Michael F. Bird, Academic Dean and Lecturer in Theology
Ridley College, Melbourne, Australia

Through Jesus of Nazareth, Christianity is deeply entrenched in Judaism. That is commonplace today. This Handbook on the Jewish Roots of the Christian Faith, however, is unique in two ways. No other work covers such a wide range of relevant topics from Old Testament covenants and Israelite kingdoms to modern debates about Messianism. Moreover, several of the authors are Messianic Jews, clearly showing that this movement now has a voice in scholarly discussion.

Rainer Riesner, Professor Emeritus of New Testament
University of Dortmund, Germany

The question of the Jewish roots of Christian faith comes with historical as well as theological implications, demanding not only knowledge but also due sensitivity. Craig A. Evans and David Mishkin have, together with their coworkers, admirably succeeded in doing precisely this. A comprehensive handbook may appear as a contradiction in terms. Through its brief and concise contributions the book is, indeed, a handbook, but the way it highlights the questions and issues that come into play in this field is really complete. The book will be a most helpful and needed tool for students, pastors, and teachers.

Karl Olav Sandnes, Professor, New Testament
MF Norwegian School of Theology, Religion and Society

Craig Evans and David Mishkin are to be heartily congratulated for this very helpful compendium on the Jewish roots of Christianity, a subject that is much too often neglected in theological discussions. There can be little doubt that the first subject covered—God's covenant with Abraham, Moses, and David—is most crucial for understanding the central role played by Jesus as the Messiah in the New Testament Scriptures. Moreover, Old Testament prophecy, Jewish feasts, atonement, and the Temple are core topics for comprehending Jesus' ministry as the Messiah in whom the Old Testament Scriptures find fulfillment. The section on the Jewish roots of Jesus and his early followers is mandatory reading for anyone interested in the historical background of the Christian faith.

Pieter Gert van der Veen, PhD habil.
Protestant Faculty of Mainz University, Germany

A
Handbook
on the
Jewish
Roots
of the
Christian
Faith

A Handbook on the Jewish Roots of the Christian Faith

Edited by

Craig A. Evans

and David Mishkin

HENDRICKSON
PUBLISHERS

A Handbook on the Jewish Roots of the Christian Faith

© 2019 by Craig A. Evans and David Mishkin

Hendrickson Publishers Marketing, LLC
P. O. Box 3473
Peabody, Massachusetts 01961-3473
www.hendrickson.com

ISBN 978-1-68307-164-8

Printed in the United States of America

First Printing—March 2019

Library of Congress Cataloging-in-Publication

A catalog record for this title is available from the Library of Congress.
Hendrickson Publishers Marketing, LLC ISBN 978-1-68307-164-8

Contents

Acknowledgments — xi

Contributors — xiii

Abbreviations — xv

Introduction — 1
    David Mishkin

Part I: The Soil

Chapter 1: God's Plan for Israel

1.1   The Kingdom and the Covenants — 9
    Noam Hendren

1.2   The Abrahamic Covenant — 13
    Seth D. Postell

1.3   The Mosaic Covenant — 17
    Kevin Chen

1.4   The Davidic Covenant — 22
    Brian J. Kinzel

1.5   The New Covenant — 28
    Noam Hendren

Chapter 2: God's Plan for the Nations

2.1   The Nations in the Torah — 34
    Yohanan Stanfield

2.2   The Nations in the Prophets — 40
    Brian J. Kinzel

2.3   The Nations in the Writings — 45
    Kevin Chen

Chapter 3: Messianic Prophecies

3.1   The Messiah in the Torah — 50
    Seth D. Postell

3.2   The Messiah in the Prophets — 55
    Michael L. Brown

3.3   The Messiah in the Writings   59
      Brian J. Kinzel

3.4   New Testament Use of the Old Testament   65
      Craig A. Evans

Chapter 4: Appointed Times

4.1   The Sabbath   72
      Eitan Bar

4.2   Passover, Unleavened Bread, Firstfruits   74
      Erez Soref

4.3   Shavuot   80
      Golan Brosh

4.4   The Fall Feasts   83
      Noam Hendren

4.5   Purim   89
      Golan Brosh

4.6   Hanukkah   92
      Eitan Bar

Chapter 5: Tabernacle and Temple

5.1   Atonement in the Old Testament   96
      Michael L. Brown

5.2   Salvation in the Old Testament   101
      Michael L. Brown

5.3   Jesus and the Tabernacle/Temple   105
      George H. Guthrie

Part II: The Roots

Chapter 6: The Jewish World of Jesus

6.1   The Jewish Land and Archaeology of Jesus   115
      Sheila Gyllenberg

6.2   Jewish Groups in the First Century   123
      Jim R. Sibley

6.3   Jewish Literature of the Second Temple Period   130
      Sheila Gyllenberg

6.4   The Jewish Institutions   138
      Andreas Stutz

6.5   Messianic Expectations   144
      Andreas Stutz

Chapter 7: The Jewish Life and Identity of Jesus

7.1   The Life and Ministry of Jesus   151
      Craig A. Evans

7.2   Son of Man: Daniel 7   157
      Andreas Stutz

7.3   "I Am" Statements   159
      Andreas J. Köstenberger

7.4   Trials and Crucifixion   164
      Andreas J. Köstenberger

7.5   Early Jesus-Devotion   171
      Larry W. Hurtado

Chapter 8: The Jewish Teachings of Jesus

8.1   Jesus as Rabbi   178
      Andreas J. Köstenberger

8.2   The Lord's Prayer   184
      Scot McKnight

8.3   The Sermon on the Mount   188
      Scot McKnight

8.4   Parables of Jesus   193
      Russell Morton

Part III: The Trunk

Chapter 9: The Jewish Disciples

9.1   The Jewish Disciples in the Gospels   203
      Andreas J. Köstenberger

9.2   The Jewish Disciples in the Book of Acts   206
      Jim R. Sibley

9.3   The Jewishness of the Book of Hebrews   214
      George H. Guthrie

9.4   Jews and Judaism in the Gospel of John   221
      Craig A. Evans

Chapter 10: The Jewish Paul

10.1 Paul's Life   226
      Jason Maston

10.2 Paul in Modern Scholarship   232
      Brian S. Rosner

10.3 Paul's View of the Law   238
      Brian S. Rosner

10.4 Paul's View of Israel and the Nations   244
      Jim R. Sibley

Chapter 11: The Jewish Message: Resurrection

11.1 Resurrection in the Old Testament   250
      Kevin Chen

11.2 Resurrection in the Second Temple Period   255
      Jason Maston

11.3 Resurrection in Paul's Theology   261
      Paul T. Sloan

11.4 Jewish Perspectives on the Resurrection of Jesus   266
      David Mishkin

Part IV: The Branches

Chapter 12: The Parting of the Ways

12.1 Early Judaism   275
      David Mishkin

12.2 Early Christianity   281
      Jason Maston

12.3 The Middle Ages   288
      Ray Pritz

Chapter 13: The Mending of the Ways

13.1 Jewish Believers in Jesus in Modern Israel   295
      Erez Soref

13.2 Jewish and Arab Believers in Jesus in Modern Israel   301
      Erez Soref and Thomas Damianos

Index of Modern Authors   309
Index of Ancient Sources   315
Figures   341

Acknowledgments

Several people need to be thanked for the completion of this volume. A few years ago, Seth Postell, the academic dean of Israel College of the Bible (ICB), had the idea for an online video course on the Jewish Roots of Christianity. It is a popular topic that has been addressed from various perspectives. But a scholarly overview of all of the relevant issues was lacking. David put together the online course, which was only able to cover each topic briefly. A number of reading assignments were needed to supplement the material, but there was no single book which included all of the topics covered in the class. Thus, the idea for this book was born. Erez Soref, the president of ICB, saw the value in it and readily endorsed it. The present book is not only a companion for this specific course, but is meant to be a stand-alone work and a scholarly contribution to the discussion. Craig was approached soon afterward, and the project was underway. We'd like to thank Hendrickson Publishers, and specifically Jonathan Kline, for their enthusiasm. Our editor at Hendrickson, Tirzah Frank, provided a keen eye for detail, thoughtful clarifying questions and, most of all, patience. Finally, the twenty-four authors whose articles are included here are the ones who ultimately made this book what it is.

Craig A. Evans
Houston Baptist University

David Mishkin
Israel College of the Bible

Contributors

Eitan Bar (DMin in progress, Dallas Theological Seminary), Israel College of the Bible

Golan Brosh (DMin in progress, Dallas Theological Seminary), Israel College of the Bible

Michael L. Brown (PhD, New York University), FIRE School of Ministry

Kevin Chen (PhD, Golden Gate Baptist Theological Seminary), Union University

Thomas Damianos (PhD in progress, Central University of Nicaragua), Israel College of the Bible

Craig A. Evans (PhD, Claremont Graduate University; DHabil, Karoli Gaspar Reformatus University), Houston Baptist University

George H. Guthrie (PhD, Southwestern Baptist Theological Seminary), Regent College

Sheila Gyllenberg (PhD, Bar Ilan University), Israel College of the Bible

Noam Hendren (ThM, Dallas Theological Seminary), Israel College of the Bible

Larry W. Hurtado (PhD, Case Western Reserve University), University of Edinburgh

Brian J. Kinzel (PhD in progress, Bar Ilan University), Israel College of the Bible

Andreas J. Köstenberger (PhD, Trinity Evangelical Divinity School), Midwestern Baptist Theological Seminary

Jason Maston (PhD, Durham University), Houston Baptist University

Scot McKnight (PhD, University of Nottingham), Northern Seminary

David Mishkin (PhD, University of Pretoria), Israel College of the Bible

Russell Morton (ThD, Lutheran School of Theology at Chicago), Ashland Theological Seminary and Asbury Theological Seminary

Seth D. Postell (PhD, Golden Gate Baptist Theological Seminary), Israel College of the Bible

Ray Pritz (PhD, Hebrew University), The Bible Society in Israel

Brian S. Rosner (PhD, Cambridge University), Ridley College

Jim R. Sibley (PhD, Southwestern Baptist Theological Seminary), Israel College
of the Bible

Paul T. Sloan (PhD, University of St. Andrews), Houston Baptist University

Erez Soref (PsyD, Wheaton Graduate School), Israel College of the Bible

Yohanan Stanfield (PhD, Hebrew University), Lech L'cha

Andreas Stutz (PhD in progress, Southwestern Baptist Theological Seminary),
Israel College of the Bible

Abbreviations

General Abbreviations

Aram.	Aramaic
BCE	before the Common Era
ca.	circa
CE	Common Era
cf.	compare
ch(s).	chapter(s)
d.	died
e.g.	*exempli gratia*, for example
Eng.	English
esp.	especially
ESV	English Standard Version
et al.	*et alii*, and others
frag.	fragment
i.e.	*id est*, that is
Heb.	Hebrew
LXX	Septuagint
MT	Masoretic Text
NASB	New American Standard Bible
NET	New English Translation
NIV	New International Version
NJPS	*Tanakh: The Holy Scriptures: The New JPS Translation according to the Traditional Hebrew Text*
NRSV	New Revised Standard Version
par.	parallel
passim	here and there
pl.	plural
P.Oxy.	Papyrus Oxyrhynchus
RSV	Revised Standard Version
s.v.	*sub verbo*, under the word
v(v).	verse(s)
x	times

Ancient Sources

DEAD SEA SCROLLS

CD	Cairo Genizah copy of the *Damascus Document*
1QH^a	*Hodayot^a*
1Q35	*Hodayot^b*
1QM	*War Scroll*
1QS	*Rule of the Community*
4Q169	*Nahum Pesher*
4Q174	*Florilegium*
4Q246	*Apocryphon of Daniel*
4Q266	*Damascus Document^a*
4Q285	*Sefer ha-Milhamah*
4Q317	*AstrCrypt*
4Q319	*Otot*
4Q320	*Calendrical Document A*
4Q321	*Calendrical Document B^a*
4Q385	*Pseudo-Ezekiel^a*
4Q386	*Pseudo-Ezekiel^b*
4QMMT	*Halakhic Letter*
4Q394	*Halakhic Letter^a*
4Q398	*Halakhic Letter^e*
4Q399	*Halakhic Letter^f*
4Q500	*Benediction*
4Q521	*Messianic Apocalypse*
11Q13	*Melchizedek*
11Q19	*Temple Scroll^a*

APOSTOLIC FATHERS

Barn.	*Epistle of Barnabas*
Did.	*Didache*
Diogn.	*Epistle to Diognetus*

EUSEBIUS

Chron.	*Chronicle*
Dem. ev.	*Demonstration of the Gospel*
Hist. eccl.	*Ecclesiastical History*

HIPPOLYTUS OF ROME

Haer.	*Refutation of All Heresies*

IGNATIUS

Magn.	*To the Magnesians*

JEROME

Vir. ill.	*De viris illustribus*

JOSEPHUS

Ag. Ap.	*Against Apion*
Ant.	*Jewish Antiquities*
J.W.	*Jewish War*
Life	*The Life*

JUSTIN MARTYR

1 Apol.	*First Apology*
Dial.	*Dialogue with Trypho*

PHILO

Decalogue	*On the Decalogue*
Dreams	*On Dreams*
Good Person	*That Every Good Person Is Free*
Spec. Laws	*On the Special Laws*

SUETONIUS

Vesp.	*Vespasian*

TACITUS

Hist.	*Histories*

TERTULLIAN

Adv. Jud.	*Against the Jews*

Journals, Series, and Reference Works

AB	Anchor Bible
ABD	*Anchor Bible Dictionary.* Edited by David Noel Freedman. 6 vols. New York: Doubleday, 1992
ABRL	Anchor Bible Reference Library
ApOTC	Apollos Old Testament Commentary
ASOR	American Schools of Oriental Research
ATDan	Acta Theologica Danica

AzTh	Arbeiten zur Theologie
BA	*Biblical Archaeologist*
BAR	*Biblical Archaeology Review*
BBR	*Bulletin for Biblical Research*
BDAG	Danker, Frederick W., Walter Bauer, William F. Arndt, and F. Wilbur Gingrich. *Greek-English Lexicon of the New Testament and Other Early Christian Literature.* 3rd ed. Chicago: University of Chicago Press, 2000
BECNT	Baker Exegetical Commentary on the New Testament
BibInt	Biblical Interpretation Series
BSac	*Bibliotheca Sacra*
BZ	*Biblische Zeitschrift*
CBQ	*Catholic Biblical Quarterly*
CBQMS	Catholic Biblical Quarterly Monograph Series
CRINT	Compendia Rerum Iudaicarum ad Novum Testamentum
CTR	*Criswell Theological Review*
DJG	*Dictionary of Jesus and the Gospels.* Edited by Joel B. Green, Jeannine K. Brown, and Nicholas Perrin. 2nd ed. Downers Grove, IL: InterVarsity Press, 2013
DNTB	*Dictionary of New Testament Background.* Edited by Craig A. Evans and Stanley E. Porter. Downers Grove, IL: InterVarsity Press, 2000
DOTP	*Dictionary of the Old Testament: Prophets.* The IVP Bible Dictionary Series. Edited by Mark J. Boda and J. Gordan McConville. Downers Grove, IL: IVP Academic, 2013
DPL	*Dictionary of Paul and His Letters.* Edited by Gerald F. Hawthorne and Ralph P. Martin. Downers Grove, IL: InterVarsity Press, 1993
DSD	*Dead Sea Discoveries*
EBib	*Etudes bibliques*
EDB	*Eerdmans Dictionary of the Bible.* Edited by David Noel Freedman. Grand Rapids: Eerdmans, 2000
EDNT	*Exegetical Dictionary of the New Testament.* Edited by Horst Balz and Gerhard Schneider. ET. 3 vols. Grand Rapids: Eerdmans, 1990–1993.
EKKNT	Evangelisch-katholischer Kommentar zum Neuen Testament
EncJud	*Encyclopedia Judaica.* Edited by Fred Skolnik and Michael Berenbaum. 2nd ed. 22 vols. Detroit: Macmillan Reference USA, 2007
FRLANT	Forschungen zur Religion und Literatur des Alten und Neuen Testaments
GNS	*Good News Studies*

Herm	*Hermanthena*
HThKAT	Herders Theologischer Kommentar zum Alten Testament
HTR	*Harvard Theological Review*
HTS	Harvard Theological Studies
HUCA	*Hebrew Union College Annual*
IBC	Interpretation: A Bible Commentary for Teaching and Preaching
ICC	International Critical Commentary
IDB	*The Interpreter's Dictionary of the Bible.* Edited by George A. Buttrick. 4 vols. New York: Abingdon, 1962
Int	*Interpretation*
JAOS	*Journal of the American Oriental Society*
JBL	*Journal of Biblical Literature*
JBQ	*Jewish Bible Quarterly*
JETS	*Journal of the Evangelical Theological Society*
JJS	*Journal of Jewish Studies*
JQR	*Jewish Quarterly Review*
JR	*Journal of Religion*
JSJ	*Journal for the Study of Judaism in the Persian, Hellenistic, and Roman Periods*
JSNT	*Journal for the Study of the New Testament*
JSNTSup	Journal for the Study of the New Testament Supplement Series
JSOTSup	Journal for the Study of the Old Testament Supplement Series
JTS	*Journal of Theological Studies*
LCC	Library of Christian Classics
MSJ	*The Master's Seminary Journal*
NAC	New American Commentary
NIB	*The New Interpreter's Bible.* Edited by Leander E. Keck. 12 vols. Nashville: Abingdon, 1994–2004
NICNT	New International Commentary on the New Testament
NICOT	New International Commentary on the Old Testament
NIDB	*New Interpreter's Dictionary of the Bible.* Edited by Katharine Doob Sakenfeld. 5 vols. Nashville: Abingdon, 2006–2009.
NIDNTT	*New International Dictionary of New Testament Theology.* Edited by Colin Brown. 4 vols. Grand Rapids: Zondervan, 1975–1978
NIDOTTE	*New International Dictionary of Old Testament Theology and Exegesis.* Edited by Willem A. VanGemeren. 5 vols. Grand Rapids: Zondervan, 1997
NovT	*Novum Testamentum*

NovTSup	Supplements to Novum Testamentum
NTAbh	Neutestamentliche Abhandlungen
NTS	*New Testament Studies*
OTL	Old Testament Library
PNTC	Pelican New Testament Commentaries
RBS	Resources for Biblical Study
RevExp	*Review and Expositor*
RGG	*Religion in Geschichte und Gegenwart.* Edited by Hans Dieter Betz. 4th ed. Tübingen: Mohr Siebeck, 1998–2007
SANT	Studien zum Alten und Neuen Testaments
SBFCMi	Studium Biblicum Franciscanum, Collectio Minor
SBLSBS	Society of Biblical Literature Sources for Biblical Study
SBT	Studies in Biblical Theology
SJLA	Studies in Judaism in Late Antiquity
SNTSMS	Society for New Testament Studies Monograph Series
SNTW	Studies of the New Testament and Its World
STDJ	Studies on the Texts of the Desert of Judah
StPB	Studia Post-biblica
SUNT	Studien zur Umwelt des Neuen Testaments
TDNT	*Theological Dictionary of the New Testament.* Edited by Gerhard Kittel and Gerhard Friedrich. Translated by Geoffrey W. Bromiley. 10 vols. Grand Rapids: Eerdmans, 1964–1976.
TDOT	*Theological Dictionary of the Old Testament.* Edited by G. Johannes Botterweck and Helmer Ringgren. Translated by John T. Willis et al. 8 vols. Grand Rapids: Eerdmans, 1974–2006
TLOT	*Theological Lexicon of the Old Testament.* Edited by Ernst Jenni, with assistance from Claus Westermann. Translated by Mark E. Biddle. 3 vols. Peabody, MA: Hendrickson, 1997
TNTC	Tyndale New Testament Commentaries
TOTC	Tyndale Old Testament Commentaries
TRE	*Theologische Realenzyklopädie.* Edited by Gerhard Krause and Gerhard Müller. Berlin: de Gruyter, 1977–
TSAJ	Texte und Studien zum antiken Judentum
VT	*Vetus Testamentum*
VTSup	Supplements to Vetus Testamentum
WBC	World Biblical Commentary
WMANT	Wissenschaftliche Monographien zum Alten und Neuen Testament
WUNT	Wissenschaftliche Untersuchungen zum Neuen Testament
ZNW	*Zeitschrift für die neutestamentliche Wissenschaft und die Kunde der älteren Kirche*

Introduction

David Mishkin

It is no longer a novelty to say that Jesus was a Jew. In fact, the term "Jewish roots" has become somewhat of a cliché in books, articles, and perhaps especially on the internet. The popular interest is an outgrowth of scholarship which began over two hundred years ago, and both Christians and Jews have been involved. Each group followed a different trajectory, but the end result is undeniable: any discussion about Jesus of Nazareth must not only include but highlight the fact that he cannot be understood apart from his Jewish context. It is among the few things upon which virtually all contemporary scholars agree.

The Christian quest for the historical Jesus has been well documented (Evans 2008; Charlesworth 2014). In the beginning there was no interest in the Jewishness of Jesus as scholars were addressing more fundamental issues. This trend is usually traced back to Samuel Reimarus (at least among German scholars), whose work in the late 1700s was so radical that it was published only posthumously. Nineteenth-century figures such as David Friedrich Strauss, Ernst Renan, and many others attempted to find the "historical Jesus" as opposed to the "Christ of faith." There were two main issues, broadly speaking, that fueled this trend. The first was Enlightenment rationalism, which doubted (or outright denied) the possibility of supernatural events. The second was the fact that the canonical Gospels do not attempt to record history in the same way as modern historians (Burridge 2004). Despite the fact that they were not looking for a Jewish Jesus, their approach demanded some interaction with first-century Jewish groups, Jewish religious practices of the day, and the geography of Judea and the Galilee. The Jewish context was a peripheral reality. A seemingly endless number of authors attempted to explain who Jesus "really" was and what he "really" did. By the early twentieth century, however, this *First* (or *Old*) *Quest* was ultimately declared a failure (Schweitzer 1910).

What emerged in its wake is sometimes called the "no quest" era, largely inspired by Rudolph Bultmann's proclamation that it was impossible to construct the life of Jesus. This would have a profound effect on all subsequent New Testament scholarship. Soon afterward, any notion of a Jewish Jesus would take an even greater step backward with the arrival of the Nazi regime. Obviously, Nazis could not have a Jewish Jesus, and they went to great lengths to promote a perverted version of the New Testament's message (Heschel 2008). With the help of some of Germany's leading theologians, they formed the Institute for the Study and Eradication of Jewish Influence on German Religious Life. Galilean residents, it was declared, were actually "Aryans" and only the residents of Judea (whom Jesus spoke against) were Jews. Infamously, Walter Grundmann declared that Jesus "was no Jew" (Grundmann 1941, 165–75). An intricate web of absurdities and propaganda was needed in this attempt to deny the Jewishness of Jesus. Ironically, the grand scope of this project illustrates how thoroughly Jewish the New Testament actually is. The Jewish aspects cannot simply be dismissed by providing an alternative explanation for one or two verses.

The first hint of progress came in the 1950s when some scholars (including students of Bultmann's) began to declare that it *is* possible to know at least some things about Jesus. This is usually regarded as the start of the *Second* (or *New*) *Quest* for the historical Jesus. There was still no specific focus on the Jewishness of Jesus, but again, placing him in history meant placing him in context. It would be about three more decades before scholars were ready to interact more seriously with the world of Second Temple Judaism. This was one of the key factors leading to the *Third Quest* (Witherington 1997), which has focused on understanding Jesus as a Jew in a Jewish world.

Jewish scholarship on Jesus had different motivations, although its roots may also be traced to the late 1700s. The Enlightenment was giving way to a new Europe and a new situation for Jews (Mendes-Flohr and Reinharz 2011). They would no longer be confined to ghettos, and in some places (particularly in Germany) they were even allowed to enter public universities. This opened up a whole new world, leading to the emergence of Reform Judaism in the nineteenth century. A number of traditional (Orthodox) Jewish ideas were challenged. The belief in the transmigration of the soul replaced the concept of bodily resurrection, the concept of the messiah was no longer an individual but an era, and the Tanakh (Old Testament) was seen more as a human than a divine creation (Meyer 1995). At this time, Jewish scholars first began to interact with the New Testament. Since much of the "Christian" scholarship of the day was critical and not necessarily bound to a faith commitment, Jewish scholars were able to join the conversation. As Christian scholars were busy searching for the historical Jesus, Jewish scholars had broader objectives. Pioneers such as Abraham Geiger were more concerned with how the Jewish community should interact with Christendom as a whole than with deciphering the identity of the man from Nazareth. Nevertheless, the Jewish study of Jesus begins here.

In the twentieth century, Jewish scholars began to interact directly with the historical Jesus. Books by Claude Montefiore, Joseph Klausner, David Flusser, Geza Vermes, and others set the standard. A number of books have documented this trend, which is often referred to as the Jewish "reclamation" of Jesus (see Jacob 1974; Hagner 1984; Homolka 2015). The *Third Quest* was in some ways an *outgrowth of* this interest among such Jewish scholars. At the same time, the *Third Quest* also served as a *catalyst for* the wave of Jewish scholars that followed. This field of study has grown exponentially in the early years of the twenty-first century, as demonstrated by the publication of the *Jewish Annotated New Testament* (Levine and Brettler 2011). This is the work of fifty Jewish scholars commenting on each book of the New Testament, along with a number of additional articles. The Jewishness of Jesus is here presumed and even Paul is understood to be a Jew, although he has not quite been "reclaimed" to the extent that Jesus has.

But, what does the Jewishness of Jesus actually mean, and why is this important to both Christians and Jews? These are among the questions which are addressed in this volume. This is not the first book on the Jewish roots of the New Testament and the Christian faith (see Wilson 1990; Schwartz 1992; Scott 2000; Bauckham 2010; Johnson 2017). But, it is unique in several ways. First, it is a "handbook," which means it is meant to provide a scholarly but accessible overview of a variety of relevant topics. It is also multi-authored. About half of the contributors are (or have been) on the faculty of Israel College of the Bible. Most of these authors are Jewish and/or Israeli citizens, and believers in Jesus as the Messiah. This perspective complements the perspectives of the traditional Jewish and Christian communities, which were mentioned above. Finally, the scope of topics covered below is vast. The primacy of the Jewish Jesus (as opposed to the coincidentally Jewish Jesus of past research) is not an end in itself. It raises questions regarding history and theology, but it also has ramifications for current events. The word "Roots" in the title is meant to have an overarching connotation, referring not only to antecedence but also to an ongoing interconnectedness.

We begin in "The Soil." The new appreciation of the Jewish Jesus must recognize the importance of *his* Bible, the Tanakh (note: in this volume authors may variously use the terms Old Testament, Tanakh, Hebrew Scriptures, or Hebrew Bible). Debates throughout history have often centered on a small handful of verses and whether or not they find their fulfillment in the New Testament claims. But, the subject is much greater than this. The New Testament authors immersed their message in the words and themes of the Tanakh. This is hardly a peripheral issue, and as will be seen below, the Tanakh itself provides the best commentary and explanation of its own intentions. An understanding of Jewish exegesis is valuable as well.

The following section, "The Roots," grows naturally from the soil. This section covers first-century beliefs, practices, literature, institutions, and geography. It also examines the life and teachings of Jesus. These are the issues that are usually addressed in works about the Jewish roots of Jesus and the New Testament. The articles provide a succinct summary of the latest scholarship.

The next section, "The Trunk," focuses on the immediate aftermath of the life of Jesus. This includes his resurrection and the movement that emerged from it. It was nothing if not a Jewish movement, and it was understood to be a continuation of God's plan throughout the Tanakh. But, were the benefits meant to be only for Jews? This question dominated the very first church council in history (Acts 15), and it was decided that, based on God's plan throughout the Tanakh, gentiles could join the fold without needing to become Jews. Paul was tasked with bringing the message to the gentiles, yet he neither forgot his own people nor excluded them from his message.

Finally, we arrive at "The Branches," which begin in the years immediately following the early church. There has been much discussion about the so-called "parting of the ways" (Dunn 1991; 1992; Boyarin 2004; Yuval 2006). Prior to the *Third Quest* it was commonly assumed that with the coming of Jesus, "Judaism" and "Christianity" naturally and immediately developed as two mutually exclusive entities. Actually, the process took not just decades but centuries. As the Jewish people were dispersed from Israel (as the land is called in Matt 2:20–21), and as the gentile movement became dominant, the Jewish roots of Christianity began to dissipate. The message became less Jewish, non-Jewish, and then all too quickly anti-Jewish. The corporate remnant of Jewish believers in Jesus would disappear by the fourth century, only to return in the modern period. By the Middle Ages, any semblance of a Jewish Jesus was at best seen as a historical oddity, and the Jewish community had no interest in the non-Jewish, "European" Jesus being proclaimed by those who were persecuting them. This history of persecution is long and painful and must never be forgotten (Carroll 2001; Cohen 2007). But, it is not the end of the story.

There has also been a *mending of the ways*. In the first one hundred years or so after Jesus, Jews were still living in the land of Israel and there were still Jewish followers of Jesus. In the last century or so, both of these patterns have been restored. The reality of the modern state of Israel presents challenges that are undoubtedly controversial and complicated. But, the return to the land after an extended (almost nineteen hundred years) exile is at the very least an unprecedented situation in history that, along with the scriptural record, must be addressed by those who take the Bible seriously (and is compelling evidence for those who do not!). Similarly, the re-emergence of Jewish believers in Jesus has presented its own set of challenges, and their history has become a topic of academic interest (Skarsaune and Hvalvik 2007; Pritz 1992; Sobel 1974; Jones 2012; Cohn-Sherbok 2001; Harris-Shapiro 1999; Darby 2010). The contemporary remnant, particularly in the United States and Israel, is becoming more difficult to ignore.

This collection of articles is meant to be a comprehensive yet concise primer on the Jewish roots of the Christian faith. It does not claim to be the final word on the subject, although it does seek to highlight the topics that should be considered in this field of study. Knowledge of the Jewish roots of Christianity is valuable to the extent that it sheds light on both the New Testament itself and Jewish-Christian relations (in history and today).

Works Cited

Bauckham, Richard. 2010. *The Jewish World around the New Testament*. Grand Rapids: Baker Academic.

Boyarin, Daniel. 2004. *Borderlines: The Partitioning of Judaeo-Christianity*. Philadelphia: University of Pennsylvania Press.

Burridge, Richard A. 2004. *What Are the Gospels?* 2nd ed. Grand Rapids: Eerdmans.

Carroll, James. 2001. *Constantine's Sword: The Church and the Jews—A History*. Boston: Houghton Mifflin.

Charlesworth, James H., ed. 2014. *Jesus Research: New Methodologies and Perceptions—The Second Princeton Prague Symposium on Jesus Research*. Grand Rapids: Eerdmans.

Cohen, Jeremy. 2007. *Christkillers: The Jews and the Passion from the Bible to the Big Screen*. Oxford: Oxford University Press.

Cohn-Sherbok, Daniel. 2001. *Messianic Judaism: A Critical Anthology*. London: Bloomsbury Academic.

Darby, Michael R. 2010. *The Emergence of the Hebrew Christian Movement in Nineteenth-Century Britain*. Leiden: Brill Academic.

Dunn, James D. G. 1991. *The Parting of the Ways: Between Christianity and Judaism and Their Significance for the Character of Christianity*. London: SCM Press.

———, ed. 1992. *Jews and Christians: The Parting of the Ways A.D. 70 to 135*. WUNT 66. Tübingen: Mohr Siebeck.

Evans, Craig A., ed. 2008. *The Routledge Encyclopedia of the Historical Jesus*. Oxford: Routledge.

Grundmann, Walter. 1941. *Jesus der Galiläer und das Judentum*. 2nd ed. Leipzig: Wiegand.

Hagner, Donald. 1984. *The Jewish Reclamation of Jesus*. Grand Rapids: Zondervan, 1984.

Harris-Shapiro, Carol. 1999. *Messianic Judaism: A Rabbi's Journey through Religious Change in America*. Boston: Beacon Press.

Heschel, Susannah. 2008. *The Aryan Jesus: Christian Theologians and the Bible in Nazi Germany*. Princeton University Press.

Homolka, Walter. 2015. *Jesus Reclaimed: Jewish Perspectives on the Nazarene*. New York: Berghahn.

Jacob, Walter. 1974. *Christianity through Jewish Eyes*. Cincinnati: Hebrew Union College.

Johnson, Jeffrey D. 2017. *Jewish Roots: 101*. Eugene, OR: Wipf and Stock.

Jones, F. Stanley, ed. 2012. *The Rediscovery of Jewish Christianity: From Toland to Bauer*. Atlanta: SBL Press.

Levine, Amy-Jill, and Marc Brettler, eds. 2011. *The Jewish Annotated New Testament.* Oxford: Oxford University Press.

Mendes-Flohr, Paul, and Jehuda Reinharz, eds. 2011. *The Jew in the Modern World, a Documentary History.* Oxford: Oxford University Press.

Meyer, Michael A. 1995. *Response to Modernity: A History of the Reform Movement in Judaism.* Detroit: Wayne State University Press.

Pritz, Ray. 1992. *Nazarene Jewish Christianity: From the End of the New Testament Period until Its Disappearance in the Fourth Century.* Jerusalem: Magnus.

Schwartz, Daniel R. 1992. *Studies in the Jewish Backgrounds of Christianity.* WUNT 60. Tübingen: Mohr Siebeck.

Schweitzer, Albert. 1910. *The Quest of the Historical Jesus.* Translated by W. Montgomery. London: A. & C. Black.

Scott, J. Julius, Jr. 2000. *Jewish Backgrounds of the New Testament.* Grand Rapids: Eerdmans.

Skarsaune, Oskar, and Reidar Hvalvik, eds. 2007. *Jewish Believers in Jesus: The Early Centuries.* Peabody, MA: Hendrickson; Grand Rapids: Baker Academic.

Sobel, B. Z. 1974. *Hebrew Christianity: The Thirteenth Tribe.* New York: Wiley & Sons.

Wilson, Marvin R. 1990. *Our Father Abraham: Jewish Roots of the Christian Faith.* Grand Rapids: Eerdmans.

Witherington, Ben, III. 1997. *The Jewish Quest: The Third Search for the Jew of Nazareth.* Downers Grove, IL: IVP Academic.

Yuval, Israel. 2006. *Two Nations in Your Womb.* Berkeley: University of California.

PART I: THE SOIL

CHAPTER 1

God's Plan for Israel

1.1 The Kingdom and the Covenants

Noam Hendren

The absolute and universal sovereignty of God is declared from the first verse of the book of Genesis: "In the beginning God created the heavens and the earth." As the creator of all that exists, God is the absolute Lord of the universe and all that is in it: "The heavens are Yours, the earth also is Yours; the world and all it contains, You have founded them" (Ps 89:11 NASB). As Ps 24:1 declares, "The earth is the LORD's and all it contains, the world, and those who dwell in it." Nevertheless, in the climax of the creation account, God revealed his intent to rule the earth not directly but through human intermediaries created in his image (see Gen 1:26–28; cf. Pss 8; 115:15–16).

Humankind as a whole, male and female, received this mandate from the Lord to fill the earth with life, to bring it under their authority and to rule it as God's representatives (Ross 1988, 112–13). Having been created in God's image (Gen 1:26) and filled with his life (2:7), human beings were fully equipped to fulfill their mandate. Adam and Eve, the perfect couple, were placed in a perfect environment—the garden of Eden—where they were given meaningful work: to nurture and protect the garden, and to extend its borders to cover the entire earth (cf. 1:28, "fill the earth and subdue it"; Hamilton 1990, 139–40). They maintained a perfect relationship with one another, transparent and loving (2:25), and with their Creator, who walked with them there (cf. 3:8). This is the situation concerning which God reflected in Gen 1:31, "God saw all that He had made, and behold, it was very good."

The blessed conditions described in Gen 2 embody God's original, intended purpose for the creation: perfect humankind created in the image of God was to rule over a perfect creation as God's representatives. This is the archetype of the "kingdom of God on earth" as God himself intended it to be (Merrill 1987, 298). The ultimate fulfillment of God's original purpose for humanity and the world becomes the central theme of the Scriptures and of human history: "Your kingdom come. Your will be done, on earth as it is in heaven" (Matt 6:10).

The Fall

Humankind's sinful rebellion against their loving Creator plunged humanity and the world into a renewed chaos, corrupting their nature and bringing them under the curse. Genesis 3 describes the immediate effects of sin on humans and the world which was under their dominion: Adam and Eve experienced true moral guilt (v. 7), alienation from God (vv. 8–10), and alienation from one another (vv. 11–12). Their physical existence would be characterized by painful labor in a cursed world, and ultimately they would die (vv. 16–19). Finally, they experienced separation from the presence of God, expelled from the garden of Eden. Thus, they were cut off from access to the tree of life and the life of God (v. 24).

The Promise

But God was not willing to abandon his plan or the people whom he had made. As he pronounced the curse he also promised and provided redemption. Whereas the serpent had used the woman to bring sin and the curse into the world, God would use her to bring a redeemer, a "seed" who would destroy the satanic interloper, just as a man would kill a snake (Gen 3:15; Kaiser 2009, 43). This promise contains within it the first ray of hope in an otherwise desperate situation: If the source of sin in the world would one day be destroyed, perhaps sin's cursed effects would likewise be reversed and creation itself restored (Vlach 2017, 68–69).

The "seed of the woman" introduces the theme of redemption in the Scriptures. As God intended to rule his perfect world through perfect human beings, so God would raise up a redeemer through fallen humankind. This theme would be developed in the promise to Abraham that "in your seed all the nations of the earth shall be blessed" (Gen 22:18; see 18:18–19); and later in the promise to David that his "seed" would become God's priest and king, restoring humanity and the world to its original "kingdom of God" state (1 Chr 17:14; cf. Isa 11:1–10).

Along with this promise of ultimate redemption, God made an immediate provision for Adam and Eve. "The LORD God made garments of skin for Adam and his wife, and clothed them" (Gen 3:21). According to God's commandment (Gen 2:17), Adam and Eve should have been put to death on the very day that they ate from the tree of the knowledge of good and evil, but God in his grace had another plan. God took an innocent animal and, killing it, made garments of skin to cover the nakedness of Adam and Eve. A death did in fact take place on that day; but it was the death of an innocent substitute which allowed the sinful couple to live on. Substitutionary atonement, as later reflected in the sacrificial system of the Torah, became the divine means for restoring sinful human beings to a limited relationship with the holy God (Merrill 2006, 228). A full and final restoration would require something more.

The Parade of Shame

In spite of God's redemptive act, sinful rebellion continued to dominate human life from that day on. Genesis 4–11 presents the degradation of humanity and vividly demonstrates the need for divine redemptive intervention. Beginning with Cain's murder of Abel, the downward spiral of sinful human beings is laid out before us.

Human sin brings human death, as in the "genealogy of death" from Adam to Noah, which closes each generation with the words "and he died" (Gen 5). The curse of sin is pervasive and, like a steamroller, irresistible. The only exception is Enoch, who "walked with God; and he was not, for God took him" (Gen 5:24), thus introducing another central theme of the Scriptures: to experience God's blessing, even in a world under the curse, one must "walk with God," living in holy fellowship with him (Ross 1988, 174–75).

Universal rebellion brought about universal destruction in the flood (Gen 6–8). But, although God had scoured the world with water, the sinfulness of human beings immediately resurfaced. The renewal of the creation covenant (8:21–9:17) proved illusory. Noah was found lying drunk and naked in his tent, and his son Ham put him to public shame. Noah, in turn, cursed Canaan, Ham's son (Gen 9:20–25). The cycle of sin and curse had resumed and quickly swelled to renewed worldwide rebellion, leading to divine judgment at the Tower of Babel (Gen 11).

Humanity's steady descent had reached a new nadir. Sinful rebellion following sinful rebellion had demonstrated people's total inability to redeem themselves and return to Eden. The absolute necessity of divine intervention—if there was to be any hope for human beings and the world—was now clear beyond all doubt.

The Kingdom and the Covenants

God's intervention began with the call of Abraham, and in three short verses he laid out his plan for world redemption (Gen 12:1–3). God chose Abraham and his descendants to become the object and instrument of his restored blessing in the world, a calling formalized by an unconditional covenant (Gen 15). The Abrahamic covenant formed the bedrock of Israel's unique role in God's redemptive plan and the guarantee that the nation would ultimately fulfill her mission (Lev 26:42–45; Isa 41:8–9; Luke 1:71–75; Rom 11:28–29). The Abrahamic covenant would be further explicated and ultimately realized through three subsequent covenants (Merrill 1987, 297).

In the Sinai covenant, God revealed the conditions under which Israel would enter into her blessing and fulfill her role as "a kingdom of priests," bringing the promised kingdom blessings to the world (Exod 19:4–6; Lev 26:3–13). God also promised that in spite of Israel's rebellion he would bring the nation through severe judgments to sincere, universal national repentance and national redemption "in the latter days" (Deut 4:25–30; 30:1–9; cf. Lev 26:14–45).

In the covenant with David, as illuminated by the prophets, God promised to raise up a redeemer, the seed of David, who as a priest would bring spiritual restoration for wayward Israel and for the world (2 Sam 7:11–16; Isa 49:3–9; 52:13–53:12; 59:16–20); and as judge and king would restore the world to its pristine Edenic state, reestablishing the kingdom of God on earth (Isa 9:1–7; 11:1–10; Jer 23:5–6). The Chronicler summarized the prophetic revelation concerning the priest-king Messiah (Zech 6:11–13; Ps 110) as he rephrased the conclusion of the Davidic covenant: "I will cause him to stand in my house [i.e., to serve as priest] and in my kingdom forever; his throne will be established forever" (1 Chr 17:14, literal translation; cf. 1 Kgs 12:32; 2 Chr 5:14).

In view of Israel's consistent failure to fulfill the demands of the Torah at Sinai, and in his gracious allegiance to his covenant with Abraham, God promised to inaugurate a new covenant, bringing national repentance and spiritual transformation by the outpouring of the spirit of God on the nation (Jer 31:33–34; Ezek 36:24–27; Isa 59:17–20; Zech 12:10–13:6). This transformation would enable Israel to perfectly fulfill the righteous demands of God's Torah and thus to inherit his blessing and become his channel for world redemption, as originally promised to Abraham (Isa 60:1–3, 20; 61:6–9; Ezek 36:27–31; Zech 8:11–13, 20–23).

Works Cited

Hamilton, Victor P. 1990. *The Book of Genesis: Chapters 1–17*. NICOT. Grand Rapids: Eerdmans.

Kaiser, Walter C., Jr. 2009. *The Promise-Plan of God: A Biblical Theology of the Old and New Testaments*. Grand Rapids: Zondervan.

Merrill, Eugene H. 1987. "Covenant and the Kingdom: Genesis 1–3 as Foundation for Biblical Theology." *CTR* 1:295–308.

————. 2006. *Everlasting Dominion: A Theology of the Old Testament*. Nashville: B&H Academic.

Ross, Allen P. 1988. *Creation and Blessing: A Guide to the Study and Exposition of Genesis*. Grand Rapids: Baker Book House.

Vlach, Michael J. 2017. *He Will Reign Forever: A Biblical Theology of the Kingdom of God*. Silverton, OR: Lampion Press.

1.2 The Abrahamic Covenant

Seth D. Postell

Genesis 15 and the making of the Abrahamic covenant is the literary summit of the patriarchal narratives (Gen 12–50). (Actually, a more appropriate name would be "Abramic covenant," as it is made prior to the change of name to Abraham.) From this passage, we can see the landscape of the entire Torah (Pentateuch), and even beyond. This passage picks up on and relates to the three key themes introduced in the first chapter of Genesis—blessing (Gen 15:5; see Gen 1:28; 9:1), seed (Gen 15:3–5; see Gen 1:28; 3:15; 4:25; 9:1, 26), and land (Gen 15:7, 18; see Gen 1:28; 2:10–14). It should be noted that although the word "bless/ing" does not appear in Gen 15, the promise of abundant seed is directly related to the divine blessing in Genesis (Gen 1:22, 28; 9:1; 17:20; 28:3). This passage also anticipates the story of Israel's exodus out of Egypt (Gen 15:13–14) as well as Israel's eventual conquest of the land as recorded in the book of Joshua (Gen 15:16). The making of the Abrahamic covenant comes within the context of two specific promises: the promise of a seed (Gen 15:1–5) and the promise of the land (Gen 15:6–18). The land aspect of the Abrahamic covenant is emphasized in Gen 15:7–21, while the seed aspect is the focus of Gen 17.

The hinge verse joining the promise of the seed with the promise of the land appears in Gen 15:6: "And he believed in the Lord, and he credited it him *as* righteousness" (author's translation). The Abrahamic covenant is given within the context of Abram's faith. At first sight, this chapter presents the recipient of the covenant (Abram) as one who is struggling over God's unfulfilled promises. In fact, every time God refers to a promise in Gen 15, Abram retorts with a question (see Gen 15:2–3 and Gen 15:8).

These questions are so atypical of Abram, the man who has silently obeyed up until this point, that the author is compelled to note that faith was a quintessential quality of Abram's experience with God. The theme of faith appears again within the context of the Mosaic covenant (Exod 19:9). It comes as no surprise, therefore, that the promise of the land is rescinded from the wilderness generation, including Moses and Aaron, because they do not believe (Num 14:11; see 20:12).

The Relationship of the Abrahamic Covenant in Genesis 15 and 17

Before we discuss the meaning of the Abrahamic covenant within its larger literary context, it is important to explain the relationship of Gen 15 and 17 since both narratives describe the making/establishing of a covenant with Abram/

Abraham. Because of the presence of these two separate covenant narratives, some scholars suggest that Gen 15 and 17 represent two distinct covenants, the former an unconditional covenant and the latter a conditional covenant (Williamson 2007; Alexander 2012). The major problem with this view, as is well pointed out by others (Niehaus 2013; Gentry and Wellum 2015; Todd 2017), is the fact that all other passages in the Hebrew Bible (as well as the New Testament) only and always refer to one covenant God made with Abraham, a covenant that was subsequently reconfirmed to Isaac, Jacob, and their descendants (Exod 2:24; Lev 26:42; 2 Kgs 13:23; 1 Chr 16:16; Ps 105:9; Acts 3:25).

How are we to understand, then, the literary and theological relationship of Gen 15 and 17? Why is there an additional covenant in Gen 17 when one has already been made in Gen 15? Are there theological differences between these two covenants, i.e., unconditional vs. conditional covenant? In terms of the need for a second installment of the Abrahamic covenant, it is essential to note that Gen 17 follows the story of Abram and Hagar (Gen 16). In Gen 16, Sarai impatiently pushes her Egyptian maidservant on Abram, who silently acquiesces to her plan. The literary parallels between Sarai's taking of Hagar to give to Abram (Gen 16:3) with Eve's taking of the forbidden fruit to give to Adam (Gen 3:6) suggest that Gen 16 is intended to be understood as a fall narrative (Sailhamer 1992). The literary context suggests that it is best to consider Gen 17 as a covenant renewal that comes in the wake of Abram's failure to trust God's promise specifically concerning the seed, much as Exod 34 is a renewal of the Sinai covenant in light of Israel's worship of the golden calf in Exod 32.

In terms of the added conditional aspects of the Abrahamic covenant in Gen 17 which were not originally part of the covenant in Gen 15 (e.g., circumcision; Gen 17:9–14), it is necessary to consider the fact that the unconditional nature of God's earlier promises to Abram and his seed already contain elements of conditionality (Gen 12–15). For instance, the promises in Gen 12:2–3 are contingent upon Abram's obedience to "go forth" from his land (Gen 12:1). In Gen 15, Abram is commanded to bring and prepare the covenantal sacrifice (Gen 15:9). Jeffrey Niehaus (2013, 260–61) explains the conditional aspects of God's unconditional covenant with Abraham quite well when he writes,

> The Abrahamic covenant is both unconditional and conditional. It is unconditional in the sense that the Lord, having instituted it, will see it through until it has accomplished its purpose. It will not fail. It is conditional in the sense that any individual who participates in it may drop out of it by covenant-breaking. That is, the individual may fail.

It is best, therefore, to regard Gen 17 as a covenant renewal which focuses on the specific area of Abram's lapse of trust: the seed. And though there are certain conditions placed upon individuals to enjoy the benefits of the covenant,

God is unconditionally committed to fulfill all his promises and purposes to Abraham with respect to the seed and the land (Rom 11:28–29).

The Purpose of the Abrahamic Covenant

The purpose for the Abrahamic covenant can only be appreciated within the context of the plot of the Primeval History (Gen 1–11). According to Gen 1:28, blessing, seed, and land are integral parts of God's plan for creation. The first chapter of the Torah describes the protological *blessing* of God (Gen 1:22, 28; 2:3) and the penultimate chapter of the Torah refers to blessing five times (Deut 33:1, 11, 13, 20, 24). The Torah begins and ends with blessing and therefore any attempt to understand the Torah's plot must include God's priority to bless Israel and the nations. [See Figure 1.]

Likewise, the opening chapter mentions "land" twenty-one times. The land theme also appears in the final two chapters of the Torah (Deut 33:13, 16–17, 28; 34:1–2, 4). Just as the Torah begins and ends with divine blessing, so the Torah begins and ends with a focus on the importance of the land. Finally, filling the land (earth) through human procreation appears in the first chapter of the Torah in the context of God's blessing (Gen 1:28). This theme also appears in the concluding chapters of the Torah (Deut 30:5, 16).

Genesis 2:4–11:26 not only explains how God's very good purposes for creation were disrupted by rebellion and disobedience, but also paves a literary-theological trail to the resolution of the problem through a specific line of Adam's descendants. Genesis 2 focuses on the gift of a land (Gen 2:10–14) as well as the gift of a wife as part of God's plan for filling the land (Gen 2:18, 21–24). Genesis 3 tells the sad story of rebellion and disobedience that directly undermines God's original purposes. Firstly, instead of blessing we are now introduced to the antithetical problem of the curses of disobedience. The word curse (*'arar*) appears five times in the Primeval History (Gen 3:14, 17; 4:11; 5:29; 9:25) and another nineteen times at the end of the Torah (Deut 27:15–26; 28:16–20). Secondly, marital conflict, as well as pain and suffering in childbirth, are introduced, an obvious antithesis to the original blessing of marriage and procreation. Finally, Adam and Eve are thrust out of the land God gave them (Gen 3:23–24), and exile becomes another major antithesis to the divine plan of giving the land to his people.

The Torah's solution to the curses of disobedience is a chosen seed (Gen 3:15; 4:25; 5:29; 9:26). God's pledge to bring about a solution to the curses of disobedience is through the making of a covenant (Gen 9:8–17). God's choice of Abram (an individual seed) through whom humanity will be blessed or cursed (Gen 12:1–3), the promise of a land (Gen 12:7), and the making of the Abrahamic covenant (Gen 15:18) must all be understood through the lens of this redemptive story. The Abrahamic covenant provides God's unconditional commitment to restore the blessing through the provision of the seed and the land. The Abrahamic covenant is deeply rooted in the faithfulness of God, who alone passes between the pieces of the parted animals to signify his unilateral commitment to ensure the fulfillment of the covenant with all its promises (Gen 15:9–17; see Jer 34:18–19).

To summarize, the Abrahamic covenant was made in the context of Abram's faith (Gen 15:6), and God required from Israel, the covenant people, this same faith to enjoy the promises of this covenant. Faith is so important to this covenant that when Moses and Aaron "did not believe" (Num 14:11; 20:12), they were not permitted into the land that the covenant promised (Gen 15:7). This theme of faith and the Abrahamic covenant becomes one of Paul's major theological points in his discussions of the gospel (e.g., Rom 4:1–5; Gal 3:6). Also, the relationship of Gen 17 with Gen 15 reveals that the circumcision narrative is portrayed as a covenant renewal in light of Abram's failure to trust God for the provision of a seed through Sarai (Gen 16). The purpose of the Abrahamic covenant is to fulfill God's commitment to restore creation through the seed of Abraham. The apostle Paul notes that "seed" can be understood both collectively and individually. Collectively, Paul assures the believers in Rome that God will save Israel (the collective seed) because of his unchanging covenant promises to Abraham (Rom 11:28–29). Individually, Paul well notes that the fate of the collective seed is inseparably bound to the individual seed (Gal 3:16). The idea of the Abrahamic covenant's fulfillment through an individual seed is already well rooted in the Old Testament, where we see the literary-theological relationship between the Abrahamic and the Davidic covenants (see articles below). Because of the faithfulness of this individual seed of Abraham, Isaac, Jacob, Judah, Perez, and David, the hope of the collective seed (Israel) is assured.

Works Cited

Alexander, T. Desmond. 2012. *From Paradise to the Promised Land: An Introduction to the Pentateuch*. Grand Rapids: Baker Academic.

Gentry, Peter J., and Stephen J. Wellum. 2015. *God's Kingdom through God's Covenants: A Concise Biblical Theology*. Wheaton, IL: Crossway.

Niehaus, Jeffrey. 2013. "God's Covenant with Abraham." *JETS* 56:249–71.

Sailhamer, John H. 1992. *The Pentateuch as Narrative: A Biblical-Theological Commentary*. Grand Rapids: Zondervan.

Todd, James M. 2017. *Sinai and the Saints: Reading Old Covenant Laws for the New Covenant Community*. Downers Grove, IL: InterVarsity Press.

Williamson, Paul R. 2007. *Sealed with an Oath: Covenant in God's Unfolding Purpose*. Downers Grove, IL: InterVarsity Press.

1.3 The Mosaic Covenant

Kevin Chen

The Mosaic covenant refers to the covenant that the Lord made with the Israelites at Mount Sinai (or, Horeb) as narrated in the Pentateuch. As such, it includes the most extensive legal codes in the Bible. These codes encompass not only moral and civil concerns but also the entire Levitical system including the tabernacle, sacrifices, and Aaronic priesthood. A proper understanding of this covenant requires careful attention to terminology, literary context, its relationship to the Abrahamic covenant, and its relationship to the law.

Terminology

The Mosaic covenant, as it is often called, is named after its mediator, Moses. It is also often referred to as the Sinai(tic) covenant because of its institution at Mount Sinai. Hebrews 8:13 refers to this covenant as "old" (KJV) or "obsolete" (NIV, NASB). Second Corinthians 3:14–15 relatedly refers to the veiled reading of the "old covenant" and of "Moses" (NIV). The latter designation is likely a reference to the Pentateuch, which deals with this covenant among others (e.g., Noahic, Abrahamic, new [see Deut 30:6]).

The Mosaic covenant is closely associated with the giving of the law at Mount Sinai (see below), and these two realities are directly linked in Heb 8:4–7 and contrasted with the new covenant in Heb 8:7–13. Likewise, though Paul does not often refer to the Mosaic covenant using the word "covenant" (see Gal 4:24 NIV for an exception), he does contrast the gospel with "the law" (e.g., Rom 3:21; Gal 5:4 NIV; see also "the letter" in Rom 2:27–29; 7:6; 2 Cor 3:6–7 NASB). Schreiner (2007, 67) explains that Paul's use of the term *nomos* ("law") most often refers to the Mosaic law, especially its commands. This use of "the law" should not be automatically equated with the Pentateuch, also frequently referred to in the Bible as "the Law [of Moses]," of which the Sinai law is a part (see Rom 3:21 for both uses of the term). A clear understanding of the Mosaic covenant, the so-called "old covenant era," and "the law" is also important in relation to what is known as the "Old Testament" Scripture. Despite similar terminology, the meaning of the Old Testament ("all Scripture" in 2 Tim 3:16 NASB) should not be assumed to be the "old covenant" without proof, since this meaning should be sought exegetically.

Literary Context and Institution

The Israelites' arrival at Mount Sinai in Exod 19:1–2 was shortly followed by the Lord's charge to "diligently listen to my voice" and "keep my covenant" in

Exod 19:5 (author's translation; for similar combinations of such terminology, see Exod 23:21–22, 32; Judg 2:2, 20; 2 Kgs 18:12; Jer 11:10). The Israelites were also specifically commanded to prepare themselves to meet the Lord on the third day (Exod 19:10–11). When the time came, the Lord's manifestation of himself was accompanied by thunder, lightning, thick clouds, a loud trumpet sound, fire, smoke, earthquake, and even the Lord's own voice (Exod 19:9, 16–19; Deut 4:10–12, 33, 36; 5:4). The Israelites' hearing of the divine voice involved their direct reception of the Ten Commandments (Exod 20:1–17; Deut 5:4–22). The foundational role of the Decalogue to the "covenant" is strongly implied by their appositional relationship in Deut 4:13, the inscription of the Decalogue on stone tablets (Exod 24:12; 31:18; 34:1, 28–29; Deut 5:22; 9:10), and the storage of these tablets in the ark of the covenant (Deut 10:1–5, 8; see Exod 25:16), which was the centerpiece of both the tabernacle (Exod 25:10–22) and the entire sacrificial system.

The giving of the Ten Commandments is also inextricably linked to the installation of Moses as a mediator between Israel and the Lord. After hearing the Decalogue directly from God, the Israelites were terrified and were granted their request that Moses mediate for them (Exod 20:18–21; Deut 5:23–31). This mediation is a key aspect of the Mosaic covenant (John 1:17; 7:19; Gal 3:19–20). Moses proceeded to ascend Mount Sinai alone and received the so-called "Covenant Code" from the Lord (Exod 20:22–23:33). After reporting these commands to the people (Exod 24:3), Moses ratified the covenant by writing down the Lord's words, building an altar, having sacrifices offered, reading "the Book of the Covenant" to the people, and sprinkling "the blood of the covenant" upon them (Exod 24:4–8 NIV; Heb 9:18–20). Moses was then summoned to ascend the mountain again, where he would receive the stone tablets (Exod 24:12–15; 31:16) and instructions concerning the tabernacle (Exod 25–31). Before the Israelites left the wilderness of Sinai in Num 10:11–13, they would receive many more commandments from the Lord (see Leviticus and Numbers). Their stay at Mount Sinai (Exod 19–Num 10) also makes plain that the Mosaic covenant, even early on, was a covenant that was repeatedly broken (Exod 32:1–6; Lev 10:1–3; 17:7; 24:10–12), despite the Israelites' promises to the contrary (Exod 19:8; 20:19; 24:3, 7). This sober reality contrasts with the new covenant, which provides for the law to be written on the heart so that it will not be broken (Jer 31:31–34; Heb 8:6–13).

Although originally spoken to the next generation of Israelites, most of Deuteronomy also concerns the same Mosaic covenant. Deut 4:9–13 treats this new generation as though they too were at "Horeb" (i.e., Sinai), witnessed the theophany, and heard the Ten Commandments directly. Accordingly, not only were their parents who had since died in the wilderness parties to this covenant, but so were they (Deut 4:23; 5:2–3). Like the exodus (Josh 24:17; Judg 2:1), the Mosaic covenant involved Israel corporately, including future generations. As in the Sinai narrative (see Exod 20:1–17), the Decalogue again plays a foundational role in Deuteronomy (Deut 4:13; 5:6–22), and both Moses' mediation (Deut 5:23–28; see 1:5) and the breaking of the covenant are key elements (Deut 4:3; 9:8–21; 29:4; 31:16–22). Unlike earlier legislation, Deuteronomy notably includes the Shema (Deut 6:4–5) and more extensive instructions concerning life in the promised land (Deut 12–26). The blessings for obedience and curses for disobedience (culminating in exile, death, and shame) in Deut 27–28 recall the consequences for the same in Lev 26. As was the case for the Covenant Code (Exod 24:4, 7), Moses wrote down all the Lord's words in a book (Deut 31:24–26).

These points of contact support Hafemann's (2007, 47) comment that Deuteronomy "focus[es] on Israel's covenant relationship with God, now carried on in terms of the Sinai covenant." Similarly, Gentry and Wellum (2012, 378) assert that it is "a *supplement* to—and not a replacement for—the covenant at Sinai." The one clarification that I would make related to these insights is that Deuteronomy is not entirely focused on the Mosaic covenant and its continuation, since it also has an eschatological outlook. Though infrequently self-evident in the bulk of Deuteronomy (e.g., Deut 4:30; 18:15–19), this outlook is emphasized in its final chapters (e.g., Deut 30:1–14; 31:29; 32:1–43; 33:1–29; 34:10–12) and is directly linked to the new covenant in Deut 30:6.

Relation to the Abrahamic Covenant

Whereas the relationship of the Mosaic covenant to Deuteronomy and its contrast with the new covenant are relatively easy to discern, its relationship to the Abrahamic covenant is more complex. This is because it has both significant continuity and significant discontinuity with this covenant. The former is noticeable in Gen 15, when the Lord made a covenant with Abram. By predicting Israel's enslavement in Egypt for 400 years (v. 13) and their eventual possession of the promised land (vv. 16, 18–21), the Gen 15 covenant overlaps with core elements of the Mosaic covenant. The fulfillment of the promise of land to Abraham and his "seed" is a major theme in the exodus (Exod 2:24; 3:6–9, 15–17; 6:2–8) and journey to the promised land (Exod 32:13; 33:1; Lev 26:42; Num 32:11), which included the planned stop at Mount Sinai (Exod 3:12). The Lord's declaration of having "brought [Israel] out of the land of Egypt, out of the house of slaves" at the beginning of the Decalogue (Exod 20:2, author's translation; Deut 5:6; see Gen 15:7) is a reminder of where they had come from and where they were going, all in fulfillment of the covenant promises made to Abraham. Instructions concerning circumcision are another connecting line between the Abrahamic and Mosaic covenants (Gen 17:10–14; Lev 12:3).

On the other hand, Paul strongly contrasts the covenant promises made to Abraham and "the law" in Gal 3. As in Rom 4:2–3, Paul in Gal 3:6 roots the gospel and justification by faith apart from works in the example of Abraham and Gen 15:6 ("Then he believed in the LORD; and He reckoned it to him as righteousness," NASB). Paul further explains that the law brings curse, justifies no one, and is not based on faith (Gal 3:10–12; see Rom 4:15). Neither did the law include the "promise" of the Spirit (Gal 3:2; see Rom 8:1–15), who is given as a result of the Messiah's redemptive, substitutionary death on the cross (Gal 3:13–14; see Acts 2:33). The covenant "promises" made to Abraham are fulfilled through this individual messianic "seed" (Gal 3:16), not through the law (Gal 3:18; see Rom 4:13–14). The giving of the law at Mount Sinai 430 years after the institution of the Abrahamic covenant "does not revoke [it] in order to nullify the promise" (Gal 3:17, author's translation). Insofar as this Mosaic "law" is part of the Mosaic covenant (see Gal 4:24), this covenant thus must also be significantly *dis*continuous with the Abrahamic covenant promises and the gospel that it announced in advance (Gal 3:8).

The Mosaic Covenant and the Law Given at Mount Sinai

It could seem self-evident that the Mosaic covenant and the law given at Mount Sinai are one and the same. After all, Deut 5:2 plainly states, "The LORD our God made a covenant with us at Horeb" (NIV), the same site as the giving of the law. The prefacing of the giving of the law with a charge to "keep my covenant" (Exod 19:5 NIV) could suggest an identification of the Mosaic covenant with the law. Further supporting such a relationship are the references to "the Book of the Covenant" and "the blood of the covenant" (Exod 24:6–8 NIV) in connection with the Covenant Code (Exod 20:22–23:33). The "law" would then be a shorthand way of referring to this covenant for Paul and the author of Hebrews. Although this reasonable position doubtless has many adherents, there are several influential scholarly perspectives which have for different reasons distinguished between the law and the Mosaic covenant.

The frequent use of Hittite suzerain-vassal treaties as an interpretive framework for understanding the Mosaic covenant relates to one of these perspectives. Mendenhall's influential work demonstrated that there are similarities between these Hittite treaties and some biblical covenants, especially the use of the formal elements of preamble, historical prologue, stipulations, provision for deposit in the temple and periodic public reading, list of gods as witnesses, and the curses and blessings formula (Mendenhall 1954, 58–60). Concerning the relationship of the Mosaic covenant to the law, the use of Hittite treaties as an interpretive framework would suggest that the law, which corresponds to "stipulations," is a significant part of the Mosaic covenant but not identical with the covenant itself. Mendenhall (1954, 59) adds that the "I-Thou" form of address characteristic of the "historical prologue" shows that the "covenant form is still thought of as a personal relationship, rather than as an objective, impersonal statement of law." As a representative example of Mendenhall's influence, Kline (1972, 48) believes that legal corpora in the Old Testament correspond to "treaty stipulations," which were a "central element in ancient treaties" (see also Hafemann 2007, 32). Though coming from a very different perspective (an argument for "covenantal nomism" as characteristic of Palestinian Judaism in 200 BCE–200 CE), Sanders's (1977, 419–28) point that the law was given to Israel in the context of an existing covenant and of divine grace is also relevant here (see also Schreiner 2007, 73). The pioneering work of Mendenhall and Sanders in their respective ways thus each suggests a subtle distinction between the law and the Mosaic covenant.

From yet another perspective, Wellhausen observed that Jer 7:21–23 distinguishes between the Lord's command to "listen to my voice" when he brought Israel out of Egypt (v. 23) and the later commands concerning "burnt offering and sacrifice" (v. 22). For Wellhausen (1994, 58), this is evidence that Jeremiah "opposes the Torah to the cultus." But even for those who reject Wellhausen's documentary hypothesis, his textual observations regarding Jer 7:21–23 remain relevant to the question of whether the Mosaic covenant is identical to the law given at Mount Sinai. Theological conservatives can see for themselves that "listen to my voice" in Jer 7:23 is probably an allusion to Exod 19:5 including its reference to "my covenant" (see also Exod 15:26; 23:21–22), with both contexts also promising a blessed relationship with the Lord. Jeremiah 7:21–23 can thus be interpreted as suggesting that the laws concerning "burnt offering and sacrifice" (e.g., Lev 1–7) were a secondary addition to the original command that the Lord gave to listen to his voice and keep his covenant in Exod 19:5. [See Figure 2.]

Even further back in the history of interpretation, one of the fathers of covenant theology, Johannes Cocceius (1603–1669), argued that the ceremonial law was deliberately added by the Lord as a result of the sin of the golden calf in Exod 32 (see Lee 2009, 120–21, 128–29). He based his argument on passages such as Jer 7:22–23 (see above), Jer 31:32 (concerning which Cocceius interprets *ba'alti bam* as describing an oppressive rule [*dominationem*]; see Cocceius 1675, 3:104), Ezek 20:25 ("I also gave them statutes that were not good" NASB; see Cocceius 1675, 3:80–81), Rom 5:20 ("the Law snuck in"; see Cocceius 1675 4:90), and Gal 3:19 ("Why the Law then? It was added because of transgressions" NASB; see Cocceius 1675, 4:50–51). Among recent interpreters, Sailhamer (1995, 272–89; 2009, 40–48, 351–54), drawing upon Cocceius but without relying on the category of "ceremonial law," has relatedly argued that laws were added to the Mosaic covenant as a result of Israel's transgressions. Prior to these transgressions, the simple focus on listening to the Lord's voice (Exod 19:5; see 15:26) resembled the Abrahamic covenant (Gen 26:5; see Lee 2009, 127–28). The identification of the Mosaic law with the Mosaic covenant may continue to be commonplace, but the preceding alternative perspectives provide nuance and possible areas for further study.

Works Cited

Cocceius, Johannes. 1675. *Opera Omnia*. 8 vols. Amstelodami: Johannis à Someren.

Gentry, Peter, and Stephen Wellum. 2012. *Kingdom through Covenant: A Biblical-Theological Understanding of the Covenants*. Wheaton, IL: Crossway.

Hafemann, Scott. 2007. "The Covenant Relationship." Pages 20–65 in *Central Themes in Biblical Theology: Mapping Unity in Diversity*. Edited by Scott Hafemann. Grand Rapids: Baker.

Kline, Meredith. 1972. *The Structure of Biblical Authority*. Grand Rapids: Eerdmans.

Lee, Brian J. 2009. *Johannes Cocceius and the Exegetical Roots of Federal Theology: Reformation Developments in the Interpretation of Hebrews 7–10*. Göttingen: Vandenhoeck & Ruprecht.

Mendenhall, George. 1954. "Covenant Forms in Israelite Traditions." *BA* 17:50–76.

Sailhamer, John. 1995. *Introduction to Old Testament Theology: A Canonical Approach*. Grand Rapids: Zondervan.

———. 2009. *The Meaning of the Pentateuch*. Downers Grove, IL: InterVarsity Press.

Sanders, E. P. 1977. *Paul and Palestinian Judaism: A Comparison of Patterns of Religion*. London: SCM.

Schreiner, Thomas. 2007. "The Commands of God." Pages 66–101 in *Central Themes in Biblical Theology: Mapping Unity in Diversity*. Edited by Scott Hafemann. Grand Rapids: Baker.

Wellhausen, Julius. 1994. *Prolegomena to the History of Israel*. Repr., Atlanta: Scholars Press.

1.4 The Davidic Covenant

Brian J. Kinzel

The Davidic covenant is a promise Yahweh made to David that he would have an everlasting dynasty. It is the basis for the messianic hope—that a coming king from the line of David will rule in Zion over Israel and all the nations, and that this king will usher in an age of righteousness, justice, and peace. By all accounts the Davidic covenant is a major watershed in biblical history (Brueggemann 1990, 253; 1997, 604–6) as well as one of the most significant aspects of biblical theology (von Rad 1962, 307–8; Kaiser 2008, 117). The Davidic covenant is first and primarily described in 2 Sam 7(// 2 Chr 17). Though the word "covenant" (*brit*) is not mentioned there, it is in other passages that refer to this promise

(2 Sam 23:5; 2 Chr 13:5; Ps 89:4). The Davidic covenant amplifies God's previous promises of a king to Abraham (Gen 17:6, 16; 35:11), to the tribe of Judah (Gen 49:10), and through Balaam (Num 24:17). The Psalms and the Prophets continue the theme of this message (e.g., Pss 2; 89; Isa 9:5–6; 11; 55:3; Jer 33:14–26; Ezek 34:23–24; 37:24–25; Hos 3:5; Amos 9:11). The New Testament then records that Jesus came as this promised king, "the Messiah, the son of David" (Matt 1:1 NASB; cf. Luke 1:32; Rom 1:3; Rev 5:5; 22:16).

Summary of 2 Samuel 7

Historical Circumstances. In 2 Sam 5 David is anointed as king over all the tribes, conquers Jerusalem, builds his own "house" (5:11; *bayit*=palace), and subdues the Philistines. Because of these victories, in chapter 6 David is able to move the ark of the covenant into Jerusalem. David is portrayed as a worshiper (6:12–19) and thus a fitting replacement for Saul (6:20–23).

David's Desire (7:1–3). The account begins by noting that Yahweh had given David rest from his enemies. Speaking to Nathan the prophet, David explains that his "house" is permanent and of cedar, but the ark of God was only in a tent. Kings in the ancient Near East commonly built temples to their gods, and David's dialogue reflects that cultural expectation, even though David refrains from asking directly (Bergen 1996, 335; Anderson 1989, 114–15). The prophet Nathan affirms David's unstated desire by acknowledging that God is with David.

The Revelation of the Promise (7:4–17). Through the oracle of Nathan, God rejects David's desire to build a "house" (7:5; *bayit*=temple), but in contrast bestows remarkable promises on David. There are at least nine specific elements in this promise.

(1) Yahweh's choice of David (7:8–9a). God's choice of and blessing on David serve as the preface to the promises.

(2) A great name for David (7:9b). Not since Abraham had God promised to make a man's name great (Gen 12:2), and the parallel is unmistakable.

(3) A place for God's people (7:10a).

(4) Rest and peace from all enemies (7:10b–11).

(5) A "house" for David (7:11; *bayit*=dynasty).

(6) A descendent who will build a "house" for Yahweh (7:12–13a; *bayit*=temple).

(7) A descendent whose kingdom will be established forever (7:13b).

(8) A father-son relationship with David's descendants (7:14).

(9) Permanent mercy that includes an eternal house, kingdom, and throne (7:15–16).

David's Prayer of Thanks (7:18–29). David's effusive response of thanksgiving explains these specific elements, and indicates that these promises have an eternal and worldwide fulfillment (Block 2003, 40–41). Though "forever" (*ad olam*) can mean an indefinite period of time and also refer to conditional promises, in his response David uses this phrase to refer to other eternal and irrevocable promises. In 7:24 the same phrase refers to God's choice of the nation of Israel. In 7:25 David asks God to confirm the promises "forever" so that God's name will be glorified "forever." The call of the nation of Israel and the praise of God's name both concern all of time and all of the world. David's response links the promises with the establishment of the nation in the exodus, and the nation's mission to glorify the name of Yahweh on earth. Specifically, 7:19 states that this promise concerns all of humankind (Kaiser 1995, 80). Though seminal here, both the eternal and universal aspects of the promises are expanded later in the prophets and psalms.

Nature of the Promises in the Davidic Covenant

The most striking feature of the promises in the Davidic covenant is that David's house, kingdom, and throne will continue forever (7:16). However, the promise of an enduring dynasty is held in tension with the demand for obedience upon the individual heirs to the throne, and this tension has produced much discussion. God promised to deal with David's heirs as a father would a son, meaning that he would apply corrective discipline to them when they did not obey. But in 7:15 God reassures David that even the sinful failures of future heirs will not annul the promise of an eternal dynasty. Previously, Samuel told Saul that his dynasty was rejected because of his failures, even though it might have endured "forever" (1 Sam 13:13–14). God assures David that his dynasty will not be so rejected because "My lovingkindness shall not depart from him, as I took it away from Saul" (2 Sam 7:15).

Relation to the Sinaitic Covenant. Many have commented how the Davidic covenant appears to differ fundamentally from the Sinaitic covenant (Mendenhall 1962, 718; Levenson 1979, 205–10). The Sinaitic covenant is full of commands for the nation to obey, and in that covenant the blessings promised to Israel depended on the nation's obedience. However, 2 Sam 7 emphasizes the remarkable and expansive promises David received. Many critical scholars are content to explain differences between the Sinaitic and Davidic covenants as contradictions, and as evidence of different stages of redaction of the biblical text that reflect differing traditions in ancient Israel (e.g., Tsevat 1963). This issue is summarized by two closely interrelated questions: (1) what is the literary form of the Davidic covenant, and (2) is the Davidic covenant conditional or unconditional?

Literary Form. Many writers have compared the Davidic covenant and Sinaitic covenant on the basis of different literary forms. The former is often grouped together with other biblical covenants, like the Noahic covenant (Gen 9:8–17), the new covenant (Jer 33), and especially the Abrahamic covenant (Gen 12:1–3). These covenants are termed royal-grants or promissory covenants, in which God promises to fulfill the conditions unilaterally without obligation upon the recipient. Attempting to better interpret these critical texts, biblical scholars have sought to find analogies to their literary form from the cultures around ancient Israel. Whereas the covenant renewal in Deuteronomy follows the Hittite suzerain-vassal treaty pattern, scholars noted that the so-called grant covenants had no clear precedent in the ancient Near East (Hillers 1969, 105–6). Weinfeld explained that the Davidic covenant was a promissory grant, and that it differed fundamentally from the Sinaitic covenant. He believed that he found extrabiblical parallels to the promissory covenants in Babylonian *kidduru* boundary stones, which describe the land a king gave to a loyal subject. Weinfeld (1970, 185) wrote, "Like the royal grants in the Ancient Near East so also the covenants with Abraham and David are gifts bestowed upon individuals who excelled in loyally serving their master." He based this assertion on several phrases used in *kidduru* documents that he believed paralleled the biblical examples. Weinfeld's proposal gained wide acceptance and is repeated in many sources. Knoppers (1996) challenged this proposal, saying that the *kidduru* stones have no clear likeness to the Davidic covenant. He asserted also that the *kidduru* documents themselves actually did not have one common form, and the linguistic parallels between them and the covenants of grant were not convincing. Avioz (2012, 47, 50) wrote that the Davidic covenant does have characteristics of the vassal treaties, but cautions that the biblical writers did not always closely adhere to such patterns. These assessments reinforce what previous scholars had noted—no close analogies to the Davidic covenant have been found outside the Bible, and interpretation of the Davidic covenant does not depend entirely on its literary form.

Conditional or Unconditional. As mentioned, many have observed that the Davidic covenant and other promissory grants in the Bible look very different from the Sinaitic covenant. However, the Law anticipated the Davidic covenant with a promise of royal status to both Abraham (Gen 17:6, 16) and to Judah (Gen 49:10), and also with regulations for the monarchy (Deut 17). The Davidic covenant assumes that David's heirs will be judged according to the standard of the law (e.g., 2 Sam 7:14, ". . . when he commits iniquity, I will correct him . . ."). Rather than a rigid dichotomy, both the law and the Davidic covenant include elements of conditionality (demands for man to meet) and unconditionality (promises for God to fulfill). Grisanti (2009, 240) notes, "An unconditional covenant is not necessarily without conditions just as a conditional covenant can have unconditional elements" (cf. Waltke 1988). The unconditional aspects of the Davidic covenant include God's choice of David, a great name, rest from enemies, a place for the people, an everlasting dynasty, and an eternal throne (Steinmann 2014, 28). The conditional element is that the heirs of David were punished when they disobeyed.

In the Prophets and the Psalms

The many messianic prophecies written after 2 Sam 7 testify to the importance of the Davidic covenant, for these prophecies stem from the promise of David's eternal dynasty. Both in the psalms and in the prophets the seminal ideas in the Davidic covenant are developed and elucidated. Though most messianic prophecies have some reference to the Davidic covenant (e.g., Pss 2; 110), there are several important texts that specifically mention David and his covenant.

Isaiah. This prophecy has three important references to the Davidic covenant. (1) Chapter 9 includes the momentous prophecy of the birth of the prince of peace. This child is born to rule, for the government rests on his shoulders, and he rules on the throne of David (9:5–6 [Eng. 6–7]). (2) Chapter 11 promises a shoot and branch from the root of Jesse that will judge righteously and with omniscient knowledge (11:1–5). The prophet describes that the peace of this king's reign encompasses all nature so that even "the wolf will dwell with the lamb" (11:6). (3) In chapter 55 the prophet includes a promise to those who repent that they will share in the blessings of the Davidic covenant. Isaiah 55:4–5 describes that David's future heir is served by gentile nations and glorified by God.

Jeremiah. The prophet mentions briefly in 23:5–6 and 30:9 that God will raise up an heir to the throne of David, the righteous branch in whose reign Israel will dwell in safety. Yet chapter 33 is Jeremiah's important contribution to the understanding of the messiah. The chapter describes Israel's restoration and cleansing during a time of abundance and safety. Part of this is the rule of the righteous branch of David (33:14–26). Several times this section mentions that the Davidic covenant cannot be broken, and that David will not lack a man to sit on the throne.

Ezekiel. Chapter 37 starts with the vision of the valley of dry bones, which describes the resurrection and return of the nation to the land. Part of their restoration is the reunification of the kingdoms so that they will "no longer be divided into two kingdoms" (v. 22). The Davidic messiah will reign as shepherd king over this renewed people. Ezekiel 37:25 reads "and David My servant will be their prince forever," showing that not only is the Davidic dynasty eternal but also the messiah will reign eternally.

Psalm 89. This psalm begins by referring to the Davidic covenant (vv. 4–5). It recounts both the future glory of the anointed heir of David, and also the difficulties of the present Jerusalem. The actual historical setting is elusive, but was a time of severe devastation in Jerusalem, with the walls broken down and enemies plundering the city (vv. 38–51). The beginning of the psalm promises that God will uphold his covenant promises to David forever (vv. 1–4), including victory over all enemies (vv. 22–23) and worldwide reign (vv. 25, 27). The trouble of Jerusalem described in the psalm vividly illustrates the truth that God promised to punish the Davidic heirs who failed to uphold the law, but the psalm also affirms the eternal nature of the promises in the Davidic covenant.

Psalm 132. This psalm illustrates the connection between the Davidic covenant and the role of Zion as the messiah's capital. As a "song of ascents," the psalm recounts how David brought the ark into Jerusalem, and made the city the spiritual center of his kingdom. David is both the servant of Yahweh and his anointed (v. 10). The psalm expresses the tension between God's promise to David (v. 11) and the demand that his heir obey the covenant (v. 12).

Works Cited

Anderson, A. A. 1989. *2 Samuel.* WBC. Dallas: Word.

Avioz, Michael. 2012. "The Davidic Covenant in 2 Samuel 7: Conditional or Unconditional?" Pages 43–51 in *The Ancient Near East in the 12th–10th Centuries BCE: Culture and History.* Edited by Gershon Galil, Ayelet Gilboa, Aren M. Maeir, and Dan'el Kahn. Münster: Ugarit-Verlag.

Bergen, Robert D. 1996. *1, 2 Samuel.* NAC. Nashville: Broadman & Holman.

Block, Daniel I. 2003. "My Servant David: Ancient Israel's Vision of the Messiah." Pages 17–56 in *Israel's Messiah in the Old Testament and the Dead Sea Scrolls.* Edited by Richard S. Hess and M. Daniel Carroll R. Grand Rapids: Baker.

Brueggemann, Walter. 1990. *First and Second Samuel.* IBC. Louisville: John Knox.

———. 1997. *Theology of the Old Testament: Testimony, Dispute, Advocacy.* Minneapolis: Fortress Press.

Grisanti, Michael. 2009. "The Davidic Covenant." *MSJ* 10:233–50.

Hillers, Delbert R. 1969. *Covenant: The History of a Biblical Idea.* Baltimore: John Hopkins.

Kaiser, Walter C., Jr. 1995. *The Messiah in the Old Testament.* Grand Rapids: Zondervan.

———. 2008. *The Promise Plan of God.* Grand Rapids: Zondervan.

Knoppers, Gary N. 1996. "Ancient Near Eastern Royal Grants and the Davidic Covenant: A Parallel?" *JAOS* 116:670–97.

Levenson, Jon D. 1979. "The Davidic Covenant and Its Modern Interpreters." *CBQ* 41:205–19.

Mendenhall, George E. 1962. "Covenant." *IDB* 1:714–23.

Rad, Gerhard von. 1962. *Old Testament Theology.* Translated by D. M. G. Stalker. New York: Harper & Row.

Steinmann, Andrew E. 2014. "What Did David Understand About the Promises in the Davidic Covenant?" *BSac* 171:19–29.

Tsevat, Matitiahu. 1963. "Studies in the Book of Samuel III." *HUCA* 34:71–82.

Waltke, Bruce K. 1988. "The Phenomenon of Conditionality within Unconditional Covenants." Pages 123–40 in *Israel's Apostasy and Restoration.* Edited by A. Gileadi. Grand Rapids: Baker.

Weinfeld, Moshe. 1970. "The Covenant of Grant in the Old Testament and in the Ancient Near East." *JAOS* 90:184–203.

1.5 The New Covenant

Noam Hendren

The term "new covenant" is one of the names given to the promised eschatological transformation of Israel by the outpouring of the spirit of God. Otherwise referred to as an "everlasting covenant" (Isa 55:3 NASB; Jer 32:40; Ezek 16:60) and a "covenant of peace" (Ezek 34:25; 37:26), the only specific reference to the "new covenant" in the Old Testament is found in Jer 31:31–34, which details most of the essential elements of the promised transformation and sets it in the context of God's overall plan of redemption, as laid out in the Abrahamic, Sinaitic, and Davidic covenants. The purpose of this covenant is to enable Israel to perfectly keep the requirements of covenant relationship with God and thus to fulfill their calling as God's channel of blessing to the nations.

God chose Abraham and his descendants that they might become his instrument to restore humanity and the world to their original blessed state (Gen 12:3b; Sailhamer 1992, 139). At Sinai, God gave his Torah to transform Israel from a nation of slaves into a "holy nation" and a "kingdom of priests" (Exod 19:5–6) prepared to bring the knowledge of God and his salvation to the nations of the world. God promised to bless the nation in her land, restoring garden of Eden conditions there, if Israel would truly walk in his commandments (Lev 26:3–12; Sailhamer 1992, 364). Nevertheless, Moses predicted that future generations of Israelites would abandon the ways of the Lord and turn to idols, and as a result they would be driven out of the land into exile (Deut 4:25–28; 30:1; 31:16–21, 29).

The Need for a New Covenant

The subsequent records of Israel's national experience confirmed Moses' prophetic warning. Israel's refusal to listen to the voice of the Lord and to keep his covenant led to the exile of the ten northern tribes through the Assyrians and the exile of Judah through the Babylonians in 586 BCE. For the prophet Jeremiah, this was a direct fulfillment of God's covenant sanctions (see Jer 11:7–8). Israel's demonstrated inability to keep the requirements of the Sinai Covenant necessitated a new and unconditional covenant, one which would enable Israel to become truly and totally devoted to the Lord their God so that he might bless them and use them to bless the world. Such a new covenant was promised in Jer 31:31–34.

Jeremiah presents the new covenant, firstly, as one that would be enacted sometime in the future, coinciding with the fulfillment of the Abrahamic covenant's promises to Israel, regathered and blessed in her land (31:1–14). Secondly, this new covenant would be made with the people of Israel specifically and exclusively ("the house of Israel and . . . the house of Judah"). Thirdly, this covenant would be "new" in contrast to the Sinai covenant, which the people of Israel had consistently broken throughout their history, although the two covenants shared a common goal: the fulfillment of the righteous requirements of relationship with God (Keown et al. 1995, 132; Eichrodt 1961, 59; Bright 1976, 194–96).

The "newness" of Jeremiah's new covenant vis-à-vis the Sinai covenant is specified in verses 33–34. In contrast to Sinai's external law which Israel had proven incapable of keeping, God's unconditional promise to embed his law in their hearts would make devotion and obedience to God irresistible, their natural impulse (Keown et al. 1995, 135). The result would be a perfectly restored relationship between Israel and her God ("they will all know me"; Hillers 1969, 121–24), as God himself removes the barrier of sin which had caused him to hide his face from a sinful nation (Deut 31:17–18).

The reason for God's gracious promise is his fundamental commitment to bless Abraham's seed in spite of Israel's consistent rebellion (Deut 31:35–36). These verses reflect the promise of Lev 26:44–45, which links God's refusal to ultimately destroy sinful Israel with his faithfulness to the covenant promises made to their forefathers. Jeremiah's new covenant as a whole reflects God's eschatological promise to transform Israel by "circumcising their hearts" that he might bless them in the promised land (Deut 30:6–9; cf. 10:16; Jer 4:4; 9:25–26 [Heb. 24–25]).

While the designation "new covenant" is unique to Jeremiah, the description of a future covenant of promise that would transform the people of Israel and allow them to inherit the Abrahamic promises is not (see Isa 54:10; 55:3; 61:8–9;

Ezek 16:60–63; 34:24–27; 37:26; note also Jer 32:37–41). Jeremiah's contemporary Ezekiel gives a parallel account with a crucial addition. In chapter 36 of his prophecy, Ezekiel reveals God's motivation behind his promised end-time intervention as well as the nature of the transforming force and its specific effects.

Ezekiel, like Jeremiah, is unequivocal in his condemnation of Israel's national rebellion and frames it as the antithesis of Israel's national calling: to glorify God among the nations of the world (Ezek 36:22–23). The profanation of God's name resulted from his presumed inability to protect his people from defeat and exile (36:20–21), when in fact Israel's exile was imposed by God as a result of national sin (36:16–19). According to Ezekiel's version of the new covenant, God's action would deal with both the cause and the effect, resulting in the restoration of God's holy reputation.

God's intervention would begin with the regathering of Israel from the exile, thus eliminating the effect of Israel's sin and its resulting profanation of God's name (v. 24). This would be followed by Israel's national cleansing from her sin and impurity which had defiled the land and led to her expulsion from it (v. 25). This spiritual cleansing parallels Jeremiah's statement, "I will forgive their iniquity and their sin I will remember no more" (31:34). Similarly, Ezekiel's description of Israel's transformation parallels Jeremiah's, with a heart of stone being replaced by a heart of flesh (Ezek 36:26–27).

Explaining the metaphor of a heart transplant, Ezekiel reveals that it is the indwelling spirit of God who will bring about Israel's change of heart, not only enabling but impelling Israel to walk faithfully in God's ways (v. 27; cf. 11:17–20). The use of the singular "heart" along with the plural "you" indicates that the indwelling and resultant transformation will be collective: true of the entire nation and all the individuals in it (Eichrodt 1970, 500). Thus, the entire nation will experience the resulting blessings, both spiritual ("so you will be My people, and I will be your God") and physical (36:28–30), and her land will be transformed to a garden of Eden, the archetypical place of blessing (36:35; cf. Lev 26:4–12; Taylor 1969, 227). The linkage between the eschatological outpouring of God's transforming spirit and the new covenant is again made in Ezek 37:14–26.

The promised outpouring of the Spirit and the resulting restoration of Edenic conditions also appears a number of times in the book of Isaiah. Chapter 32, which amplifies certain elements of the messianic prophecy of chapter 11 (Grogan 2008, 676–79), describes the outpouring of the Spirit upon Israel, resulting not only in the transformation of the desolate land but of the nation itself, to experience the righteousness and peace of the kingdom of God (32:15–18; cf. 44:3–5). Isaiah 59 shares a similar context to the Jeremiah and Ezekiel passages: Israel's national sin and resulting experience of judgment (59:1–18). This passage places the outpouring of the Spirit in the context of the coming of the divine redeemer to a repentant nation (Isa 59:20–21).

The identification of the coming redeemer with the Lord God himself is clear from the context (Isa 59:16–19). The Lord, who is coming to establish righteousness through judgment, will himself be the intercessor that a sinful Israel so desperately needs (v. 16b). Because Israel ("Zion") will have turned to God in true national repentance (59:20), God comes to her not as her judge but as her redeemer (cf. Jer. 24:7; von Rad 1965, 212). Addressing the nation collectively ("you" is in the singular), the Lord promises that his outpoured Spirit would transform Israel for all generations to come (59:21). The expression "put My words in your mouth" means to "teach by heart" (Christensen 2002, 776; cf. Deut 31:19) and is parallel to Jeremiah's "write My law on their heart." Both expressions indicate the internalization of God's word and the will to perform it (cf. Deut 30:14).

The result of this Spirit-produced national transformation is detailed in the following verses, unfortunately separated from the previous section due to an inopportune chapter division (see Isa 60:1–3). Israel's spiritual transformation will kindle the light and glory of God upon her, enabling her to fulfill her calling as a light to the gentiles: to receive and to transmit the blessing of the knowledge of the one true God and his salvation to the world. Isaiah goes on to describe the blessed conditions which will prevail as a result (Isa 60–61): the nations of the world will ascend to Jerusalem to worship the one true God (Isa 60:3–11) and honor Israel as the "priests of the LORD" (61:6–9; cf. Exod 19:6).

The New Covenant in the New Testament

The new covenant promise to Israel, as presented in the Tanakh, appears primarily in the Gospels and the early chapters of Acts, where it is consistently linked with the establishment of God's kingdom on earth, as the prophets foretold. John the Baptist's call to his fellow Judeans to "repent, for the kingdom of heaven is at hand" is connected both with the coming judgment and with the outpouring ("baptism") of God's spirit by the soon-to-appear Messiah (Matt 3:2, 11–12). So also Jesus' post-resurrection promise to the eleven that this baptism would soon take place elicited their very reasonable question, "Lord, is it at this time You are restoring the kingdom to Israel?" (Acts 1:6). The apostle Paul, in predicting Israel's eschatological national repentance and salvation (Rom 11:26–27), supports his confident declaration by appealing to the new covenant promise of Isa 59:20–21, reinforced by 27:19 and parallel to Jer 31:33–34 (Harrison and Hagner 2008, 178).

In apparent contrast, in the upper room Jesus had promised his disciples that his imminent sacrificial death would—in some sense—inaugurate the new covenant (Luke 22:20), providing forgiveness of sins (Matt 26:28). This promise was also accompanied by the promise of God's indwelling spirit

(John 14:16–17, 26). Nevertheless, the clear differentiation between this in-auguration and the future coming of the kingdom, both in the upper room narratives and in Acts 1:6, calls for careful consideration. The new covenant promise of total transformation, as predicted in the prophets, is still anticipated in the New Testament as a distinctly future event, tied to the return of Jesus to establish his kingdom on the earth (see Acts 1:9–11; 14:22; 1 Cor 13:12; 15:43–53; Phil 3:20–21; Col 3:4).

In his first sermon, Peter cited Joel's promise of the eschatological out-pouring of the Spirit upon Israel (Joel 2:27–3:1 [Heb. 2:27–4:1]) to explain the miraculous speech exhibited by Jesus' Jewish followers (Acts 2:15–21). Jesus, the risen redeemer himself, had poured out the Spirit (vv. 32–33; cf. Isa 59:20–21), and Peter promised his hearers that all who call upon him as Lord and Messiah would be likewise endowed (Acts 2:38). In all likelihood, the believers' expecta-tion of the imminent return of Jesus (see, for example, 1:6–11; 3:19–26; 14:22; Rom 13:11–12; 1 Thess 1:9–10) caused them to view their experience of the indwelling Spirit as but a short interim phase between the present age and the age to come (cf. Heb 6:4–5; Rom 8:23).

The essential contrast between the Sinai covenant and the new covenant inaugurated by Jesus' sacrificial death is detailed extensively by the author of Hebrews (chs. 8–10), with the latter making the former "obsolete" (8:13). Paul, whose writings consistently juxtapose the Torah as a rule of life with the in-dwelling Spirit as the source of transforming empowerment for believers (Rom 7–8; Gal 3–5; et al.), can therefore refer to the apostles as "servants of a new covenant" (2 Cor 3:6). Surprisingly, given the designation "the New Testament" to the apostles' teaching, the term "new covenant" rarely appears in it (Luke 22:20; 1 Cor 11:25; 2 Cor 3:6; Heb 7:22; 8:6–10, 13; 9:15; 10:16, 29; 12:24; 13:20), though the key elements of the new covenant—forgiveness, transformation, the knowledge of God, and the indwelling of the Spirit—are all prominent in the New Testament.

Works Cited

Bright, John. 1976. *Covenant and Promises*. Philadelphia: Westminster Press.

Christensen, Duane L. 2002. *Deuteronomy 21:10–34:12*. WBC 6B. Grand Rapids: Zondervan. Accordance electronic edition.

Eichrodt, Walther. 1961. *Theology of the Old Testament*. Vol. 1. Philadelphia: Westminster Press.

————. 1970. *Ezekiel: A Commentary*. Philadelphia: Westminster Press.

Grogan, Geoffrey W. 2008. *Isaiah*. Pages 433–863 in vol. 6 of The Expositor's Bible Commentary. Edited by Tremper Longman III and David E. Garland. Rev. ed. Grand Rapids: Zondervan.

Harrison, Everett F., and Donald A. Hagner. 2008. *Romans*. Pages 19–273 in vol. 11 of The Expositor's Bible Commentary. Edited by Tremper Longman III and David E. Garland. Rev. ed. Grand Rapids: Zondervan.

Hillers, Delbert R. 1969. *Covenant: The History of a Biblical Idea*. Baltimore: Johns Hopkins University Press.

Keown, Gerald L., Pamela J. Scalise, and Thomas G. Smothers. 1995. *Jeremiah 26–52*. WBC 27. Grand Rapids: Zondervan. Accordance electronic edition.

Rad, Gerhard von. 1965. *Old Testament Theology*. Vol. 2. Translated by D. M. G. Stalker. New York: Harper & Row.

Sailhamer, John H. 1992. *The Pentateuch as Narrative*. Grand Rapids: Zondervan.

Taylor, John B. 1969. *Ezekiel: An Introduction and Commentary*. TOTC 22. Downers Grove, IL: InterVarsity Press. Accordance electronic edition.

CHAPTER 2

God's Plan for the Nations

2.1 The Nations in the Torah

Yohanan Stanfield

In the books of the Torah the nations are part of a story, a story that begins in the garden of Eden with Adam and Eve, the progenitors of all who follow. The story is focused around the hope for "the seed" (Patterson 2018), a hope that springs from the ashes of the serpent's success in corrupting the forebears of humankind to do what their Creator had forbidden. God's declaration to the serpent, that the seed of the woman will be at enmity with his seed (Gen 3:15), is the starting point of the story and infuses the successive narrative with an underlying expectation for "the seed." This expectation is expressed by Noah's father at his birth (Gen 5:29)—could this son be the one to restore what was lost? Before this point there is no clearly defined idea of "nations," and humanity is taken as a whole, as "man" (Gen 6:5–6 NASB). It is with Noah's sons that the separation into "nations" starts, and the separation itself is in reference to the seed motif, for it is Shem, rather than his two brothers, who is the son of blessing, that is, the chosen seed (Gen 9:25–27). In the very next chapter (Gen 10) appears the first list of different nations coming from Noah's sons. But still the whole world ("*aretz*"; Gen 11:1) was united by one language. It was human pride at the tower of Babel that brought God to divide the people by languages. The scene is thus set for God's calling of Abram (Abraham) and his promise that through him God would bless all the families of the world (Gen 12:1–3). This promise is then focused on Abraham's seed (Isaac and the seed coming from him, Gen 22:16–18). In the thought of the Torah there is now a clear division: Israel and the nations.

The nations take on two roles: (1) opponents to God's planned blessing through Abraham's seed; and (2) recipients of the blessing that will come through this seed. The first is seen in the whole story of Israel's bondage in Egypt and subsequent passage to the promised land of Canaan: the opposition of Pharaoh (Exod 1–15), of Amalek (Exod 17:8–13), of Balak king of Moab (Num 22–24), and of the kings Sihon and Og and their nations (Num 21:21–35). The opposition of the nations to God's plan to bless through Israel is largely connected with their alignment to idols rather than to the Lord. Thus, Egypt's magicians call on their gods to oppose Moses (Exod 7:8–8:15), the daughters of Moab draw the sons of Israel after their gods (Num 25:1–3), and the people of Israel are repeatedly warned of the potential danger of fraternizing with the nations of Canaan who would lure them after their gods (e.g., Deut 7:1–6).

The second role, recipients of the blessing that will come through Abraham's seed, is made clear in the promise to Abraham (Gen 12:3; 18:18; 22:18). This key point in the story is highly significant in that it focuses the promise of blessing through a particular family and seed (Israel), but it is for the good of all the nations. The repetition of this promise to Isaac and his seed (Gen 26:4) and to Jacob and his seed (Gen 28:14) only strengthens the importance of God's commitment to bless all the nations and identifies the family line through which this blessing would come (Isaac not Ishmael, Jacob not Esau). [See Figure 3.]

From this point of the story narrated in the Torah, however, the focus becomes Abraham, Isaac, and Jacob's family—the people of Israel. Our attention is, therefore, concentrated on the continuing story of the "seed." The nations are mentioned when they relate to Israel, and some individuals from the nations are singled out (positively or negatively) as they relate to Israel. In several cases the kings, as representatives of the nations, are used, against their own wills, to fulfill God's will and bring him glory (Pharaoh, Exod 9:16; Balak with Balaam, Num 22–24), thus demonstrating the Lord's sovereignty over all the nations. In general, however, it is not until the end of the Torah that we find a key to understand its message as far as the blessing that will come on the nations is concerned. This key is found in links between the end of Deuteronomy and the beginning of Genesis, and in particular in the Song found in Deut 32.

In the last chapters of Deuteronomy there are elements that seem to link the story of Israel to the beginning of the Torah. The two ways, that of life and that of death, which the Lord sets before Israel as they are about to enter the land (Deut 30:15–20) set up an equivalence with the two trees in the garden of Eden, one leading to death and the other called the tree of life. Israel entering the land is here portrayed in a similar position to Adam and Eve in the garden of Eden (on the equivalence of Israel and Adam in the Torah cf. Postell 2011). In Deut 31 we are told that Israel will not follow God's way because of their "inclination" (Deut 31:21, author's translation). This word is used as a common noun in only three places in the Torah, here and the story of the flood in Gen 6:5 and 8:21, where it describes the evil inclination of the heart of humankind. Israel's problem is, therefore, being phrased in terms of the problem of the whole of humanity—the evil intent of the heart. It is in the Song of Deut 32 that we are led to understand the significance of the equivalence set up by these links (for a short commentary on the Song cf. McConville 2002, 444–62; for a book-length commentary cf. Knight 1995).

The Song *Ha'azinu* (Deuteronomy 32)

The Song starts with a call to all creation to hear the story that is about to be presented (v. 1) and ends with a call for all people to rejoice because of what God has done as portrayed in the Song (v. 43).

The Song starts with a call to acknowledge God's greatness ("Ascribe greatness to our God . . ." vv. 3b–4 NASB) and ends with a call to understand who God is ("See now that I, I am He, and there is no god besides Me" v. 39 NASB).

The Song starts with a description of the corruption of Israel ("He [the people] acted corruptly towards Him [God] . . ." v. 5, author's translation) and ends with a description of God atoning for that sin (". . . and He [God] atoned His land, His people" v. 43, author's translation).

Thus the Song is framed in a way that directs the reader to the heart of its message—the story of God's greatness in his relations with his people Israel, exemplified in his turning them from a rebellious people to a redeemed people.

The Nations in the Song of Deuteronomy 32

In the text of the Song the nations play a role vis-à-vis Israel, appearing at certain key points.

In verses 8–9 the nations are given an inheritance and allotment, while Israel itself is the Lord's inheritance. The emphasis on the Lord as "Elyon," meaning "Most High," highlights the fact that he is sovereign over all the nations and that there is no rival to him. So, if the main point is to show God's goodness to Israel, we also learn that all the nations are his. He is over all and decides the lot of all.

Verses 26–27 are pivotal to the story presented in the Song. The reason that God decides not to obliterate the remembrance of Israel as just punishment for their "forgetting" him (v. 18) is to avoid the possibility that the "enemy" would presume that they succeeded against God or that the story of Israel to this point was not his doing. The foolishness of this potential thought, that the nations could defeat the people of the Lord in their own strength, is emphasized in the next verses. But in verses 28–29 a deliberate ambivalence allows for the description of the foolish nation to apply both to the nations and to Israel. There is now no difference in the character of Israel from that of the nations who do not know the Lord. But the other side of the coin is the terrible fact that the Lord has "sold" his people. This is the place to which Israel comes. The terrible nature of the spiritual forces to which Israel turns is described in verses 32–34, and the lot which the Lord has prepared for these forces and those that follow them is presented in verse 35. Israel has become like the other nations by turning to their gods. But God will intervene at the point at which Israel comes to a place of hopelessness (v. 36) and by asking some pointed questions will expose the futility of their turning to other gods (vv. 37–38).

The revelation described in the final movement of the Song, verses 39–43, involves both Israel and the nations. While the call, "See now that I, I am He, and there is no god besides Me," (NASB) is addressed directly to Israel, this is a revelation that is final, full, and all-encompassing. All will know who the Lord is, both Israel and the nations. His intervention will involve both a just reckoning and retribution on those who opposed his purpose and plan in Israel (vv. 40–42) and the saving of his people through an act of atonement (v. 43). The final verse of the Song brings the nations and Israel together in a surprising way. In the ancient versions (including Qumran) and translations there are many alternative versions to the text of this verse, which have led scholars to multiple suggested solutions. None of those solutions are able to answer all the difficulties raised, and in my opinion, it is better to stay with the Masoretic text (Stanfield 2012, 223–29). There is also a question as to the meaning of the first sentence of verse 43. The verb can be a command either to rejoice or to make others rejoice, and the subsequent two words can be taken in several ways. Some of the main suggestions are:

- O nations, praise his people
- Give praise, O nations, his people
- O nations, make his people rejoice

There are major theological implications attached to each understanding. The implication of the first understanding (O nations, praise his people) is that the nations are now active in praising what the Lord has done by saving his people. The implication of the second (Give praise, O nations, his people) is that the nations themselves are now included as "his people." The implication of the third (O nations, make his people rejoice) is that the nations are given an active place in encouraging Israel and causing them to see what the Lord has done and is doing for them. What is common to them all is a positive place that the nations are now given in acknowledging the Lord and his salvation, whether in his people, as his people, or with his people as an encouragement to them. The Song ends, then, with the nations taking a positive role in the Lord's purpose of bringing glory to himself through what he does in Israel.

Israel's Story as the Key for the Story of the Nations

We have looked at how the nations are presented in the Song, treating the text as a unit in itself. We can now return to the indications of an intertextual relationship between the Song and the opening of the Torah. Within the context of this relationship the reader is led by the text itself to understand that Israel's story is also the key to understanding what the Torah is saying concerning God's dealings with humanity as a whole.

Let's start by looking at the main markers that lead the reader to this understanding.

(1) The context is the whole created order. The Song's opening call to the heavens and the earth immediately creates a resonance with the creation story and the first verses of the book of Genesis. This is not enough in itself to generate a meaningful link but it does set the scene by indicating that the heavens and earth which God created are now being called on as witnesses.

(2) Israel's formation is described in terms that link it with creation in Gen 1. The only two places in the Torah in which the words "land" (*eretz* or *aretz*) and "waste" (*tohu*) appear together are in the description of Israel's beginning in Deut 32:10 ("He found him in a desert *land* (*eretz*), And in the howling *waste* (*tohu*) of a wilderness" NASB) and in the story of creation ("the *earth* (*eretz*) was *formless* (*tohu*) and void," Gen 1:2 NASB). The fact that in both texts the Lord is described as "hovering" (author's translation; again a word used in the Torah only in Deut 32:11 and Gen 1:1) confirms the link. Israel's formation is being presented in the same terms as the creation. The question, of course, is why? It seems that Israel is being presented as a microcosm, a representative. But to understand what the Song is doing with this we have to continue to think about the additional links.

(3) Israel's sin and salvation are described in the same way as humanity's sin at the flood and Noah's means of escape. The Song in Deut 32 is framed by two words that in Hebrew are the only verbs in the Song in the singular piel form—*shichet* ("acted corruptly," v. 5), the first word in the Song that describes Israel's sin, and *kipper* ("he atoned," v. 43), which is the last verb in the Song describing God's solution for the sin of the people—atonement. Given that a close reading of the Song finds it characterized by numerous inner verbal and semantic linkages, this link is neither accidental nor inconsequential. In fact, its significance is demonstrated when we look at all the other occurrences of the verb translated in verse 5 "acted corruptly" in the Torah that are related to a human agent. These occurrences are the sin of humankind at the flood (Gen 6:11–12), the sin of Onan son of Judah (Gen 38:9) and the sin of Israel in the incident of the golden calf (Exod 32:7). In every one of those instances the word describes

sin the result of which was God's punishing the sinner, or sinners, by death. However, in two instances out of the three (the flood and the golden calf), we find God saving individuals or sparing the nation and in both cases this sparing from destruction is linked to the same Hebrew root translated "atone," in the case of Noah the command to "cover" the ark with "covering/pitch" (Gen 6:14) and in the case of Israel Moses' atoning for the people (Exod 32:30). Thus, the verb "acted corruptly" is used in each case that the Torah has dealt with sin deserving destruction and its way of escape. Now these are the descriptions that frame the Song. In verse 5 it is the people that act corruptly toward God, leading to the whole story presented to us in the body of the Song. In verse 43, the last statement of the Song, it is God who atones for his land and his people. In this framing of the Song is the whole story of sin and its solution. Just as the beginning of Israel is described in Deut 32 in terms of the original creation, so also the sin of Israel is described in the Song in terms of the sin that brought the judgment of the flood.

Thus, we can see significant links between Israel's story in the Song and between the story of creation and the flood.

But why should Israel's beginning be framed in terms of the creation? Here the place of the Song at the end of the Torah and the solution presented for Israel's sin are crucial. The Song does tell the story of the relationship of the Lord with Israel and the various roles that the nations play in that story. But the intertextual links lead us to additional significance. Israel is a representative. Israel's story represents the story of the world. From Israel's "creation" to Israel's sin and the atonement that God provides we find that by forging links with the beginning of the Torah we are presented with God's way of solving the wider situation brought about in the beginning.

In this sense, Israel's story, though significant in itself, is also representing God's way for his creation, for humankind, for all. The Song closes the Torah, therefore, with a severe portrayal of sin, Israel's and the world's, and yet this is only to present the solution that the Lord will give both for Israel and the nations—atonement.

Works Cited

Knight, George A. F. 1995. *The Song of Moses: A Theological Quarry*. Grand Rapids: Eerdmans.

McConville, J. G. 2002. *Deuteronomy*. ApOTC 5. Leicester: Apollos.

Patterson, Todd L. 2018. *The Plot-structure of Genesis: 'Will the Righteous Seed Survive?' In the Muthos-logical Movement from Complication to Dénouement*. BibInt 160. Leiden: Brill.

Postell, Seth D. 2011. *Adam as Israel: Genesis 1–3 as the Introduction to the Torah and Tanach*. Eugene, OR: Pickwick.

Stanfield, Yohanan. 2012. "The Song 'Ha'azinu' and Its Presence in Isaiah 1–39" [Hebrew]. PhD diss., Hebrew University of Jerusalem.

2.2 The Nations in the Prophets

Brian J. Kinzel

Israel's prophetic literature referred extensively to foreign nations, and over many periods of history, from at least ca. 780 BCE (Jonah) to ca. 450 BCE (Malachi). This article focuses on the writing prophets (Isaiah to Malachi). The prophets frequently wrote about the superpowers of the ancient Near East (Egypt, Assyria, Babylon, and Persia), and also dedicated major sections of their writings to the topic of the nations (e.g., Isa 13–23; Jer 46–51; Ezek 24–32). Some prophets wrote almost entirely about foreign powers (e.g., Jonah and Nahum [Assyria and Nineveh], Obadiah [Edom]). In regard to history, the fact that the prophets so often mention non-Israelite peoples shows that ancient Israel was not isolated from the nations around them. Instead, Israel was often caught up in international conflicts that raged both around and within their borders. In regard to biblical theology, the promise to Abraham (Gen 12:1–3) highlights God's worldwide intentions for the nation of Israel. According to that promise, nations can expect God's favor if they treat Israel well, dire results for abusing Abraham's seed, and also worldwide blessing stemming from Abraham. Furthering this theme, in the Law Israel was called to be a kingdom of priests representing God to the nations (Exod 19:4–5; Deut 4:5–7; 26:16–19). As Oswalt (1986, 36) notes about Isaiah's portrayal of God, "Zion may be his throne, but the earth was his stage." The prophets asserted repeatedly that Yahweh alone is God, and rules over all peoples (Cook 2013, 566; Brueggemann 1997, 492). The book of Jeremiah described Yahweh as "King of the nations" (10:7 NASB), and Daniel's prophecy stated, "The Most High is ruler over the realm of mankind" (4:17).

Terminology

The most important Hebrew terms used in prophetic literature to refer to non-Israelite peoples are "nation" (*goy*) and "people" (*am*). "Nation" emphasizes geopolitical affiliation, and "people" ethnic identity (Hulst 1997, 913–14). Even so, the terms are synonymous, and are both used to describe Israel as well as other peoples, but the plural *goyim* typically describes gentile nations. The nations are designated by a mixture of eponyms (e.g., Esau=Edom), tribal names (e.g., Medes), gentilics (e.g., Sidonians), and toponyms (e.g., Mount Seir=Moab). In addition to the four empire-nations mentioned above, Israel's surrounding neighbors are mentioned frequently (e.g., Amalek, Amorites, Ammon, Aram, Canaanites, Edom, Midian, Moab, and Philistines). Distant nations are also mentioned (e.g., Isa 66:19 mentions Tarshish [southern Spain], Put [Libya], Lud [northern Africa?], Meshech [southeast Asia Minor], Tubal [central Asia Minor], Javan [Greece], and the distant coastlands). Not surprisingly, cities are frequently mentioned, since they were the seats of government (e.g., Babylon, Damascus, Gaza, Nineveh, Tyre).

The Nations as the Enticers of Israel

The book of the covenant (Exod 21–23) includes a warning to Israel regarding the gentile nations: "You shall make no covenant with them or with their gods" lest the people of God be ensnared by them (Exod 23:32, 33; cf. Deut 12:29–31; 13:6–11). The writing prophets frequently applied this injunction by rebuking the people of the covenant for forsaking the one true God and instead worshiping idols. Thus, the prophets present the gentile nations as enticing and tempting Israel to enter into political alliances and follow after foreign gods.

Isaiah presents the house of Jacob as filled with both economic and religious influences from "children of foreigners" (2:5–8). The most obvious proof of this influence was that the idols of foreign gods were set up for worship in Judah. The people sinned so grievously in their idolatry that Isaiah even compared them to Sodom and Gomorrah (1:9–10; 3:9). In addition to idolatry, Israel and Judah were tempted to enter political alliances forbidden by the law. Judah was often tempted to enter into a political alliance with Egypt in response to the dire threats from Assyria and Babylon. Isaiah warned Judah against a treaty with Egypt (chs. 30–31). Hezekiah faced the threat of Assyria, and Isa 36–38 recounts the Assyrian invasion of 710 BCE. The Assyrian official assumed that the Judeans resisted the Assyrian juggernaut based on support and protection from Egypt (36:6–9). Hezekiah resisted the Assyrians and was rewarded with a miraculous deliverance. But later the Judean king succumbed to the overtures of the Babylonian emissaries, and was thus promised judgment at the hand of Babylon (ch. 39).

So important were *Jeremiah's* prophecies about the surrounding countries that his commission states, "I have appointed you a prophet to the nations" (1:5). Jeremiah prophesied during the collapse of the Assyrian empire, and advised

Judah to submit to the Babylonian rule. Hence, he viewed Judah's alliance with the anti-Babylonian forces (Egypt, Assyria) as forsaking the Lord. Like Isaiah, Jeremiah warned Judah against such an alliance, and presented it as an enticement away from the Lord (e.g., 2:18, "But now what are you doing on the road to Egypt, to drink the waters of the Nile? Or what are you doing on the road to Assyria, to drink the waters of the Euphrates?"). In chapter 27, Jeremiah warns Judah and her surrounding countries (v. 3) to submit to Babylon. The book records Jeremiah's severe conflict with a group of false prophets who encouraged the alliance against Babylon (27:9–10, 14, 16–17). Jeremiah even advised the Judean exiles, "Seek the welfare of the city where I have sent you into exile, and pray to the LORD on its behalf; for in its welfare you will have welfare" (29:7).

Writing in exile in Babylon, *Ezekiel* described Jerusalem as "at the center of the nations" (5:5), nations that will be witnesses to God's judgment on idolatrous Judah (5:8). Ezekiel described the idolatry in Jerusalem as "abominations" (8:9), and mentions the women "weeping for Tammuz" (8:14), the Sumerian god of fertility made popular by the Babylonians. He presented Judah's idolatry not as an enticement by the foreign powers, but with Judah taking the initiative as a harlot (with Egypt, 16:26; Assyria, 16:28; and Babylon, 16:29). This idolatry had persisted from the time of the exodus because Israel did not "forsake the idols of Egypt" (20:8). The parable of the two sisters (ch. 23) also presents Israel's and Judah's idolatry as spiritual adultery with foreign nations (Assyria, Egypt, Babylon). Like Isaiah and Jeremiah, Ezekiel also believed the anti-Babylonian alliance with Egypt and Assyria was rebellion against the Lord (e.g., 17:11–21).

Daniel represents the life of the exiles, and the enticement to integrate with the nations. Instead of accepting the "daily ration from the [Babylonian] king's choice food," Daniel "made up his mind that he would not defile himself with the king's choice food" (1:8). In the same way, Daniel's three companions refuse to worship Nebuchadnezzar's golden image, but are miraculously saved from the fiery furnace (ch. 3), just as Daniel is saved from the lions' den (ch. 6).

Hosea condemns the idolatrous Baal worship as spiritual adultery, symbolized by his marriage to "a wife of harlotry" (1:2). He also explains foreign alliances as defection from the Lord. Rather than seeking God, "Ephraim mixes himself with the nations" (7:8), and "They call to Egypt, they go to Assyria" (7:11).

The Nations as Enemies

Very often the prophets portray the nations as enemies of Israel and of God, and thus under threat of divine judgment. Since God has created the nations, they must answer to him (Block 1997, 4:971). The nations are judged for a wide variety of offenses. Pride and violence are often mentioned as the reasons for divine judgment.

In regard to *pride*, the prophets condemned both nations and their rulers. Isaiah pronounced doom "against everyone who is proud and lofty" (2:12). Pride and idolatry usurp God as the correct object of worship, but in the day of judgment "the LORD alone will be exalted" (Isa 2:11, 17). Isaiah condemned both Assyria and its king for self-willed arrogance (Isa 10:5–19). In pride, Assyria failed to recognize God's sovereign plan and control—that God wielded the Assyrian war machine as the rod of his anger against his people (10:3, 5). Jeremiah denounced Moab for pride (Jer 48) describing this sin extensively (i.e., arrogance, haughtiness, self-exaltation, boasting; 48:26, 29–30, 48). This mirrors Isaiah's assessment of Moab as guilty of pride (Isa 16:6). Daniel described God's judgment on proud and boastful rulers. Because of his boastful words, Nebuchadnezzar lost his mind (Dan 4:30–33) until he acknowledged God's sovereignty and that "He is able to humble those who walk in pride" (4:37). The evil ruler called the "little horn" was characterized by boastful speech, and thus his destruction in the fires of judgment is foretold (Dan 7:8, 11).

Violence is among the most often mentioned sins against society for which the prophets condemn the nations. Even though God used nations and rulers as instruments of his punishment against Israel and Judah, the nations are still accountable to their Creator for their own sins (e.g., Assyria, Isa 10). Thus, even though Isaiah warned Judah that divine judgment would come from an invader in the north (1:13–16; 6:22–26), Jeremiah still condemned Babylon also for violence against Jerusalem (Jer 51:34–36). Nahum pronounced woe on the Assyrians in Nineveh, "the bloody city," because of its ruthless warfare (Nah 3:1–3). Amos described the cruelty of Israel's neighbors, including the Arameans (1:3–5), the Philistines (1:6–8), the Phoenicians (1:9–10), and the Edomites (1:11–12). Amos also condemned Moab for inhumane treatment of Edom on its southern border. Habakkuk censured Babylon for looting and violence against the peoples it conquered (2:4–20).

One of the most widespread literary forms used in the prophets to express judgments against the nations is *collections of oracles*. While the origin of this genre is debated, clearly these collections have implications primarily for Israel and Judah, not for the nations themselves (Cook 2013, 565–66). These catalogues of judgments against nations around Israel and Judah are found in most of the prophets (e.g., Isa 13–23; Jer 46–51; Ezek 24–32; Amos 1–2).

Universal Judgment. Aside from the catalogues of oracles and other various judgments, the prophets also included the idea of universal judgment against humanity and the world. These judgments are often general but still not global (e.g., against idolatrous coastlands, Isa 41:1, 5–7). This theme of universal judgment is also in the setting of apocalyptic judgment that falls on the entire world (Dumbrell 1997, 397–99). Daniel's prophecy well illustrates this apocalyptic genre, which is found in many of the writing prophets (e.g., Isa 24–27; 34–35; Ezek 38–39; Joel 3; Zech 9–14).

The Nations as Worshipers

The prophets often wrote that God desires to bless all the nations, whom he called to worship along with Israel (Donaldson 2009, 235–36). Jonah's prophecy shows that the Lord offers forgiveness to any nation that will repent, even the ruthless Assyrians in Nineveh (Block 1997, 4:970). While the book of Jonah is evidence of God's ongoing concern for all the nations, most of the prophet's predictions of the salvation of the world concern the far future. Amos writes that when God will restore the "fallen booth of David," all the nations that are called by his name will be included in his plan of redemption (9:11–12).

Some of the most important statements about the salvation of the gentiles come from Isaiah. In 2:1–4, Isaiah describes how "in the last days" all nations will stream to glorified Zion to learn the law, resulting in worldwide peace (// Mic 4:1–3). Isaiah predicted that the nations will turn to the messianic "root of Jesse" (11:10), who will usher in perfect righteousness and Edenic peace. In the midst of oracles of judgment, Isaiah writes that Egypt "will even worship with sacrifice and offering, and will make a vow to the LORD and perform it" (19:21), and "the Egyptians will worship with the Assyrians" (19:23).

In chapters 40–66 Isaiah frequently describes how, in addition to worshiping with Israel, the nations will serve Israel, bringing the exiles back to their land (60:9; 66:20), paying homage to Israel, building up Zion, and contributing to the prosperity of the chosen people (60:10; 61:4). The coastlands wait for the law from the servant of the Lord (42:4), who is appointed as "a light to the nations" (42:6) so that his salvation "may reach to the end of the earth" (49:6). God calls "all the ends of the earth" to turn to him for salvation (45:22). The messianic heir of David is a "witness to the peoples"; to him the nations of the earth will turn because God will glorify him (55:4–5). When the dispersed of Israel are gathered back to the land from exile, the eunuchs and foreigners who keep the covenant also are included. God declares of the temple, "For My house will be called a house of prayer for all the peoples" (56:7). [See Figure 4.]

The *New Testament* expands the theme of the salvation of the nations. Jesus called his disciples to "make disciples of all the nations" (Matt 28:19; cf. Luke 24:47). In Acts, Saul was called as the apostle to the gentiles (9:15). Compelled by a vision, Peter visited Cornelius, and declared to him "all the prophets bear witness" that anyone among the nations who believes will receive forgiveness (Acts 10:43; cf. 10:34–35). The Jerusalem Council confirmed that God called the gentiles to salvation based particularly on the "words of the Prophets" (Acts 15:15).

Works Cited

Block, Daniel I. 1997. "Nations/Nationality." *NIDOTTE* 4:965–71.

Brueggemann, Walter. 1997. "The Nations as Yahweh's Partner." Pages 492–527 in *Theology of the Old Testament*. Minneapolis: Augsburg Fortress.

Cook, P. M. 2013. "Nations." *DOTP* 563–68.

Donaldson, Terence L. 2009. "Nations." *NIDB* 4:231–38.

Dumbrell, William J. 1997. "Apocalyptic Literature." *NIDOTTE* 4:394–99.

Hulst, A. R. 1997. "עַם/גּוֹי *'am/gôy* people. " *TLOT* 2:896–919.

Oswalt, John. 1986. *The Book of Isaiah 1–39*. NICOT. Grand Rapids: Eerdmans.

2.3 The Nations in the Writings

Kevin Chen

The theology of the nations in the Writings is essentially the same as it is in the Torah and Prophets, where, as "sons of Adam," the nations are created in the image of God, just like their forefather was (Gen 1:27; 9:6; Isa 45:12). The ultimate destiny of the nations is to be blessed through the Messiah (Gen 18:18; 22:18; Jer 4:2) and to live under his perfect rule forever (Gen 49:10; Isa 9:7; Zech 9:10). At the same time, the nations will also experience the just punishment of the Messiah, and those individuals among the nations who resist him to the end will suffer a crushing defeat (Num 24:17; Isa 34:2). This explains why some passages describe the nations as the enemies of the Lord and his people (Num 24:8, author's translation, "he devours the nations, his enemies"), whereas others describe them as part of the Lord's people (Zech 2:11, "many nations will join themselves to the Lord on that day, and they will be my people"). All these truths likewise apply to Israel, which is a "nation" (Gen 12:2; Exod 19:6; Isa 1:4). Israelites who are rebellious to the end will be punished as the Lord's enemies (Num 14:22–23; Isa 1:24), but a humble remnant will be saved (Num 14:24; Isa 1:27; 4:2–4). Below, the Writings will be shown to teach these same things.

Although the English word "nation" in the Old Testament is generally used to translate the Hebrew term *goy*, several other terms have significantly overlapping meanings and also bear on a theology of the nations. These include "people" (*'am*), "tribe" (*mishpachah*), "nation" (*le'om*), "humanity" (*'adam*), "sons of Adam," "[all] the earth," and "ends of the earth."

The Nations in the Writings

Probably the richest source for a theology of the nations in the Writings is the Psalter. The value of the Psalter for this purpose is heightened even more when studied as a coherent work (Wilson 1985), even one with an eschatological message (Mitchell 1997). If Pss 1–2 are an integrated introduction to the Psalter (Cole 2013), then the two references to "nations" (*goyim, le'umim*) in Ps 2:1 immediately indicate the importance of the nations in the Psalter. Their raging, plotting, and taking counsel "against the Lord and against his Messiah" depict the nations and their kings as the Lord's enemies (vv. 1–2). Their resistance is futile because the Messiah has been installed by the Lord on Zion (vv. 3–6) and will have "the nations as [his] inheritance, and the ends of the earth as [his] possession" (v. 8). Possession of the nations is likewise one aspect of the messianic kingdom in Amos 9:11–12, and possession of enemy gates is part of the Abrahamic covenant promises in Gen 22:17 and 24:60. In Ps 2:7, the statement "You are my son" is a direct reference to the fulfillment of the Davidic covenant, which itself involves fulfillment of the Abrahamic covenant through a messianic "seed" (2 Sam 7:8–16). Kings and nations who resist the Messiah to the end will be dashed to pieces, but those who wisely serve him will be blessed along with all those who take refuge in him (Ps 2:9–12). Psalm 2 thus concisely expresses the truths that the nations are currently in rebellion against the Lord and as such subject to his holy wrath, but they are offered protection if they serve the Messiah, who will ultimately rule the earth.

Another psalm that weaves together the destiny of the nations and the messianic kingdom is Ps 72, which also plays an important role in the Psalter as the concluding psalm of Book II (Pss 42–72). Unlike Ps 2, this psalm emphasizes the salvation of the nations, without ignoring their being judged (Ps 72:9, "his enemies will lick dust"). The references to "Solomon" in the psalm title and to "the son of a king" in verse 1 direct attention to the fulfillment of the Davidic covenant, rather than to David himself. As the psalm unfolds, it becomes increasingly apparent that the kingdom being described exceeds even Solomon's kingdom at its greatest heights (Kraus 1989, 81; Mitchell 1997, 85). For example, dominion "from sea to sea, and from the river to the ends of the earth" (v. 8) was never enjoyed by Solomon, but this same phrase characterizes the Messiah's rule in Zech 9:10. Neither did "all kings bow down" to Solomon nor did "all nations serve him" (Ps 72:11). Though many sought to hear his wisdom and brought gifts (1 Kgs 10:1–10, 23–25), 1 Kgs 11:14–40 describe Hadad, Rezon, and Jeroboam as his persistent enemies. Much less was Solomon known for his care for the poor and needy (Ps 72:12–13) but rather for laying a heavy burden upon the people (1 Kgs 12:4; see Kidner 1973, 256–57). Indeed, it is the Messiah's "name" that will endure forever, and in him that all nations will be blessed in fulfillment of the Abrahamic covenant (Ps 72:17; see Gen 12:2; 2 Sam 7:9).

Modern commentators sometimes interpret these verses as a glorified description of Solomon (Tate 1990, 222–23), but taking the words of the text at face value is generally more reliable for interpretation, and it leads here (and elsewhere in the Psalter, e.g., Ps 2:8; 16:10–11; 21:4) to a messianic interpretation and the promise of salvation for all nations in him (Kidner 1973, 254).

Furthermore, if the Psalter bears a unified message, then passages such as Ps 22:27 ("let all the tribes of the nations bow down before you") and Ps 67:3–4 ("let the peoples praise you, all of them. Let the nations be glad and shout for joy") can be understood in terms of the nations' eschatological worship of the Messiah and joy in him. Earlier, the "sons of Adam" had turned away from the Lord (Ps 14:1–3; 53:1–3) and subjected themselves to the divine sentence of death (Ps 90:3), but ultimately "all nations which you have made will come and worship you, O Lord" (Ps 86:9). These consistent references to the "nations" as corporate entities suggest that the Lord's judgment and salvation are carried out without ignoring national identity. At the same time, individual identity and responsibility are still the primary basis for judgment (Ps 2:12; Ezek 18:4). Thus, some individuals from every nation will be judged and some will be saved, even as sanctified national identities apparently endure in the kingdom of the Messiah (Rev 21:24, 26; 22:2), who will rule the nations forever.

Another book in the Writings that is a rich source for a theology of the nations is Daniel. From start to finish, the nations are a major part of this book due to Israel's exile among them (e.g., Dan 1:1–2). This scattering had been foretold by Moses (Deut 4:27) and led to the nations reproaching both the Lord and Israel (Ps 79:10, "Why should the nations say, 'Where is their God?'"). The defeat of Israel was readily interpreted as a defeat of the Lord, who was thought to be inferior to other deities (Dan 1:2; see Isa 36:18–20; Goldingay 1989, 15). The interrelatedness of the conflict between Israel and Babylon with the conflict between the Lord and other gods parallels the Lord's judgment of both the Egyptians and their gods on the Passover (Exod 12:12). Corresponding conflicts in both the physical and spiritual realms are also implied by reference to angelic battles involving the "prince of Persia" and "the prince of Greece" (Dan 10:13, 20; see Miller 1994, 285–86, 288). The book of Daniel also soberly describes brutal persecution by the nations (Dan 3:6; 6:7; 11:33–35). Their comparison to "beasts" (Dan 7:3–7) suggests a blurring of the distinction between man and animal, thus serving as a fitting description of their debasement.

Nevertheless, the book of Daniel repeatedly demonstrates the Lord's sovereignty over the nations and their gods by delivering his people, humbling gentile kings, and declaring his eternal kingdom. Daniel 2 may serve as a representative example. The inability of Nebuchadnezzar's wise men to interpret his dream suggests the futility of Babylonian gods as well as providing the perfect setup for the Lord to show his own wisdom and power (vv. 1–11). Since Daniel was also subject to the subsequent death sentence upon the wise men, he asked for time and called Hananiah, Mishael, and Azariah together to seek the Lord for mercy and revelation (vv. 12–18). After their prayer was answered (v. 19), Daniel praised the Lord as the one who "removes kings and raises up kings" (v. 21). Nebuchadnezzar himself honored Daniel and acknowledged that "your God is the God of gods and Lord of kings" (v. 47). Relatedly, the meaning of the dream is that the Lord's kingdom will crush all human kingdoms, fill the earth, and endure forever (vv. 34–35, 44–45). Nebuchadnezzar did not immediately turn away from idolatry and oppression (Dan 3), but his humiliating experience of insanity led to a striking confession of the greatness of the Lord and his eternal kingdom (Dan 4). There is hope, then, even for the most wicked of gentile kings. Many of them, like Belshazzar (Dan 5), will be arrogant to the end, but Nebuchadnezzar gradually had a change of heart. Darius also seems to have always been favorably disposed toward Daniel (Dan 6:3, 14, 16, 18–20, 23) and could only be duped into putting him in harm's way (vv. 4–9, 12–15).

Chronicles likewise includes the nations within its scope. This can be seen through its beginning and ending, as well as several passages in between. By beginning with Adam (1 Chr 1:1) and including others that are not part of Israel's line (e.g., vv. 5–16), Chronicles shows an interest in the entire human race (Merrill 2015, 91). By concluding with the edict of the Persian king Cyrus (2 Chr 36:22–23), the Lord's salvation plan, including the building of the Temple, is shown to involve his sovereign use of gentile kings (Japhet 1993, 1076–77). Thus, even in Chronicles' focus on the Davidic dynasty and the future, temple-building king to come from that line (1 Chr 17:11–14; 2 Chr 36:23), it is framed by and hence related to two non-Israelite rulers. The psalm sung when the ark was successfully brought into Jerusalem emphasizes the theme of the nations (1 Chr 16:7–36; see Klein 2006, 364). The opening lines include a call to "make known among the peoples his works" (v. 8). The Lord's protection over Israel while they went "from nation to nation" (v. 20; see v. 35) was not only for their benefit but calls for worldwide praise, "Sing to the Lord, all the earth. . . . Declare his glory among the nations, his wonders among all the peoples" (vv. 23–24; see v. 31). He is exalted over "all the gods of the peoples" (v. 26) and deserves the honor of "tribes of peoples" (v. 28; see v. 30). The Lord rules from heaven "over all the kingdoms of the nations" (2 Chr 20:6), and the Temple was intended to be a house of prayer not only for Israel but for them as well (2 Chr 6:32–33; see Isa 56:7).

Other books in the Writings relate to the theme of the nations in varying ways. So-called "wisdom books" (Job, Proverbs, Ecclesiastes, and perhaps Song of Songs) can be thought of as indirectly relating to the nations through their subject matter, which is of general interest (Waltke 2004, 50–55). These books are less focused on issues that specifically concern Israel and more on problems that humanity generally encounters. The wisdom they offer is for all people (i.e., the nations). Ruth directly concerns the theme of the nations through the sojourn of Elimelech's family in Moab and Ruth's Moabite heritage (Ruth 1:1–4). Her marriage to Boaz resulted in her inclusion in the Davidic and messianic line and depicts the inclusion of the nations in the messianic kingdom (Ruth 4:18–22). Lamentations focuses on the judgment of Jerusalem/Zion at the hands of the nations (Lam 1:3, 10), but it also refers in passing to the judgment to come upon all nations (Lam 1:21–22; 4:21–22). Esther emphasizes the Lord's protection of his exiled people from the murderous plot of Haman, an infamous example of an enemy from the nations. Hostility from the nations is also found in Ezra-Nehemiah in the form of opposition to the building of both the Temple and Jerusalem's walls, but the Lord's sovereign purposes prevail.

The Writings contain a rich theology of the nations that is in essential unity with that of the Torah and the Prophets. As descendants of Adam, the nations are also created in the image of God. However, they have turned away from the Lord wholesale and are consequently subject to his holy wrath. Their sins include idolatry and sometimes also brutal persecution of the Lord's people, which will be avenged. Nevertheless, those among them who take refuge in the Messiah will receive mercy and citizenship in his kingdom. He will rule the nations forever in peace and in justice.

Works Cited

Cole, Robert L. 2013. *Psalms 1–2: Gateway to the Psalter*. Sheffield: Sheffield Phoenix.

Goldingay, John. 1989. *Daniel*. WBC. Dallas: Word.

Japhet, Sara. 1993. *I & II Chronicles*. OTL. Louisville: Westminster John Knox.

Kidner, Derek. 1973. *Psalms 1–72: An Introduction and Commentary*. TOTC. Downers Grove, IL: InterVarsity Press.

Klein, Ralph. 2006. *1 Chronicles*. Hermeneia. Minneapolis: Fortress.

Kraus, Hans-Joachim. 1989. *Psalms 60–150: A Continental Commentary*. Translated by Hilton C. Oswald. Minneapolis: Fortress.

Merrill, Eugene. 2015. *A Commentary on 1 & 2 Chronicles*. Grand Rapids: Kregel.

Miller, Stephen. 1994. *Daniel*. NAC. Nashville: Broadman & Holman.

Mitchell, David. 1997. *The Message of the Psalter: An Eschatological Programme in the Book of Psalms*. Sheffield: Sheffield Academic.

Tate, Marvin. 1990. *Psalms 51–100*. WBC. Dallas: Word.

Waltke, Bruce. 2004. *The Book of Proverbs: Chapters 1–15*. NICOT. Grand Rapids: Eerdmans.

Wilson, Gerald. 1985. *The Editing of the Hebrew Psalter*. Chico, CA: Scholars Press.

CHAPTER 3

Messianic Prophecies

3.1 The Messiah in the Torah

Seth D. Postell

The New Testament makes some extraordinary claims about messianic prophecy in the Torah. In a dispute with the religious leaders, Jesus argues that Moses, and not he, would be their accuser for not believing in him (John 5:45). For, in his words, "if you believed in Moses, you would believe in me. For he wrote about me" (John 5:46, author's translation). Earlier in John's Gospel, Philip urges Nathanael to come and meet the Messiah of whom Moses wrote (John 1:45). In Luke 24 (vv. 27, 44), Jesus explains to his disciples how he has fulfilled the prophecies of Moses (see Matt 5:17). In Acts, Paul continually defends his message as the fulfillment of the prophecies of Moses (Acts 24:14; 26:22; 28:23). In Rom 10:4, Paul emphatically states that the Messiah is the goal of the law (Jewett and Kotansky 2007), and goes on to argue that the Torah predicted the message Paul was proclaiming (Rom 10:6–8; see Deut 30:12–13). The writer of Hebrews argues that Moses testified about future messianic realities (Heb 3:5), and even chose reproach for the sake of Christ (the Messiah) as a far greater treasure than all the riches of Egypt (Heb 11:26). Even a cursory reading of the New Testament reveals how important the Torah was for the new messianic faith, serving as a key witness for faith in Jesus as the Messiah.

Although the messianism of the Torah was obvious to Jesus and his early followers, many of Jesus' modern disciples, scholars and laypeople alike, are hard-pressed to identify just two or three messianic prophecies in the Torah, let alone explain how to defend the New Testament's huge claims about the Torah's message. In fact, some scholars even argue that the precious few verses in the Torah that have been interpreted messianically in the New Testament and the church were not intended by the historical author to be messianic prophecies. The early church's messianic interpretation of the Torah, they say, is not an interpretation of the grammatical-historical meaning of the text, but an added layer of meaning from a later period in the history of interpretation. The conservative textual commentary *The NET Bible Notes* (Harris 2005), for example, claims that the messianic interpretation of Gen 3:15 is "allegorical" (so also John Calvin) and that Gen 49:10 and Num 24:17 refer literally to the

Davidic dynasty and only secondarily or ultimately to the Messiah (i.e., not intended to be messianic by the historical author). Daniel Block (2004, 439) takes Deut 18:15, the "prophet like Moses" passage, as a reference to "Israelite prophecy in general." An examination of the Torah's structure, however, reveals something else.

Conflict in the Plot in the Introduction and Conclusion of the Torah

A literary inclusio is a common feature in biblical literature. An inclusio is a literary device which uses an intentional repetition of words, phrases, and themes at the beginning and the end of a literary work, which helps us to identify the work's primary concerns (Patzia and Petrotta 2002). An inclusio can be used to bracket literary units of all sizes, from an individual psalm (e.g., Ps 8:1, 8) to a pericope (Gen 1:1–2:3), to whole books (e.g., Isa 1; 65–66). The Torah is no exception. It begins and ends with intentional repetitions of words, phrases, and theological themes.

The introduction (Gen 1–11) and the conclusion of the Torah (Deut 31–34) share a number of repeated words and themes which not only show that the Torah is a self-contained book, but also serve to highlight its message (Postell 2011). Among the many repetitions, two common themes stand out. First, the Torah begins and ends with a prophetically pessimistic view of humans' ability to obey God's commandments. The word "inclination" (*yetzer*), which comes from the verb "to fashion/shape," only appears three times in the Torah: in the introduction (Gen 6:5; 8:21) and in the conclusion (Deut 31:21). In each case, the word highlights a human bent to rebel against God.

This inclination to do evil is reinforced by the storyline of the Primeval History (Gen 1–11) as well as by Moses' prophetic outlook at the end of the book. Even a cursory look at the storyline of Gen 1–11 reveals a perspective which is very similar to the end of Deuteronomy, and contains a plot remarkably similar to Israel's biblical history as recorded in the Former Prophets (Joshua, Judges, 1–2 Samuel, 1–2 Kings). God prepares a special land and brings Adam into it (Gen 2:10–15). According to Gen 1:28, Adam (and Eve) are called to subdue (conquer) this land. Adam is given one commandment (Gen 2:16). If he keeps it, he will enjoy God's blessing (Gen 1:28) and continue living in the land. Sadly, Adam and Eve quickly disobey God's commandment, experience the curses for disobedience, are cast out of this land, and eventually die in exile. Likewise, the Torah ends with the certainty that Israel will quickly disobey God's commandments by turning to other gods (Deut 31:16–21; see 4:25–26), will experience the curses of disobedience (Deut 28:15–68; see Lev 26:14–41), will be cast out of the land, and will die in exile (Deut 30:1).

An important insight that comes from this prophetic anticipation of disobedience and exile is that the law is not offered in the storyline of the Torah as the means for achieving God's blessing. Though God promises blessings for obedience to the law, the absolute certainty of Israel's disobedience and exile in the storyline serve to highlight the major conflict in the plot. In fact, disobedience seemingly reverses all forward progression toward achieving the blessings of obedience: this trend is visible when the Israelites worship the golden calf (Exod 32), offer strange fire (Lev 10), and fail to trust God's promises about the land of Canaan (Num 13–14). We can confidently say that exile from the promised land because of disobedience is the primary conflict in the Torah's plot. This conflict finds expression in the curses at the beginning and end of the Torah (Gen 3:14, 17; 4:11; 5:29; 9:25; etc.). It is the antithesis of God's ultimate purpose for humanity: blessing (Gen 1:22, 28; 2:3; 5:2; 9:1; etc.). This storyline paves the way for the coming of a hero (an individual seed) who will resolve the conflict of the curse and usher in God's blessing.

The second common theological theme at the beginning and end of the Torah is hope: namely, a prophetic (and poetic) note of hope despite human disobedience. The Torah begins and ends with blessing (Gen 1:28; Deut 33) even under the threat of the curses of disobedience. Despite Moses' prophecies in Deut 32 that Israel would rebel against her God, the chapter ends with the hope of Israel and the nations rejoicing together in God's work of salvation and atonement (Deut 32:43). This hope for Israel and the nations is impossible to understand apart from God's earlier promises to Abram: namely, that through him and his seed all nations (including Israel) will be blessed (Gen 12:2–3; 18:18; 22:18; Num 24:9). Moreover, the blessing of Moses (Deut 33) concludes with an amazingly optimistic note: Israel is a saved people living safely in the promised land (Deut 33:26–29). This unexpected and hopeful ending compels the reader to look for the conduit (hero) by which this prophetic optimism will be achieved. Our search for a hero leads us back to familiar ground—those passages traditionally understood as messianic (cf. Gen 3:15). But when viewing these few messianic verses from this larger perspective, we gain a much deeper appreciation for their disproportional importance, which far exceeds their number.

Conflict Resolved by a Hero in the Last Days: The Structure of the Torah

Quality over quantity is the driving factor in one's search for the Torah's message. Three things stand out when we look at the Torah's macrostructure. First, in key moments throughout the storyline of the Torah, the author has inserted poems, almost all of which focus on divine blessing and the vanquishing of hostile forces through a promised seed (Sailhamer 1992). Though the word "messiah" does not appear in these poems, they are profoundly universal in scope, anticipating a final defeat of hostile forces and blessings to Abraham's seed as well as to all the nations of the earth. Second, three of the Torah's major poems (Gen 49:11; Num 24:14; Deut 31:28–29) focus on events that will take place in "the last days" (Sailhamer 1992). In addition to being universal in scope, therefore, these poems are overtly eschatological. In each of the last day poems, moreover, the spotlight shines on a king from the tribe of Judah who will conquer the forces of evil and rule over Israel and the nations (Gen 49:8–10; Num 24:7–9, 17–19; Deut 33:7). Given the universal and eschatological orientation of these poems, and the prophetically hopeful perspective in the Torah's conclusion, it is quite reasonable to assume that these passages are messianic in the fullest sense of the meaning, and that this messianism is by design of the historical author, who identified the king in these poems as the hero of the Torah's story.

The Prophet like Moses as the Torah's Redeemer

As mentioned above, some have suggested that Deut 18:15 is not a messianic prophecy (contrary to the New Testament's interpretation). This conclusion fails to grasp the importance of this passage in the larger storyline of the Torah (Moses the prophet-redeemer). It also fails to consider the way in which Deut 18:15 is interpreted in the final chapter of the Torah (Deut 34:10), as well as in the remainder of the Hebrew Bible, particularly in Isaiah's famous Servant Songs in Isa 40–55.

Exile, as we have shown, is the antithesis of God's ultimate purpose to bless his people by making them fruitful and giving them the land (Gen 1:28; 9:1; 28:3–4; 35:11–13; see also Exod 1:7). Adam and Eve's disobedience resulted in curses and exile from the land. God's choice of Abram (and his seed) with its promises (Gen 12:1–3; 15:1–20) is strategically aligned with God's purposes to redeem creation from Adam and Eve's sin. In light of the earlier chapters of Genesis (1–11), God's decision to bring Abram and his seed back to the land from whence Adam and Eve were exiled (cf. Gen 2:10–14 with 15:18) and to conquer it by defeating their enemies (Gen 22:17; 24:60) can be traced back to the acorn-like promise in Gen 3:15: "And I will put enmity between you and the woman, and between your seed and her seed. He will strike you in the head, and you will strike him on the heel." The seed of the woman, which in the storyline of the Torah includes both the collective and the singular aspects, is called, among other things, to return to the land and conquer the people's enemies. Moses' calling must be understood within this larger perspective. Moses is portrayed as a seed of the woman whom God chooses to bring his people out of exile and back to the promised land.

Given the end of the Torah's focus on the certainty of exile from the land as well as a future return, the obvious implication is the need for another

Moses-like figure to bring Israel back from exile. It comes as no surprise, therefore, that the Torah concludes with a couple of rather strategic allusions to this Moses-like figure. In Deut 30, for instance, we see a clear prophecy that God would scatter Israel among all the nations (30:1), but at some future point (Deut 4:30 identifies this period as "the last days"), God will regather the people and circumcise their hearts to obey (30:2–10). Deuteronomy 30:11–14 speaks about "this commandment," presumably to love God with a circumcised heart (30:6), as something quite different than what the Israelites experienced during the days of Moses. This commandment will "not be far" (v. 11), a likely allusion to the distance between the people of Israel and the burning mountain in Exod 20:18. It will also "not be heaven," so they will need to ask for someone to "go up" and get it so that they can hear it and "do it"; again, these are all strong allusions to Moses going up Mount Sinai to bring the law to his people (see Exod 19:3, 8, 23–24; 31:18). Furthermore, this commandment will be beyond the sea so that someone would need to cross the sea and bring it to the people, once again an obvious allusion to the crossing of the Red Sea. *Targum Neofiti*, an early Aramaic targum of the Torah, translates Deut 30:12 with a clear allusion to Moses: "The Torah is not in the heavens, saying, 'O that we had one like Moses the prophet who would go up to the heavens and take it to us and make us hear the commandments and keep them.'"

Deuteronomy 34:10, another allusion to Deut 18:15, makes it clear that the prophet like Moses had not yet come. Two things are quite striking about this verse. First, Moses is long dead (Deut 34:6). We do not know how long after Moses' death this passage was written, but enough time passed for the author to state categorically that a prophet like Moses had never arisen (Blenkinsopp 1977). This statement could only have been made by someone who had compared all the prophets to Moses. Second, Deut 34:10 makes it clear that in spite of the promise in Deut 18:15 that God would raise up a prophet like Moses, this prophet had never come. In other words, the author of Deut 34 provides invaluable insight into how later biblical authors interpreted Moses' words in Deut 18:15. They did not understand this as a general reference to the prophets, but as a specific reference to an individual.

Support for this understanding of Deut 34:10 can be found in Isa 40–55, commonly known as Isaiah's "new exodus." Gordon P. Hugenberger (1995) has convincingly argued that the servant of the Servant Songs (Isa 42:1–4; 49:1–6; 50:4–9; 52:13–53:12) may best be understood with reference to the promise of the prophet like Moses. It is clear this figure's primary role is to provide spiritual and physical redemption for exiled Israel. Hugenberger not only points to the number of allusions to the exodus narrative in Isa 40–55, but also shows how the Servant Songs, like the Torah passages, portray a royal, priestly prophet who will be God's instrument in redeeming Israel from their physical and spiritual exile. Therefore, when we consider Deut 18:15, it is clear this passage is best interpreted messianically in its larger literary and canonical context. This prophet like Moses, like the messianic king in the Torah's poems, is the hero of the Torah story, not because of how frequently he appears but because of his vital importance for resolving one of the major conflicts in the plot of the Torah.

Works Cited

Blenkinsopp, Joseph. 1977. *Prophecy and Canon: A Contribution to the Study of Jewish Origins*. Notre Dame: University of Notre Dame Press.

Block, Daniel I. 2004. *Deuteronomy*. The NIV Application Commentary. Grand Rapids: Zondervan.

Harris, W. Hall, ed. 2005. *The NET Bible Notes*. Richardson, TX: Biblical Studies Press. Accordance electronic edition, version 4.1.

Hugenberger, Gordon P. 1995. "The Servant of the Lord in the 'Servant Songs' of Isaiah." Pages 105–40 in *The Lord's Anointed: Interpretation of Old Testament Messianic Texts*. Edited by Philip E. Satterthwaite, Richard S. Hess, and Gordon J. Wenham. Grand Rapids: Baker Books.

Jewett, Robert K., and Roy D. Kotansky. 2007. *Romans: A Commentary on the Book of Romans*. Hermeneia. Minneapolis: Fortress Press.

Patzia, Arthur G., and Anthony J. Petrotta. 2002. "Inclusio." Page 63 in *Pocket Dictionary of Biblical Studies*. A. G. Patzia and A. J. Petrotta. Downers Grove, IL: InterVarsity Press.

Postell, Seth D. 2011. *Adam as Israel: Genesis 1–3 as the Introduction to the Torah and the Tanakh*. Eugene, OR: Pickwick.

Sailhamer, John H. 1992. *The Pentateuch as Narrative: A Biblical-Theological Commentary*. Grand Rapids: Zondervan.

3.2 The Messiah in the Prophets

Michael L. Brown

There are no explicit references to "the Messiah" in the Prophets, but the prophetic books are filled with messianic expectation. This is in keeping with the rest of the Tanakh, in which (1) the choosing of Abraham and his descendants is destined to affect the whole world (first stated in Gen 12:1–3); (2) the prophets spoke of a time characterized by the universal knowledge of God when nations would live in peace and harmony, with Israel at the center (e.g., Isa 2:1–4); and (3) these promises were connected to the rule of a future son of David (e.g., Isa 11:1–16). Yet, in virtually all cases, this future hope was described without reference to "the Messiah." (Daniel 9:24–27 refers to *an* anointed one and not *the* anointed one. It is also not part of the section "Prophets" in the traditional Jewish canon.)

Former Prophets

The books of Joshua and Judges do not contribute to the discussion in a major way, other than to establish the need for a king to rule the unruly nation and for a successor to Moses to lead Israel into the promised land (possibly symbolic of the need for something to succeed the Sinaitic covenant). The books of 1 and 2 Samuel build on this with the rise and fall of Saul, Israel's first king, followed by the coronation of David, the eponymous ancestor of the messiah (see Ezek 34:23–34; 37:24–25; Hos 3:5; cf. Block 2003). It is to David, then, that the dynastic promises are given (2 Sam 7:12–16), and it is a descendant of Jesse, David's father, who will rule the world in the beatific messianic era (Isa 11:1).

As to whether David himself spoke about the Messiah, a minority of scholars suggest that 2 Sam 23:1 should be understood as saying that David's last words, recorded in the verses that follow (2 Sam 23:2–7), are about the anointed one (*mashiakh*) rather than about David. As rendered by Rydelnik (2010, 40), "These are the last words of David: the declaration of David son of Jesse, and the declaration of the man who was raised up concerning the Messiah [Anointed One] of the God of Jacob, and the Delighted One of the songs of Israel." If this were true, it would call for a major paradigm shift in modern scholarship on the antiquity of the messianic hope in Israel (cf. Fitzmyer 2007; see also Boda 2007; Acts 2:25–31).

The messianic promises are renewed to David's son Solomon in 1 Chronicles (17:11–14; 22:10), but because of Solomon's moral and spiritual failures, it is only David's name that receives that honor (1 Kgs 11:1–13; see also 1 Kgs 9:4–9; 1 Chr 28:7). In keeping with this emphasis, in later rabbinic literature the Messiah is often called *ben David*, the son of David, not *ben Shlomo*, the son of Solomon, and it is on the throne of David, not the throne of Solomon, that the messiah will sit.

This narrative of failure continues throughout 1 and 2 Kings, culminating in the destruction and exile of the northern kingdom of Israel (2 Kgs 17) and the southern kingdom of Judah (2 Kgs 25), including the destruction of the Temple in Jerusalem. And all this happened despite the Herculean reform efforts of King Josiah (see 2 Kgs 22–23) and the earlier efforts of King Hezekiah (2 Kgs 18–19). Thus, the people of Israel, scattered and broken, with no Davidic monarch to rule over them, find themselves in desperate need of a deliverer—the ultimate deliverer, the greater David, the Messiah himself. The rest of the prophetic books, from Isaiah to Malachi, intersect with and build on these realities, more fully developing the messianic hope.

Latter Prophets

Isaiah looks forward to a time of universal peace, when all nations will stream to Jerusalem to learn from the Lord (Isa 2:1–4; cf. Mic 4:1–4). That era is associated directly with the Davidic Messiah in Isa 11:1–16. Under his rule, the Lord promises, "They shall not hurt or destroy in all my holy mountain; for the earth shall be full of the knowledge of the Lord as the waters cover the sea" (Isa 11:9 ESV). See also the promises of the Davidic Branch, in whose days Judah will be saved and Israel will dwell securely (Jer 23:5–6; 33:14–16), living in obedience to God and enjoying his bounty (Ezek 34:23–31). At that time, Israel and Judah will be reunited, with the Lord's sanctuary reestablished in their midst (Ezek 37:15–27; cf. further Ezek 40–48). As a result of this, "Then the nations will know that I am the Lord who sanctifies Israel, when my sanctuary is in their midst forevermore" (Ezek 37:28). For other prophecies describing aspects of the messianic era, see Isa 60:1–22; Jer 3:16–18; Hos 3:5; Zech 14.

It should be noted, however, that the prophets often saw these messianic promises unfolding on the immediate horizons of history—that is to say, in the very near future as opposed to the very distant future. Thus, it is on the heels of the fall of the archenemy Assyria, which had exiled Northern Israel and threatened to do the same to Judah, that the prophecy of Isa 9:6–7 (Heb. 5–6) is spoken, where the birth of the Davidic king (possibly Hezekiah) is announced with messianic grandeur, as if he himself would be the greater David. His failure to live up to these lofty, even superhuman expectations allows later readers to reread these promises to Isaiah's generation as pertaining to the messianic era. This would be similar to Ps 2, originally an enthronement psalm celebrating the Davidic king, God's son, in Jerusalem, but with ultimate application to the Messiah, God's Son, who will rule the world from Jerusalem.

Similarly, Isa 11:1–16 follows the prophecy of Assyria's demise (see Isa 10:5–34), while it would seem that Jeremiah expected to see his messianic prophecies fulfilled on the heels of the return from Babylonian exile (and/or the nation's repentance), which he also prophesied (see, e.g., Jer 3:12–18; 23:1–6; 24:5–7; 30:1–24; 33:2–16; cf. also 1 Pet 1:10–12). The same holds true for the plans of the temple in Ezek 40–48, which the prophet was to show to his contemporaries in exile to make them ashamed of their sins (Ezek 43:10–11). Those temple plans included instructions that appear to assume that Ezekiel would serve in this rebuilt temple (see, e.g., Ezek 43:18–27). See also Hag 2:21–23, where the raising up of Zerubbabel, Haggai's contemporary and the grandson of King Jeconiah (thus, a potential heir to the Davidic throne), will take place when God overthrows the thrones of kingdoms. This principle helps us to recognize how later Jewish writers, especially the writers of the New Testament, could find messianic references in seemingly obscure places, such as Isa 7:14: they expected key promises given to Davidic kings that did not reach their fulfillment in their day to be fulfilled through the Davidic Messiah. Accordingly, Isa 7:14 is read by Matthew in light of the larger messianic complex in Isa 7–11; cf. Matt 1:23 with Isa 7:14; Matt 2:23 with Isa 11:1 (an apparent play on the word *netzer* with reference to other verses as well); and Matt 4:13–16 with Isa 9:1–2 (Heb. 8:23–9:1; see further 9:6–7 [Heb. 9:5–6]).

But just as Israel's history is marked by suffering, so also the Messiah's mission is marked by suffering, and just as David was a priestly king (see esp. Ps 110:4), so the Messiah is a priestly king. In keeping with this, in Zech 6:12–15 the Branch, which is a title of the Messiah son of David in Jer 23:5–6 and 33:15–16, is typified by the high priest Joshua sitting on a throne and wearing a crown, rather than the governor (and son of David) Zerubbabel. And since it fell on the high priest to intercede for his people, taking their sin on his shoulders and making atonement for them, this too is part of the Messiah's mission (see further Rose 2000).

This picture emerges most clearly in Isa 40–53, where "the servant of the Lord," an individual Israelite (Isa 42:1–7, 19; 49:1–7; 50:10; 52:13–53:12) rather than the nation as a whole (Isa 41:8–9; 42:19 [2x]; 43:10; 44:21 [2x]; 45:4; 48:20), dies for the sins of his people. This same servant delivers his people from bondage and becomes a light to the nations (Isa 42:6; 49:6), even while appearing to fail in his mission to Israel (Isa 49:4–6), a mission that is marked by suffering (Isa 50:6–7). Yet he will be highly exalted (Isa 52:13, 15) but only after enduring terrible disfigurement (Isa 52:14). And during his time of greatest agony, his own nation will misinterpret his pain, thinking that he is being wounded for his transgressions rather than suffering for theirs (Isa 53:4–6). Instead, he will make many righteous by becoming a guilt offering on their behalf, bearing their sins and pain (Isa 53:10–12).

Zechariah also alludes to the Messiah's humble origins (see Zech 9:9, in contrast with Dan 7:13–14; Isa 11:4—but note that he begins as a stump in Isa 11:1), and speaks of the time when the nation would mourn over the one whom they pierced, leading to their redemption (Zech 12:10–13:1). As priest, then, the Messiah suffers for the sins of his people; as king, he rules and reigns over them. It is the priestly ministry that empowers his kingship, is accomplished first, and includes aspects of divine purging and judgment (see Mal 3:1–6).

Works Cited

Block, Daniel I. 2003. "My Servant David: Ancient Israel's Vision of the Messiah." Pages 17–56 in *Israel's Messiah in the Bible and the Dead Sea Scrolls*. Edited by R. S. Hess and M. Daniel Carroll R. Grand Rapids: Baker.

Boda, Mark J. 2007. "Figuring the Future: The Messiah in the Prophets." Pages 35–74 in *The Messiah in the Old and New Testaments*. Edited by Stanley E. Porter. Grand Rapids: Eerdmans.

Fitzmyer, Joseph A. 2007. *The One Who Is to Come*. Grand Rapids: Eerdmans.
Rose, Wolter H. 2000. *Zemah and Zerubbabel: Messianic Expectation in the Early Postexilic Period*. JSOTSup 304. Sheffield: Sheffield Academic Press.
Rydelnik, Michael. 2010. *The Messianic Hope: Is the Hebrew Bible Really Messianic?* NAC Studies in Bible & Theology 9. Nashville: B&H Academic.

3.3 The Messiah in the Writings

Brian J. Kinzel

In the canon of the Hebrew Bible, the Writings constitute eleven books: Psalms, Proverbs, Job, Song of Songs, Ruth, Lamentations, Ecclesiastes, Esther, Daniel, Ezra-Nehemiah (counted as one book), and Chronicles (also connected as one book). They include some very significant references to the messiah. Ruth gives the genealogy leading to David, the founder of the messianic dynasty (4:18–22). The chronicler's history was recorded after the fall of the Davidic dynasty in Jerusalem in 586 BCE, and it repeats the account of the covenant God made with David (1 Chr 17 // 2 Sam 7). The promise given to David (that his heir will reign forever) is repeated in 2 Chr 21:7. This indicates that the Davidic covenant had a central place in the expectations and hopes of the community that returned to the land of Israel from exile. This eschatology lacked the details given in the Prophets (Williamson 1977, 154); even so, the account in Chronicles supports (1) "Israel's identity as Yahweh's people" and (2) "the possibility of Israel's future existence" (Kelly 1996, 156–57; see 1.4). The most significant references to the messiah in the Writings are in the Psalms and Daniel. The prophecy in Dan 7 describes how a human figure called the "son of man" receives dominion over the earth from the "Ancient of Days." Jesus then used "son of man" as his self-designated title (see below, article 7.2).

Overview of the Messiah in the Psalms

Many psalms have been read as messianic, and the New Testament uses them extensively to identify Jesus as the expected messiah. One of these is Ps 2, which describes the world-wide rule of the messiah (cf. 2:2 ESV "his Anointed"). Another is Ps 110, which is the most quoted portion of the Hebrew Bible in the New Testament. Of those psalms typically understood as messianic, some are called "royal psalms" because they feature a ruler: either David, the king, or the anointed. This group includes Pss 2, 18, 20, 21, 45, 61, 72, 101, 110, and 144, as well as two that mention the Davidic covenant specifically, Pss 89 and 132.

Not all of the royal psalms refer to a future messiah, however (e.g., 20, 21). The category of "royal psalms" does not actually describe a specific literary genre or function. Instead, these psalms include various forms and purposes, and are grouped according to their content (Mowinkel 2004, 46–47). Other psalms are considered messianic, but lack a clear reference to a royal figure, including some that the New Testament applies to Jesus as the messiah (e.g., Pss 8, 16, 22, 40, 97, 102, 118).

Canonical Shape of the Psalter. The psalms are a collection of individual compositions, and every section of the collection includes messianic psalms. Earlier critical scholars viewed the order of the collection as gradual and random (Mowinkel 2004, 196); they preferred to interpret each psalm according to its literary genre (i.e., form criticism) with little thought to its position in the canon. Since 1985 there has been increasing awareness that the final canonical order of the book reflects an intentional interpretive strategy (Wilson 1985). The collection certainly reflects the beliefs of the Jewish people during the Second Temple period, when the order of the canon was fixed. Especially noteworthy, Pss 1–2 serve as an introduction, and thus Ps 2 introduces the figure of the messiah as a major theme in the collection (Cole 2013, 183–85). There also is broad agreement that the messiah is a prominent theme in the psalms (Crutchfield 2003); some believe that messianic psalms form the overriding theme for the collection (Mitchell 2006). Though there is disagreement about the meaning of their order (e.g., Longman 2013, 224), the inclusion of psalms that speak of a messiah and the Davidic covenant (e.g., Pss 89 and 132) show that after the return from exile, the Jewish people had a belief in a future heir of David.

New Testament Interpretation of the Psalms. The New Testament frequently quotes from messianic psalms in reference to the life, death, and resurrection of Jesus. The New Testament writers thus interpret the psalms to mean that Jesus was the fulfillment of Israel's messianic expectation. They explain these psalms in at least two ways.

(1) Predictive Prophecy. Psalms 16, 110, and 118 especially are used to prove that Jesus' ministry was previously predicted. In his sermon at Pentecost, Peter quotes Ps 16 (Acts 2:25–28), and explains that David wrote not of his own experiences, but of the resurrection of Jesus. Peter indicates the predictive element of the psalm by pointing out that David never rose from the dead. "Being therefore a prophet . . . he foresaw and spoke about the resurrection of the Christ . . ." (Acts 2:30–31). Peter then uses Ps 110 to show that Jesus' ascension to heaven was also predicted (Acts 2:34–35). The author of Hebrews uses Ps 110 to show that the priestly ministry of Jesus had been predicted (Heb 7–10). The synoptic gospels record that Jesus quoted from Ps 118:22–23 to prove to the Jewish leaders that their rejection

of the messiah had been predicted: "The stone that the builders rejected has become the cornerstone; this was the Lord's doing, and it is marvelous in our eyes" (Matt 21:42 // Mark 12:10–11 // Luke 20:17).

(2) Typological Fulfillment. The New Testament also cites psalms that have no clear reference to a messianic figure, and applies them to the life of Jesus, but not as fulfillment of a prophecy. For example, when Jesus cleansed the Temple of merchants and money changers (John 2:13–17), the gospel account quotes Ps 69:9, "Zeal for your house will consume me." Though Ps 69 did not predict this event from Jesus' ministry, the disciples viewed their master's zeal as an application of the principle expressed.

Jewish Interpretations. In the Second Temple and rabbinic periods, Jewish writers interpreted royal psalms as messianic: a future king and heir of David would rule Israel, defeat her enemies, and usher in the idyllic conditions described in the prophets (Ginsberg et al. 2007, 110–12). As Harris (2008, 845) expresses, "In the exegetical traditions of both ancient Judaism and Christianity, particular psalms were read as containing significant allusions to the person and career of the Messiah." However, in the medieval period Jewish commentators began to move away from a messianic interpretation of the psalms. That is, they interpreted the royal psalms as describing a past messiah (e.g., the historical figure of King David) instead of alluding to a future messiah. In his commentary on the Psalms, the great Jewish writer Rashi continued this trend. For most of the royal psalms, Rashi deemphasized messianic interpretation as part of his famous contextual "simple" hermeneutic. Part of his motivation was anti-Christian polemic, desiring to show that correct philology proves that the Christian messianic interpretation of the psalms was not the original meaning (Harris 2008, 848). According to Gruber (2007, 182), Rashi explained the psalms so that "no Jew need be intimidated into giving up the ancestral faith because of the assertion that one historical figure, namely Jesus of Nazareth, is known to Christians as the 'son of God.'" The standard Jewish understanding to this day is that the royal psalms refer not to an eschatological or future messiah, but instead to "the anointed one of God, the earthly king of Israel" (Sarna 2007, 670).

Christian Interpretations. Interpreters in the church have used different methods to show that Jesus was the intended subject of the messianic psalms. They are divided on two questions: (1) which psalms actually refer to the messiah, and (2) which psalms were originally intended to refer to the messiah. While there is general agreement about the first question, there remains a clear division over the question of authorial intent. On the one hand, most modern commentators agree with Rashi that the psalms were not originally written with an inspired prophetic meaning, but rather to describe David or another figure in the ancient world. On the other hand, most Christian commentators still think that Jesus fulfilled the messianic hope of these psalms.

The majority position of evangelical interpreters is that the psalms were not intended originally by the author to describe a future messiah, but a deeper meaning (*sensus plenior*) was added later, either by the editors of the psalter (i.e., those who compiled them in their present order), by the New Testament, or by both (Craigie 1983; Tate 1990; Allen 2002; VanGemeren 2012). In this vein, Waltke (1997, 1108) writes that the psalms "were always pregnant with messianic expectation" but only "became full blown messianic psalms" after they were edited. Other commentators believe that the psalms give evidence that the original author wrote about a future messiah, and not the past anointed king of Israel (Kidner 1975a; 1975b). However, commentators apply different rules to different psalms. Delitzsch (1996, 41–43) has five explanations about the authorial intent of the royal psalms. For example, he believed Ps 110 to be truly intended as a prophecy about the messiah, while Pss 2 and 45 were indirectly "royal" (they refer to the historic king and are applied as types to Jesus in the New Testament). His approach is not unusual, and commentators often interpret individual psalms differently.

Survey of Selected Messianic Psalms

Psalm 2. Many commentators view this psalm as polite exaggeration ("court style") applied to the king of Israel on the occasion of his coronation; thus, the mention of messiah in verse 2 does not mean the psalm was in any way originally intended to be messianic (Craigie 1983, 65–67). However, the description of the anointed goes far beyond what was expected of or allowed for a human heir of David. This psalm presents the messiah on the same level as God himself as the ruler of the entire world, and not just of Israel. The "nations" and "peoples" (v. 1) follow the kings and rulers in rebellion against "the LORD and against his Anointed" (v. 2). God rules in the heavens. First, he declares the anointed as his rightful heir ("you are my son"), and then installs him as king in Zion. The house of David ruled over Israel and Judah, but this heir rules over all the nations (vv. 7–9). Though the presence of an Aramaic word for "son" in verse 12 is variously explained, it is obvious that worship and submission to Yahweh are synonymous with submission to the rule of the anointed son. In summary, it seems unlikely that the psalmist would be so bold as to equate God's universal reign and judgment with the reign of a human heir of David.

Psalm 16. Peter quotes from 16:8–11 in his sermon at Pentecost (Acts 2) as proof of the resurrection of Jesus. Verse 10 is particularly important: "For you will not abandon my soul to Sheol, or let your holy one see corruption." Commentators explain Peter's quotation in two ways. (1) Deeper Meaning. Many commentators believe that David wrote of his own experiences in this psalm, and Peter then provided the *sensus plenior* that was not originally intended by David. (2) Prophetic Meaning. A minority of commentators think that Peter quoted this psalm as proof of the prophetic prediction of the resurrection (e.g., Kidner 1975a, 103); this means that the psalm presents an unrealized ideal that does not describe David's personal experiences. Just as David did not always set the Lord before him nor was he unshaken, so David did not expect that his body would be raised from the dead and thus not decompose in the grave. Instead, in 16:7–11 David wrote about a future heir who would indeed not see corruption in the pit.

Psalm 22. The gospel accounts record that Jesus quotes from 22:2 (Eng. v. 1) during his crucifixion (Matt 27:46 // Mark 15:34). In addition, 22:12–19 (Eng. vv. 11–18) is widely considered a prophetic description of Jesus' experience on the cross, including the remark that "they divide my garments among them, and for my clothing they cast lots" (v. 18). The details in this section closely match the crucifixion. Believing scholars either explain this as a true prediction, or assign this to the traditional deeper meaning revealed in the New Testament. Delitzsch (1996, 193) writes that "the hyperbolic element is changed into the prophetic." Either way, this psalm has long been used as an apologetic support of a messianic understanding. The MT diverges from the versions at verse 17 (Eng. v. 16). The ancient translations (LXX, Syriac, Vulgate) all read, ". . . they pierced my hands and my feet." But the MT reads, ". . . as a lion . . . my hands and my feet." The difference between "pierced" and "lion" is the vowels, which were standardized in the Christian era. Very probably the MT reading was chosen to avoid having the text sound like a Christian tradition. Most English translations follow the versions with the reading "they pierced" (Rydelnik 2010, 44–46).

Psalm 110. The New Testament refers to this psalm several times, and it is often interpreted as a direct prophecy of the future messiah. The psalm has several elements that indicate that it was originally intended to describe an eschatological ruler and not simply a human heir of the house of David. (1) The psalm begins with the pronouncement "The LORD says" (*ne'um YHWH*), which introduces the psalm as a prophetic oracle. Prophecy of this type typically addresses future events. (2) As indicated by the New Testament quotations of verse 1, David refers to the ruler described as "my lord," pointing to the ruler's superior status (Matt 22:41–45 // Mark 12:35–37 // Luke 20:41–44; Acts 2:34–35; Heb 1:13). (3) Yahweh also designates this ruler as "a priest forever after the order of Melchizedek" (v. 4). Neither David nor any other of his heirs served as priests, and this role was denied the kings of Israel. (4) The psalm looks forward to the judgment of the nations and defeat of all enemies (vv. 5–7).

Works Cited

Allen, Leslie C. 2002. *Psalms 101–150*. Rev. ed. WBC. Waco, TX: Word.

Cole, Robert L. 2013. "Psalms 1–2: The Psalters Introduction." Pages 183–96 in *The Psalms: Language for All Seasons*. Edited by Andrew J. Schmutzer and David M. Howard, Jr. Chicago: Moody.

Craigie, Peter C. 1983. *Psalms 1–50*. WBC. Waco, TX: Word.

Crutchfield, John C. 2003. "The Redactional Agenda of the Book of Psalms." *HUCA* 74:21–47.

Delitzsch, Franz. 1996. *Psalms*. Vol. 5 in Biblical Commentary on the Old Testament. Translated by J. Martin et al. 25 vols. Edinburgh, 1857–1878. Repr., 10 vols. Peabody, MA: Hendrickson.

Ginsberg, Harold Louis, David Flusser et al. 2007. "Messiah." *EncJud* 14:110–15.

Gruber, Mayer I. 2007. *Rashi's Commentary on Psalms*. Philadelphia: Jewish Publication Society.

Harris, Robert A. 2008. "Rashi and the 'Messianic' Psalms." Pages 845–62 in *Birkat Shalom: Studies in the Bible, the Ancient Near Eastern Literature, and Postbiblical Judaism Presented to Shalom M. Paul on the Occasion of His Seventieth Birthday*. Edited by Chaim Cohen, Victor Avigdor Hurowitz, Avi Hurvitz, Yochanan Muffs, Baruch J. Schwartz, and Jeffrey H. Tigay. Winona Lake, IN: Eisenbrauns.

Kelly, Brian E. 1996. *Retribution and Eschatology in Chronicles*. JSOTSup 211. Sheffield: Sheffield.

Kidner, Derek. 1975a. *Psalms 1–72: An Introduction and Commentary*. TOTC. London: Inter-Varsity Press.

———. 1975b. *Psalms 73–150: An Introduction and Commentary*. TOTC. London: Inter-Varsity Press.

Longman, Tremper III. 2013. "From Weeping to Rejoicing: Psalm 150 as the Conclusion to the Psalter." Pages 219–30 in *The Psalms: Language for All Seasons*. Edited by Andrew J. Schmutzer and David M. Howard, Jr. Chicago: Moody.

Mitchell, David C. 2006. "Lord, Remember David: G. H. Wilson and the Message of the Psalter." *VT* 56.4:526–48.

Mowinkel, Sigmund. 2004. *The Psalms in Israel's Worship*. Translated by D. R. Ap-Thomas. Grand Rapids: Eerdmans. First published 1962 by Basil Blackwell.

Rydelnik, Michael. 2010. *The Messianic Hope: Is the Hebrew Bible Really Messianic?* NAC Studies in Bible & Theology 9. Nashville: B&H Academic.

Sarna, Nahum M. et al. 2007. "Psalms." *EncJud* 16:663–83.

Tate, Marvin E. 1990. *Psalms 51–100*. WBC. Dallas: Word.

VanGemeren, Willem A. 2012. *Psalms*. The Expositor's Bible Commentary. Rev. ed. Grand Rapids: Zondervan.

Waltke, Bruce K. 1997. "Psalms." *NIDOTTE* 4:1096–1112.

Williamson, H. G. M. 1977. "Eschatology in Chronicles." *TynBul* 28:115–54.
Wilson, Gerald H. 1985. *The Editing of the Hebrew Psalter*. Chico, CA: Scholars Press.

3.4 New Testament Use of the Old Testament

Craig A. Evans

Nothing demonstrates more deeply the Jewish roots of the Christian movement than the observation of the ubiquity of Old Testament passages, language, and themes in the writings that make up Christian Scripture. The Old Testament is quoted or alluded to in every New Testament book except Philemon and 2 and 3 John, three brief personal letters. The Old Testament appears in the New Testament in every conceivable manner. It is quoted with introductory formulas ("it is written") and without. It is paraphrased and alluded to. Sometimes the allusions comprise no more than a word or two. Other times the New Testament reflects Old Testament themes, structures, and theology. The New Testament writers appeal to the Old Testament for apologetic, moral, doctrinal, pedagogical, and liturgical reasons (Lindars 1961; Barrett 1970; France 1971; Smith 1972; Shires 1974; Longenecker 1975; Hanson 1980; Carson and Williamson 1988; Beale and Carson 2007).

Corroboration from the Dead Sea Scrolls

Not long after the publication of several texts, it became apparent that the Dead Sea Scrolls were important for understanding the New Testament's use of Old Testament Scripture (Fitzmyer 1961). In Matt 11:3, an imprisoned John the baptizer sends messengers to ask Jesus: "Are you the coming one or shall we look for another?" (author's translation). Jesus replies with allusions to various passages from Isaiah: "Go and report to John what you hear and see: the blind receive sight and the lame walk, the lepers are cleansed and the deaf hear, and the dead are raised up, and the poor have the gospel preached to them" (Matt 11:4b–5; cf. Luke 7:22). Jesus has alluded to Isa 26:19; 35:5–6; and 61:1. He clearly means to reply to John's question in the affirmative, but was his reply messianic? Evidently it was, for we find the same passages clustered in a text from Qumran, in which similar activities are understood to take place when God's Messiah comes, whom "heaven and earth will obey" (cf. 4Q521 frag. 2 ii 1–12). This fragmentary scroll, which dates to the middle of the first century BCE, provides important documentation of messianic belief held among Jews living in Israel a generation or two before the time of Jesus' ministry. Simply by alluding to the same Isaianic passages, Jesus has brought eschatology and messianism to his hearers' minds.

In his parable of the wicked vineyard tenants (Mark 12:1–9), the contents and context of which reflect sharp conflict between Jesus and the religious authorities of his day, Jesus alludes to Isaiah's song of the vineyard (Isa 5:1–7), reflecting an understanding that cannot wholly derive from either the LXX or the Hebrew. Why should Jesus' opponents have understood his parable as directed against them (Mark 12:12), since Isa 5:1–7 is directed against all of Judah? The targum, however, provides the missing link. According to its para-phrase, God built an "altar" and a "sanctuary" (instead of a "watchtower" and "wine vat") for his people. But because of his people's sin, God will destroy their "sanctuaries." This threat of the destruction of the Temple and altar makes the Isaianic passage particularly relevant for the Temple authorities of Jesus' day. In view of the targum's interpretation, therefore, Jesus' use of Isa 5 in his parable is particularly appropriate, and the hostile reaction of his religious opponents is perfectly understandable. That Isa 5:1–7 was in fact applied specifically to Jerusalem's Temple is attested in 4Q500 frag. 1, a scroll from Qumran that dates to the first century BCE.

Matthew and John

All four New Testament Gospels engage Old Testament Scripture in a way that shows that the latter was foundational for the former. The Gospels of Matthew and John, the two most Jewish Gospels, appeal frequently and formally to the Old Testament to show that this or that prophecy has been fulfilled. But Old Testament Scripture is not only quoted formally; it is often echoed here and there in ways that import patterns, themes, and perspectives into the Gospel narratives. The ways in which the Gospels engage Israel's ancient Scripture create continuity between the old stories of covenant, promises, and prophecies and their fulfillment in Jesus and his community (Hays 2016).

Matthew's citations of the Old Testament, customarily introduced with a fulfillment formula (1:22; 2:15, 17, 23; 4:14; 8:17; 12:17; 13:14, 35; 21:4; 27:9), cannot be fully understood apart from an appreciation of Jewish approaches to the interpretation of Scripture. Space permits only one example. In Matt 2:13–15 the evangelist tells the story of the holy family's flight to Egypt, the place where they were to remain "until the death of Herod" (v. 15a). Jesus' de-parture from Egypt, Matthew tells us, fulfills the prophecy: "Out of Egypt have I called my son" (v. 15b). The quotation comes from Hos 11:1b, but from the Hebrew, not the LXX (". . . I called his children"). Matthew's Greek translation is quite literal, but his application is problematic. Hosea, as the context makes quite clear, is looking back to the exodus, not to a future deliverance. Indeed, the Hosean context is judgmental, not salvific. Moreover, God's "son" is Israel (see Hos 11:1a), not Israel's Messiah. If Hos 11:1 is not messianic, why has the evangelist applied the passage to Jesus?

The reference in Hos 11:1a to Israel as a "child" (MT: *na'ar*) or "infant" (LXX: *nēpios*) may explain in part why the evangelist perceived the relevance of this passage for the infancy narrative. But by itself the text is neither messianic nor predictive. However, when read in light of the similar passage from LXX Num 24:7–8a ("There shall come a man out of his seed, and he shall rule over many nations . . . God led him out of Egypt"), its messianic and predictive potential becomes clear. Matthew is not appealing to Hos 11:1b only, but to LXX Num 24:8a as well.

Appealing to one text, interpreted in the light of another, is a form of exegesis that is not foreign to Jewish exegetical practices of the time. A messianic application of the text is also facilitated by the assumption that references to David may sometimes be taken as references to all of Israel. This is seen clearly in *Midrash Psalms* 24.3 (on Ps 24:1): "Our Masters taught: In the Book of Psalms, all the Psalms which David composed apply either to himself or to all of Israel." The midrash goes on to say that in some instances the Davidic Psalm may have application for the "Age to Come" (the messianic age).

If David and Israel were thus identified, and if David was also understood as a type for the Messiah (see Matt 1:1, 17), it is not hard to see how Matthew saw messianic potential in Hos 11:1. The saying of Rabbi Yohanan, though uttered in the post-New Testament era, probably reflects what was assumed by many in the first century: "Every prophet prophesied only for the days of the Messiah" (*b. Berakhot* 34b). Moreover, rabbinic exegesis of Hos 11:1 itself may shed further light on why Matthew would apply this Old Testament passage to the infant Jesus. In several passages (*Sifre Deuteronomy* §305 [on 31:7]; *Exodus Rabbah* 43.9 [on 32:7]; *Numbers Rabbah* 12.4 [on 7:1]; *Deuteronomy Rabbah* 5.7 [on 16:18]; *Pesiqta Rabbati* 26.1–2) the rabbis understand Hosea's reference to "son" as a reference to Israel's innocence and youth, even infancy. Matthew has not exegeted Hos 11:1 in a strict linguistic, contextual, and historical sense. His is an exegesis of typology and "resignification," that is, finding a new element or dimension in the older tradition. This aspect of his exegesis conforms completely with what is observed in the Jewish exegesis of his day. Matthew has (re)interpreted Scripture in light of what God has accomplished (or "fulfilled") in his Messiah.

At first glance John's use of the Old Testament appears to be about the same as Matthew's. Like Matthew, the fourth evangelist formally quotes the Old Testament several times, many times in "fulfillment" of something. But in other important ways the Old Testament functions quite differently in John. Even in the case of the quotation formulas, John's purpose runs along very different lines. Unlike Matthew, John's formulas appear to make up a pattern, a pattern that accentuates the theological development of the Gospel narrative.

In the first half of his Gospel, the evangelist introduces Scripture in a variety of ways, though usually using the word "written" (1:23; 2:17; 6:31, 45; 7:38, 42; 8:17; 10:34; 12:14). In the second half he invariably introduces Scripture "in order that it be fulfilled" (12:38, 39–40; 13:18; 15:25; 19:24, 28, 36, 37).

What is the meaning of this pattern? The answer may be deduced from the summary in 12:37 and the citation that follows in verse 38: "Though he had done so many signs before them, yet they did not believe in him, in order that the word of Isaiah . . . be fulfilled. . . ." The "signs" to which reference is made are those of the first half of the Gospel. The scriptural citations in the first half of the Gospel demonstrate that Jesus conducted his ministry in keeping with scriptural expectation ("as it is written").

It is not until Jesus is rejected, despite his signs, that the Scriptures are said to be "fulfilled." It is in Jesus' rejection and crucifixion that the Scriptures find their ultimate fulfillment. Far from proving that Jesus did not fulfill the Scriptures, and so could not be Israel's Messiah, Jewish unbelief and obduracy specifically fulfilled Isa 53:1 ("Lord, who believed . . . ?") and Isa 6:10 ("He blinded their eyes . . ."). With each action taken against Jesus, including the treachery of Judas, Scripture is fulfilled. It is apparent that the fourth evangelist wishes to show that it is in Jesus' passion, his "hour of glorification" (17:1), that the Scriptures are truly fulfilled.

Mark and Luke

The Gospels of Mark and Luke take somewhat different approaches. Unlike Matthew and John, Mark rarely quotes the Old Testament outside of what is likely the tradition that he received. Other than the conflated quotation of LXX Exod 23:20 // Mal 3:1 // LXX Isa 40:3 at the opening of his account (Mark 1:2–3), and a few allusions in the passion (15:24, 29, 36), Old Testament quotations are limited to statements of Jesus (4:12; 7:6–7, 10; 8:18; 11:17; etc.). It is likely that even the citation in 1:2–3 and the allusions in the passion are traditional elements also. But this is not to say that the Old Testament is unimportant to the evangelist. In many places Old Testament passages and themes underlie the Markan narrative.

An interesting example of the presence of allusions and echoes is seen in the story of the transfiguration (Mark 9:2–8), which at several points parallels Sinai tradition: (1) The phrase "after six days" (v. 2) alludes to Exod 24:16, where after six days God speaks. (2) Just as Moses is accompanied by three companions (Exod 24:9), so Jesus is accompanied by Peter, James, and John (v. 2). (3) In both accounts, epiphany takes place on a mountain (v. 2; Exod 24:12). (4) Moses figures in both accounts (v. 4; Exod 24:1–18). It is also interesting to note that on one occasion Joshua (LXX: "Jesus") accompanied Moses on the mountain

(Exod 24:13). (5) Jesus' personal transfiguration (v. 3) probably parallels the transfiguration of Moses' face (Exod 34:29–30). Matthew and Luke have apparently seen this parallel, for they draw a closer correspondence by noting the alteration of Jesus' "face" (Matt 17:2; Luke 9:29). (6) In both accounts the divine presence is attended by a cloud (v. 7; Exod 24:15–16). Some believed that the cloud which had appeared to Moses would reappear in the last days (see 2 Maccabees 2:8). (7) In both accounts the heavenly voice speaks (v. 7; Exod 24:16). (8) Fear is common to both stories (v. 6; Exod 34:30; cf. *Targum Pseudo-Jonathan* Exod 24:17). (9) Mark's "Hear him" (v. 7), unparalleled in Exod 24, probably echoes Deut 18:15.

How much of this is tradition and how much of it reflects the work of the Markan evangelist is hard to say, but the many allusions show that in the transfiguration of Jesus and in the heavenly voice that recognizes him we witness significant continuity between the great moment of Sinai and a second great moment. The first moment in history witnessed the ratification of a formal covenant between God and his people Israel; the second moment in history adumbrated the ratification of the promised new covenant, foretold in Jer 31 and in the Words of Institution (Mark 14:22–25) and fulfilled in the death of Jesus on the cross (Mark 15:33–39).

In the writings of the Lukan evangelist, the Old Testament functions in ways that are clearly distinct from the other three Gospels. Luke does not punctuate the tradition with proof texts like Matthew and John; rather, he punctuates his narrative with speeches that are often made up almost entirely of Old Testament words and phrases (esp. the speeches and canticles in the birth narrative). Another distinctive feature is Luke's dependence upon the LXX. Indeed, the evangelist deliberately imitates the style of the Greek Old Testament.

This imitation does not simply involve style; it involves substance. One of the clearest examples of this imitation is seen in Jesus' birth narrative: (1) The angelic announcement of 1:32–33 alludes to the Davidic covenant (2 Sam 7:9–16) and finds a remarkable parallel in an Aramaic text from Qumran (i.e., 4Q246 1:1–2:9). (2) The progress reports in 2:40 and 2:52 echo the similar reports of the young Samuel (1 Sam 2:26; 3:19; and of John the Baptist in Luke 1:80). Indeed, at other points in the narrative there are echoes of the Samuel story (cf. 1 Sam 1:22 with Luke 2:22; 1 Sam 2:20 with Luke 2:34). (3) The Magnificat itself (1:46–55; cf. also Anna's song in 2:36–38) is modeled to a certain extent after Hannah's song of thanksgiving (1 Sam 2:1–10), which in the targum is eschatologized.

Paul and Hebrews

Paul quotes the Scriptures some one hundred times and alludes to them many more times. The Dead Sea Scrolls and the targumim—both vital sources for understanding Jewish interpretation of Scripture in late antiquity—have recently aided our understanding of Paul's use of the Old Testament.

One of the most debated issues in Pauline theology has to do with the background of Paul's criticism of those who advocate "works of law" (*erga nomou*). Is Paul criticizing an actual position held by some of his Jewish contemporaries, or has he created a straw man in his polemic in Gal 2–3 and Rom 4? The publication of 4QMMT (= "Some of the Works of the Law") has offered dramatic proof that the position that Paul attacked was indeed held in his time.

According to 4QMMT, if the faithful observe the law properly, especially with respect to the "works of the law" about which the author(s) of this letter wrote, they "will rejoice in the end time" when they discover that their obedience "will be reckoned to (them) as righteousness" (4Q398 frags. 14–17 ii 7 = 4Q399 frag. 1 ii 4). Paul, of course, argues in precisely the opposite direction, contending that it is faith, not works of the law, that will result in being reckoned righteous.

There are only two passages in the Hebrew Bible where we find "reckoned" and "righteousness" juxtaposed; they are Ps 106:30–31 and Gen 15:6. In the first passage Phineas the priest is reckoned righteous because of his zeal for the law (i.e., his work of law), while in the second passage Abraham is reckoned righteous because of his faith in God. Paul appeals to Abraham, while the priestly author of 4QMMT appeals to the example of Phineas! Among other things, 4QMMT's "works of the law" include avoiding gentile food (e.g., 4Q394 frags. 3–7 i 7–8: "you shall not eat Gentile grain"), which is exactly what Peter did at Antioch and was criticized for (Gal 2:12). We now know why Paul spoke of "works of law" (Gal 2:16) in response to Peter's decision to stop eating food with gentile believers.

The author of Hebrews has developed his own style of typological exegesis, in which he compares Christ and the church to Old Testament figures and institutions. Unlike midrash, pesher, or even allegory, typology is primarily interested in biblical *events* and not the biblical *text*. The author cites or alludes to the Old Testament approximately sixty times, usually following the LXX, and often citing the Psalter. His most important typological comparisons include Moses-Christ (3:2–6), Melchizedek-Christ (7:1–28), and old covenant-new covenant (8:1–9:28). The discovery of 11Q13 ii (*Melchizedek*), which anticipates the arrival of an eschatological Melchizedek, who in some sense is divine, clarifies why the author of Hebrews found it useful to appeal to this Old Testament worthy to develop the theme of Jesus' superior priesthood.

The life, death, and resurrection of Jesus became for early Christians the hermeneutical key for their interpretation and application of Old Testament Scripture. Since Scripture could be relied on for clarification of eschatological events, and since Jesus was the eschatological agent, there could be no doubt that the Scriptures were fulfilled in him. The vital importance of Jewish Scripture for Jesus and the early Christians is amply demonstrated by how frequently virtually every writing in the New Testament appeals to this Scripture. In short, there would be no New Testament without Israel's ancient and sacred writings. This fact above all else demonstrates how deeply rooted Jesus and his followers were in Jewish faith and Scripture.

Works Cited

Barrett, C. K. 1970. "The Interpretation of the Old Testament in the New." Pages 377–411 in *From the Beginnings to Jerome*. Vol. 1 of *The Cambridge History of the Bible*. Edited by P. R. Ackroyd and C. F. Evans. Cambridge: Cambridge University Press.

Beale, G. K., and D. A. Carson, eds. 2007. *Commentary on the New Testament Use of the Old Testament*. Grand Rapids: Baker Academic.

Carson, D. A., and H. G. M. Williamson, eds. 1988. *It Is Written: Scripture Citing Scripture*. Cambridge: Cambridge University Press.

Fitzmyer, Joseph A. 1961. "The Use of Explicit Old Testament Quotations in Qumran Literature and in the New Testament." *NTS* 7:297–333.

France, R. T. 1971. *Jesus and the Old Testament*. London: Tyndale.

Hanson, Anthony Tyrrell. 1980. *The New Testament Interpretation of Scripture*. London: SPCK.

Hays, Richard B. 2016. *Echoes of Scripture in the Gospels*. Waco, TX: Baylor University Press.

Lindars, Barnabas. 1961. *New Testament Apologetic*. Philadelphia: Westminster.

Longenecker, Richard N. 1975. *Biblical Exegesis in the Apostolic Period*. Grand Rapids: Eerdmans.

Shires, Henry M. 1974. *Finding the Old Testament in the New*. Philadelphia: Westminster.

Smith, D. M. 1972. "The Use of the Old Testament in the New." Pages 3–65 in *The Use of the Old Testament in the New and Other Essays: Studies in Honor of William Franklin Stinespring*. Edited by James M. Efird. Durham, NC: Duke University Press.

CHAPTER 4

Appointed Times

4.1 The Sabbath

Eitan Bar

Leviticus 23 outlines the seven feasts of the ancient biblical year (as will be discussed in the articles immediately following). There is also one special day each week. The pattern is clear: seven special days in one year, one special day out of each seven day period. The seventh day, of course, is the Sabbath (or *Shabbat*), which comes from the Hebrew word for "rest" or "cease" (Fruchtenbaum 2014; Millgram 2018).

In the Tanakh

The Sabbath first appears in the account of creation. On the seventh day God "ceased" from working (Gen 2:1–3). This day was sanctified, made holy. After the first six days of creating/preparing the land, God rested—or ceased. This final day of the week is marked off differently than the others. After each of the previous days the text says that "it was evening and morning, the X day." But after the seventh day there is no such comment. This "day" did not come to a close. This final day was meant to describe life in the garden, or the setting for humanity in fellowship with God. This situation did not last long. Genesis 3 explains humanity's sin and separation from God, which created a breach of the Sabbath. The restoration of this breach is the theme of the remainder of the Bible, with its ultimate fulfillment to be realized in the future (this history is summarized in Heb 4).

The concept of the Sabbath appears again in Exod 16, in the story of the manna from heaven. Here it is declared that the Sabbath is to be remembered and no work is to be done (manna collected on this day was not edible). It is in the giving of the law that the Sabbath became prominent. The decree to remember the Sabbath and keep it holy is one of the ten commandments (Exod 20:8–11). The day is blessed by God. This commandment is reiterated in Deut 5:12–15. Here it is commanded that the Sabbath is to be "observed," not just remembered. It is also stated that the reason for observing the Sabbath is related to the redemption from slavery in Egypt. The scope of this redemption (both as a remembrance and a foreshadowing) is seen in the concept of the Sabbatical Year (see Lev 25 and 26). For one year out of seven the land would "rest" (from producing crops), financial debts were cancelled, and slaves (indentured servants) were set free. In addition, after every seven series of seven years (the year after forty nine years, or fifty years) there was the Year of Jubilee, which always began on the Day of Atonement (Lev 25:1–10).

Jesus and the Sabbath

During the Second Temple period, a variety of regulations and customs emerged regarding the observance of the Sabbath (see Robinson 2014). The day itself still held a preeminent place in the Jewish world. This is seen in the life of Jesus as well, and some of his words and deeds on the Sabbath were among his most controversial. For example, while Jesus and his disciples were out in a grain field, they became hungry and began to pick heads of grain to eat. The Pharisees saw this and accused them of breaking the Sabbath. This was a question of authority—who has the right to decide what constitutes "work"? The law of Moses says that lighting a fire is forbidden (Exod 35:1–3), but exactly what else is forbidden is less clear. Jewish tradition has provided a running commentary, and the later rabbis would spend a considerable amount of time on this question (see below, article 12.1). Jesus responded to his accusers by not only appealing to Scripture, but also taking the opportunity to proclaim something about himself, something even more startling than a Sabbath infringement. He said "the Son of Man is Lord of the Sabbath" (Matt 12:8 NASB; cf. Mark 2:28; Luke 6:5). The title "Son of man" is a reference to Dan 7:13–15, which speaks of a divine, anointed figure. Jesus used this term again at his trial and was accused of blasphemy (Mark 14:62–64).

Immediately before declaring himself the Son of Man, Jesus also said that "the Sabbath was made for man, and not man for the Sabbath" (Mark 2:27). This has a parallel in rabbinic literature. It is understood that saving a human life takes priority over Sabbath prohibitions. In a discussion of when it is permissible to break the Sabbath, it was concluded that the Sabbath "is committed to your hands, not you to its hands" (*b. Yoma* 85b). The Sabbath itself is important, but there is something greater still. Jesus claimed to be the very rest that the Sabbath foreshadows. He said: "Come to Me, all who are weary and heavy-laden, and I will give you rest. Take My yoke upon you and learn from Me, for I am gentle and humble in heart, and you will find rest for your souls" (Matt 11:28–29).

The Sabbath in Israel Today

The modern state of Israel was not founded as a religious nation. Nevertheless, the Sabbath and the festivals provide a framework for life for both the secular and the religious. Starting at sundown on Friday afternoon, the Sabbath begins. Actually, it begins a few hours before this so as to guarantee that no transgressions of the Sabbath are committed. There is no public transportation and virtually all places of business are closed (coffee shops and some restaurants are an exception, and there have recently been great debates about such issues).

The day is enjoyed differently in different communities. It is a family day, a day of rest. For the very religious, it is a day filled with prohibitions. The Mishnah (*Shabbat* 7:2) famously outlines thirty-nine categories of what constitutes "work." The details arising from these general categories are endless and are still being written in the modern world. For example, it is forbidden (for Orthodox Jews) to drive a car, since the ignition creates a spark. Moses prohibited lighting a fire, and since it is not good to do anything that approaches what is forbidden, it is forbidden even to create the "spark" of the engine. For the same reason, hotels that cater to the religious have "Shabbat elevators" which stop at every floor so there is no need to push the button on Saturday.

Most Israeli believers in Jesus worship on Saturday morning. This is partly because of the reality that Sunday morning is the beginning of the work week. But it is also to remember the Sabbath. The earliest followers of Jesus (Acts 20:7), who were Jewish, met on Sundays to commemorate the resurrection. But this was not a replacement for the Sabbath. Believers in Jesus inherit a Sabbath rest, and are free to worship collectively on any day they choose.

Works Cited

Fruchtenbaum, Arnold G. 2014. *The Sabbath*. San Antonio, TX: Ariel Ministries.
Millgram, Abraham E., ed. 2018. *The Sabbath Anthology*. The JPS Holiday Anthologies. Repr., New York: Jewish Publication Society.
Robinson, Richard A. 2014. *Christ in the Sabbath*. Chicago: Moody Publishers.

4.2 Passover, Unleavened Bread, Firstfruits

Erez Soref

Leviticus 23 outlines the seven feasts of the biblical year. The first three (Lev 23:4–14) all occur within a one-week period in the spring. Passover is celebrated on one night and the Feast of Unleavened Bread lasts the entire week, although these two are often discussed interchangeably. In the middle of this week is the celebration called Firstfruits. These three need to be seen together, and all of them foreshadow the life and message of Jesus.

Passover in the Pentateuch

Exodus 12 tells the story of Passover. After being enslaved by the Egyptians for some four hundred years, God provided a way of deliverance for the children of Israel. This happened in the month of Nisan, the first month of the year. Beginning on the tenth day of the month, each household was to take an unblemished lamb and keep it until the fourteenth day of the month. At twilight, the "whole assembly" of Israel was to kill it and then place the blood on both the doorposts and the lintel of each house. They were to eat it along with matzot (unleavened bread) and bitter herbs, and none of it was to remain in the morning. They were instructed to eat it in the following way: "with your loins girded, your sandals on your feet, and your staff in your hand; and you shall eat it in haste—it is the LORD's Passover" (Exod 12:11 NASB). This was part of the tenth and final plague on Egypt, the slaying of the firstborn. Pharaoh had been warned. As a result of his hardness of heart, it was time for God to execute judgment, and only those who placed the blood upon their doors in obedience would be spared.

Prior to the exodus, God referred to himself as, for example, "the God of Abraham, Isaac and Jacob," or more directly as "I AM." At the giving of the Ten Commandments, however, God introduced himself as follows: "I am the LORD your God, who brought you out of the land of Egypt, out of the house of slavery" (Exod 20:2). This was a defining event which underscored God's character and his sovereignty. This designation is used not only dozens of times in the Torah (Pentateuch) itself, but throughout the Tanakh (some examples include Josh 24:5; Judg 2:1; 1 Sam 10:18; 2 Sam 7:6; 1 Kgs 8:16; Ps 81:10; Jer 2:6; Dan 9:15; Amos 2:10; Mic 6:4).

Passover in the Gospel of John

Each of the four Gospels presents Jesus going to the cross during Passover. The Gospel of John, in particular, uses the typology of lambs and Passover in a dramatic way (for questions about chronology, see Carson 1991, 424–76 and 571–631). John's Gospel records three Passovers during Jesus' ministry, while the others each record one. Jesus is first introduced by John the Baptist as "the Lamb of God who takes away the sin of the world" (John 1:29). This is a curious statement and it is not immediately clear what his original listeners might have thought. The events of Exod 12 do not immediately speak of atonement, yet they certainly speak of redemption for the children of Israel who placed the blood on their doors in obedience. John the Baptist's words speak of redemption not just for the children of Israel, but for the "world."

Others who heard the words "lamb of God" may have thought about the *Akedah*, the story in Gen 22 of Abraham and Isaac on Mount Moriah. When

Isaac asked where the lamb was, Abraham responded that "God will provide for Himself the lamb for the burnt offering, my son" (Gen 22:7–8). But there is no explicit reference to atonement there either. To understand the words of John the Baptist we need to remember that he was a Jew who understood Jewish ways of communicating (it is perhaps better to refer to him as *Yohananon the Immerser*). He was not only combining themes from throughout the Tanakh to make his point but also tapping into Jewish exegetical tradition.

There is a very interesting midrash called *Sefer HaYesher* (*Akadat Itzak*), which may stem from the early centuries CE, and perhaps even the Second Temple period (see Dan 2005, 121–22). According to this commentary, Isaac asks Abraham to bind him tightly so none of his bones would be broken. This, it is explained, was so that he would be a sacrifice known as *ha-olah* (usually rendered "burnt offering," as in Lev 7:37), and that he would specifically be an acceptable sacrifice without blemish, so that he could atone for the future sins of Israel. The command in Exod 12:46 to not break any of the bones of the lambs does not contain an explanation, although this midrash links it with being an unblemished sacrifice. John's Gospel also refers to the Exodus passage when he says that none of Jesus' bones were broken (John 19:36). But there is more. In the same midrash, when God tells Abraham not to kill Isaac, Abraham sees a ram in the bushes. This commentary says that this ram was prepared before the creation of the world. This too fits perfectly with the prologue of the Gospel of John (1:1) as well as other passages in the New Testament (1 Pet 1:20; Rev 13:8). The midrash continues by saying that the "lamb" (the one which was just referred to as a ram) was prepared before the beginning of the world to substitute for Isaac. The *Sefer HaYesher* was probably written after the Gospel of John, and it seems very unlikely that it would have been directly influenced by the Gospel of John. The two sources may be alluding to existing Jewish interpretations which equated a spotless lamb with expiation of sin.

The Development of the Seder in Jewish Traditions

Judaism is uniquely a matter of both ethnicity and religion, and the exodus and subsequent Sinai event is the point at which that merge happened. The celebration of the Passover meal evolved over the years and it is not always clear when all of the traditions appeared (Bock 2017). The meal is called a seder ("order"), which is outlined in a small book called a *haggadah* ("the telling"), which includes the story, Scripture passages, prayers, and traditions. There are different versions in the modern world, but a few constants appear in every seder around the world. For example, the evening is outlined by four cups of wine. There are variations regarding what each of the four cups represents, but generally the first cup refers to sanctification, and being set apart for God. The second is often called "plagues," and is a time to tell the story. The third cup is taken after the meal, where it is said, "May he who makes peace in the high places make peace for us!" The last cup is called *hallel* or "praise," after the songs and psalms of thanksgiving. Psalms 113–118, much of which point to the Messiah, feature heavily at the end of the seder, much of which points to the Messiah.

There is a seder plate containing six items of food: the "bitter herbs" of horseradish; salt water to represent tears; lettuce and parsley; a lamb shankbone; an egg; and a sweet mixture of apple, nuts, and wine called *charoset*, which reminds us of the mortar that the Hebrew slaves used with the bricks when they were forced laborers. Neither the charoset nor the egg appear in the Bible. It is now customary to dip the parsley or lettuce into the salt water, which reminds us of the tears of Israel's suffering in Egypt, and to make a "sandwich" with matzo, horseradish, and charoset. Ten drops of wine are spilled to represent the ten plagues, and there are set readings, stories, songs, and prayers that can go on long into the night.

Some of these traditions emerged in the days of Jesus, and there is much evidence that the Greco-Roman symposiums had an influence on the Passover celebration at this point (Levine 1988, 103; Stein 1957, 13–17). A symposium was a celebratory feast with a philosophical discussion, beginning with a ceremonial cup of wine (and punctuated with a few other toasts during the event). It was often held in honor of a deity, a dignitary's birthday, or a similar annual event. There was an address or explanation as part of the meal; a sweet mixture of apple, nuts, and wine was standard symposium fare; and at the end of the night, songs were sung in praise of the deity or person being honored. Sound familiar? At such events it was customary to dip elements of the food and recline at a low table rather than sit upright, which we also see in the Last Supper. It might seem strange to think that such a biblical and God-ordained event could have been influenced by other cultures in this way, but the Jewish sages seem to have absorbed the more harmless elements of the contemporary celebrations happening around them, without permitting ungodly aspects to permeate the feast.

An example of this is the tradition of the *Afikomen*. The Greek word means "that which comes after." In a Passover seder, three matzot are put in a napkin, and the middle piece, known as the Afikomen, is broken. Half of the Afikomen is hidden away, and the children have to hunt for it after the meal, redeeming it for sweet treats as a prize. However, originally the word was connected with activities that were typically at the end of a symposium—"that which comes after" meant heavy drinking, debauched behavior, and revelers going house to house causing trouble on the streets. The Jewish sages were naturally keen to keep the holy and family-like qualities of the seder, so the whole family was involved; it was not restricted to men (as symposiums were). They were careful to adopt some symposium practices while avoiding the inherent dangers. These include gluttony (according to *Pesahim* 119b–120a, "You should not call for more food after Passover *dessert* [Afikomen]). Even in the tradition of the Afikomen, the Messiah can be found, since there is great significance in unleavened bread, as will be seen below.

The Feast of Unleavened Bread

The Passover meal marks beginning of the weeklong "Feast of Unleavened Bread." Israel was commanded to eat bread with no yeast (*hametz*) in it for a whole week. But why? The most obvious answer is a reminder of the swift exodus from Egypt, when there was no time for the bread to rise: "They baked the dough which they had brought out of Egypt into cakes of unleavened bread. For it had not become leavened, since they were driven out of Egypt and could not delay, nor had they prepared any provisions for themselves" (Exod 12:39). But if they knew it would be a bit of a rush, surely they could have started the bread-making process earlier? Possibly, but the unleavened bread speaks symbolically of haste. It is a powerful symbol that helps to bring the ancient story alive today in our own homes in a very concrete way. However, haste is not the only reason for unleavened bread. In fact, the imperative to get rid of all the leaven is made quite clear throughout the rest of the chapter:

> In the first month, on the fourteenth day of the month at evening, you shall eat unleavened bread, until the twenty-first day of the month at evening. Seven days there shall be no leaven found in your houses; for whoever eats what is leavened, that person shall be cut off from the congregation of Israel, whether he is an alien or a native of the land. You shall not eat anything leavened; in all your dwellings you shall eat unleavened bread. (Exod 12:18–20)

As is the case in many situations, the New Testament develops this idea further. First Corinthians 5:6–8 draws the parallel between *hametz* and sin—particularly the sin of pride.

> Your boasting is not good. Do you not know that a little leaven leavens the whole lump of dough? Clean out the old leaven so that you may be a new lump, just as you are in fact unleavened. For Christ our Passover also has been sacrificed. Therefore let us celebrate the feast, not with old leaven, not with the leaven of malice and wickedness, but with the unleavened bread of sincerity and truth.

The idea of being puffed up with pride is also mentioned elsewhere by Paul in 1 Cor 4:18; 8:1; and Rom 11:21–31. The symbolism is clear—risen bread, puffed up with leaven, is reminiscent of sinful pride, and unleavened matzo is humble, simple, and pure. There is actually enough leaven in the air to have an effect on dough, so special efforts have to be taken to prevent it from rising. The bread has lines scored across it and holes pierced through it to help keep it flat. This reminds us of how Jesus, humble, pure, and sinless, was striped and pierced as he gave his own life for the ultimate Passover sacrifice.

Bearing in mind that this striped, pierced bread points to Jesus, the Afikomen tradition becomes all the more poignant. Three matzot are placed in a cover, which can speak to us of the Father, Son, and Holy Spirit—with the middle piece, the "Son," being taken out, broken, and hidden away for a while. Later in the evening this Afikomen is brought back out from the dark hiding place, and represents redemption for those that find it. During the Passover meal, part of the ceremony is to eat the matzo bread together and remind each other by saying, "This is the bread of affliction that our fathers ate in Egypt." It symbolizes affliction, slavery, and lack of luxury. It is designed, along with the whole Passover meal, to help the children of Israel reenact the Passover event, year after year, each generation telling the story to the next. At his final celebration of Passover, Jesus would hold this matzo up and add something new, saying to his followers, "This is My body which is given for you; do this in remembrance of Me" (Luke 22:19). Today as we take the Lord's Supper, it reminds us of Jesus' death until he comes again, just as the unleavened bread is reminiscent of the mighty deliverance from Egypt. It is no coincidence that Jesus' death was at the time of the Passover sacrifice, for the whole Passover story was a grand echo of an even greater redemption to come, planned by the same composer who orchestrated the exodus.

Firstfruits

The festival of Firstfruits comes in two installments: The first waving of firstfruits ("*Reshit Katzir*," Lev 23:10) is to be done on the day after the Shabbat of Passover. Fifty days later, as part of the Feast of Shavuot/Pentecost, there is another waving of the firstfruits ("*bikurim*," Lev 23:17). In Lev 23:10–11, God says,

> When you enter the land which I am going to give you and reap its harvest, then you shall bring in the sheaf of the first fruits [*Reshit Katzir*] of your harvest to the priest. He shall wave the sheaf before the LORD for you to be accepted; on the day after the sabbath the priest shall wave it.

Jesus was crucified at Passover and rose again on Sunday, coinciding with this ordinance of firstfruits. This fact was not missed by the apostle Paul, who drew the following parallel: "But now Christ has been raised from the dead, the first fruits of those who are asleep" (1 Cor 15:20).

Right after Passover, farmers would go out and look at their harvest to find the buds that sprang first. They would have special ribbons to mark those buds, and for the next fifty days they would tend their crop, paying careful attention to the ones they had marked. On the Sunday after Passover, the farmer would walk around again, and those buds that were ready to be presented would be cut right away, taken to the Temple, and waved before God for the first waving of the *Reshit Katzir*. Then, on the fiftieth day, the farmer would cut all his marked plants but nothing else. Rather than only bringing ten percent, the entire crop of firstfruits was taken and left in the Temple. The farmer could do this with joy and faith, because he knew that when firstfruits were given to God, the entire harvest would be blessed.

Works Cited

Bock, Darrell. 2017. *Messiah in the Passover*. Grand Rapids: Kregel.
Carson, D. A. 1991. *The Gospel According to John*. Grand Rapids: Eerdmans.
Dan, Yosef. 2005. *Sefer HaYesher* [Hebrew]. Jerusalem: Bialik.
Levine, Lee I. 1988. *Judaism and Hellenism in Antiquity: Conflict or Confluence?* Seattle: University of Washington Press.
Stein, Siegfried. 1957. "The Influence of Symposium Literature on the Literary Form of the Pesah Haggadah." *JJS* 8:13–17.

4.3 Shavuot

Golan Brosh

After the three spring festivals and before the three fall festivals, there is one special day. It is called the Feast of Weeks (*Shavuot* in the Hebrew), and is also known as Pentecost (from the Greek). It was one of the three times a year (along with Passover and Sukkot; see Exod 23:14–17) when all the men of Israel were required to go up to Jerusalem and offer sacrifices.

Overview

The date of Shavuot is determined by its relationship to Passover. At the Feast of Firstfruits (after the Sabbath that falls during Passover/Unleavened Bread), the counting begins. For this reason the common name for this holiday is the Feast of Weeks. Leviticus 23:15–16 says: "You shall also count for yourselves from the day after the sabbath, from the day when you brought in the sheaf of the wave offering; there shall be seven complete Sabbaths. You shall count fifty days to the day after the seventh sabbath; then you shall present a new grain offering to the Lord" (NASB; cf. Deut 16:9).

It is also known by other names, including the Feast of Harvest or Firstfruits (*Hag Hakatzir* or *Yom HaBikurim*). This is a bit confusing. As mentioned in the previous article, the English word "firstfruits" is usually used for both the holiday during Passover (Lev 23:10) and the offering during the celebration of the Feast of Weeks (Lev 23:17). There are two different Hebrew words used (*Reshet Katzir* and *Bikurim*, respectively), and both refer to the harvest and a different aspect of that which is first gathered. *Hag HaKatzir* is meant specifically to highlight the timing of the wheat harvest. Yet another name for Shavuot is based on tradition. It is known as the Feast of the Giving of the Torah (*Hag Matan Torah*). This is based on the tradition that the five books of Moses (the Torah) were given on this day (see below).

Traditions

The celebration of this feast in the Bible involves pure animals being sacrificed, as it is written in Lev 23:18–20:

> Along with the bread you shall present seven one year old male lambs without defect, and a bull of the herd and two rams; they are to be a burnt offering to the Lord, with their grain offering and their drink offerings, an offering by fire of a soothing aroma to the Lord. You shall also offer one male goat for a sin offering and two male lambs one year old for a sacrifice of peace offerings. The priest shall then wave them with the bread of the first fruits for a wave offering with two lambs before the Lord; they are to be holy to the Lord for the priest.

It is clear that this was originally very much a "meat" holiday. According to later rabbinic teachings, meat and dairy are not to be consumed during the same meal. Today, however, Shavuot is very much a "dairy" holiday. Everyone eats mainly dairy products and the highlight of the day is cheesecake. This is a good example to how far tradition can deviate from the original biblical commandments. According to a rabbinic tradition, the Torah is likened to milk and honey (*Tanhuma*), and the Torah was given on Shavuot/Pentecost (*Tana Debai Eliyahu*). Perhaps this is the reason for the dairy nature of this holiday. It is customary to wear white clothes, although this custom is also part of the Feast of Trumpets and Passover. Another tradition is reading through the book of Ruth, as this story takes place during Shavuot. Finally, a rabbinic tradition (Jerusalem Talmud, *Hagigah*) says that King David was born and died on this holiday. This might very well have been the reason that Peter mentioned David's burial during his speech on Pentecost (Acts 2:29).

There are numerous traditions in modern Israel, especially in the kibbutz movement, regarding Shavuot. In one such ceremony, all the children dress up in white with flower wreaths on their heads and gather outside the dining hall. Then, a procession with tractors and carts with representatives of different agricultural products made by the kibbutz passes by. The peak of the ceremony comes with the arrival of the last cart—carrying all the newborn babies and their mothers of the last year.

In the New Testament

As mentioned above, the Feast of Shavuot was prophetically fulfilled in the New Testament in Acts 2:1–4, which says:

> When the day of Pentecost had come, they were all together in one place. And suddenly there came from heaven a noise like a violent rushing wind, and it filled the whole house where they were sitting. And there appeared to them tongues as of fire distributing themselves, and they rested on each one of them. And they were all filled with the Holy Spirit and began to speak with other tongues, as the Spirit was giving them utterance.

There are parallels between the giving of the law and the events of Acts 2. When Moses received the law the people had grown tired of waiting and began worshiping the golden calf. As a result, three thousand men died by the sword and paid a bitter price (Exod 32:28). By contrast, after the Holy Spirit was poured out, three thousand people experienced new life in Jesus the Messiah (Acts 2:41). Rabbinic tradition offers some interesting comments as well. A passage in the Mishnah says that at the giving of the law (which was commonly thought to be on Shavuot), the words went out in "70 tongues" (*Sotah* 7.7). Also, the Babylonian Talmud records that Rabbi Yochanon said the same thing. In response, Rabbi Ishmael declared: "just as a hammer is divided into many sparks, so every single word that went forth from the Holy One, blessed be He, split up into seventy languages" (*Shabbat* 88b). Another midrash called *Mekhilta de Rabbi Ishmael* quotes Rabbi Akiva as saying that the people of Israel saw actual fire coming out of the mouth of God at the giving of the law. All of these passages are brought together by Moshe Weinfeld (2001, 113–16), who taught at Hebrew University, to show that this tradition is well grounded in the Second Temple era. Weinfeld explicitly refers to the book of Acts several times to demonstrate that God's words appearing "like tongues of fire" was a common Jewish understanding.

Work Cited

Weinfeld, Moshe. 2001. *The Decalogue and the Recitation of the Shema* [Hebrew]. Tel Aviv: Hakibbutz Hameuchad.

4.4 The Fall Feasts

Noam Hendren

The feasts of the Lord, as laid out in Lev 23, can have agricultural, historical, or religious-prophetic significance; and sometimes a combination of all of these. The three fall festivals (although one of these is a fast day) reflect all three areas of significance, with an emphasis on the fulfillment of God's redemptive purposes.

The Feast of Trumpets/Rosh Hashanah

The fall feasts begin on the first day of the seventh month with "a memorial proclaimed with blast of trumpets" (Lev 23:24 ESV). The significance of this special day is originally laid out rather laconically in Lev 23:23–25. Numbers 29:1–6 adds a list of special sacrifices to be offered on this day, but there is no further discussion of the significance or practice of "the Feast of Trumpets." In fact, nowhere in the Scriptures is there any indication that the day was actually commemorated in biblical times. Nevertheless, in Rabbinic Judaism this day has become one of the most sacred days of the religious calendar, the beginning of the High Holidays: Rosh Hashanah (literally: the head of the year), the Jewish New Year. According to Jewish tradition, on this day God judges every human being to see if they are worthy to be inscribed in the "Book of Life" for the coming year. There is, however, no evidence that a fall new year festival was ever celebrated during the First or Second Temple periods (see Safrai and Stern 1974, 2:843–44; VanGemeren 1997, 3:1019–20, s.v. "ראש השנה").

Later tradition aside, what is the most likely significance and intent of the Feast of Trumpets as given in the Torah? It must be related to the act of blowing the trumpet as a memorial and, secondly, to the placement of this holiday in the divine calendar. Though later rabbinic tradition specifies that the instrument must be a shofar (a ram or goat horn), Lev 23 makes no mention of a specific instrument. The first questions are: Why were instruments trumpeted in biblical times, and who is the object of this "memorial" or reminder?

Numbers 10 gives four reasons for blowing trumpets:

(1) To assemble the people at the tent of meeting (10:2–3).

(2) To cause the tribes to break camp and set out during the desert wanderings (10:2, 5–6).

(3) To call for God's help in threat of war: "that you may be remembered before the LORD your God" (10:9 NASB).

(4) To call for God's attention at appointed times—including new moons and the feasts—to witness the nation's obedience in fulfilling his ordinances: "They shall be as a reminder of you before your God" (10:10 NASB).

The Feast of Trumpets is designated "a holy convocation" (Num 29:1 NASB); thus, the assembling of the people before the Lord is clearly intended. Similarly, in view of the coming Day of Atonement, an appeal to God for his attention and help is significant. The special sanctity of that day and the serious repercussions for not fulfilling its precise requirements were clear: improper approach to the presence of God in the holy of holies could result in instant death (Lev 16:1–2, 13). Similarly, the failure of a person to properly "humble himself" on this day would cause him to be "cut off from his people" (Lev 23:29–30 NASB). Thus, while the Day of Atonement carried great promise, it also threatened severe judgment for disobedience.

On Shabbat Shuva, the Sabbath day that falls between Rosh Hashanah and the Day of Atonement, Joel 2:15–27 is read in every synagogue. This passage captures the significance of the blowing of trumpets on Rosh Hashanah as a preparation for the coming Day of Atonement. The chapter opens with the call to "blow a trumpet in Zion" as a warning of the coming judgment of God upon his people. To avert this judgment, the trumpet is again blown to summon the people to national repentance and as an appeal to God to "spare your people" (Joel 2:12–17 ESV; cf. VanGemeren 1997, 1:1080, s.v. "זכר").

Maimonides, the medieval Jewish rabbi and philosopher, summarizes:

> Although the blowing of the trumpet on the New Year's Day is an ordinance of Scripture, it also bears a symbolical significance, as if calling: Ye sleepers, awake from your sleep; and ye who are in a deep slumber, arise; search into your actions, turn with repentance, and remember your Creator! (*Mishneh Torah*, Repentance 3:3–4)

Yom Kippur: The Day of Atonement

In contrast to Rosh Hashanah, the Day of Atonement is given detailed treatment in the Torah. Leviticus 23:26–32 summarizes the requirements of the day for the people and states its purpose: "to make atonement for you before the LORD your God" (ESV). Leviticus 16 goes much further, giving precise, step-by-step instructions for the high priest's actions—and the people's participation—on this unique day.

The Day of Atonement constitutes the climax of the sacrificial system detailed in the book of Leviticus. The sacrifices mandated in Lev 1–7 were necessitated by God's taking up residence in the midst of his people in the tabernacle (Exod 40:34–38; cf. 25:8–9). As the most holy God, the Lord would not dwell in the midst of a sinful people. Following the golden calf episode, God had declared, "You are an obstinate people; should I go up in your midst for one moment, I would destroy you" (Exod 33:5 NASB). His presence in the tabernacle therefore required daily sacrifices, both communal and personal, in order to maintain or restore a right standing before God.

The sin and guilt offerings in particular (Lev 4–5) made atonement for unintentional sins. Openly rebellious sins could only be atoned for—and thereby not "defile the land/sanctuary"—by the death of the perpetrator (Num 15:22–36; 19:13; 35:31–34). But whether through oversight or neglect, many personal and community sins would not have been properly atoned for, which allowed for an accumulation of guilt and moral uncleanness resulting in God's judgment or even withdrawal from his people (Lev 15:31; 20:3; Num 19:13, 20; Ezek 5:11; 36:17). Yom Kippur provided yearly atonement for the nation and a cleansing of God's dwelling place from the defilement of a sinful people (Lev 16:16).

The procedure of the Day of Atonement parallels that for the ceremonial cleansing of a man or a house which has been healed from "leprosy" (Lev 14:1–8, 48–53). In the latter, two birds are used: the first is slain and its blood is used to sprinkle the one being cleansed, while the other bird is set free alive, symbolizing the total removal of defilement. On the Day of Atonement two goats are chosen (Lev 16:7–10): One goat is slaughtered and its blood is used by the high priest to sprinkle and thereby cleanse the tabernacle and its furniture, beginning with the "mercy seat" or "atonement cover" (*kapporet*) resting on the ark of the covenant (Lev 16:15–19, 32–33). The high priest lays his hands upon the second goat and confesses the sins of the nation, symbolically making this goat the nation's sin-bearer. He then sends the "scape-goat" into the wilderness, carrying with it the sins of the nation and thus completing the atonement ritual (16:20–22).

For their part, the people of Israel were full, though passive, participants in the events of the day. While the high priest represented them in the atonement rituals, the people expressed their sincere repentance and earnest appeal for God's mercy by "afflicting their souls" and abstaining from all work (Lev 16:29; 23:29–30). This self-deprivation would include fasting (cf. Isa 58:3, 10; Ps 35:13) and perhaps the wearing of sackcloth. The book of Jonah, which is traditionally read in the synagogue on this day, describes the repentance of the people of Nineveh in similar terms (Jonah 3:5–9). According to the Mishnah, washing, anointing with oil, wearing sandals, and marital relations were also forbidden (*Yoma* 8:1; see Hartley 1992, 242).

No descriptions of the commemoration of Yom Kippur are found in either the Hebrew Bible or the New Testament. The only sign that the day was kept is found in the oblique reference in the book of Acts 27:9: "The voyage was now dangerous, since even the fast was already over" (NASB). But the central elements of the Day of Atonement are highlighted in Heb 9–10, as a limited foreshadowing of the ultimate sacrifice provided by Jesus.

In parallel to the earlier spring festivals, the Day of Atonement seems to prefigure another event in God's redemptive calendar. The prophets speak of a day in which the nation's sins will be cleansed in preparation for Israel's inheritance of God's kingdom promises. In Zech 3, this future cleansing was prefigured by prophetic pre-enactment, with the high priest, Joshua ben Jehozadak, representing the sinful nation (Zech 3:3–5). Zechariah 3:9–10 summarizes the result, "I will remove the iniquity of that land in one day. 'In that day,' declares the LORD of hosts, 'every one of you will invite his neighbor to come under his vine and under his fig tree'" (NASB).

Similarly, the new covenant promise in Jer 31:31–34 states, "'They will all know Me, from the least of them to the greatest of them,' declares the LORD, 'for I will forgive their iniquity, and their sin I will remember no more'" (NASB). This ultimate "Day of Atonement" will enable Israel to enjoy the fulfillment of God's eternal covenant with Abraham: a holy nation walking in relationship with her God and enjoying his blessing to the full in the land of promise (see Jer 31:1–14; cf. Rom 11:25–29).

Sukkot: The Feast of Booths

The Feast of Booths, or Tabernacles (*Sukkot*) was the final pilgrimage feast in the religious calendar and the preeminent holiday of the seventh month, perhaps even of Israel's entire sacred year (Hartley 1992, 381). Leviticus 23:39 designates it as "the feast of the LORD" and later it is referred to simply as "the feast" (1 Kgs 8:2 NASB; cf. John 7:1). Israel was commanded to keep the feast "to the LORD" with singular rejoicing (Deut 16:14–15) and it was chosen as the holiday at which the law of Moses would be read to all the people—men, women, and children—every sabbatical year (Deut 31:10–13). This was most likely because it was the best-attended pilgrim feast and ideal for entire families. It followed the work-intensive harvest season, and usually occurred during good travel conditions: the roads were baked dry by the long, rainless summer, and moderate fall temperatures were the norm.

The Feast of Booths has multiple associations in the Scriptures. The book of Exodus emphasizes the agricultural significance of the holiday, naming it "the Feast of Ingathering" (23:16–17 ESV; 34:22–23 ESV), and similarly Deuteronomy recognizes it as a feast of thanksgiving and joy following the harvest, celebrating the abundant provision of the Lord (16:13–15). While recognizing its links to the harvest season, Lev 23:41–43 emphasizes the historical rationale for dwelling in booths for seven days: namely, as a reminder of God's care and provision for Israel during the wilderness wanderings (Hartley 1992, 381). The addition of a "solemn assembly" immediately following the holiday gave it its eight-day character (Lev 23:36; cf. Neh 8:18).

God himself had dwelt in a temporary dwelling in the midst of his people during the wilderness wanderings. This fact, as well as subsequent historical developments, gave the Feast of Booths unique religious and prophetic significance. Both the dedication of Solomon's Temple (1 Kgs 8:1–2) and of the rebuilt altar following the Babylonian exile (Ezra 3:1–4) coincided with this holiday, giving it a temple association. Later still, Ezra read the Torah in the vicinity of the Temple, which moved the people to resume the celebration of the feast, even erecting booths in the Temple courts (Neh 8:14–18). It is likely that the later eight-day celebration of Hanukkah, the rededication of the Temple, was styled after the Feast of Booths, as indicated in 2 Maccabees 10:6–8 and 1:18–36 (Moore 1971, 2:46–50; Edersheim 1958, 334–35).

The prophetic promises of the Lord's return to dwell among his people with the establishment of his kingdom on earth were naturally linked with this feast. In the Torah, God had promised that if Israel would truly walk in his ways, "I will put my tabernacle in your midst and I will not abhor you. I will walk among you, and I will be your God and you will be my people" (Lev 26:11–12 NET). The language used shows an intentional allusion to the garden of Eden, God's original "tabernacle" on earth, where he walked with Adam and Eve (Gen 3:8). John picks up this theme when he writes, "And the Word became flesh, and dwelt among us . . ." (John 1:14 NASB), using the Greek term *skenoō*, "take up residence," derived from the noun *skēnē*, "temporary quarters, . . . tent, hut" (BDAG). The prophet Zechariah echoes this promise and the wilderness experience in Zech 2:4–5, 10. The fulfillment of this promise with the establishment of the kingdom is predicted in Zech 14, where the kingdom association of the Feast of Booths also is made explicit.

> And the LORD will be king over all the earth; in that day the LORD will be the only one, and His name the only one. . . . Then it will come about that any who are left of all the nations that went against Jerusalem will go up from year to year to worship the King, the LORD of hosts, and to celebrate the Feast of Booths. (Zech 14:9, 16 NASB)

The New Testament agrees emphatically, anticipating God's rule in the midst of his people: "Behold, the tabernacle of God is among men, and He will dwell among them, and they shall be His people, and God Himself will be among them" (Rev 21:3 NASB).

By the first century, a number of ceremonies had developed which expressed the people's prayer that the kingdom associations of the feast would be realized in their day. The first was the illumination of the Temple, which began on the evening following the first day of the feast. Huge candlesticks were set up in the courts of the Temple, illuminating the entire city and symbolizing the light of the coming kingdom of God. The roots of this ceremony may be connected with the *Shekinah*, the manifest glory of God, which filled the Temple at its dedication under Solomon (1 Kgs 8:10–11), was removed prior to the destruction of the First Temple (Ezek 10–11), and will be restored to the Temple with the establishment of the kingdom of God (Ezek 43:1–9; cf. Zech 2:4–5, 10–11).

While the Levites played music on the steps leading down to the court of women, sages and other leading men danced until dawn before the crowds. Concerning the nightly spectacle, the Mishnah remarks, "Whoever has not seen the rejoicing of the water-drawing [*Beit HaShoeva*] has never seen rejoicing in his life" (*Sukkah* 5:1).

As morning came, the water libation was performed (*Sukkah* 4:9–5:1). Having filled a golden flagon with water drawn from the pool of Siloam, at the time of the morning sacrifice the priest would pour out the water at the base of the altar, to the cheers of the masses who had accompanied him. This act constituted a prayer for the outpouring of the Holy Spirit upon Israel at the inauguration of the kingdom of God, in accordance with the verse from Isaiah, "Therefore you will joyously draw water from the springs of salvation" (Isa 12:3 NASB; *Sukkah* 5:1; 55a).

Immediately the crowds began a recitation of the Hallel Psalms, Pss 113–118, and, waving palm branches, they circled the altar chanting the words from Psalm 118:25–26, "Save us, we pray, O LORD!" and "Blessed is he who comes in the name of the LORD!" In Jesus' day, languishing under the Roman occupation, the people were desperate for the coming of God's kingdom and the Messiah who would liberate them. Each day of the feast the spectacle would be repeated, but on the seventh day, *Hoshana Rabbah*—the "great Hosanna"—they circled the altar seven times. In a final, desperate appeal, with one voice they cried out for God's salvation.

On that last, great day of the feast, John tells us,

> Jesus stood and cried out, saying, "If anyone is thirsty, let him come to Me and drink. He who believes in Me, as the Scripture said, 'From his innermost being will flow rivers of living water.'" But this He spoke of the Spirit, whom those who believed in Him were to receive. (John 7:37–39 NASB)

Works Cited

Edersheim, Alfred. 1958. *The Temple: Its Ministry and Services*. Grand Rapids: Eerdmans.

Hartley, John E. 1992. *Leviticus*. WBC 4. Grand Rapids: Zondervan. Accordance electronic edition, version 2.5.

Moore, George Foot. 1971. Vol. 2 of *Judaism in the First Centuries of the Christian Era*. New York: Schocken Books.

Safrai, S., and M. Stern, eds. 1974. Vol. 2 of *The Jewish People in the First Century*. Philadelphia: Fortress Press.

VanGemeren, Willem A., ed. 1997. *NIDOTTE*. Grand Rapids: Zondervan. Accordance electronic edition, version 2.4.

4.5 Purim

Golan Brosh

The festival of Purim is not one of the yearly biblical feasts mentioned in Lev 23. However, it is a memorial to events in the Bible and a celebration is commanded. The New Testament does not mention Purim.

In the Bible

After the Babylonian captivity, the Persian army conquered the Babylonians and allowed the Jews to return to Jerusalem and begin rebuilding the Temple (as seen in the books of Ezra and Nehemiah). Some Jews, like Mordecai, remained in Persia (modern Iran). A wicked man named Haman rose up in the ranks of the government and wielded enormous influence on King Ahasuerus. He wanted supreme power, and he also wanted to destroy the Jewish people. Mordecai's niece (technically, cousin) was Esther, a young woman who would be instrumental in foiling Haman's plot and saving the Jews from destruction. It is a rich plot, full of intrigue and suspense.

The word *purim* is the plural of *pur*, which refers to the "lots" (or "destiny") that were cast (Est 9:24–26). The scroll of Esther is one of only two books in the Bible (along with Song of Songs) which does not mention the name of God (although in the LXX there is a reference to "the Lord" in 6:1). In Hebrew there is an obvious play on words with two of the book's heroes. First, the name "Esther" could represent the alleged absence of the Lord from the story, as in Hebrew the same word refers to God hiding his face from his people. Ezekiel 39:23–24 (NASB) says:

The nations will know that the house of Israel went into exile for their iniquity because they acted treacherously against Me, and I hid My face from them; so I gave them into the hand of their adversaries, and all of them fell by the sword. According to their uncleanness and according to their transgressions I dealt with them, and I hid My face from them.

The Hebrew word here for "hid" (*ester*) is identical to Esther's name.

Second, scholars have recognized that the names Esther and Mordecai resemble the figures of the Babylonian gods Ishtar and Marduk (Ahitov 2001, 32). Hence, the book mentions Esther's Hebrew name—Hadassah (Est 2:7)—as if to emphasize that she was indeed Jewish and not pagan. Likewise, Mordecai is the only figure in the Bible who is called (Mordecai) "the Jew" (5:13; 6:10), emphasizing both his Jewishness and his piety.

Rabbinic Traditions

According to the book of Esther, there are but three definite customs to Purim, which is celebrated each year on the 14th of the month of Adar (usually in March). The first custom is for the Jews to make Purim a day of feasting and joy; the second is to send portions (of food) to one another; and the third is to give gifts to the poor (Est 9:22).

The Rabbis later added additional customs. The Talmud, for example (*b. Megillah* 7b), says that "a man is obligated to get drunk on Purim to the point where he can no longer distinguish between cursed Haman and blessed Mordecai." This inability to tell friend from foe is illustrated in the same passage, which continues: "Rabba and R. Zira were celebrating Purim together; they got drunk; then, Rabba stood up and slaughtered R. Zira! The next day, he prayed over him and resurrected him. After a year, Rabba invited R. Zira to join him again for the Purim feast, but R. Zira refused and said: not every time miracles occur." From this tragic episode we get the modern expression "not every day is Purim," meaning: do not count on good things, or miracles, to happen on a regular basis.

The sages also embraced foreign traditions inspired by pagan carnivals (Bar-Navi 1993, 72). Thus, the celebrations of Purim over the centuries were greatly influenced by pagan festivals from the Middle Ages and especially by the urban Catholic carnival in Europe (Helman 2007, 85). The assimilation of pagan elements into the Purim holiday, as it is celebrated even today in the Jewish world, brought about several obvious similarities between Purim and the traditional carnival:

(1) The tradition of wearing masks and costumes was adopted by the sages directly from masquerades in ancient Europe (Belkin 2002, 60–61); for example, the "Clandes" festival (Flusser 1981, 13), which is mentioned in the Talmud (*b. Avodah Zarah* 6a, 8a).

(2) The tradition of the Adloyada Parade was influenced by a common practice in Catholic and secular festivals all over Europe through the Middle Ages (*Illustrated Lexicon* 1987, 199).

(3) These pagan parades included the tradition of wearing masks for the purpose of laughing at and mocking the boring routine of everyday life (Regev 2011, 269, 383).

(4) In addition to the masquerades and parades, the pagan carnivals included an excess consumption of alcoholic beverages (Ahitov 2001, 8, 69). Not surprisingly, scholars have traced the roots of this behavior to celebrations in ancient Greece (sixth century BCE) dedicated to the mythological god of wine (Sokman 2007, 14). This well explains the commandment from the Talmud mentioned earlier, which encourages, and in fact requires, the excessive drinking of wine during Purim.

(5) The final similarity has to do with an old rabbinic custom according to which dolls in the shape of Haman were cast into a huge bonfire that men were dancing around (Prawer 1975, 541; Rapell 1990, 229). The Babylonian Talmud even associates this tradition with the evil practice of the Canaanite Moloch, which included burning actual people. Tractate *Sanhedrin* 64b records an argument between the sages over whether the tradition of burning Haman-shaped dolls was too similar to the pagan practice of the Moloch. In any case, the Jewish tradition of burning dolls and dancing close to the fire during Purim is an ancient remnant of pagan traditions which were common among foreign folks who celebrated their festivals in a similar manner (Belkin 2002, 41–42).

Modern Customs

Purim today has four main characteristics: (1) wearing costumes; (2) eating *hamantaschen* (this is a Yiddish word for a triangular pastry; its Hebrew name, *oznei haman*, means "Haman's ears"); (3) singing the traditional songs; and (4) the public reading of the scroll of Esther (where children are instructed to make a big noise every time the word "Haman" is mentioned). Along with this is often a *Purim Spiel*, which is a fun dramatization of the events of the story. Such plays are traced back to 1555 CE in the writing of a Jewish-Polish scholar (Belkin 2002, 66–67).

Purim is known as the holiday of fun, laughter, and costume parties. The reason for the celebration is rooted in the history recorded in the book of Esther, according to which the Jews overcame the threat of destruction once again.

Indeed, the biggest feasts (e.g., Passover and Hanukkah) have a similar theme which we in Israel joke about, saying all the major Jewish holidays boil down to three main points: "They tried to kill us; we won; let's eat!"

Works Cited

Ahitov, Shmuel. 2001. *Scripture to Israel: Scientific Commentary to the Tanakh: The Book of Esther* [Hebrew]. Tel Aviv: Am Oved.

BarNavi, Eli, ed. 1993. *Historical Atlas of the History of the Jewish People* [Hebrew]. Tel Aviv: Yidiot Sepharim.

Belkin, Ahuva. 2002. *The Purim Spiel: Searching through the Jewish Folk Theater* [Hebrew]. Jerusalem: Mosad Bialik.

Flusser, David. 1981. Vol. 1 of *Sefer Yosifun* [Hebrew]. Jerusalem: Mosad Bialik.

Helman, Anat. 2007. *Light and Sea Surrounded It: Culture of Tel Aviv during the British Mandate* [Hebrew]. Haifa: Haifa University.

An Illustrated Lexicon of Judaism and Zionism [Hebrew]. 1987. Tel Aviv: Misrad Habitachon.

Prawer, Joshua, ed. 1975. Hebrew Encyclopedia 27 [Hebrew]. Jerusalem: Hebrew Encyclopedia Publishing.

Rapell, Yoel. 1990. *The Feasts of Israel: Practical Encyclopedia for Shabbat* [Hebrew]. Rananna: Misrad HaBitachon.

Regev, Moti. 2011. *Sociology of Culture: General Introduction* [Hebrew]. Rananna: Open University.

Sokman, Rahel. 2007. "Carnival in Venice" [Hebrew]. *Terminal: Journal for Art in the 21st Century* 31:14–15.

4.6 Hanukkah

Eitan Bar

Hanukkah is not a biblical feast, as it is a remembrance of events that happened after the writing of the Tanakh and before the writing of the New Testament. But it was celebrated by Jesus, and it brings a message that is very much in line with the biblical narrative: the survival of the Jewish people.

The History

The events of Hanukkah are recorded in the books of 1 and 2 Maccabees. In the year 167 BCE King Antiochus IV Epiphanes of the Seleucid (Greek) Empire conquered Jerusalem and turned the Temple into a pagan shrine. The leader of the Hasmonean dynasty was Judah the Maccabee, the oldest son of the priest named Mattiyahu. Three years later, in 164 BCE, Judah and his men fought back. According to 1 Maccabees 4:36–49, they defeated the much larger army, entered the Temple, and began to purify it. The 25th of the Jewish month of Kislev (usually in December) was set for the rededication. Second Maccabees 2:12 mentions an eight-day ceremony which was meant to be analogous to Solomon's dedication of the Temple. The celebration is called both *Tabernacles* (2 Maccabees 1:9) and *Tabernacles and fire* (2 Maccabees 1:18). This latter term was a memorial to the fact that fire accompanied the consecration of the Temple led by Judah, just as it accompanied the consecration of the Temple in the days of old (2 Maccabees 1:18–36).

Josephus does not use the term *Hanukkah*. He refers to the festival as "lights," explaining that the right to serve God came like a sudden light (*Ant.* 12.325). After the destruction of the Temple, new traditions emerged. The Talmud (*Shabbat* 21b) explains that each man and his household should kindle one light, whereas among the "the zealous" each individual must kindle a light. The school of Shammai said that the celebration should start with eight lights and work progressively down to one light by the end of the eight days. Hillel, by contrast, said that one light should be kindled on the first night and increased each night. Later in the same passage, further historical reasons for the celebration of Hanukkah are given. The Hasmoneans entered the Temple and discovered there was only enough (undefiled) oil to last for one night. Miraculously, this oil lasted for eight nights. According to Shmuel Safrai (1995, 218), former professor of Jewish history at Hebrew University, there is no mention of this miracle in any sources until this talmudic passage. More recently an Israeli historian (Hevlin 2009, 93) suggested that the miracle of the oil burning for eight days is part of the rabbinic narrative that sought to lessen the importance of their rivals the priests (Maccabees). Ironically, the secular pioneers of modern Israel went back and reclaimed the Maccabean narrative. One of their theme patriotic songs (*Anu Nosim Lapidim*, "We Carry Torches"), from the 1930s, has this refrain: "A miracle never happened, we never found the oil." This was a way of applauding the heroics of the Maccabees as an example for their own current struggles to reclaim the land of Israel (Meltzer 2007, 376; see also Rappaport 2004, 155).

In the New Testament

The third of the three Fall Feasts is Tabernacles (or *Sukkot*), which during the time of the Second Temple was celebrated in Jerusalem with elaborate displays of both water and lights. The Gospel of John alludes to some of these customs in 7:37–38 (see the discussion above, 4.4). According to John, Jesus remained in Jerusalem after this feast at least until the celebration of Hanukkah. A key term in these passages is "light" (8:12; 9:5).

Beginning in John 10:22, Jesus was at the Temple during Hanukkah. Most English translations refer to it as "the Feast of Dedication." The crowd wanted him to identify himself: "How long will You keep us in suspense? If You are the Christ, tell us plainly" (10:24 NASB). The answer he gave was not what they expecting, nor what they wanted. A direct answer in the affirmative (as he gave in John 4:26) might have been misconstrued in this context. The crowd was in Jerusalem celebrating the victory of the Maccabees. It might have seemed like the perfect time for Jesus to reveal his messiahship and begin a revolt against their Roman oppressors. But he gave them more than they asked for, and made one of his most outrageous statements ("I and the Father are One," John 10:30). This statement is all the more ironic during Hanukkah, as they were celebrating the defeat of the madman (as Antiochus is known in Jewish history) who claimed to be God.

Traditions

The most recognizable symbol of Hanukkah is the eight branch *hanukia* (or menorah), which symbolizes the story of the oil mentioned in the Talmud. The *savivon* (Hebrew for "around") is a spinning top that is used for children's games during the holiday. It is often called a *dreidel* (from the Yiddish word for "to turn"). Each of the four sides has a Hebrew letter, representing the words in the following phrase: "a great miracle happened there." In the land of Israel it is slightly changed to "a great miracle happened *here*." Traditional foods vary around the world. Jews from Eastern Europe are used to eating *latkes* (potato pancakes) while Jews in the Middle East prefer *suvganyot* (which are basically donuts). While it is a joyful celebration, there is also a serious message. As with Passover and Purim, Hanukkah is a testament of God's promise to preserve his people (see Jer 31:35–37).

Works Cited

Hevlin, Rina. 2009. *Jewish-Israeli Time: The Jewish Holiday as a Key to Identity Discourse* [Hebrew]. Tel Aviv: HaKibbutz Hameuchad.

Meltzer, Yoram. 2007. "Nationalizing and Secularizing Ancient Holidays and Creating New Ones/Hanukkah" [Hebrew]. Pages 374–78 in *New Jewish Time: Jewish Culture in a Secular Age, An Encyclopedic View*. Edited by Yeramiah Yovel. Jerusalem: Keter Publishing.

Rappaport, Uriel. 2004. *The First Book of Maccabees: Introduction, Hebrew Translation, and Commentary* [Hebrew]. Jerusalem: Yad Ben Zvi Press.

Safrai, Shmuel. 1995. "The Relationship between the Aggaddah and the Halacha" [Hebrew]. Pages 215–34 in *From the End of Biblical Times Up to the Redaction of the Talmud*. Edited by Arieh Kasher and Aaron Oppenheimer. Tel Aviv: Bialik Institute.

CHAPTER 5

Tabernacle and Temple

5.1 Atonement in the Old Testament

Michael L. Brown

The concept of atonement in the Hebrew Scriptures is integrally related to the root *k-p-r*, "to atone, expiate," although there is considerable scholarly debate as to the fundamental meaning of the root (see Averbeck 1997; Maass 1997; Lang 1995; Janowski 1982; Levine 1974). Does it mean "to cover," in which case atonement refers to the covering over of sins (cf. Jer 18:23 with Neh 3:37)? Does it mean "to pay a ransom," in which case atonement emphasizes the ransoming of the guilty party through the payment of an innocent party (cf. Lev 17:11 with Exod 30:12)? Or does it mean "to wipe away, remove," in which case atonement speaks of the removal of guilt and sin (cf. Isa 6:7, where *k-p-r* is parallel with *s-w-r*, "to take away, remove")?

Blood and Substitution

Although one cannot be dogmatic, a good argument can be made for the last view for two primary reasons. First, both people and inanimate things (like the tabernacle) are objects of expiation in the Old Testament (cf. Exod 29:36; 30:10), suggesting the concepts of "cleansing" and "purging" (cf. Lev 16:19, where the altar, having been expiated by blood, is now "cleansed"; and note that the NJPS renders *k-p-r* in verses like Exod 30:10 with "purify" and "purification"). Second, other texts with *k-p-r* found in non-cultic settings point to the concept of "removal," which again is in keeping with the idea of "wiping away" (cf. Rashi to Gen 32:21; see also Isa 28:18, with LXX and *Targum*; Isa 47:11; and Prov 16:14, where *k-p-r* more likely means "remove" than "atone"). Thus, when sin, guilt, and uncleanness are expiated, they are wiped away and removed from sight, resulting in the cleansing of the object of expiation (Brown 1998). More broadly, Averbeck states (1997, 2:704, with reference to Lev 10:10–11), "the results or benefits of making atonement fall into three main categories: consecration (relating to the distinction between the holy and the common), purification (relating to the distinction between the unclean and clean), or forgiveness (relating to the issue of 'all the decrees of the Lord'), respectively."

Throughout the Torah, this process is integrally related to the blood of sacrificial animals, which relates at least in part to the concept of substitution, or "life for life" (cf. Rashi to Lev 17:11). In keeping with this, of the 112 times that *k-p-r* occurs in the Tanakh, more than half of them (66x) are found in Leviticus and Numbers (respectively, 48x and 18x), the key Torah books dealing with blood sacrifices and priestly ministry. Note also that *dam*, blood, occurs roughly 90x in Leviticus, which is *the* book of atonement in the Tanakh, representing almost one in three occurrences for "blood" in the Old Testament (for discussion of the alleged apotropaic aspects of blood, cf. Levine 1974). Even in the case of Israelites too poor to afford an animal sacrifice for a sin offering, their grain offerings were mingled with the blood sacrifices on the altar (see Lev 5:11–13). There is, then, an intimate connection between blood sacrifices and atonement, to the point that *Targum Onkelos* to Exod 24:8 changes Moses sprinkling blood on the people to ratify the covenant to Moses sprinkling blood on the altar for their atonement. Note also the rabbinic term "the altar of atonement" (cf. *Mishneh Torah, Hilkhot Teshuvah*, 1:3), and cf. Hebrew *kapporet*, from *k-p-r*, which is rendered as "place of atonement," "mercy seat," or "cover" (over the ark), and found 26x in the Old Testament, primarily in Exod (see, e.g., Exod 25:17–22).

In contrast, emphasis on the important concept of repentance is primarily found outside of Leviticus and Numbers, indicating that atonement is connected more closely with the cultus, while other aspects of getting right with God found expression outside of an exclusive temple context (cf. also Ezek 43:20, 26; 45:15, 17, 20, all in cultic contexts with *k-p-r*). An Israelite, then, could repent and ask God for mercy at any time and place, although this act might also call for sacrificial offerings and he might choose to recite penitential psalms in the Temple (note Ps 51:17–19). But by law and design, an Israelite could only offer a sacrifice at the Temple, the place where he would also experience cultic atonement with the help of the priests and Levites. Thus atonement preceded forgiveness (see Lev 4:20, 26, 31; 19:22; Num 15:25). Not only so, but the people of Israel were admonished to direct their prayers toward the Temple in Jerusalem when supplicating the Lord and asking for forgiveness (1 Kgs 8:29–30; 2 Chr 6:20–21). Even 2 Chr 7:14, a *locus classicus* for national forgiveness based on repentance and prayer, is predicated on 2 Chr 7:12: "Then the LORD appeared to Solomon in the night and said to him: 'I have heard your prayer and have chosen this place for myself as a house of sacrifice [*bet zevah*]' " (ESV). See also Dan 9:24, in the context of the rebuilding of Jerusalem and the Second Temple, where one of the six divine goals to be accomplished was "to atone for wickedness."

Central, then, to Israel's atonement system was the Temple (or, originally, tabernacle), where blood sacrifices were offered and the high priests interceded for the nation (Exod 28:29–30). And central to this was Yom Kippur, the Day of Atonement, the only time each year when the high priest would enter the Most Holy Place (Lev 16:2–3). He would then offer a bull as a sin offering to "make atonement for himself and for his house" (Lev 16:6 ESV), also sprinkling the bull's blood, along with the blood of a male goat (which had been designated "for the Lord") on the various cultic items. "Thus," Lev 16:16 reads, "he shall make atonement for the Holy Place, because of the uncleannesses of the people of Israel and because of their transgressions, all their sins. And so he shall do for the tent of meeting, which dwells with them in the midst of their uncleannesses" (ESV). So, the nation's sin polluted and defiled God's holy dwelling place, because of which it had to be expiated by blood, pointing again to the concept of "cleansing," since the tabernacle/ Temple itself bore no moral guilt.

The rest of the day's ceremonies focused on a second male goat, which was not slaughtered and was designated *la'azazel*, variously rendered "for Azazel" (understood to be the name of a wilderness demon) or "for the scapegoat" (see already LXX; cf. NET translation notes to Lev 16:8). The high priest would "lay both his hands on the head of the live goat, and confess over it all the iniquities of the people of Israel, and all their transgressions, all their sins. And he shall put them on the head of the goat and send it away into the wilderness by the hand of a man who is in readiness" (Lev 16:21). Thus, the corporate sins of the nation were transferred to this goat, which then carried them into the desert, also highlighting the aspect of substitution. In this way, Israel's sin was expiated and removed by these sacrificial animals, while God's holy dwelling and holy items were also expiated by blood (see further Wright 1992).

Restoration

As for the connection between atonement and restoration, note that the Year of Jubilee began on the Day of Atonement, at which time "release" (*deror*) was proclaimed throughout the land (see Lev 25:1–11). More broadly, note the connection between forgiveness and healing in the beatific vision of Isa 33:24: The forgiveness of sin (and, by implication, the absence of sin) would remove sickness, one of the direct results of sin (cf. also Isa 53:4–6; Pss 6:1–2; 41:1–4; 103:3; Matt 8:16–17; Mark 2:1–12; Jas 5:14–16).

As for the substitutionary element of atonement, see Deut 21:8, where, in the case of an unsolved homicide, a heifer was to be offered in sacrifice, accompanied by this prayer, "Accept atonement, O LORD, for your people Israel, whom you have redeemed, and do not set the guilt of innocent blood in the midst of your people Israel, so that their blood guilt be atoned for" (ESV). Note that this concept of substitutionary atonement could carry over to an intercessor as well, as seen in Exod 32:30, where Moses says to the nation after the golden calf incident at

Mount Sinai, "You have sinned a great sin. And now I will go up to the Lord; perhaps I can make atonement for your sin" (ESV). In the prayer that follows, Moses offers his own life in place of the sinning nation: "Alas, this people has sinned a great sin. They have made for themselves gods of gold. But now, if you will forgive their sin—but if not, please blot me out of your book that you have written" (Exod 32:31–32 ESV). Here, Moses offers himself, as one not guilty at Sinai and as the nation's leader, in place of the guilty nation, an offer which God declines. However, in Num 8, we see that one of the functions of the Levites was to take the place of the people of Israel. And so, in Num 8:10–12, the people lay their hands on the Levites, setting the Levites aside as a wave offering, and then the Levites lay hands on the heads of bulls, which make atonement for them. So the Levites take the place of the people (see further Num 8:19, discussed below), while the bulls take the place of the Levites.

This concept is found again in Num 25, but in this case, it was the public execution of representative sinners (an Israelite man named Zimri and a Midianite woman named Cozbi, whom Aaron's son Phineas thrust through with a spear) that assuaged God's wrath and stopped a plague. As described in verses 11 and 13, "Phinehas the son of Eleazar, son of Aaron the priest, has turned back my wrath from the people of Israel. . . . He was jealous for his God and made atonement for the people of Israel" (ESV). From this we see the explicit connection between atonement and turning away wrath, reflected also in the word "propitiation" (cf. Greek *hilasmos*; see 1 John 2:2; 4:10). Compare also 2 Sam 21:3, where atonement must be made for the bloodguilt of the household of Saul, guilt that has caused a famine. See further Num 8:19, where the Levites are given "to make atonement for the people of Israel, that there may be no plague among the people of Israel when the people of Israel come near the sanctuary" (ESV), and Num 16:46 (Heb. 17:11), where the Lord instructs Aaron to take coals from the altar, put them on his censer, and run into the midst of the sinning people to "make atonement for them, for wrath has gone out from the Lord; the plague has begun" (ESV).

Also significant is Num 35:28, where the death of the high priest, the chief intercessor for the nation, frees the unintentional manslayer from exile in the city of refuge, thereby providing a substitutionary payment for the blood that was shed. Otherwise, the only acceptable payment for blood was the blood of the killer (Num 35:33), but since he did not deserve death, the death of the high priest took his place. Accordingly, the Talmud (*m. Makkot* 2:6; *b. Makkot* 11b; see also *Leviticus Rabbah* 10.6) asks the question: Isn't it the exile of the innocent manslayer [in the city of refuge] that expiates? The answer is no; "It is not the exile that expiates, but the death of the high priest." And Jacob Milgrom (1990, 294) comments: "As the High Priest atones for Israel's sins through his cultic [i.e., ritual] service in his lifetime (Exod. 28:36; Lev. 16:16, 21), so he atones for homicide through his death" (for the broader rabbinic concept that the death of the righteous atones for the sin of the generation, see, e.g., *b. Mo'ed Qatan* 28a; *Leviticus Rabbah* 20.12; *y. Yoma* 2:1; *Pesiqta of Rab Kahana* 26.16; cf. also *Exodus Rabbah, Terumah* 35.4).

Interestingly, in verses where God is the subject of *k-p-r*, translators often render the verb with "forgive" rather than "atone," since the Lord is not making atonement for sins but rather providing atonement. Hence, *k-p-r* in Deut 21:8; 2 Chr 30:18; Pss 65:4[3]; 79:9; Jer 18:23 means "pardon" or "provide expiation." As Averbeck (1997, 2:691) notes: "These occurrences of the vb. suggest that God himself could affect atonement for his people if he so desired, and that people could call upon him to do so. The fact that modern EVV often translate the vb. *kpr* in these passages with some form of the word 'forgive' assumes that there is a close connection between 'atone' and 'forgive' (the latter is usually Heb. *slḥ* . . .)." Yet in some of these cases, blood sacrifices are still involved (and note the animal offering in Deut 21:1–8). In the words of Maass, "Yahweh grants atonement (2 Chron 30:18), the agents are the priests, the medium is the blood ceremony, the beneficiary Israel." However, in other cases Maass (1997, 2:631) observes, "Human action (besides prayer and contrition) is not considered, apparently because it is inconsequential. . . . If guilt becomes too great, Yahweh intervenes and 'atones' ([Ps.] 65:4)" (see also Pss 78:38; 79:9). Lang (1995, 7:300) calls this "Divine Atonement," noting that "The active use of *kipper* with God as subject is associated primarily with the language of prayer" (see further Deut 32:43, although there are some textual difficulties).

In cultic atonement texts, almost no emphasis is put on acts of repentance or contrition (aside from the call for national self-affliction in Lev 16, traditionally taken to mean fasting; and aside from the many penitentiary prayers for forgiveness associated with the Temple, such as 1 Kgs 8 // 2 Chr 6). For confession accompanying sacrificial rites, see Lev 5:5; Num 5:7; and note Isa 6:7, where the prophet's lips are cleansed with coals from the altar after his confession of sin. Consequently, his sin is removed (*s-w-r*) and wiped away (*k-p-r*). In Isa 27:9, it is Israel's destruction of idolatrous altars that will result in its iniquity being removed and wiped away (with the same two verbs). Note also Prov 16:6, where iniquity is wiped away (*k-p-r*; others, "atoned for" or "forgiven") by loving-kindness and truth.

Works Cited

Averbeck, Richard E. 1997. "*kpr.*" *NIDOTTE* 2:689–710.

Brown, Michael L. 1998. "*Kippēr* and Atonement in the Book of Isaiah." Pages 189–202 in *Kî Barukh Hû': Ancient Near Eastern, Biblical, and Judaic Studies for Baruch A. Levine.* Edited by R. Chazan, W. W. Hallo, and L. H. Schiffman. Winona Lake, IN: Eisenbrauns.

Janowski, B. 1982. *Sühne als Heilsgeschehen: Studien zur Sühnetheologie der Priesterschrift und zur Wurzel KPR im Alten Orient und im Alten Testament.* WMANT 55. Neukirchen-Vluyn: Neukirchener Verlag.

Lang, B. 1995. "*kipper.*" *TDOT* 7:288–303.

Levine, B. A. 1974. *In the Presence of the Lord: A Study of Cult and Some Cultic Terms in Ancient Israel.* Leiden: Brill.

Maass, F. 1997. "*kpr* pi., to atone." *TLOT* 2:624–35.

Milgrom, Jacob. 1990. *Numbers.* JPS Torah Commentary. Philadelphia: Jewish Publication Society.

Wright, D. P. 1992. "Day of Atonement." *ABD* 2:72–76.

5.2 Salvation in the Old Testament

Michael L. Brown

Salvation in the Old Testament is both personal and corporate, physical and spiritual, although the primary emphasis is on salvation in this world more than in the world to come. But that does not mean that salvation was conceived primarily in material terms. Rather, salvation was viewed holistically as an act of divine intervention: The God who saved from earthly enemies also saved from spiritual enemies, and the Lord who delivered from sickness also delivered from sin.

The Scope of Salvation

There is not a clear emphasis on "saving the soul" in the Old Testament (in the New Testament, see, e.g., 1 Cor 5:5), but there are semantic parallels in the terminology of salvation in the Old Testament and New Testament. Thus, in the space of just two chapters in Luke, Greek *sōzō*, the equivalent to Hebrew *yasha'*, is used in four different contexts: in Luke 7:50 it is used with reference to being *saved from sin* (see 7:36–50); in 8:36 with reference to being *saved from demons* (see 8:26–39); in 8:48 with reference to being *saved from sickness* (see 8:43–48); and in 8:50 with reference to being *saved from death* (see 8:49). Accordingly, what W. Radl (1990–1993) states about the use of *sōzō* can largely be said about *yasha'*: "That from which one is saved . . . include[s] mortal danger, death, disease, possession, sin and alienation from God, and eternal ruin." Therefore, Yahweh in the Old Testament and Jesus in the New Testament are Saviors who forgive, deliver, heal, and resurrect, both temporally and eternally. (According to the lexicons, the fundamental range of meaning for *yasha'* includes "to deliver, save, help"; see especially Sawyer and Fabry 1990.)

The Tanakh recounts how God saved his people from the Egyptians (see Exod 14:30 ESV, "Thus the LORD saved [*yasha'*] Israel that day from the hands of the Egyptians, and Israel saw the Egyptians dead on the seashore"). And as he saved Israel from Egypt, so he saved them again and again throughout the centuries (e.g., Pss 28:9; 107:13, 19, all with *yasha'*). In light of these great past acts of salvation, the psalmist cried out to the Lord to save him from his own present enemies (e.g., Ps 18:27[28]). Thus, Israel's deliverance from hostile forces (normally sinful nations) and the psalmist's deliverance from hostile forces (normally human enemies, sickness, sin, or demonic attack) were not simply a matter of physical, earthly salvation. Rather, these saving, delivering acts of God were part of a larger spiritual picture of God's reign over nature and of his reign over all competing spiritual powers. That's why, in Ps 18, David's deliverance is viewed as a mighty triumph of God over evil men as well as over the forces of death and destruction. In Exod 15, Israel's deliverance from Egypt is depicted as Yahweh's victory over the gods of Egypt, Pharaoh and his army, and the forces of nature (see Exod 12:12; 15:3–4, 7–12; of course, the gods were often associated directly with forces of nature).

Thus, in Exod 14:13 Moses tells Israel they will see God's salvation (from the pursuing Egyptians) and in 15:2 he proclaims in song (after the Egyptians were drowned in the sea), "The LORD . . . has become my salvation." Similarly, in Judg 15:18, Samson speaks of "this great salvation" after killing one thousand Philistines. These are all acts of God's deliverance from earthly enemies (similar examples are found passim in Old Testament texts). For examples of personal "salvation," cf. Ps 3:8, where the psalmist declares that "Salvation belongs to the LORD," after crying out, "Arise, O LORD! Save me, O my God! For you strike all my enemies on the cheek; you break the teeth of the wicked" (Ps 3:7; see further Pss 18:2, 35, 46, 50; 21:1, 5; 25:5; 27:1, 9; 38:22; 42:5, 11; 43:5; 60:5; 62:1–2, 6–7; 69:20; 70:4; 71:15; 85:9; 88:1; 108:6; 118:14–15, 21; 140:6; again, all in the primary context of deliverance from earthly enemies). In contrast, humankind cannot be trusted to save (Ps 60:11; 108:12; 146:3; see also 119:155, where salvation is far from the wicked).

Salvation and the Kingdom of God

It would be wrong, however, to see "salvation" only in terms of individual or corporate deliverance from temporal danger or threat. It also speaks of God's wider acts of salvation, as he manifests his royal authority on the earth, thereby demonstrating that he is God of gods and King of kings. No other deity or power can compete with him in character or power or might. His salvific acts testify to who he is, revealing his righteousness, his strength, his love, and his faithfulness.

The psalmist declares, "By awesome deeds you answer us with righteousness, O God of our salvation, the hope of all the ends of the earth and of the farthest seas" (Ps 65:5). Indeed, the Lord reigns in the midst of the earth, performing acts of deliverance and salvation, resisting and defeating the powers of chaos, both natural and supernatural. See Ps 74 (note especially vv. 12–23; see further below) and Ps 95, where the people are exhorted to praise the rock of their salvation in verse 1 because

> The Lord is a great God, and a great King above all gods. In his hand are the depths of the earth; the heights of the mountains are his also. The sea is his, for he made it, and his hands formed the dry land. (vv. 3–5)

This deserves the attention of the whole world.

> Oh sing to the Lord a new song, for he has done marvelous things! His right hand and his holy arm have worked salvation for him. The Lord has made known his salvation; he has revealed his righteousness in the sight of the nations. He has remembered his steadfast love and faithfulness to the house of Israel. All the ends of the earth have seen the salvation of our God. (Ps 98:1–3)

> Oh sing to the Lord a new song; sing to the Lord, all the earth! Sing to the Lord, bless his name; tell of his salvation from day to day. Declare his glory among the nations, his marvelous works among all the peoples! For great is the Lord, and greatly to be praised; he is to be feared above all gods. For all the gods of the peoples are worthless idols, but the Lord made the heavens. Splendor and majesty are before him; strength and beauty are in his sanctuary. (Ps 96:1–6)

In other contexts, "salvation" seems to have a more spiritual emphasis, emphasizing either forgiveness of sin and/or right relationship with God, perhaps even beyond this world (see Ps 91:16). For "salvation" in relation to forgiveness and reconciliation, see Ps 51:14 (in David's prayer of repentance after committing adultery and murder, referring to the Lord as the "God of my salvation"). See also Ps 132:16, where it is the priests whom the Lord clothes with salvation (cf. *Metzudat David*; others, however, see this simply as a promise of protection; cf. NET; note that NJPS has "victory" rather than "salvation").

Sawyer and Fabry (1990, 6:459–60) summarize the significance of "salvation" in the Psalter and related texts:

> Nearly half of the Psalms contain 1 or more occurrences of *yšʿ*. . . . The subject is always God, except where God is contrasted to the vanity of human aid . . . or the inadequacy of military might. . . . The uniqueness of God's saving power is also expressed in several passages . . . and the same exclusiveness is implied in the expression *ʾelōhê yišî*, "God of my salvation" . . . and in metaphors such as *ṣûr yešuʿātî*, "rock of my salvation" . . . *māgēn yišʿekā*, "shield of your salvation" . . . and *qeren-yišʿî*, "horn of my salvation."

In the Major and Minor Prophets, where *yasha'* occurs 100x, the root is used "to affirm adamantly that only Yahweh saves (Isa 59:16; 63:1, 5). Only he has a known track record as Savior (43:[11]–12; 63:9), a claim no other gods (45:20; 46:7), astrologers (47:13), or kings (Hos 13:10) can make. Yahweh never lacks the power to save (Isa 59:1), though his inaction may leave that impression (Jer 14:19; cf. 8:20)" (Hubbard 1997, 2:558). Note that Yahweh as Savior (Isa 43:11) is the one who forgives and wipes away sins: "I, I am he who blots out your transgressions for my own sake, and I will not remember your sins" (Isa 43:25). Also, in Isa 26:18, the concept of "salvation" (in the plural) may be connected to the future resurrection of the dead, where Israel makes this confession: "We were with child, we writhed in labor, but we gave birth to wind. We have not brought salvation to the earth, and the people of the world have not come to life" (NIV). Compare also NJPS, "We have won no victory on earth; the inhabitants of the world have not come to life!" (Others, however, render v. 18b differently; cf. NET, "We cannot produce deliverance on the earth; people to populate the world are not born"; ESV, "We have accomplished no deliverance in the earth, and the inhabitants of the world have not fallen." If ESV is correct, the "deliverance-salvation" that Israel was to accomplish would include the defeat of the wicked. Cf. also the differing interpretations in the commentaries of Rashi, Ibn Ezra, Radak, and Malbim.)

The concrete reality of God's salvation in the Old Testament reminds us, however, that salvation in the New Testament should not be treated as an abstract theological category, even when speaking of personal salvation. Rather, it depicts people being saved in a tangible and real way: saved from sin, saved from demonic powers, saved from damnation, and saved from wrath. And in both the Old Testament and New Testament, salvation is directly connected to Yahweh's reign. Thus, in the midst of the chaos of this world, Ps 74:12 declares, "Yet God my King is from of old, working salvation in the midst of the earth" (ESV). He is the one who sets things in order (74:16–17) and defeats both spiritual and natural enemies (74:13–15, 18–23). Similarly, in Isa 35, it is the announcement of God's coming with vengeance that paves the way for the return of the Jewish exiles, accentuated by miracles of healing and natural transformation (Isa 35:1–10).

This, then, breaks into a new and greater level with the announcement of the inbreaking of the kingdom of God with the ministry of Jesus, the bearer of God's salvation. As noted by Mueller, and reflecting the consensus of New Testament scholarship, the acts of deliverance and healing in Jesus' ministry were an element in the struggle for the establishment of eschatological salvation. He writes: "His exorcism of demons, and with it the victorious struggle against Satan on earth, are visible signs of the advent of the eschatological time of salvation in which God alone will reign" (Seybold and Mueller 1981, 117–18). Accordingly, Peter looks to the words of Joel to proclaim that, in this new era of the Spirit's outpouring, "it shall come to pass that everyone who calls upon the name of the Lord shall be saved" (Acts 2:21, quoting Joel 2:32 [3:5]; the rendering of this verse in Joel in the NJPS underscores the very real nature of this salvation: "But everyone who invokes the name of the LORD shall escape; for there shall be a remnant on Mount Zion and in Jerusalem, as the Lord promised. Anyone who invokes the LORD will be among the survivors"). And since Jesus "brought life and immortality to light through the gospel" (2 Tim 1:10), the eternal salvation that was hoped for and hinted at in the Old Testament (see Pss 16:11; 17:15; 36:9; Prov 12:28; more explicitly, Dan 12:2–3) becomes an assured reality in the New Testament (e.g., Acts 2:47; 15:11; 16:30–31; Rom 5:9–10; 1 Cor 1:18; 15:2; Eph 2:5–8; 1 Tim 1:9).

Works Cited

Hubbard, Robert L., Jr. 1997. "*yš*," *NIDOTTE* 2:556–62.
Radl, W. 1990–1993. "*sōzō*, rescue, save, preserve, help." *EDNT* 3:319–20.
Seybold, Klaus, and Ulrich B. Mueller. 1981. *Sickness and Healing*. Translated by Douglas W. Stott. Nashville: Abingdon.
Sawyer, J. F. A., and H. J. Fabry. 1990. "*yš*," *TDOT* 6:441–63.

5.3 Jesus and the Tabernacle/Temple

George H. Guthrie

A Jewish midrash from the second half of the first millennium considers the land of Israel the very navel of the world, Jerusalem the center of the land, the Temple the center of Jerusalem, and the stone in the holy of holies the world's foundation (*Tanhuma, Kedoshim* 10). Although God himself stands as *the* center of the story of Scripture, the spaces he has crafted for people to interface with himself thread their way through the heart of that story, from very beginning to very end, bearing witness to the fact that God desires human beings to know his presence and to experience it in special places.

The Dwelling of God in the Hebrew Scriptures

In recent scholarship, the garden of Eden often is read as foreshadowing the tabernacle and the Temple, especially the holiest place of those institutions. Like the tabernacle, for example, the garden only has one entrance, is guarded by cherubim, and faces east. In priest-like fashion, the first man "cultivates" and "keeps" the garden (Gen 2:15), the same terms used of the priests "working" in relation to and "watching over" the tabernacle (Num 3:7–8; 8:25–26; 1 Chr 23:32; Walton 2001, 148–49; Schachter 2013, 73–77). After the fall and expulsion of people from Eden, the biblical narrative turns to the establishment of a people whom God will draw back into his presence (Gen 17:1).

During the wilderness era, God gave his people laws, including instructions for building a mobile worship space referred to as a "dwelling place" for God (e.g., Exod 25:9; 26:1), or the "tent" (e.g., Exod 26:7, 9, 11–14), or the "sanctuary" or "holy place" (Exod 15:17; 25:8; 30:13, 24; 36:1, 3–4, 6). Through this structure, God's people would experience his presence in the center of their camp, draw near to him, and thus know human flourishing and transformation (e.g., Num 4:15; 2 Sam 6:6–7). With a tree-like lampstand and guardian cherubim, the tabernacle harkens back to the garden, perhaps serving as an indication of God's desire that people be restored to his presence, this restoration ultimately mediated through his people to the whole world (Fretheim 2010, 271–72). Yet the people of Israel do not mediate the glory of God well, ultimately forsaking God's covenant, rejecting his rule over them, and turning once again from his presence. Thus, God hides his face from them (Deut 31:15–18): "He abandoned the tabernacle of Shiloh, the tent he had set up among humans" (Ps 78:60 NIV). [See Figure 5.]

The vision for a holy place of worship is reborn in the "man after God's own heart" (1 Sam 13:14; 16:7; 1 Kgs 8:17–18). Yet, as a man of war, David is not allowed to build the temple (1 Chr 22:8), and the task falls to his son Solomon. Upon completion of the First Temple, glory fills it, but Solomon's spiritual collapse is imminent (1 Kgs 10:14–11:11), and his idolatrous failure sets a pattern that will plague the people of God for centuries (Hays 2016, 63–103). Brief moments of reform are swallowed up in overwhelming patterns of rebellion; so, God leaves his temple and brings judgment on it at the hands of the Babylonians (2 Kgs 25:8–12; Ezek 10:18). Upon return from exile in 538 BCE, a second temple is initiated, with the prophets Haggai and Zechariah motivating the people to complete the project. This second temple, however, has no ark of the covenant (Jer 3:16), and the glory of God never fills it.

Longing for an Eschatological Temple

At this point in the unfolding narrative of Scripture, the prophets begin to speak of an eschatological sanctuary associated with a new covenant God will make with the people, a sanctuary whose glory will be greater than that of the First Temple (Hag 2:9). Thus, God's vision for a sanctuary among his people will not be fully realized in the Second Temple in Jerusalem (see Ezek 37:26; cf. Zech 6:12–13). This brings us to a strand of thought in Second Temple Judaism that reflects dissatisfaction with the Temple in Jerusalem, as if that institution was compromised and in need of restoration or replacement with an eschatological temple. Some trace the antipathy toward the Temple to Ezek 40–48, with its vision of a new temple located in the new Jerusalem, a heavenly temple that would descend on Zion (Wise 1992, 813–14).

In Second Temple Judaism, for instance, *1 Enoch* and *Jubilees* both express the belief that the current Temple is polluted and will be replaced by an eschatological temple (*1 Enoch* 89:73; 90:28–29; *Jubilees* 1:17, 27). *Testament of Levi* 15:1 and *Testament of Moses* 6:8–9 foretell of judgment against the Temple (cf. Tobit 14:5; Sirach 36:19–20; *Testament of Benjamin* 9:2), while *Psalms of Solomon* hopes specifically in a messiah who will cleanse the whole of Jerusalem, supposedly including the Temple (*Psalms of Solomon* 2:2–3; 17:22, 30; Chanikuzhy 2012, 398; Keener 1999, 561). At Qumran, Nathan's oracle to David (2 Sam 7:10–14) is interpreted eschatologically and in light of Exod 15:17, which speaks of the house that God would build (4Q174 1:2–7), with the "the Shoot of David" as his agent (Juel 1977, 172–73). The literature of earliest Christianity understands this longing for a Messiah who would put right the Temple to be fulfilled pre-eminently in the person of Jesus of Nazareth.

Jesus and Herod's Temple

In terms of an institution, it is Herod's Temple that sets the backdrop for the ministry of Jesus. Originally built after the return from exile in the latter sixth century BCE, the Second Temple was greatly enhanced by Herod the Great. A brilliant builder, Herod began work on the Temple in 20–19 BCE. The work, carried out by approximately ten thousand lay workers and one thousand specially trained priests, went on throughout the earthly ministry of Jesus and continued until 63 CE, just a handful of years before the sanctuary and its complex would be destroyed by the Romans in 70 CE. In first-century Judaism, there simply was no more important institution than the Temple in Jerusalem.

Jesus' own relationship with the Temple was multifaceted. On one level, the Gospels reflect a positive attitude toward the Temple as the special place of God's dwelling. For instance, Jesus' parents follow the purification rites required in the law by taking the baby Jesus to the Temple and offering sacrifice there (Luke 2:22–24). Jesus referred to the Temple as God's "house" (Matt 12:4; Luke 2:49; 6:4) and, in his teaching, could speak of appropriate and inappropriate oath-taking in relation to the sanctuary (Matt 23:16–22). For Jesus and his disciples, the Temple was a place of worship and ministry (Betz 1997, 461; Wise 1992, 816). [See Figure 6.]

Nevertheless, the Gospels record words and actions by Jesus that raised significant concerns about the legitimacy of the temple cult and those who administrated it. These words and actions, therefore, are consonant with larger concerns about the Temple in broader Second Temple Judaism, and ultimately point to the hope for an eschatological temple established by a Messianic figure. Particularly, we can consider Jesus' negative posture toward the Temple along three lines: Jesus' apocalyptic prophecies concerning the destruction of the Temple, Jesus' action in "cleansing" the Temple, and Jesus' sayings concerning the destruction and rebuilding of the Temple.

First, apocalyptic prophecies concerning the destruction of the Temple are found in the Olivet Discourse in Matt 24:1, 15; Mark 13:2–3, 14; and Luke 21:5–6. In these synoptic parallels, the disciples of Jesus comment on the magnificence of the buildings in the Temple complex and its impressive stones—a sentiment common in the Judaism of the day (e.g., Josephus, *J. W.* 6.267; *b. Bava Batra* 4a). Yet, the comment by his disciples prompts Jesus to note that those large beautiful stones will be toppled in a coming destruction of the Temple, a prophecy fulfilled when the Romans destroyed Jerusalem in 70 CE. Rather than a retrospective prophecy concocted after the Temple's demise, Jesus' words are very much in line with both the sentiments of his day and the biblical prophets concerning judgment on Jerusalem and her Temple (Keener 1999, 561–62).

Second, Jesus' action in "cleansing" the Temple is found in all four Gospels (Mark 11:15–17; Matt 21:12–13; Luke 19:45–46; John 2:14–17). In the Synoptic Gospels, Jesus arrives in Jerusalem for his final Passover week. Mark records that upon arriving in Jerusalem Jesus entered the Temple courts late in the day, looked around, and left for an evening in Bethany (Mark 11:11). The next day, Jesus enters the Temple complex, driving out both sellers and buyers, overturning the tables of the money changers and the benches of the dove sellers, and not allowing anyone to carry goods through the Temple courts (Mark 11:15–16). He then, in Mark 11:17, comments on his actions by pointing to twin passages from the prophets: "My house will be called a house of prayer for all nations" (cf. Isa 56:7) and "But you have made it 'a den of robbers'" (cf. Jer 7:11).

Matthew follows Mark closely, focusing attention on both sellers and buyers, the turning over of the money changers' tables and the benches of those selling doves, and the scriptural comments from Isaiah and Jeremiah (Matt 21:12–13). Luke's terse account focuses on the sellers, without any reference to the money changers (Luke 19:45–46). John's more dramatic account also focuses on the sellers (of "cattle, sheep and doves"), but as in Mark and Matthew, Jesus' ire is turned on the money changers as well. In the Fourth Gospel, the scriptural comment on the event comes from Ps 69:9, a passage remembered afterward by his disciples: "Zeal for your house will consume me" (John 2:17 ESV), a comment that recently has been understood as the zeal of the religious leaders that led to Jesus' death (Bryan 2011, 482–86).

The particular import of the Temple action has been hotly debated in New Testament scholarship (for a summary of the positions see Collins 1999, 2–6;

Chanikuzhy 2012, 401). Interpretations include, for example, that Jesus' act in the Temple consisted of a protest against Herod and his secular authority (e.g., Betz 1997, 464–69), a protest against trade in the Temple as a form of desecration (Eppstein 1964; cf. Zech 14:20), or a cleansing action in light of a corrupt Temple priesthood. The Temple action has also been understood as a symbolic, prophetic act heralding the Temple's destruction (e.g., Sanders 1985, 61–76), and/or a messianic act proclaiming that the Jerusalem Temple had failed in its eschatological mission to the nations (Bryan 2011, 492). The best understanding perhaps lies in reading Jesus' action as both a prophetic, eschatological act and a cleansing action against the commercialization and corruption of Temple worship (Evans 1997, 435–39).

Finally, a third set of passages focus on Jesus' sayings concerning the destruction of the Temple and the rebuilding of a temple not made with human hands (Matt 26:61; 27:40; Mark 14:57–58; 15:29–30; John 2:18–22). In Matthew and Mark these words are found on the lips of the enemies of Jesus, first at his hearing before the Sanhedrin and then as he hangs upon the cross. The words clearly stand at the center of the accusations against Jesus. Yet, the saying by Jesus himself is presupposed rather than recorded.

In John, the Temple is the center of religious existence for the Jews and especially the place of God's self-manifestation (Lieu 1999, 51–69), and in that Gospel the pericope on the Temple's destruction and rebuilding follows on the heels of the Temple cleansing event and in answer to the religious leaders asking Jesus to explain his basis of authority. The destruction and building of a temple are offered as the "sign" that will demonstrate Jesus' authority to do the Temple cleansing (John 2:18–19). John interprets Jesus' words as referring to his body, which the leaders would "destroy" and which would be raised from the dead (John 2:21–22).

In John's Gospel, therefore, the writer presents Jesus as replacing the Temple and its cult. Jesus is the new temple, a thought that echoes the allusion to the tabernacle in 1:14, Jesus having "tabernacled" among people. So, for John, Jesus is "the locus of the Divine dwelling with humankind, the 'place' where the name of God abides or dwells" (Attridge 2010, 262–63). This would have been especially poignant to John's audience in the latter first century CE, after the destruction of the Temple in Jerusalem.

Jesus and the Eschatological Temple

The balance of the New Testament presents the eschatological temple in two primary forms: (1) the church as the new temple; and (2) the apocalyptic, heavenly temple. As to the former, in the Corinthian correspondence, Paul speaks of the church as God's temple in three places. In 1 Cor 3, the apostle uses a "building" metaphor, pointing out that the Corinthians are God's building, and he and Apollos are builders building the church on the true foundation, Jesus Christ (3:10–15). Then in 3:16–17 he states plainly, "Do you not know that you are a temple of God . . . ?" (NASB). In 6:19 the assertion is repeated, this time in the context of warning against sexual immorality: "Do you not know that your body is a temple of the Holy Spirit who is in you . . . ?" (NASB). In 2 Cor 6:14–18, a key moment in the letter as the apostle brings his treatise on authentic ministry to a close, Paul warns against idolatry, stating that there can be no agreement between the temple of God and idols, and adds, "For we are the temple of the living God" (6:16, author's translation). This assertion he follows immediately with a catena of passages from the Jewish Scriptures, beginning with a conflation of Lev 26:11–12 and Ezek 37:27: "I will live among them and walk around, and I will be their God, and they will be my people" (author's translation). The temple imagery, therefore, consistently points to God's presence among his people (Guthrie 2015, 353).

Similarly, in Ephesians Paul speaks of the church as "a holy temple in the Lord" (2:21 ESV) built on the foundation of the apostles and prophets, with Jesus himself as the chief cornerstone (2:19–22). Again, God dwelling among his people by the Spirit is central to the imagery. First Peter 2 extends the imagery. Not only are believers "being built into a spiritual house" but they are also the holy priesthood approaching God with spiritual sacrifices (vv. 4–8).

Finally, we have noted already that Jesus' replacement of the Temple in Jerusalem with himself is an important theme in John's Gospel. Yet the Gospel carries this thought a step further, anticipating the "church as temple" idea in John 14:1–3. Mary Coloe argues convincingly that when Jesus speaks of the Father's "house" and the "place" he goes to prepare for his disciples, he alludes to his building of the people of God as an eschatological temple where God would dwell. She rightly points out that throughout John 14 *God* is the one who dwells or remains: "The action therefore is not the believers coming to dwell in God's heavenly abode, but the Father, the Paraclete, and Jesus coming to dwell with the believers. It is a 'descending' movement from the divine realm to the human, not an 'ascending' movement from the human to the divine" (2009, 376). [See Figure 7.]

Works Cited

Attridge, Harold W. 2010. "Temple, Tabernacle, Time, and Space in John and Hebrews." *Early Christianity* 1:261–74.

Betz, Hans Dieter. 1997. "Jesus and the Purity of the Temple (Mark 11:15–18): A Comparative Approach." *JBL* 116:455–72.

Bryan, Steven M. 2011. "Consumed by Zeal: John's Use of Psalm 69:9 and the Action in the Temple." *BBR* 21:479–94.

Chanikuzhy, Jacob. 2012. *Jesus, the Eschatological Temple: An Exegetical Study of Jn 2,13–22 in the Light of the Pre-70 C.E. Eschatological Temple Hopes and the Synoptic Temple Action*. Biblical Exegesis and Theology 58. Leuven: Peeters.

Collins, Adela Yarbro. 1999. "Jesus and the Jerusalem Temple." Paper presented at the International Rennert Guest Lecture Series, Jerusalem, May 5.

Coloe, Mary. 2009. "Temple Imagery in John." *Int* 63:368–81.

Eppstein, Victor. 1964. "The History of the Cleansing of the Temple." *ZNW* 55:42–58.

Evans, Craig. 1997. "Jesus in Context: Temple, Purity, and Restoration." Pages 395–439 in *Jesus in Context: Temple, Purity, and Restoration*. By Bruce Chilton and Craig A. Evans. Leiden: Brill.

Fretheim, Terence. 2010. *Exodus*. IBC. Louisville: Westminster John Knox.

Guthrie, George H. *2 Corinthians*. 2015. BECNT. Grand Rapids: Baker Academic.

Hays, J. Daniel. 2016. *The Temple and the Tabernacle: A Study of God's Dwelling Places from Genesis to Revelation*. Grand Rapids: Baker Books.

Juel, Donald. 1977. *Messiah and Temple: The Trial of Jesus in the Gospel of Mark*. Missoula, MT: Scholars Press.

Keener, Craig S. 1999. *A Commentary on the Gospel of Matthew*. Grand Rapids: Eerdmans.

Lieu, Judith. 1999. "Temple and Sypagogue in John." *NTS* 45:51–69.

Sanders, E. P. 1985. *Jesus and Judaism*. Philadelphia: Fortress.

Schachter, Lifsa Block. 2013. "The Garden of Eden as God's First Sanctuary." *JBQ* 41:73–77.

Walton, John H. 2001. *Genesis*. The NIV Application Commentary. Grand Rapids: Zondervan.

Wise, M. O. 1992. "Temple." Pages 811–17 in *Dictionary of Jesus and the Gospels*. Edited by Joel B. Green, Scot McKnight, and I. Howard Marshall. Downers Grove, IL: InterVarsity Press.

PART II: THE ROOTS

CHAPTER 6

The Jewish World of Jesus

6.1 The Jewish Land and Archaeology of Jesus

Sheila Gyllenberg

What do we know about the geographical settings of the ministry of Jesus, and the material culture of his day? How do these help us to place the Gospel accounts in context?

The Land of Israel in the Time of Jesus: Political Boundaries

In 333 BCE the Persians (who had conquered the Babylonians) were themselves conquered by the king of Macedonia, Alexander the Great. Alexander's conquest brought Greek ideas to the ancient Near Eastern cultures. This fusion is known as Hellenism. New cities were established, governed by officials elected by the local elite. These cities promoted the study of philosophy, rhetoric, and sciences such as physics, math, and astronomy. Town planning followed the rules of Hippodamus of Miletus (who himself was influenced by earlier Persian town planning). Streets were laid out on a systematic grid (orthogonally), and public buildings were concentrated in the center of the city.

After Alexander's death his kingdom was divided. Much of the southern Levant, including the territories that had once been the heartland of Judah and Israel, soon came under the control of the dynasty of the Ptolemies, who ruled from Egypt. In contrast, the northern Levant became part of the empire of the Seleucids. The Seleucid Empire, at its height, stretched from India and Afghanistan to Asia Minor. In 198 BCE the Seleucids wrested control of the land of Israel from the Ptolemies. Under the Seleucids the process of Hellenization intensified and was embraced enthusiastically by some of the elites in Jerusalem, including some of the high priestly families. Hellenistic values included religious syncretism and eschewing circumcision. The reaction against the Hellenizing leadership led to the Maccabean revolt. Within two decades a new Jewish religious-political leadership, the Hasmonean dynasty, had been established. Ironically, under the Hasmoneans hellenization of the material culture continued steadily, with Hellenistic architecture, town planning, and decorative elements predominant.

The Hasmonean kings brought more and more of the Southern Levant under their control. By the time of Aristobulus I (104–103 BCE), Galilee was again controlled by Jerusalem, and in the days of Alexander Janneus [Yannai] (103–76 BCE) much of the coastal plain and Transjordan was under Hasmonean control.

The Jewish communities of Lower Galilee and around the Sea of Galilee flourished at this time, including Capernaum, Magdala, Sepphoris, and Gamla. Hellenistic ideas of local, elected leadership led to the establishment of public buildings to meet community needs. These included *proseuchē* (prayer houses) and synagogues, which served both as places of Torah study and of community decisions. The synagogue at Magdala, on the shores of the Sea of Galilee, is one of our best preserved examples of a synagogue from the period. It is tentatively dated to the first half of the first century CE (Evans 2015, 18–23). It is a small two-room structure, decorated with frescoes without human or animal forms, with benches around the walls of both rooms. An elaborately carved stone slab may have served as a place to lay out a Torah scroll. [See Figure 8.]

The arrival of the Romans under Pompey and their eventual appointment of Herod as king over Judea, Samaria, Idumea, Galilee, and some parts of Transjordan accelerated the trend of Greco-Roman architecture and town planning in the land. In 20 BCE, Herod initiated an ambitious program to renovate the Temple (*Ant.* 15.380). He constructed a massive trapezoidal platform to expand the courtyard, which was surrounded by colonnaded porticos. A large basilica ("king's building") graced the southern end, with pillars so massive that it took three people to join arms around them (*Ant.* 15.413). Construction of the Temple courts continued long after his death. Josephus states that Herod built the cloisters and courtyards in eight years (*Ant.* 15.420). However, elsewhere he mentioned the completion of the Temple in the last year of the procurator Albinus (i.e., 64 CE; *Ant.* 20.219). Also, a coin found sealed under the southwestern corner of the retaining wall has confirmed that the platform was still under construction in the year 18 CE (Reich and Shukron 2011). Substantial remains of the platform Herod built are visible today in the Western Wall prayer area, around Robinson's Arch; in the Western Wall Tunnel excavations; and at other points along the southern and eastern retaining walls (see Ritmeyer 2006, 15–137 for a detailed discussion of all the Herodian remains on and around the Temple Mount). [See Figure 9.]

Ten thousand paid workers were hired for the project, boosting the economy and leading to expansion of the city. Excavations under the Jewish Quarter have exposed large homes with fine masonry, frescoes, mosaics, decorative columns, and even a *peristyle* courtyard (colonnaded, interior garden). Herod commissioned a new northern wall to be built, which Josephus called the "second wall." Herod built a magnificent port city at Caesarea Maritima (including a temple to the gods of Rome) and rebuilt Sebaste (ancient Samaria). In addition Herod established Antipatris (named after his father) at an important crossroad with springs ("Aphek" of 1 Sam 4:1; 29:1) on the route between Jerusalem and Caesarea (Paul spends the night there in Acts 23:31). He added palaces for himself and his many wives in Jerusalem, Caesarea, Herodion, Jericho, and Masada. He also refurbished and beautified many of the former Hasmonean palaces (Netzer 2006). His three-tiered palace cascading down the north cliff at Masada, the great artificial mountain at Herodion (on which he built his mausoleum), his many pools, bath-houses, and banquet halls, were all decorated with mosaic floors, frescoes, and decorative columns. His architecture is almost always devoid of human and animal forms that would have offended the observant elite who would be his guests, who followed a strict interpretation of the second commandment.

After his death his kingdom was divided among three of his sons. Archeleus ruled over Judea, Samaria and Idumea. Antipas, ruler of Galilee and Perea, continued his father's tradition of city building by establishing his capital, Tiberias, on the western shores of the Sea of Galilee. Philip, the ruler of areas northeast of the Sea of Galilee (Paneas, Gaulanitis, Batanea, Trachonities, Auranitis—today's Golan Heights and parts of Syria), built Caesarea Philippi. All of the Herodian rulers and some of their family members, as well as three of the Roman emperors who were their patrons and three of the Roman prefects/proconsuls for Judea, are known to us from extra-biblical sources (Mykytiuk 2017).

Locations Named in the Gospel Narratives

Our knowledge of the political divisions and important towns of the first century CE is based largely on the first-century Jewish historian Josephus. The New Testament, in contrast, shows very little interest in the "where" of its narrative. Various locations in Jerusalem are mentioned (the Temple, the pool of Siloam, the pools of Bethesda, the Mount of Olives, and Golgotha). Some of these are known from the Mishnah and other early rabbinic sources (for example, the pool of Siloam; John 10:23; Acts 3:11; Shiloah in *t. Arakhin* 2.6), or from the Qumran Copper Scroll (the pools of Bethesda; John 5:2). Others are only mentioned in the New Testament: Golgotha (the place of the skull; Matt 27:33; Mark 15:22; John 19:17), Gethsemane (the place of the oil press; Matt 26:36; Mark 14:32), the Beautiful Gate (Acts 3:2), and Solomon's Portico (John 10:23; Acts 3:11). Outside of Jerusalem, just over twenty places are mentioned by name in the Gospels. [See Figures 10–11.]

Luke often shows more interest in details of geography than the other Gospel writers. For example, he is the only Gospel writer to place the feeding of the five thousand in a specific location (near Bethsaida; Luke 9:10). In addition, only Luke consistently uses the Greek term for a freshwater lake (the Lake of Gennesaret; Luke 5:1) to describe the Sea of Galilee, an appellation also used by Josephus. Matthew and Mark, in contrast, use the term for a salt-water sea (the Sea of Galilee; Matt 4:18; 15:29; Mark 1:16; 3:7; 7:31), which is never used in Josephus, early rabbinic sources, or classical writers (when they mention this body of water). Notley has suggested that the use of this term (*thalassa*) for "sea" in Matthew and Mark is chosen purposely to link this body of water with Isa 9:1, where both the Septuagint and Matthew's quotation of it (Matt 4:15) include it in the description of a great light shining upon people sitting in darkness (Rainey and Notley 2006, 353). The Gospel of John uses the term "the Sea of Galilee of Tiberias" (John 6:1).

The location of many important events, such as the Sermon on the Mount (Matt 5), the transfiguration (Matt 16; Mark 9), Jesus' baptism, and his wilderness temptation (Matt 4:1–11; Mark 1:12–13; Luke 4:1–13) are recorded with only vague references to locations. Thus it was up to pilgrims to identify these sites. However, pilgrims only began to arrive in significant numbers some three hundred years after the events, once Christianity became a tolerated, and then the official, religion of the Roman Empire. Eusebius, the fourth-century CE Bishop of Caesarea, had already begun the process of identifying both Old and New Testament sites. His research has been preserved in his work *The Onomasticon*. But the arrival of full-fledged pilgrimage accelerated the need to mark holy sites. For example, Joseph of Tiberias, a fourth-century Jewish believer in Jesus, is sometimes credited with building churches that mark various events from the Gospel—such as the feeding of the five thousand at Tabgha (Pixner 1985, 198) or the purported House of Peter at Capernaum (Murphy-O'Connor 1998, 220). However, Joseph's mandate from Constantine was to build churches in Jewish communities where there had previously been no church: Tiberias, Sepphoris, Capernaum, and Nazareth. At three of these we have evidence for believers of Jewish descent living among and interacting with the Jewish community. Thus, one could argue that Joseph set out to establish places of local worship, rather than to mark "holy sites" for pilgrims (see Goranson 1990, 73–125).

Of the specific places named in the Gospels, most have been identified based on the modern Arabic names for villages and ruins. Tall Hum was identified as Kfar Nahum (Capernaum in English, from the Latin transliteration). Aenon and Salim, two minor locations that are mentioned in connection to John the Baptist, have similarly been identified. In Bethlehem, Nazareth, Tiberias, Jericho, and Nain the modern towns have preserved the first century CE names. Bethany of Mary and Martha is today called al-Azariah, recalling their brother Lazarus (*al-Azar* in Arabic), who was raised from the dead there.

For at least the last four hundred years, Cana has been identified with the modern town of Kfar Kenna. Several churches commemorate the first miracle of Jesus, and another church commemorates Nathaniel (also identified with the disciple Bartholomew) who was from Cana (John 21:2). The town had Jewish residents in the Byzantine period, confirmed by an Aramaic dedicatory inscription from a synagogue or another public building. By the fifth century the town may have already been a destination of pilgrimage (Hoade 1984, 720–22). However, according to Josephus, Cana of the first century CE was in the plain of Asochis, today called the Beit Netofa Valley. Khirbet Qanah is a mound of ruins several miles away from Kfar Kenna on the north side of the Beit Netofa Valley. Most scholars think it is a more likely choice for the Cana of the Gospels than the modern town that is slightly south of the valley (Rainey and Notley 2006, 352). Excavations started in Khirbet Qanah in 1998 unearthered a large public building, identified as a first-century or early second-century CE synagogue (McCollough 2013).

Another uncertain identification is the town of Bethsaida, home of Andrew, Peter, and Philip (and perhaps James and John). According to Josephus, Bethsaida was located in the territory of Philip the Tetrarch, near the Sea of Galilee, and was elevated to be a *polis* (a city with all the necessary public buildings dictated by Greek architectural principles). Excavations at et-Tell unearthed Hellenistic remains, including several elite courtyard houses, one of which was dubbed the "House of the Fishermen" because of supposed remains of stone anchors, net weights, and fishhooks. But the height of this tell and its distance from the shore of the lake have caused many to question its identification as Bethsaida (see Notley's discussion in Rainey and Notley 2006, 356–59). Recent excavations at nearby el-Araj have unearthed early Roman period pottery and architectural elements under a Byzantine layer (Aviam 2016). The distance between the two sites (about 1.5 miles) does not preclude both being part of the same site—an older settlement on the tell and a newer settlement nearer to the shore, dating to Philip's transformation of the city into a *polis*.

At Chorazin (Khirbet Karraza) excavations have focused on the town center from the Byzantine period, including an impressive synagogue made of basalt. Whatever remained from the time of Jesus may be in the northeast quadrant of the ruins, which has not been excavated. There has been speculation that a small, square building with columns and benches, mentioned in an unpublished report by J. Ory from the 1926 excavations, may be a synagogue from this earlier village (Foerster 1981, 26). [See Figure 12.]

Excavations at Nazareth have brought to light only scanty evidence for settlement in the first century CE: a rock-cut/stone-built courtyard house under the Byzantine "Church of the Nutrition" (by tradition, the house in which Jesus was raised; Dark 2012); and a few walls from houses under the nearby Marian Center. The finds included many fragments of dishes carved from chalk, common to Jewish communities throughout the country (Adler 2016, 240–45). In addition, many fragments of Kfar Hananya ware have been found (typical pottery in Jewish villages in Galilee). *Kokh* tombs (*loculi* burials) were carved into the bedrock under the "Church of the Nutrition" house a short time after it was no longer in use (Dark 2015, 57). This type of tomb is commonly found in Jewish communities of the first century CE, especially in the southern part of the country. Although no substantial public buildings have survived centuries of city expansion, the Gospel of Luke tells us that there was a synagogue in Nazareth in the first century CE, which has not been found. This could be due to the scattered nature of excavations within a living city, or to the synagogue's small size or poor construction.

Material Remains and Jesus Research

No remains conclusively connected to Jesus have been found in the sites mentioned in the New Testament. Even the earliest places of veneration cannot be proven to be the actual sites of events, despite their being hallowed by 1700 or even 1800 years of worship. This is true of the house-cave marking the meeting of Mary and the angel Gabriel (in the Church of the Annunciation in Nazareth), the birth cave of Jesus (in the Church of the Nativity in Bethlehem), the cave where Jesus taught his disciples about his second coming (in Queen Helena's Eleona Church, now part of the Pater Noster Convent), and the crucifixion/burial/resurrection sites (in the Church of the Holy Sepulcher in Jerusalem; see Hanauer 1892 for an early discussion; Walker 1999). The rooms of the first-century house at the center of St. Peter's Church in Capernaum may have been used by Jesus as his home during his ministry years, but there is only circumstantial archaeological evidence (Murphy-O'Connor 1998, 218). [See Figures 13–14.]

Likewise, the so-called "Jesus Boat" (a small, wooden fishing boat dating to the first century CE that was found in the lake-bed off the Plain of Gennesaret) could have belonged to anyone. The Talpiot burials, excavated in the 1980s and later popularized as the secret "tomb of Jesus' family" (Jacobovici and Pellegrino 2007), could be the tomb of any Jewish family of the period. The names found engraved on ossuaries there (Yehosef, Yudah, Miriam, Yeshua) are among the most common Jewish names known to us from historical and archaeological sources of the period. Other purported evidence that this was Jesus' tomb (such as the x-mark on the "Yeshua, son of Yehosef" ossuary and supposed Jewish-Christian symbols over the tomb's entrance) have been shown to be unfounded (Evans 2015, 181–89).

However, study of the Herodian-period material remains can tell us much about the audience to whom Jesus was bringing the Gospel of the kingdom (see McRay 1991; Rousseau and Arav 1995; Charlesworth 2006; and Evans 2012; 2015). First, archaeological finds suggest subtle differences within the Jewish community regarding purity issues. There were those concerned with maintaining a high level of ritual purity, evidenced by stoneware serving and storage vessels (preferable to ceramic ware, which had to be broken when ritually defiled; Exod 11:33). Another indication of concern for purity is the use of Kfar Hananya ware (pottery made by Jewish potters, with no hint of contamination by idolatry). Surveys of the area between Nazareth and Sepphoris, for example, have found a statistical difference between percentages of stoneware and Kfar Hananya ware on the Nazareth side of the valley and on the side nearer to the more-hellenized, and larger, city of Sepphoris (Dark 2015, 60). In addition, we can note the presence of ritual baths for dealing with ritual impurity in day-to-day life and not only in association with temple worship (Adler 2016, 240–45). [See Figures 15–16.]

Second, excavations have brought to light a surprisingly high standard of living, even in small towns such as Magdala. Likewise, in Nazareth, multiple large storage silos associated with even simple homes suggest a degree of prosperity. Even Capernaum, with its thin-walled "insula-style" (surrounded on four sides by parallel sets of streets) housing complexes, seems to have had a thriving industry producing grinding stones made from the local basalt, in addition to the local fishing industry. Assuming the basalt substructure under the western wall of the later limestone synagogue is indeed part of a first-century CE synagogue, this would also be an indication of wealth.

Whereas scholars of past generations speculated that a severely depressed economy proved fertile ground for the rise of a mass movement of unfortunates following Jesus, oppressed by the taxation necessary for the opulent lifestyle and building projects of the Herodians, the archaeological evidence arising from the Galilean villages suggests a different picture. Even in the minor towns and villages, a degree of prosperity is evident in the Jewish communities of Galilee (Chancey 2011, 20).

Third, concurrent with the large portion of the Jewish population that embraced high standards of ritual purity, Hellenistic ideas of town planning, architecture, and self-government (by synagogue) were part of the fabric of everyday life, both in Jerusalem and in outlying small towns. The Gospel accounts should be read with this complex fabric of daily life in mind.

Works Cited

Adler, Yonatan. 2016. "Between Priestly Cult and Common Culture: The Material Evidence of Ritual Purity Observance in Early Roman Jerusalem Reassessed." *Journal of Ancient Judaism* 7:228–48.

Aviam, Mordechai. 2016. "First Season of Excavations at Tel el-Araj." *Assemblies of God*, Sept. 12. https://news.ag.org/news/first-season-of-excavations-at-el-araj.

Chancey, Mark. 2011. "Disputed Issues in the Study of Cities, Villages and the Economy in Jesus' Galilee." Pages 53–67 in *The World of Jesus and the Early Church*. Edited by Craig A. Evans. Peabody, MA: Hendrickson.

Charlesworth, James H. 2006. *Jesus and Archaeology*. Grand Rapids: Eerdmans.

Dark, Kenneth. 2012. "Early Roman-Period Nazareth and the Sisters of Nazareth Convent." *The Antiquaries Journal* 92:37–64.

―――. 2015. "Has Jesus' Nazareth House Been Found?" *BAR* 41.2:54–63, 72.

Evans, Craig A. 2012. *Jesus and His World: The Archaeological Evidence*. Louisville: Westminster John Knox.

―――. 2015. *Jesus and the Remains of His Day*. Peabody, MA: Hendrickson.

Foerster, Gideon. 1981. "Synagogues at Masada and Herodium." Pages 25–29 in *Ancient Synagogues Revealed*. Edited by L. I. Levine. Jerusalem: Israel Exploration Society.

Goranson, Stephen Kraft. 1990. "The Joseph of Tiberias Episode in Epiphanius: Studies in Jewish and Christian Relations." PhD diss., Duke University.

Hanauer, James E. 1892. "Notes on the Controversy Regarding the Site of Calvary." *Palestine Exploration Fund Quarterly Statement* 24.4:295–308.

Hoade, Eugene. 1984. *Guide to the Holy Land*. Jerusalem: Franciscan Printing Press.

Jacobovici, Simcha, and Charles Pellegrino. 2007. *The Jesus Family Tomb: The Discovery, the Investigation, and the Evidence That Could Change History*. San Francisco: HarperCollins.

McCollough, C. Thomas. 2013. "Final Report on the Archaeological Excavations at Khirbet Qana: Field II, the Synagogue." *ASOR Blog*. Nov 11. http://asorblog.org/2013/11/19/final-report-on-the-archaeological-excavations-at-khirbet-qana-field-ii-the-synagogue/.

McRay, John. 1991. *Archaeology and the New Testament*. Grand Rapids: Baker Book House.

Murphy-O'Connor, Jerome. 1998. *The Holy Land*. Oxford Archaeological Guides. 4th ed. Oxford: Oxford University Press.

Mykytiuk, Lawrence. 2017. "New Testament Political Figures Confirmed." *BAR* 43.5:50–59, 65.

Netzer, Ehud. 2006. *The Architecture of Herod, the Great Builder*. TSAJ 117. Tübinegen: Mohr Siebeck.

Pixner, Bargil. 1985. "The Miracle Church of Tabgha on the Sea of Galilee." *BA* 48:196–206.

Rainey, Anson, and R. Steven Notley. 2006. *The Sacred Bridge*. Jerusalem: Carta.

Reich, Ronny, and Eli Shukron. 2011. "Building the Western Wall: Herod Began It but Didn't Finish it." *Israel Antiquities Authority Bulletin*. December, http://www.antiquities.org.il/article_eng.aspx?sec_id=25&subj_id=240&id=1882&module_id=#as.

Ritmeyer, Leen. 2006. *The Quest: Revealing the Temple Mount in Jerusalem*. Jerusalem: Carta.

Rousseau, John J., and Rami Arav. 1995. *Jesus and His World: An Archaeological and Cultural Dictionary*. Minneapolis: Fortress Press.

Walker, Peter. 1999. *The Weekend That Changed the World*. London: Marshall Pickering.

6.2 Jewish Groups in the First Century

Jim R. Sibley

There was a rich variety of belief and practice among the people of Israel in the first century. Most historians speak of the "judaisms" of this period in order to reflect this diversity. The different variations are often referred to as "sects," although some have argued that it is better to speak of different "schools of thought." Since they can be seen as political parties, social movements, and schools of thought, I will use the more general term "groups." While each group had roots in earlier periods, how they appear in the first century sheds light on the Gospels (Bowker 1973; Neusner 1971; Saldarini 2001).

Historical Background

The Jewish groups of the first century originated in the intertestamental period (on the difficulties associated with this terminology, cf. Scott 2000, 20), or the Second Temple period. Much attention has been given to the origin of the names of these groups and the precise times and circumstances in which they originated. While interesting, these discussions are of only marginal significance for understanding the contribution each group made to the religious life of first-century Israel.

Several points need to be made about this period of roughly four hundred years before the birth of Jesus. First of all, intertestamental Judaism is a descendant of the faith of the Hebrew Scriptures, but is not identical to it. Second, the society, culture, and faith of intertestamental Judaism were not a monolithic whole; much like first-century Judaism, intertestamental Judaism constituted a diversity of thought and practice. Third, the traditional ways of distinguishing between Jewish and Hellenistic elements in intertestamental Jewish life are too simplistic. Likewise, the four-sect division of Judaism (Pharisees, Sadducees, Essenes, and the fourth philosophy) of the first-century historian Josephus is an inadequate description of the diversities of the time (Scott 2000, 21–22). Along this line, Samaritans are often excluded in descriptions of this period (Charlesworth 2014). Finally, a distinction must be made, during this period as in the Hebrew Scriptures, between obdurate Israel and the remnant of Israel. Although the majority followed various leaders and groups with differing theologies and emphases, there was always a faithful remnant—with a "minority report."

This is all to say that generalizations are just that. Nevertheless, while generalizations about these groups must be held lightly, they are useful for a brief introductory article. What these various groups had in common was a passion for their own vision of what it meant to be God's covenant people. For some, the emphasis was placed on *ethical* purity as defined by the law of Torah and tradition. For others, the emphasis was placed on *ritual* purity usually associated with the Temple and sacrifice. The former view characterized the Pharisees and scribes, while the latter view characterized the Sadducees, priests, Essenes, Zealots, and even the Samaritans. Jesus and his followers stood in opposition to both of these approaches.

When the exiles returned from Babylon, it was with the keen awareness that their violation of the Mosaic law had resulted in the exile (cf. Ezra 9:5–15). Therefore, one priority was uppermost in their minds: Avoid God's future judgment. Consequently, following the exile they gave renewed study to the law. During the Persian period, Ezra began a process of interpretation and application of the law (cf. Ezra 7:6, 10; Neh 8:1–8). Those who returned then began to explore the practical implications of each command and formulated additional practices that were designed to keep individuals from breaking it. The initial motivation may have been honorable, but the focus shifted to the externals and to human effort, rather than a life of faith (Deut 6:4–7; 2 Chr 7:14; Mic 6:8; Matt 12:33–36; 15:7–20; 23; Rom 10:1–3). In time, for some, these traditions became as authoritative as Scripture. One of the most significant developments in Jewish intellectual life during this period was the growing conviction that the Scriptures were not sufficient or complete as a revelation from God for the faith and practice of Israel.

Likewise, the Temple, along with the sacrificial system and priesthood, needed to be restored. Renewed attention was given to the Temple and to the *cultus*. There was eventually a reaction on the part of some, perhaps associated with the Temple, against the development of extrabiblical traditions. Other theological differences also developed—regarding the source of authority for faith and practice, the relationship between God's sovereignty and human responsibility, and life after death, among other things.

Pharisees

The Pharisees began to emerge as a separate sect between 150 BCE and 130 BCE, and their focus was on the prescription of conduct for everyday life (Mason 1991, 2003). They believed their identity as the people of Israel was defined by their fidelity to a body of traditional material inherited "from the fathers." Eventually they sought to ascribe divine authority to human traditions, a belief that became more pronounced with the arrival of rabbinic authority (see below, article 12.1). This focus is most likely related to their name; the Aramaic word underlying "pharisee" means "separate." What they had in mind was separation from compromise and sin. This led to the practice of "building a fence around the Law" (*m. Avot* 1:1), which involved adding additional regulations designed to prevent people from violating the law. Jesus was severely critical of these traditions, especially when they promoted self-righteousness or contradicted the law itself (see Matt 15:1–6; Mark 7:1–17).

The Pharisees' basic doctrines included a belief in resurrection. They believed that their eternal destiny would be determined by faithfulness to Torah, by which they meant both the written law and their own traditions. The wicked would suffer eternal punishment. Although they certainly believed in human responsibility, they also held a high view of God's sovereignty (Josephus, *Ant.* 18.14; *J.W.* 2.162–163). This may be seen in Gamaliel's response to the preaching of Peter and the apostles in Acts 5:34–40. He was willing to leave the matter to God, who was directing affairs and preserving Israel. Saul of Tarsus, who was a committed Pharisee before his encounter with the risen Christ, believed in the resurrection (Acts 23:6; 24:15, 21; Phil 3:10–11) and was zealous for the "ancestral traditions" (Gal 1:14 NASB).

The Pharisees may be referenced allusively in the Dead Sea Scrolls. In the *Damascus Document* (CD), critical reference is made to those who "search for smooth things" (CD 1:18). The "smooth things" (*khalaqot*) may be a mocking reference to the Pharisees known for searching for legal traditions (*halakhot*, lit., "[ways of] walking"), as in John 5:39, where Jesus says to the Pharisees: "You [Pharisees] search the Scriptures" (NASB; cf. John 7:52). The crucifixion of eight hundred Pharisees by order of Alexander Jannaeus (Josephus, *Ant.* 13.830) appears to be referenced at Qumran in the commentary on Nahum (4Q169 frags. 3–4, col. i, lines 1–8), where again we hear of those who "search for smooth things." In rabbinic literature the Pharisees are sometimes disparaged (*m. Yadayim* 4:6) or even mocked (*m. Sotah* 3:4), usually in reference to their hypocrisy and eagerness to appear pious (*b. Sotah* 22b).

In the Gospels, the Pharisees are often paired with other groups: with Sadducees (Matt 3:7; 16:1, 6, 11–12); with scribes (Matt 5:20; 12:38; 23:2, 13–15; Mark 2:16; Luke 15:2; John 8:3); and with chief priests (Matt 21:45; 27:62). Many of these references may be explained by the Pharisees' significant representation in the Sanhedrin, the authoritative governing body. As a rule, however, because they invested their traditions with divine authority, they saw themselves as distinct from other groups. Jesus was in direct opposition to the Pharisees because he challenged this authority. He spoke of this conflict in his parable of the children in the marketplace (Matt 11:16–19) and in an extended passage in Matt 21:23–46.

Jesus often used the Pharisees as a foil to demonstrate the importance of giving attention to the heart attitudes that are expressed in actions, rather than focusing on merely external displays of piety. He criticized them for presenting displays of holiness while being consumed with pride and a desire for others' applause. By not heeding him, they were violating the very Torah they professed to keep, for Moses had written of his coming (John 5:45–47) and issued a stern warning against their refusal to acknowledge him (Deut 18:19). Jesus' most serious charge was: "You shut off the kingdom of heaven from people; for you do not enter in yourselves, nor do you allow those who are entering to go in" (Matt 23:13).

In an apocryphal story preserved in Greek in a fragment of papyrus (P.Oxy. 840), a priest in the temple precincts, identified as a Pharisee, rebukes Jesus and his disciples for entering the sacred area without having first purified themselves. The story probably does not reach back to the life of Jesus, but it does reflect the reality of both the temple precincts and Pharisaic perspectives. [See Figure 17.]

The traditions of the Pharisees continued to develop over time and were eventually written down and codified in the Mishnah (ca. 200 CE). Of the various Jewish perspectives of the first century, the Pharisees' has had the greatest continuity and impact.

Scribes

The scribes initially served secular purposes (2 Kgs 12:10; 18:18), and the kings of Israel employed them in these capacities, but increasingly scribes began to serve as experts in the study of the law of Moses (2 Kgs 22:8–10). This role was especially apparent following the return from the Babylonian exile. However, their authority could be misused. Jeremiah described the possibility of scribes leading the people astray (Jer 8:8).

In the intertestamental period, the scribes became aligned with the Pharisees. Much that has been said above about the Pharisees would apply equally to the scribes. Some were members of the Sanhedrin (Matt 16:21; 26:3). Like the Pharisees, they taught that their traditions were divinely inspired and authoritative. As the experts in traditions regarding the law, their opinions and judgments were not to be opposed. This was their main point of disagreement with Jesus. In his seven-fold woe against the Pharisees in Matt 23, Jesus included the scribes in his condemnations. The charges he brought against the Pharisees also applied to the scribes.

Sadducees

The Sadducees claimed the heritage of Zadok the priest (2 Sam 8:17; 15:24; 1 Kgs 4:4; Ezek 40:46), a proud legacy as the most faithful of the Levites. In the time of Jesus, the Sadducees were a very wealthy group associated with the Temple and the priesthood. However, in Acts 4:1 there is a clear distinction between the priests and the Sadducees. Apparently, many (perhaps most) priests were Sadducees, but many Sadducees were not priests.

In their teaching, the Sadducees not only rejected the traditions of the Pharisees but also held the five books of the Torah alone as possessing God's authority. They denied life after death (and thus also the resurrection). They denied the existence of angels and demons, and they insisted on complete freedom of the will. On one occasion, Paul exploited their disagreement with the Pharisees regarding the resurrection (Acts 23:1–10). The Sadducees were also believed by many to have been politically compromised, if not in open collusion with the Romans.

The rabbis have little regard for the Sadducees (*m. Parah* 3:3, 7), especially high priest Annas (*b. Pesahim* 57a), whom Josephus identified as a Sadducee (*Ant.* 20.199–203; Sadducees and ruling priests seem closely linked in Acts 4:1; 5:17). The rabbis even say that Sadducean women should be regarded as Samaritan women because they do not follow the oral laws regarding purity required during menstruation (*m. Niddah* 4:2).

Priests

The priesthood was instituted by God in the days of Moses, and the Torah spelled out the responsibilities and privileges of the priests. Jesus had respect for the priesthood and its lawful function. It seems his primary challenge came from the high priest, Annas, and the successors from his family. As leaders of the Sanhedrin, they led the opposition to Jesus and to his followers. Additionally, Pharisaic tradition (perhaps lacking in complete objectivity) represents the priests of the first century as morally corrupt. The Talmud describes them in a poem, listing the priestly families that abused their authority in the Temple (*b. Pesahim* 57a).

In the New Testament, priests were the teachers of the Torah (Matt 2:4; Luke 2:46), but in this they were unfaithful shepherds (Konradt 2014, 31–39). Jesus included them in his prophecy regarding his anticipated sufferings and death, which would be at the hands of the elders, chief priests, and scribes (Matt 16:21; 20:18; see also 21:15, 23, 45; etc.). Later, they would also oppose his disciples (Acts 4:1, 23; 5:24; etc.). Jesus eventually transferred their authority to the apostles (Matt 21:43, 45) and, following the resurrection, assumed for himself the role of chief priest of the new covenant (Heb 7:11–28).

Zealots

Josephus seems to ignore the Zealots' existence until the time of John of Gischala and Simon ben Giora, just prior to and during the First Jewish War (66–73 CE). But members of resistance movements probably existed as a recognizable political group earlier than Josephus indicates.

In Mark 15:7, in connection with the crucifixion account, Barabbas is introduced as one who "had been imprisoned with the insurrectionists who had committed murder in the insurrection." It also has been suggested (Stein 1993, 588; Blomberg 1992, 417) that the two "thieves" between whom Jesus was crucified should more properly be viewed as members of just such a resistance movement. In fact, one of Jesus' disciples was known as Simon the Zealot (Luke 6:15; Acts 1:13), perhaps reflecting his earlier political activism.

This group, which seems to have been most concerned with the Temple, not only rejected the Romans' right to rule over God's people, but resorted to violence to resist the occupation in general, and specifically Roman interference in temple ritual. Although Jerusalem fell in 70 CE, the last bastion of the Zealots, Masada, held out until 73 CE. After that, the Roman victory was complete, and the Zealots were crushed.

Essenes

The Essenes are not mentioned directly in the New Testament, but they surely existed at this time, and there may be allusions to the Essenes in the Gospels. Today, they are mostly associated with the discovery of the Dead Sea Scrolls at Qumran. While the identification of the Qumran community with the Essenes has been dominant, others identify the community as Sadducean. This simply illustrates the close affinities between the two. Both groups emphasized ritual purity.

However, the Essenes believed the priesthood in Jerusalem had become corrupt and the Jewish calendar was not correctly ordered. This meant that the holidays, such as Passover, would not be observed properly. So they withdrew from worship at the Temple. The Essenes rejected the Pharisaic traditions, but they did accept the inspiration of all the Hebrew Scriptures. They held to the sovereignty of God, life after death, and bodily resurrection. They were also strongly messianic, although the messiah the Essenes anticipated would respect the Zadokite high priest, who would restore worship in Jerusalem in keeping with Essenic understanding.

Many of the Essenes retreated to the Judean wilderness near the Dead Sea, where they devoted themselves to a monastic life, studied the Hebrew Scriptures, shared everything in common, and followed a strict code of conduct. There were probably groups of Essenes in other locations as well, as Josephus says. The most well-known was a neighborhood in the southwestern section of Jerusalem, near a city gate known as the Essene Gate (Pixner 1997).

Samaritans

The Samaritans were an ethnic mix of Jews from the northern tribes of Israel and the conquering Assyrians. They were disdained by the Jews in Judea, and they maintained their defiance against worship in Jerusalem. They believed they were the true heirs of the patriarchs, and their primary site of worship was Mount Gerizim. They had their own dialect of Hebrew and their own version of the Torah. It contained a commandment mandating that God be worshiped at Mount Gerizim (see John 4:20). Needless to say, the differences between the Judeans and the Samaritans ran deep. They were divided socially, politically, and theologically. In spite of these differences, the Scriptures present them as Jews—apostate Jews, but Jews all the same (Jervell 1972; Pummer 2015; and Tsedaka 2017).

Jewish Believers in Jesus

Jewish disciples of Jesus may be seen from the beginning of his public ministry until the conclusion of the book of Acts. They are referred to with different terms. In Acts 9:2, they were followers of "the Way" (cf. Acts 19:9, 23; 24:14, 22), which alluded to Isa 40:3 ("Clear the way for the LORD"). In Acts 11:26 they were called "Christians," and in Acts 24:5 they were called "the sect of the Nazarenes." This last term was used to describe Jewish believers in Jesus into the fourth century (Pritz 1988).

The Jewish believers in Jesus drew members from each of the Jewish groups of this period. Many were drawn from the Pharisees, such as Nicodemus (John 3:1–20; 7:50–51; 19:39), Saul/Paul (Acts 26:5), and others (Acts 15:5). There were also scribes who followed Jesus (Matt 8:19). Acts 6:7 says that "a great many of the priests were becoming obedient to the faith," and as mentioned previously, one of Jesus' apostles was known as Simon the Zealot.

In Mark 14:13, Jesus sent his disciples to prepare the Passover, and they were told that a man would meet them carrying a pitcher of water. This was unusual, for it was not customary for men to carry water. This may indicate that he was an Essene, for they often did not marry. Likewise, the traditional site of the upper room is in a portion of the city that likely functioned as an Essene neighborhood (Magee). More directly, Acts 8:4–8, 25 documents a great response to the preaching of the gospel among large numbers of Samaritans.

Works Cited

Bowker, John. 1973. *Jesus and the Pharisees.* Cambridge: Cambridge University Press.

Blomberg, Craig L. 1992. *Matthew.* NAC. Nashville: Broadman & Holman.

Charlesworth, James H. 2014. Review of *Outside the Bible: Jewish Writings Related to Scripture*, edited by Louis H. Feldman, James L. Kugel, and Lawrence H.

Schiffman. *Bible History Daily*, December 05. http://www.biblicalarchaeology .org/reviews/outside-the-bible/.

Jervell, Jacob. 1972. "The Lost Sheep of the House of Israel: The Understanding of the Samaritans in Luke-Acts." Pages 113–32 in *Luke and the People of God: A New Look at Luke-Acts*. Minneapolis: Augsburg.

Konradt, Matthias. 2014. *Israel, Church, and the Gentiles in the Gospel of Matthew*. Translated by Kathleen Ess. Waco, TX: Baylor University Press.

Magee, M. D. "The Essene Quarter of Jerusalem in the Time of Herod." *Ask Why!* http://www.askwhy.co.uk/christianity/0160EsseneQ1.php.

Mason, Steve. 1991. *Flavius Josephus on the Pharisees: A Composition-Critical Study*. StPB 39. Leiden: Brill.

———. 2003. *Josephus and the New Testament*. 2nd ed. Peabody, MA: Hendrickson.

Neusner, Jacob. 1971. *Rabbinic Traditions about the Pharisees before 70 AD*. 3 vols. Leiden: Brill.

Pixner, Bargil. 1997. "Jerusalem's Essene Gateway: Where the Community Lived in Jesus' Time." *BAR* 23.3:22–31, 64–66.

Pritz, Ray. 1988. *Nazarene Jewish Christianity from the End of the New Testament Period until Its Disappearance in the Fourth Century*. Jerusalem: Magnes Press; Leiden: Brill.

Pummer, Reinhard. 2015. *The Samaritans: A Profile*. Grand Rapids: Eerdmans.

Saldarini, Anthony J. 2001. *Pharisees, Scribes and Sadducees in Palestinian Society: A Sociological Approach*. Grand Rapids: Eerdmans.

Scott, J. Julius, Jr. 2000. *Jewish Backgrounds of the New Testament*. Grand Rapids: Baker Academic.

Stein, Robert H. 1993. *Luke*. NAC. Nashville: Broadman & Holman.

Tsedaka, Benyamin. 2017. *Understanding the Israelite-Samaritans: From Ancient to Modern, An Introductory Atlas*. Jerusalem: Carta.

6.3 Jewish Literature of the Second Temple Period

Sheila Gyllenberg

The three hundred years that led up to the New Testament period were a time of significant literary output in the Jewish community, both in the land of Israel and in the diaspora. The works that have come down to us span a great variety of genres, languages, and worldviews: these include biblical narratives retold and expanded, histories, short stories, wisdom literature, apocalyptic visions, Scripture exposition, and liturgical poems. The Jewish community wrote in Hebrew, Aramaic, and Greek, with Aramaic more common in the east (Parthia/

Babylon) and Greek more predominant in the west. Hebrew remained a spoken language in Judea, although the educated elite were certainly fluent in Greek, and Aramaic was spoken as well.

All the late Second Temple period literary works that have survived point to a community steeped in the earlier Israelite and Jewish writings (today collected in the Tanakh/Old Testament), even though many of their interpretations and embellishments reflect the Hellenistic culture and political struggles of their day.

Early Translations of the Scriptures

According to the *Letter of Pseudo-Aristeas*, the first translation of the Torah into Greek was made during the reign of the early Ptolemaic rulers, the dynasty that came to power in Egypt and the southern Levant following Alexander the Great's conquest of the Near East. The story recounts that a translation was undertaken by scholars brought from Jerusalem at the behest of a gentile ruler who wanted a Greek version of the Torah for his library in Alexandria. *Pseudo-Aristeas* confused the people and events from the reigns of Ptolemy I and Ptolemy II, and therefore cannot be used to date the translation. However, a third century BCE date for a Greek translation of the Torah is generally accepted. It is less clear where and when Greek translations of the Prophets (*nevi'im*) and the Writings (*ktuvim*) were made. Nor do we know how many different Greek translations of various books might have been undertaken over time in various locations during the late Second Temple period. These later Greek texts are often, somewhat erroneously, referred to as the Septuagint (LXX), because of the tradition in *Pseudo-Aristeas* that 72 elders made the first Greek translation of the Torah. Scholars have discussed at length the relationship between pre-Christian Greek translations and Greek versions (both Jewish and Christian) from the early centuries of the Christian era (see a concise summary in Peters 1992, 1096–1100). Old Testament quotations found in the Greek New Testament do not always agree with the existing texts, and there is extensive literature on whether the differences should be ascribed to variations among the early Greek translations or to other reasons (Smith 1972, 20–63; 1988, 265–91).

Translations of the Hebrew Scriptures into Aramaic, together with in-text explanations, are called *targumim*. The earliest written targumim are thought to be dated to the late third or early second century BCE (Cook 1994, 142–56; for a concise summary of alternative views see Buth 2000, 88–90) . Aramaic was the lingua franca of the Near East from the sixth century BCE until the arrival of Alexander the Great. Some have suggested that there might have been oral translations into Aramaic during public gatherings in the Babylonian and Persian periods, perhaps as early as the time of Ezra in the fifth century BCE (cf. Neh 8:8; see discussion in Chilton 2000, 903).

Hebrew, however, remained the primary language for the study of Scriptures in Judea. The Mishnah (the codification of the laws and discussions bearing on Jewish life and liturgy) was written in Hebrew at the beginning of the third century CE, long after the Temple had been destroyed and Jewish scholars had scattered from Judea. Together with the evidence from the Hebrew writings of the Dead Sea Sect (see below) and several of the Bar Kokhba letters, there is a growing consensus that Hebrew remained a spoken language throughout the first century CE.

Pseudepigrapha

During the late Second Temple period, events known from the Torah were often retold and embellished, frequently using the characters themselves as narrators. These works are called "pseudepigrapha," meaning "falsely attributed writings." Examples include *Genesis Apocryphon* and the *Testaments of the Twelve Patriarchs*. In other cases, the narrator is anonymous, but presents his work as a contemporary account of things that were actually long past. It is unknown which circles of the Jewish community considered these works authoritative. The relatively high number of manuscripts of pseudepigraphical works that were found among the Dead Sea Scrolls (fifteen scrolls of *Jubilees* and twenty scrolls from *Enoch*) and in Greek translation suggests that at least *Jubilees* and the early portions of *Enoch* were popular in various circles in the Jewish community.

Several New Testament passages use illustrations drawn from pseudepigraphical works, confirming the wide popularity of these works in the first century CE. In Jude 9 the angel Michael contends with the devil for the body of Moses. This story is not in our existing fragmentary manuscripts of the *Assumption of Moses* (also called the *Testament of Moses*), but is attributed to this work by early church fathers such as Clement, Origen, and Didymus, who presumably had access to copies. Similarly, Jude 15 closely follows *1 Enoch* 1:9, and other verses in Jude assume that portions of the *Enoch* narrative are known to the audience (Green 2009, 67–68).

Pseudepigraphy was a popular literary device in Jewish, pagan, and Christian circles over a long period of time. However, the works most relevant to understanding the background to the ministry of Jesus and the writings of the New Testament are those Jewish works that were written earlier than the destruction of the Temple. Many of these works were later rewritten, embellished, and translated into various languages. Therefore, determining their early cores is subject to a great deal of scholarly debate. However, the pseudepigrapha fragments found among the Dead Sea Scrolls (in Hebrew, Aramaic, or Greek) have confirmed the existence of some of these compositions, or at least sections of them, in the first century CE. As a result of the evidence from the Dead Sea Scrolls and from other early writings, scholars have compiled a list of early pseudepigrapha (Stone 1983; 1984; Charlesworth 1983, 1985). These include *Jubilees*, parts of *1 Enoch*, parts of *2 Enoch*, *Testament of the Twelve Patriarchs*, and *Assumption of Moses*.

Apocrypha

Many Jewish compositions of the late Second Temple period have been incorporated into the writings hallowed by the church. These works were affirmed as deuterocanonical (a secondary canon) by the Roman Catholic Church in 1546, but rejected as inspired Scripture by the Protestant movement, who called them *Apocrypha* ("hidden writings"). The Apocrypha includes history (1 and 2 Maccabees), short stories (Tobit, Judith, *Joseph and Aseneth*; additions to Esther, Daniel [such as Bel and the Dragon and Susanna], and Ezra [1 Esdras]), wisdom literature (Sirach, Wisdom of Solomon), prayers (Prayer of Azariah, Song of the Three Young Men, *Prayer of Hezekiah*), and letters (Baruch, Epistle of Jeremiah). Many of these works have only survived in Greek and Latin recensions, although the Dead Sea Scrolls have brought to light sections of the Hebrew or Aramaic versions of some of them.

Even though modern Judaism does not consider these works authoritative (and thus their Hebrew name "the outside books"), they often reflect early Jewish exegesis. It has long been recognized that a thorough familiarity with the works of the Apocrypha opens new insights into the cultural and exegetical world of the teachings of Jesus and of the New Testament writers (for recent treatments see Nickelsburg 2003; 2005; Murphy 1991; Schürer 1986–1987; Collins 1984; Charlesworth 1992).

The Dead Sea Scrolls

Beginning in 1947 a collection of scrolls and fragments of scrolls were found in eleven caves near the Dead Sea. These included various works of the Apocrypha and Pseudepigrapha, often in multiple copies, as well as works of the Jewish sect the Yahad ("togetherness"), who lived nearby at Qumran. Scrolls (or fragments of them) with portions of the Tanakh were also discovered, representing every book except for Esther (see De Troyer 2000; Talmon 1995; VanderKam 2002). Some of the scrolls include in-text commentaries (*pesharim*). Additional Scripture portions were found in the excavations at Masada and in other caves in the Judean Desert.

The sectarian work the *Damascus Document* was known to scholars before the discovery of the Dead Sea Scrolls, from a copy found in the Cairo Genizah. It gives us a cryptic history of the "Teacher of Righteousness," an esteemed figure who lived in the middle of the second century BCE. He split from, or was expelled by, a "wicked priest" who controlled the Temple in Jerusalem. The Yahad was influenced by the teachings of the Teacher of Righteousness and his followers, and was perhaps even their direct spiritual heirs. The Yahad left additional documents reflecting many of the theological ideas and halakah of the *Damascus Document*. There were hymns to be used in liturgy on the Sabbath, some of which were most likely composed by the Teacher of Righteousness (Murphy-O'Connor 1992, 341); a *Manual of Discipline*, which gave specific guidelines for their communal life; the *Temple Scroll*, which outlined the ideal temple and the calendar it was to follow; the scroll of the *War of the Sons of Light against the Sons of Darkness ["War Scroll"]*, which foresaw an apocalyptic battle and described the spiritual and practical steps needed to prepare for it; and the *pesharim*, mentioned above.

The Dead Sea Scrolls and the scrolls found at Masada and the Judean Desert caves have been pivotal in reshaping our understanding of the transmission of the Old Testament text. We can compare the Masoretic text (for which the earliest major codices date from the tenth and eleventh centuries CE) with fragments from over two hundred Scripture scrolls that are more than a thousand years older than these medieval codices. Some books of the Bible were represented by multiple copies. All of the Judean Desert texts and a few of the Qumran texts were virtually identical to the Masoretic text of the medieval codices. Other texts, associated with the sect at Qumran, had minor differences (Tov [2012, 92–93] calls these "Masoretic-like" texts). Differences that exist include missing/added conjunctions and prepositions, spelling variations (orthography), and differing sequence within the text. There are also some texts that represent variations similar to the LXX or to the Samaritan Pentateuch (Tov 2012, 92–93; Greenspoon 2000, 754). Overall, however, the Scripture texts among the Dead Sea Scrolls have reinforced scholarly confidence in the antiquity of the readings preserved in the Masoretic text.

Although no portions of the New Testament are represented among the finds (Fee 1973), the sectarian works and new portions of pseudepigrapha have revealed the diverse culture and worldviews of Jews among whom Jesus ministered. Sometimes there are similarities of exegesis, terminology, or theology between these works and the New Testament writings. Other times there is only contrast. Both the similarities and the differences are important for broadening our ideas about the society into which Christianity was birthed. Whether the shared elements are evidence of direct influence or only of writings that emerged in the same cultural milieu continues to be the subject of extensive debate (Baumgarten et al. 1981; Flusser 2007).

Philo of Alexandria

Philo, a first century CE contemporary of Jesus, was a biblical exegete and philosopher from one of the leading families in the Jewish community in Alexandria, Egypt. His works included biblical commentaries, philosophical studies, and apologetics. Forty-nine out of his seventy known works were preserved in full by the church, either in the original Greek or in Armenian translation, primarily because he was (erroneously) believed to have been an early Jewish follower of Jesus, or even a church leader (Sterling 2000, 791).

Philo's extensive literary output gives us an example of biblical exegesis and thought in the Jewish diaspora. He expressed his understanding of the nature of God and the universe in terms commonly used in Greek philosophical schools. He was particularly influenced by the school of Neo-Platonism that flourished in Alexandria at the time. His works show a thorough knowledge of the Scriptures in Greek translation, but little familiarity with exegesis of the Hebrew text (Sterling 2000, 789). He explained the Scriptures to the Greek-speaking diaspora, as well as to gentiles who were exploring the ideas of Judaism.

Although it is not possible to show a direct impact of his writings on New Testament authors, his work illustrates Hellenistic Jewish traditions and concepts that are also reflected in some parts of the New Testament, such as Colossians, Hebrews, and the Gospel of John (Hay 2000, 1052). Some of the terminology of the New Testament is also found in Philo: the agency of the Word (Logos) in creating the world (John 1), the tabernacle as a shadow of the heavenly reality (Heb 8:5), and the law as a shadow of a reality to come (Heb 10:1).

Josephus

Additional evidence for the historical, political, and cultural background of the ministry of Jesus is found in the works of Josephus Flavius. Born into a priestly family as Joseph ben Mattatiyahu in the first half of the first century CE, Josephus later became part of the leadership of the Jewish revolt against Rome. Early in the revolt, Josephus went over to the Roman side, and after the war he moved to Rome, where he wrote historical and apologetic works under the patronage of the emperors Vespasian and Titus. *Jewish Antiquities* retells the biblical narrative with interpretations and embellishments. His account of Jewish history continues through the Hellenistic period (the Maccabean revolt, the Hasmonean dynasty), followed by the civil wars and the arrival of the Romans. He gives detailed biographies of the Herodian dynasty, describing figures that appear only briefly in the New Testament, such as Herod the Great, his sons Archelaus and Antipas (the latter called only "Herod" or "Herod the Tetrarch" in the New Testament), his grandson Herod Agrippa I (also identified only as "Herod" in Acts 12), and his great-grandson Agrippa II (Acts 25 and 26). He also expands our knowledge of Pontius Pilate and Caiaphas the high priest. Other New Testament events—Jesus' life and death, the ministry and execution of John the Baptist, and the death of James the brother of Jesus—appear briefly in the tapestry that Josephus weaves. Many first-century events are retold, or expanded upon, in his account of the revolt against Rome (*Jewish War*) and in his autobiography (*The Life*).

Josephus's description of Jesus was disputed for many years due to embellishments added by Christian copyists. These additions made it seem as though Josephus had recognized the divine nature of Messiah, his miraculous powers, and his resurrection. Thanks to a medieval translation of Josephus into Arabic (in which no Christian additions are suspected), the original reading of Josephus's passage on Jesus can be reconstructed with a fair degree of certainty:

> At this time there was a wise man who was called Jesus. And his conduct was good, and he was known to be virtuous [*variant reading:* his learning was outstanding]. And many people from among the Jews and other nations became his disciples. Pilate condemned him to be crucified and to die. And those who had become his disciples did not abandon his discipleship. [They reported] that he had appeared to them three days after his crucifixion, and that he was alive; accordingly, [he was held] to be the Messiah concerning whom the Prophets have recounted wonders. And the people of the Christians, so-called after him, has to this day not disappeared. (Pines 1971)

Late Second Temple period literature expands our knowledge of the multifaceted society and religious thinking of a wide variety of Jewish groups. Through this literature, scholars can investigate the world of eschatological sectarians (the Dead Sea Sect), Greek-speaking Neo-Platonists, and early Scripture exegetes connected with the Judaism of the Temple. Greek, Hebrew, and Aramaic works were produced, with some first-century Jewish authors (such as Philo and Josephus) showing complete familiarity with Greek language and thought, while other writers produced works entirely in Hebrew (such as the *Manual of Discipline*, the *War Scroll* and the *Temple Scroll*) or in Aramaic. These Second Temple period works and early biblical translations include terms and exegetical issues similar to those of the New Testament and provide fruitful comparisons and contrasts.

Works Cited

Baumgarten, Albert, Alan Mendelson, and E. P. Sanders, eds. 1981. *Studies in Jewish and Christian Self-Definition II: Aspects of Judaism in the Graeco-Roman Period*. London: SCM.

Buth, Randall. 2000. "Aramaic Language." *DNTB* 85–91.

Charlesworth, James H. 1983, 1985. *The Old Testament Pseudepigrapha.* 2 vols. Garden City: Doubleday.

———. "Apocrypha." 1992. *ABD* 1:292–94.

Chilton, Bruce. 2000. "Rabbinic Literature: *Targumim.*" *DNTB* 902–9.

Collins, J. J. 1984. *The Apocalyptic Imagination: An Introduction to the Jewish Matrix of Christianity.* New York: Crossroad.

Cook, Edward M. 1994. "A New Perspective on the Language of Onqelos and Jonathan." Pages 142–56 in *The Aramaic Bible: Targums in Their Historical Context.* Edited by D. R. G. Beattie and M. J. McNamara. JSOTSup 166. Sheffield: Sheffield Academic.

De Troyer, Kristin. 2000. "Once More, the So-Called Esther Fragments of Cave 4." *Revue de Qumran* 19.3:401–22.

Fee, Gordon. 1973. "Some Dissenting Notes on 7Q5 = Mark 6:52–53." *JBL* 92:109–12.

Flusser, David. 2007. *Qumran and Apocalypticism.* Vol. 1 of *Judaism of the Second Temple Period.* Translated by Azzan Yadin. Grand Rapids: Eerdmans.

Green, E. Michael. 2009. *Second Peter and Jude.* TNTC 18. Edited by Leon L. Morris. Downers Grove, IL: InterVarsity Press.

Greenspoon, Leonard. 2000. "Old Testament Versions, Ancient." *DNTB* 752–55.

Hay, David B. 2000. "Philo." *EDB* 1052.

Murphy, Frederick J. 1991. *The Religious World of Jesus: An Introduction to Second Temple Judaism.* Nashville: Abingdon.

Murphy-O'Connor, Jerome. 1992. "Teacher of Righteousness." *ABD* 6:340–41.

Nickelsburg, G. W. E. 2003. *Ancient Judaism and Christian Origins: Diversity, Continuity, and Transformation.* Minneapolis: Fortress.

———. 2005. *Jewish Literature between the Bible and the Mishnah: A Historical and Literary Introduction.* 2nd ed. Minneapolis: Fortress.

Peters, M. K. H. 1992. "Septuagint." *ABD* 4:1093–1104.

Pines, S. 1971. *An Arabic Version of Testimonium Flavianum and Its Implications.* Jerusalem: The Israel Academy.

Schürer, E. 1986–1987. *The History of the Jewish People in the Age of Jesus Christ (175 B.C.–A.D.135).* 4 vols. Edited by G. Vermes et al. Edinburgh: T&T Clark.

Smith, D. Moody. 1972. "The Use of the Old Testament in the New." Pages 3–65 in *The Use of the Old Testament in the New and Other Essays: Studies in Honor of William Franklin Stinespring.* Edited by J. M. Efird. Durham, NC: Duke University Press.

———. 1988. "The Pauline Literature." Pages 265–91 in *It Is Written: Scripture Citing Scripture.* Edited by D. A. Carson and H. G. M. Williamson. Cambridge: Cambridge University Press.

Sterling, G. E. 2000. "Philo." *DNTB* 789–93.

Stone, Michael. 1983. "Why Study the Pseudepigrapha?" *BA* 4:235–43.

————. 1984. *Jewish Writing of the Second Temple Period*. Compendiarerum Iudaicarum ad Novum Testamentum 3. Assen: Van Gorcum.

Talmon, Shemaryahu. 1995. "Was the Book of Esther Known at Qumran?" *DSD* 2:249–67.

Tov, Emanuel. 2012. *Textual Criticism of the Hebrew Bible*. 3rd. ed. Minneapolis: Fortress.

VanderKam, James. 2002. "Questions of Canon Viewed through the Dead Sea Scrolls." Pages 91–109 in *The Canon Debate*. Edited by L. M. McDonald and J. A. Sanders. Peabody, MA: Hendrickson.

6.4 The Jewish Institutions

Andreas Stutz

During the time of the Second Temple, there were three Jewish institutions that were of particular importance to Judaism: the synagogue, the Sanhedrin, and the Temple. These institutions were responsible for the religious as well as the social life of the Jewish people in the first century CE. Indeed, knowing and understanding these institutions is critical for understanding many of the events reported in the New Testament. This article will introduce these three institutions individually and explain their significance for Jewish life in the era of the New Testament.

Synagogue

In Hebrew, the synagogue is usually called *bet keneset* ("house of assembly"), but also *bet tefilla* ("prayer house") and *bet midrash* ("house of learning"). In Aramaic, inscriptions have been found calling the synagogue "the holy place." On the other hand, in Greek synagogue and grave inscriptions a distinction is made between the assembly (*synagōgē*) and the assembly house, the latter being called *proseuchē* ("prayer house"), *ho hagios topos* ("the holy place"), or *ho oikos* ("the house"). Only in the New Testament period are the synagogue building (e.g., in Acts 13:14) and the actual assembly (e.g., in Acts 13:43) both called *synagōgē*.

The origin of the institution of the synagogue is widely debated. Scholars disagree on the place and time when it originated. While some assume that it should be dated back to the First Temple period (cf., for example, Weingreen 1964, 81–82), others think that it began in the time of the Babylonian exile (for example, Rabinowitz et al. 1971, 580), and still others argue for a beginning in the Hellenistic period (thus, the city gate is to be regarded as the forerunner of the synagogue, cf. Levine 2001, 500). Some facts seem to point to the latter theory, but the evidence is not yet definitive.

The earliest evidence that is occasionally related to the synagogue is very ambiguous. For example, the mentioning of *miqdash me'at* (sanctuary) in Ezek 11:16 (see *b. Megillah* 29a) and the mentioning of (*byt?*) *knsh* (= *bet keneset*, house of assembly) on an ostracon (dated to the end of the sixth century BCE, see Weingreen 1964, 70) might be references to the synagogue. From the third century BCE, clearer evidence of the existence of synagogues gradually appears (see Chilton and Yamauchi 2000, 1145–46). On the whole, therefore:

> As its [the synagogue's] birth is lost in the mists of antiquity and apparently took place unheralded, so it grew to maturity in conditions of obscurity, and makes its definite appearance about the first century of the Christian era as a fully grown and established institution. (Rabinowitz et al. 1971, 579)

According to later rabbinic tradition, there were many synagogues in Jerusalem before 70 CE: the accounts range from 394 (*b. Ketubbot* 105a) to 460 (*y. Ketubbot* 13, 1, 35c) to 480 (*y. Megillah* 3, 1, 73d). However, these numbers seem to be exaggerated. At the present time there is no way to know the number of synagogues in Jerusalem. As for the number of synagogues in the diaspora, Levine (2001, 504) estimates them to be in the hundreds if not thousands. The synagogue played an important role in the Jewish community, both socially and religiously. [See Figures 8, 12–14, 18–19.]

Regarding the social role of the synagogue, the following can be stated: (1) Legal matters were regulated in the synagogue, which is attested by Josephus Flavius (*Ant.* 14.235) and the New Testament (Matt 10:17–18 par.; 23:34; Acts 22:19). (2) According to *y. Megillah* 3.1 73d, *y. Ketubbot* 13.1 35c, and *b. Ketubbot* 105a, all the synagogues in Jerusalem had schools. (3) Occasionally synagogues or their adjoining rooms (see Reeg 2004, 1945) could serve as hostels. (4) The synagogue also collected donations—for the Temple and for the poor.

Concerning the religious role of the synagogues, the following can be said: (1) People gathered in the synagogue regularly on Sabbaths and holidays. (2) The centerpiece of the synagogue service was the public reading of the Torah (cf. Acts 13:14–15; 15:21; *Ag. Ap.* 2.175)—in first-century Israel presumably in a three- to three-and-a-half-year cycle and in the diaspora probably in a one-year cycle (see Levine 2000, 140–41). Since Hebrew had ceased to be the lingua franca, it can be assumed that in first-century Israel the Torah reading was translated (i.e., targum) and that it was read directly in Greek in the diaspora. (3) An instruction was added to the reading of the Torah (Levine 2000, 144–45). (4) After the reading of the Torah came the so-called haftarah, during which a short section was read from the prophets. This is attested in Luke 4:16–19;

Acts 13:14–15, 27. (5) The haftarah formed the basis for the sermon in Luke 4:18–19 (Levine 2000, 143).

Depending on the area there were different leadership structures and designations. The *archisynagōgos* (i.e., "leader of the synagogue") was the head of the synagogue, who held religious, financial, political, and administrative roles: "[T]he office of the archisynagogue involved overall responsibility for all facets of the institution, as, in fact, the title itself seems to convey" (Levine 2000, 391). The *archōn* (*tēs synagōgēs*; i.e., the "leader [of the Synagogue]") also held different leadership roles. The presbyters fulfilled religious and administrative tasks. The *hazzan* (cantor) was the most prominent (although not the dominant) person in a synagogue in first century Israel. He led the worship and was responsible for keeping and taking care of the scrolls (cf. Luke 4:20). While the honorary *patēr synagōgēs* (i.e., "father of the synagogue") could occasionally be associated with a role of responsibility, this seems unlikely for the title *mētēr synagōgēs* (or *matēr synagōgae*, i.e., the "mother of the synagogue"; see Levine 2000, 406). Although the above list of authorities is by no means exhaustive, it does show that there were occasional overlaps between different offices' areas of responsibility.

Jesus and the apostles regularly went to the synagogues (Luke 4:16; Acts 17:2) and taught there. Green (1997, 209) adds:

> Luke's presentation indicates not only that Jesus regularly demonstrated his piety by attendance of the synagogue on the Sabbath, but also that it was his habit to take the role of the one who read and expounded the Scriptures (cf. Acts 17:2). This phrase, "as was his custom," underscores the paradigmatic quality of this episode, both with regard to his Sabbath practices, and with regard to the content of his proclamation.

On the other hand, it was often the synagogue that opposed Jesus and his disciples. It is noteworthy that the term *synagōgē* referred to the assembly building of Jewish followers of Jesus at least up to the fourth century CE (see Riesner 1995, 207). In fact, James also distinguishes between the assembly (*ekklēsia*; Jas 5:14) and the assembly house (*synagōgē*; Jas 2:2–3).

Sanhedrin

The term *Sanhedrin* is a loanword from the Greek *synedrion* (composed by *syn* "together" and *hedra* "seat"). The older term, *gerousia* ("council"), is also found in Acts 5:21, probably epexegetic to *synedrion*. Another term is *boulē* ("council"), which is found frequently in Josephus, but not in the New Testament. The term Sanhedrin can refer to two entities: the little Sanhedrin, a local court made up of twenty-three members, and the great Sanhedrin. The present essay deals with the latter.

Almost nothing is known about the beginnings of the Sanhedrin; it "is first definitely attested in the Greek era" (Schürer 1978, 2:200). Josephus Flavius reports that in 57 BCE Aulus Gabinius divided the nation into five districts, and set a council (synedrion) over each district (*Ant.* 14.91; *J.W.* 1.169–170), seeking to weaken Hyrcanus II's political influence and Jerusalem's centrality. This situation was changed by Julius Caesar, who not only confirmed Hyrcanus II's dignity as the high priest, but also appointed him to the Ethnarch (*Ant.* 14.191). Thus, he became the head of the Sanhedrin. It can be assumed that the roles of the Sanhedrin in Jerusalem were also redefined (see Müller 1999, 34), since its members came together to accuse Herod the Great—who had previously ignored the authority of the Sanhedrin—and condemn him of murder. Later, around 37 BCE, Herod took revenge by killing forty-five of its members (according to *Ant.* 15.6, but according to *Ant.* 14.174 he killed all of its members), thus weakening the Sanhedrin. After the banishment of Archelaus, the Sanhedrin's power increased significantly. Therefore, Josephus regards the Sanhedrin as the actual Jewish authority (see Müller 1999, 35).

The Sanhedrin was made up of seventy-one members (*m. Sanhedrin* 1:6), divided into three groups. On the forefront were chief priests (*archiereis*), a category which included members of the priestly nobility and former high priests. The members of this group were associated with the Sadducees (see Porton 2000, 1053–54). As early as the first century BCE (see Schürer 1978, 2:204), scribes (*grammateis*) became part of the Sanhedrin as well. The members of the scribes belonged to the Pharisees. The chief priests and the scribes frequently engaged in a power struggle. The elders (*presbyteroi*) were the influential lay nobility, and probably all of them belonged—like the chief priests—to the Sadducees (see Lohse 1971, 862). These three groups can be found in the New Testament (Matt 16:21; 27:41). At the head of the Sanhedrin stood the high priest.

In the New Testament era, the Sanhedrin was similar to the Supreme Court, with the task of regulating both spiritual and secular affairs (Lohse 1971, 862). Outwardly, the Sanhedrin was the highest political representative of the nation: It sent correspondence to foreign states and the diaspora (see Acts 9:1–2; Bruce 1988, 180–81) and received correspondence from foreign states (Safrai 1978, 72).

On a national level, the Sanhedrin appointed the tribunals for the districts (Safrai 1978, 72). As for the jurisdiction of the Sanhedrin, its capital jurisdiction (the so-called *ius gladii*) was recognized with only two exceptions: when non-Jews crossed the Temple barrier (see *J.W.* 6.124–127) and in the case of prophecy against the Temple (cf. *J.W.* 6.300–305; but also the accusation against Jesus in Matt 26:60–63 // Mark 14:56–61; see Müller 1999, 36–38). However, the Sanhedrin had to seek formal confirmation from the Roman authorities prior to execution (see John 18:31). As for the Sanhedrin's roles in public religious life, it had to determine the new moon and the leap years. According to *b. Sanhedrin* 2:4, decisions about war also had to be made by the Sanhedrin.

This was put into practice during the revolt (66–70 CE), when the zealots took control. Josephus, as Jewish commander-in-chief of the insurgents in Galilee, received his instructions from the Sanhedrin (*Life* 62, 309–310).

The destruction of Jerusalem in 70 CE also marked the end of the Sanhedrin, since the Sanhedrin lost its authority with the destruction of the Temple (see Safrai 1981, 1:388). The Sanhedrin eventually lost its power and responsibilities as a superior Jewish authority. Rabbi Jochanan ben Zakkai, probably himself a member of the Sanhedrin before the Jewish rebellion (see Müller 1999, 39), rebuilt the Sanhedrin in Yavneh. However, this Sanhedrin "was not a political senate, but a representative tribunal, determined to take measures aimed at maintaining the continuity of tradition according to the *Pharisaic* line" (40).

The Temple

Since this essay is limited to the Jewish institutions of the New Testament period, this section will not deal with Solomon's Temple but rather with the Second Temple.

The term commonly used in the Old Testament for the Temple is *hekhal*. Later, however, *bet hammiqdash* ("holy house") became the common term. Similarly, in the New Testament the Temple is called *ho naos* ("the temple") and *to hieron* ("the holy house"). The name corresponds to the purpose: it is the house of God.

After the destruction of the First Temple around 587 BCE, the reconstruction was taken up (beginning with the altar) in 537 BCE and completed about 515 BCE. Under Antiochus Epiphanes IV the Temple was desecrated in December 167 BCE: the traditional sacrifices were stopped, the Temple was dedicated to Zeus Olympus, and pigs were sacrificed on the altar. As a result, Judas Maccabaeus conquered Jerusalem, cleaned the Temple in December 164 BCE and restored the traditional sacrificial service. In the fifteenth (*J.W.* 1.401) or eighteenth (*Ant.* 15.380) year of his reign, Herod the Great began renovating the Temple, a process that lasted until approximately 10 BCE. However, the detailed work was not completed until about 63 CE (*Ant.* 20.219). Only four years later the Jewish revolt against the Romans broke out, resulting in the destruction of the Temple in the year 70.

The Second Temple in the New Testament era had an expansive Temple court measuring 488 meters (1590 feet) in the west, 315 meters (1035 feet) in the north, 468 meters (1536 feet) in the east, and 278 meters (912 feet) in the south. Around the Temple court there were pillared halls. Particularly noteworthy is the magnificent southern portico, called Solomon's Portico. This hall—where once trade was done (Matt 12:21 par.)—was not only the headquarters of the Sanhedrin from about 30 CE on (*b. Shabbat* 15a; *b. Rosh Hashanah* 31a), but also the gathering place of the church (Acts 3:11; 5:12). The outer forecourt, also known as the "Court of the Gentiles," was accessible to both Jews and gentiles. It was separated from the inner area by a fence, on which the following inscription was found: "No alien may enter within the balustrade around the sanctuary and the enclosure. Whoever is caught, on himself shall he put blame for the death which will ensue" (Bickerman 1947, 388). In the inner part of the Temple was the court of the women (the location of Luke 2:37; Mark 12:41–44), through which the men entered the innermost forecourt, which included the forecourt of Israel and the forecourt of the priests. Here the sacrifices were slaughtered and offered. The actual Temple building consisted of two parts—the Holy Place and the Holy of Holies—separated by a hand-width-thick curtain (*m. Sheqalim* 8:5). While the Table of Showbread, the Menorah, and the incense altar stood in the Holy Place, the Holy of Holies was empty (cf. 2 Maccabees 2:5–7). The Second Temple was so magnificent that the Talmud claims: "[W]ho has not seen the building of Herod has not seen a beautiful structure" (*b. Bava Batra* 4a).

There were several officials in the Temple. The high priest had the highest position. Originally, this office was exclusively meant for the Zadokites, but that changed when the Hasmoneans seized it. Later, Herod, his descendants, and the Romans appointed and dismissed high priests (see Bateman 2012, 89–91). The priests were divided into twenty-four courses (see Luke 1:5) and served in the Temple in succession, so each served for two weeks a year. The temple captain (Acts 5:24, 26) was likely a chief priest and monitored the temple guard (Matt 26:47), which was probably at least partially made up of Levites. This guard's task was to secure the temple square.

The Temple fulfilled several purposes in the life of the Jewish people. It was the place where the various sacrifices required by law were offered. Since according to the Torah the Temple was the only legitimate place for sacrifices, many people traveled to the pilgrimage feasts (Passover, the Feast of Weeks, and the Feast of Tabernacles). According to Josephus, up to 2.6 million pilgrims gathered in Jerusalem during Passover (*J. W.* 6.422–426), but this number might be exaggerated. Furthermore, in the Temple the people were instructed in the Torah. The high priest read the Torah to the people in the Temple (*m. Yoma* 7:1). There was a *bet midrash* (a house of learning) in the Temple complex (*t. Sanhedrin* 7:1, cf. Luke 2:46), Rabbi Yohanan ben Zakkai taught in the shadow of the Temple (*b. Pesahim* 106a), and Jesus taught in the Temple (Matt 21:23; 26:55; Mark 12:35). The Temple was a place of prayer for Jews (Luke 2:37; Matt 21:13) and also for the early church (Acts 3:1). Furthermore, the Sanhedrin gathered in the Temple complex to hold court (see above).

Thus the Temple had a central role in the life of the Jewish people. Its destruction was devastating, causing confusion in the generation immediately after the war (see Safrai 1981, 1:390). It meant the cessation of the sacrifices and the pilgrimages, the impossibility of keeping numerous Old Testament commandments, and the loss of priests' relevance and power.

Works Cited

Bateman, Herbert W. 2012. *Charts on the Book of Hebrews.* Kregel Charts of the Bible. Grand Rapids: Kregel.

Bickerman, Elias J. 1947. "The Warning Inscriptions of Herod's Temple." *JQR* 37:387–405.

Bruce, F. F. 1988. *The Book of the Acts.* NICNT. Rev. ed. Grand Rapids: Eerdmans.

Chilton, Bruce, and Edwin Yamauchi. 2000. "Synagogues." *DNTB* 1145–53.

Green, Joel B. 1997. *The Gospel of Luke.* NICNT. Grand Rapids: Eerdmans.

Levine, Lee L. 2000. *The Ancient Synagogue: The First Thousand Years.* New Haven: Yale University Press.

———. 2001. "Synagogue." *TRE* 32:499–508.

Lohse, Eduard. 1971. "συνέδριον." *TDNT* 7:860–70.

Müller, Karlheinz. 1999. "Sanhedrin/Synhedrium." *TRE* 30:32–42.

Porton, Gary G. 2000. "Sadducees." *DNTB* 1050–52.

Rabinowitz, Louis I., David Davidowitch, Raphael Posner, and Benjamin Yvieli. 1971. "Synagogue: Origins and History." *EncJud* 15:579–91.

Reeg, Gottfried. 2004. "Synagoge: Antike." *RGG* 7:1944–46.

Riesner, Rainer. 1995. "Synagogues in Jerusalem." Pages 179–210 in *The Book of Acts in Its Palestinian Setting.* Edited by Richard Bauckham. Grand Rapids: Eerdmans.

Safrai, Shmuel. 1978. *Das jüdische Volk im Zeitalter des Zweiten Tempels.* Neukirchen-Vluyn: Neukirchener Verlag.

———. 1981. "Das Zeitalter der Mischna und des Talmuds (70–640)." Pages 377–469 in vol. 1 of *Geschichte des jüdischen Volkes.* Edited by Haim Hillel Ben-Sasson. 2nd ed. Munich: Beck.

Schürer, Emil. 1978. *The History of the Jewish People in the Age of Jesus Christ.* Vols. 1–3. Rev. ed. Edited by Geza Vermes and Fergus Millar. Edinburgh: T&T Clark.

Weingreen, J. 1964. "The Origin of the Synagogue." *Herm* 98:68–84.

6.5 Messianic Expectations

Andreas Stutz

The situation of the Jewish people in the first century CE was indeed miserable: they were under Roman occupation, they were ruled by a non-Davidic dynasty (the Herodians), the tribes of Israel were still scattered, and the office of the high priest was held by non-Zadokites. Out of this situation grew the deep desire for social justice, independence, restored glory, and true piety; all of which led to interest in a deliverer. It comes as little surprise that the messianic hope of that time was for a royal, ruling, sovereign messiah who would lead Israel to a new spiritual, social, and political future.

General Expectations

As is commonly known, "messiah" is a transliteration of the Hebrew term *mashiakh* (i.e., "anointed one") and "Christ" is a transliteration of the Greek term *christos* (also "anointed one"). Kings, priests, and prophets were anointed in the Old Testament. Thus, various persons could be called "anointed ones": the patriarchs (1 Chr 16:22), the high priest (Lev 4:3), and kings (Saul [1 Sam 12:5], David [2 Sam 22:51], and Cyrus [Isa 45:1]). Only in the third or second century BCE did the term receive an eschatological nuance (Evans 2000, 699) and become a technical term for a reigning end times figure.

Messianic expectation was based on passages that point to a triumphant messiah figure, for example Gen 49:10; Num 24:17; Isa 11:1–6; Ps 2; Dan 2; 7; 9. On the other hand, passages that seemed to point to a suffering messiah (like Isa 53; Zech 12:10; Dan 9:26) were largely ignored. This is confirmed in the New Testament. Jesus' announcement of his impending suffering surprises and saddens the disciples (Matt 16:21–23; 17:22–23). The figure of the suffering, crucified Christ is a hindrance to the Jewish people (1 Cor 1:23). Pilate knew that having his soldiers write down "Jesus of Nazareth, King of the Jews" in the midst of Jesus' suffering would annoy or even mock the Jewish people (John 19:19; cf. also Matt 27:11, 29; Mark 15:9, 12; Luke 23:37).

One feature of first-century messianic expectation is the appearance of rebels as end-time savior figures, as witnessed in both the New Testament and extrabiblical literature (cf., for example, Acts 5:34–39 with *Ant.* 20.97–99; Acts 21:37–38 with *J.W.* 2.261–263). In fact "one can say that all the liberation movements of the Second Temple period were messianic, whether at their base or at their roof beams" (Haggai 1969, 48–49, author's translation). These uprisings were stifled by the Roman occupying forces. Another characteristic of the imminent messianic expectation is the tense expectation found in the Qumran texts (see Betz and Riesner 1993, 119) and in *Targum Jonathan to the Prophets* (Churgin 1907, 124). This messianic expectation was not unknown to Roman historians (see Suetonius, *Vesp.* 4.5; Tacitus, *Hist.* 5.13).

On one hand, this imminent expectation was nourished by suffering (Stapleton 2006, 24–25), for "the more cramped, the poorer, and the crueler the historical reality was, the more radiant was the messianic hope" (Oberhänsli-Widmer 1998, 132, author's translation). On the other hand, Dan 9 was also influential, for, according to Josephus (*J.W.* 6.312), it was an ambiguous prophecy that made the rebels believe that "at that time" the messiah would come. Although originating from much later times, *b. Nazir* 32b obviously uses

Dan 9:24 to refer to the destruction of the Second Temple. When it comes to the details, the messianic expectations varied between the different groups, as they were differently informed, differently situated, and interpreted central Old Testament promises in a variety of ways.

Hellenistic Judaism

The messiah is expected as a ruler in such works as the *Sibylline Oracles*, the Psalms of Solomon, and *1 Enoch*. In *Sibylline Oracles* 3:652–795 (about 140 BCE, see Schiffman 1987, 238), a king from the east is announced (3:652; see Shum 1999, 59–61), who expels the hostile kings (3:661–679, referring to Ps 2:1–5) and gathers the scattered people (3:702). This king not only accomplishes political peace (3:653) but also peace in creation (3:785–795, following Isa 11:6–8). His kingdom will be an everlasting kingdom (Schürer 1973–1987, 2:502).

Messianic statements are also found in the *Testaments of the Twelve Patriarchs* (mainly second century BCE). Thus, for example, *Testament of Judah* 22:1–3 states that the eschatological kingship of Judah is to last forever. Chapter 24 describes the messiah with numerous allusions to Old Testament prophecies that were also interpreted in a messianic manner in other writings (e.g., Num 3:20; 24:17; Isa 11:1). It is noteworthy that in *Testament of Reuben* 6:7–12 a priest-messiah appears next to the king-messiah; this approach can be found in the Qumran literature (see below). The eschatological hope for the return of the tribes is attested in *Testament of Benjamin* 9:2.

In the Psalms of Solomon (first century CE) the messianic hope is intensified by the disappointment of the Hasmoneans clearly expressed in chapter 17. The poet confesses God's eternal kingship (vv. 1–3) and asks God at the same time for the promised king-messiah of the house of David (v. 21). This shows that for the writer the kingdom of the messiah is in reality a theocracy. Accordingly, the messiah is accredited with divine attributes such as "wisdom, strength, righteousness (vv. 23, 27, 37, 40), purity from sin (v. 36), and speech whose power is reminiscent of the mighty, creative, and effective power of God's Word (vv. 35–36)" (Nickelsburg and Stone 1983, 165). The poet expects the messiah to crush the enemy kings (vv. 23–24, referring to Ps 2:9) and gather the scattered people into the promised land (vv. 26–28).

In *1 Enoch* chapters 37–71 (this section is also called *Similitudes of Enoch*) the messiah is called "Son of Man" (e.g., 48:2; see also *4 Ezra* 13:3) and "chosen one" (48:6). Since there is a growing consensus among the *1 Enoch* researchers that *1 Enoch* 37–71 was written in the first century CE and perhaps even before 70 CE (see Borsch 2010, 141), these statements definitely are to be considered. For, although "Son of Man" was not used as a messianic title in the first century CE, it did serve in the writings mentioned above to describe the messiah as eternal (*1 Enoch* 52:2) and sovereign (*1 Enoch* 62; 69:26–29) based on the book of Daniel (7:13–14). These and other sources draw a clear picture: The expected messiah would be a sovereign, glorious, ruling, triumphant figure.

Also worth mentioning is the eschatological prophet figure, which is occasionally mentioned in Hellenistic Jewish literature (e.g., 1 Maccabees 4:46; 14:41; *Testament of Benjamin* 9:2). In John 1:22 this prophet is distinguished from Elijah and in John 7:40–41 from the messiah. Surely he is another precursor of the messiah, alongside Elijah. Josephus also reported on some rebels who promised signs and were obviously understood as some kind of messianic prophets (see *Ant.* 20.97; 20.169–170; 20.188; *J. W.* 2.261–263). With regard to Elijah: "In the Pseudepigrapha the idea of Elijah is strongly receding" (Strack and Billerbeck 1982–1986, 4:780, author's translation).

Dead Sea Scrolls

Although the Essene community was relatively small, it should not be underestimated. After all, according to Josephus (*Ant.* 18.20) and Philo (*Good Person* 75), their followers counted about four thousand nationwide. It is striking that "even the Essene movement . . . does not [seem] to have found a completely uniform Messiah expectation" (Betz and Riesner 1993, 119, author's translation), for, while the *Damascus Document* seems to speak of a single messiah, other writings speak clearly of two messiahs (119).

In the *Damascus Document* the "Messiah of Aaron and Israel" (CD 12:23–13:1; 14:19 [= 4Q266 frag. 18 iii 12]; 19:10–11; 20:1) is a king-messiah of the house of David (cf. the use of Num 24:17 and Amos 9:11 in CD 7:13–20) and is accordingly described in CD 7:19–20 (= 4Q266 frag. 3 iv 9), in reference to Num 24:17, as a scepter. However, the messiah is not only a king, but also a teacher of righteousness (CD 6:10–11).

Contrary to this, in other writings from Qumran there are two messiahs, with a king-messiah who is subordinate to a priestly-messiah. Thus, there may be a mention of the messiahs of Aaron and Israel (1QS 9:10–11). This expectation is based on Num 24:17, whereas "star" (i.e., the priest-messiah) and "scepter/rod" (i.e., the king-messiah) is probably understood in light of the double leadership by Joshua and Zerubbabel (Zech 6:9–16). The difference between the two Messiahs is, therefore, that "the Messiah of Aaron was expected to be superior and to dominate religious matters, while the Davidic Messiah of Israel would rule on temporal and political matters" (Schiffman 1987, 239). In this case, both messiahs are successful and radiant figures.

In addition, a messianic prophet is expected, in line with Deut 18:15–19. This prophet is the teacher of righteousness of the priestly lineage, who will rise again in the last days (see Maier and Schubert 1992, 99–101).

As in the other Jewish movements, the Essene writings do not know a suffering messiah. The attempts to find a crucified messiah in 4Q285 frag. 5 have failed. [See Figures 20–21.]

Rabbinic Judaism

One needs to be especially cautious when selecting sources, as it is all too easy to make the mistake of attributing statements from later centuries to Judaism before 70 CE. As a result of this careful selection, the number of relevant statements shrinks significantly. Some of the reliable sources that will be used in this section are *Targum Onkelos, Targum Jonathan*, and quotations of early rabbis (who taught before 70 CE).

While the messianic expectation was widespread in Rabbinic Judaism, there were also exceptions, such as Rabbi Hillel, who did not believe in a future coming of the messiah (see *b. Sanhedrin* 99a). On the other hand, there is no concrete reason to deny a messianic expectation among the Sadducees, as some have done (cf. Schiffman 1987, 240).

As with all Jewish movements, 2 Sam 7:8–16; 23:5 is the foundation and starting point for the messianic expectation in Rabbinic Judaism. There, God promises David an eternal dynasty. The hope for this descendant of David accompanies the returnees from the diaspora (see Waltke and Yu 2007, 759–60) and the people of Israel in the so-called intertestamental period. For this reason, the postexilic prophets held out the prospect of the restoration of David's line, which was interrupted by Babylonian exile. Thus, the messianic hope was in fact the expectation of the son of David. That is why Jesus is repeatedly called "Son of David" by the people (Matt 9:27; 15:22; 20:30).

The messiah expected in Rabbinic Judaism was a ruling messiah, namely a king (so all the targumim to Gen 49:10; Num 24:17) from the lineage of David (cf. targum to Isa 11:1–6), born in Bethlehem (cf. targum to Mic 5:1, but also Matt 2:4–5; John 7:41–42), who will lead the scattered people of Israel back home (cf. targum to Hos 2:2, but also Isa 11:11–12). He is the object of the hope of Israel (targum to Hos 3:5). To be sure, the *Targum Jonathan* is normally dated to the second century CE, but there can be little doubt that these fundamental expectations date back to earlier traditions—especially the targum on Mic 5:1 (see Schäfer 1980, 223).

In the rabbinic writings of the first century (or those rabbinic writings that shed light on the first century) there are no demands for signs and wonders directed to the messiah. However, it should be noted that the miracles Jesus performed awakened and strengthened messianic hopes among the people, and that he was asked to perform a sign by the Pharisees and the scribes (Matt 12:38–39; cf. John 6:30).

A suffering messiah called *mashiakh ben yosef* ("Messiah Son of Josef") can be found in rabbinic-talmudic literature only from the first or second century CE (Oberhänsli-Widmer 1998, 132). The appearance of this messianic figure next to the triumphing messiah (Son of David) in rabbinic literature may have several causes: (1) The existence of more than one messiah figure in Qumran and Hellenistic literature; (2) the destruction of Jerusalem in 70 CE and 135 CE; and (3) Scripture passages such as Isa 52:13–53:12 (see *b. Sanhedrin* 98b); Zech 12:10 (see *b. Sukkah* 52a); and Dan 9:26 (see *b. Nazir* 32b). However, the suffering servant becomes something greater in rabbinic literature during the Second Temple period. For example, the targum on Isa 53 has the suffering servant became a triumphant messiah, and in the targum of Zech 12:10 the people do not weep over the pierced messiah, but over their slain fellow countrymen. As a consequence, in messianic movements during the Second Temple period there is no claim to the Old Testament promises of the suffering messiah, with the exception of Jesus.

In light of all this, Peter's reaction in Mark 8:31–33 can be well understood: When he confessed Jesus as Messiah, he by no means expected a suffering messiah.

In John 1:21 the "attitude of the Rabbinate" (Schlatter 1960, 40) concerning the forerunners of the messiah become visible: On the one hand, Elijah (cf. Mal 4:5 [Heb. 3:23]) is expected, on the other hand the prophet promised in Deut 18:15–19 (cf. also the two witnesses in Rev 11; Schlatter 1960, 40). To be sure, in no early Jewish source is Deut 18:15–19 taken to refer directly to the messiah. This stands in contrast to the early church (Acts 3:22; 7:37) and perhaps to the Galileans (see Morris 1995, 306), for "the step from a prophet like Moses ([John] 6:14), the first Redeemer and worker of miracles, to a messianic deliverer was a short one for enthusiasts in contemporary Israel to make" (Beasley-Murray 1999, 88).

Works Cited

Beasley-Murray, George R. 1999. *John.* WBC 36. 2nd ed. Nashville: Thomas Nelson.

Betz, Otto, and Rainer Riesner. 1993. *Jesus, Qumran und der Vatikan: Klarstellung.* 3rd ed. Gießen: Brunnen.

Borsch, Frederick H. 2010. "Further Reflections on 'The Son of Man': The Origins and Development of the Title." Pages 130–44 in *The Messiah: Developments in Earliest Judaism and Christianity.* Edited by James H. Charlesworth. Minneapolis: Fortress.

Churgin, Pinkhos. 1907. *Targum Jonathan to the Prophets.* New Haven: Yale University Press.

Evans, Craig. 2000. "Messianism." *DNTB* 698–707.

Haggai (Kreuzer), Shmuel. 1969. "Messianic Movements before the Destruction of the Second Temple" [Hebrew]. *Mahanayim* 124:46–52.

Maier, Johann, and Kurt Schubert. 1992. *Die Qumran-Essener: Texte der Schriftrollen und Lebensbild der Gemeinde*. 3rd ed. Munich: Reinhardt.

Morris, Leon. 1995. *The Gospel According to John*. NICNT. Rev. ed. Grand Rapids: Eerdmans.

Nickelsburg, George W. E., and Michael E. Stone. 1983. *Faith and Piety in Early Judaism: Texts and Documents*. Philadelphia: Fortress.

Oberhänsli-Widmer, Gabrielle. 1998. "Der leidende Messias in der jüdischen Literatur." *Judaica: Beiträge um Verstehen des Judentums* 54:132–143.

Schäfer, Peter. 1980. "Bibelübersetzungen II: Targumim." *TRE* 6:216–28.

Schiffman, Lawrence H. 1987. "The Concept of the Messiah in Second Temple and Rabbinic Judaism." *RevExp* 84:235–246.

Schlatter, Adolf. 1960. *Der Evangelist Johannes: Wie er spricht, denkt und glaubt*. 3rd ed. Stuttgart: Calwer.

Schürer, Emil. 1973–1987. *The History of the Jewish People in the Age of Jesus Christ*. Vols. 1–4. Rev. ed. Edinburgh: T&T Clark.

Shum, Shiu-Lun. 1999. "The Use of Isaiah in the Sibylline Oracles, Qumran Literature and Romans (A Source-Influence Study)." PhD diss., University of Glasgow.

Stapleton, Andrew J. 2006. "First-Century Jewish Messianism and Jesus' Self-Understanding." *Journal of Theta Alpha Kappa* 30:23–40.

Strack, Hermann L., and Paul Billerbeck. 1982–1986. *Kommentar zum Neuen Testament aus Talmud und Midrasch*, vols. 1–4. Munich: Beck.

Waltke, Bruce K., and Charles Yu. 2007. *An Old Testament Theology: An Exegetical, Canonical, and Thematic Approach*. Grand Rapids: Zondervan.

CHAPTER 7

The Jewish Life and Identity of Jesus

7.1 The Life and Ministry of Jesus

Craig A. Evans

Jesus grew up in Nazareth, a small village in Galilee some four miles from the city of Sepphoris, which had enjoyed extensive development during the administration of Tetrarch Herod Antipas. Nazareth itself may well have been one of the villages founded or refounded in Galilee during the Hasmonean resettlement and "re-Judaizing" of the north following Judah's successful revolt against the Seleucids (Vermes 1973; Bockmuehl 2001).

Nazareth may owe its name to an allusion to the "Branch" or *Netser* foretold in the prophecy of Isa 11:1: "a branch shall grow out of his roots" (RSV). A number of Jews from the south migrated to Galilee in the north, which explains why we have a "Cana of Galilee," a "Bethlehem of Galilee," and a few other villages named after their older counterparts in the south. Some of the folk who founded Nazareth may well have been from Bethlehem and in all probability were from the family of Israel's famous king David. The name of their village may have been a proud reminder of this illustrious heritage. It may also explain why Joseph, the husband of Mary, the mother of Jesus, visited Jerusalem annually (Luke 2:41, author's translation: "used to go to Jerusalem every year") and why Joseph had to be in Bethlehem for a census (Luke 2:4).

Although Jewish historian and apologist Flavius Josephus does not mention the name Nazareth, ongoing archaeology has uncovered at least three private dwellings that date to the turn of the era, confirming the existence of the Jewish village in the first century BCE. The name Nazareth appears on a fourth-century inscription found at Caesarea Maritima. Claims that there was no Nazareth, that it is a Christian invention, are eccentric and are not followed by historians or archaeologists.

There is compelling evidence that Jesus was formed in the context of Israel's historic faith, as mediated by the Scriptures, read and interpreted in the synagogue. Jesus was conversant with Israel's great story and fully embraced the redemptive vision of the Prophets. He prayed the prayers of the synagogue, probably in Aramaic as well as in Hebrew. Although Greek had become widespread since Alexander's conquest, and is amply attested in inscriptions, papyri, and literary sources, in Jesus' day most Jews spoke Aramaic. Others, perhaps in the south, spoke (or at least wrote) Hebrew.

All the evidence suggests that Jesus attended the synagogue regularly and frequently. Archaeological excavations have revealed at least ten pre-70 CE synagogues in and near Galilee, including one at Magdala, the likely hometown of Mary Magdalene. Jesus not only attended synagogue services, he also preached and taught in synagogues. This likely explains why he was frequently called "Rabbi" or "Rabboni," or its Greek equivalents "master" (*epistata*) or "teacher" (*didaskalos*). Jesus refers to himself in this manner, and is called such by supporters, opponents, and non-partisans. Prior to 70 CE the designation "Rabbi" was informal, even vague, and lacked the later connotations of formal training. In the time of Jesus it was a term of respect and often implied that one's opinion, especially regarding faith and God, was very important and should be respected. That Jesus regularly taught in synagogues and was addressed as Rabbi demonstrates how deeply rooted he was in Jewish faith and tradition (Meyer 1979; Sanders 1985; Meier 1991–2016).

At about the age of thirty (Luke 3:23) Jesus began proclaiming the appearance of the kingdom of God. His ministry, however, was not limited to preaching and teaching; it also involved mighty deeds and prayers. All three of these facets formed a coherent ministry calling for Israel's repentance and prophesying a dramatic change in the human condition (Bockmuehl 1994; Wright 1996; Dunn 2003; Allison 2010).

Proclamation of the Kingdom of God

All four of the New Testament Gospels agree that Jesus proclaimed the "kingdom of God" and that this kingdom, or rule, lay at the heart of his preaching and teaching. It is now widely believed that this proclamation, "The kingdom of God is at hand; repent, and believe in the gospel" (Mark 1:15 RSV), reflects the interpretive Aramaic paraphrase of passages from Isaiah. In Aramaic, passages such as Isa 40:9 ("Behold your God!" RSV) and 52:7 ("Your God reigns" RSV) are paraphrased as "The kingdom of your God is revealed." Although this targumic reading postdates Jesus by a century or more, it is likely that his proclamation of the coming kingdom or rule of God reflects the Aramaic tradition as it was expressed in the Aramaic-speaking synagogues of Galilee in Jesus' time (Chilton 1984). [See Figures 8, 13.]

It is important to note too that the kingdom or rule of God is in itself the good news, or gospel. This is seen clearly in Isa 52:7: "How beautiful upon the mountains are the feet of him who brings good tidings, who publishes peace, who brings good tidings of good, who publishes salvation, who says to Zion, 'Your God reigns'" (RSV). What is translated "good tidings" can also be translated as "good news" or "gospel." The good news is the reign of God, or in the language of the Aramaic-speaking synagogue, the revelation of "the kingdom of God."

It is not surprising, then, that the Gospels report that Jesus routinely preached in the synagogues of Galilee (Matt 4:23; Mark 1:39; Luke 4:15). Although many if not most of the synagogue congregations welcomed Jesus and seemed to respond positively to his preaching, his preaching in the synagogue of his home village of Nazareth was not well received. The shorter version in Mark 6:1–6 provides few details, but in the longer version in Luke 4:16–30 we are told that Jesus recited Isa 61:1–2 ("The Spirit of the Lord is upon me, because he has anointed me to preach good news . . ." RSV) and declared that it was "fulfilled in your hearing" (Luke 4:21 RSV). Initially the congregation responded well to this declaration (v. 22), but when Jesus cited the examples of Elijah and Elisha, whose ministries blessed gentiles, the congregation became angry and drove Jesus from the village (vv. 23–30).

Petition That the Kingdom Come

Jesus did not limit his proclamation of the coming of the kingdom of God to preaching; he also prayed for the coming of the kingdom of God. In the famous Lord's Prayer (Matt 6:9–13) Jesus teaches his disciples:

> Pray then like this: Our Father who art in heaven, hallowed be thy name. Thy kingdom come. Thy will be done, on earth as it is in heaven. Give us this day our daily bread; and forgive us our debts, as we also have forgiven our debtors; and lead us not into temptation, but deliver us from evil. (RSV)

Interpreters have observed that Jesus' well known prayer is modeled after the ancient Aramaic Jewish prayer known as the Kaddish ("make holy"):

> May His great name be glorified and hallowed in the world which He created according to His will. May He establish His kingdom in your lifetime and during your days, and during the lifetime of the whole house of Israel, speedily and soon; and say, "Amen." (author's translation)

The form of the prayer just quoted probably dates no earlier than the medieval period, but an early form of it likely underlies Jesus' prayer. In its earliest form the Kaddish probably petitioned God to sanctify (or make hallowed) his name and establish his kingdom soon. Jesus has taken this simple two-petition prayer and has expanded it (see the shorter version in Luke 11:2–4). Jesus not only calls on God to sanctify his name and establish his kingdom, he asks God to do his will, "on earth as it is in heaven." For Jesus, this is the essence of the kingdom of God that is coming: The way things are in heaven will be the way things are on earth. Jesus envisioned an earth transformed by the glory of God. To prepare for this transformation he teaches his disciples to have faith in God and to forgive one another.

Jesus' prayer is rooted in one of Israel's ancient synagogue prayers. His message was itself a proclamation of a hope expressed by the great prophet Isaiah. The good news foretold by Isaiah was now breaking into the world in the preaching and ministry of Jesus.

Proofs of the Truth of His Proclamation

For Jesus the proof of the truth of his preaching, as well as proof that he was authorized by heaven to do this preaching, lay in his works of power, above all the exorcisms. Jesus makes this connection in his response to his critics: "But if it is by the finger of God that I cast out demons, then the kingdom of God has come upon you" (Luke 11:20 RSV). In context this reply clearly implies that his exorcisms are proof that "the kingdom of God has come upon" the generation of Jesus (Twelftree 1999).

What occasioned this reply was the accusation that Jesus was in league with the devil: "He casts out demons by Beelzebul, the prince of demons" (Luke 11:15). His critics said this because they could not deny the reality of the exorcisms (and the healings too). Jesus' works were without parallel. The crowds shouted: "We never saw anything like this" (Mark 2:12 RSV; cf. Mark 1:27 RSV: "What is this? A new teaching! With authority he commands even the unclean spirits, and they obey him").

The power, if not uniqueness, of Jesus' ministry of healing and exorcism was such that at least one contemporary exorcist began invoking Jesus' name:

> John said to him, "Teacher, we saw a man casting out demons in your name, and we forbade him, because he was not following us." But Jesus said, "Do not forbid him; for no one who does a mighty work in my name will be able soon after to speak evil of me. For he that is not against us is for us." (Mark 9:38–40 RSV)

Because the early church looked askance at outsiders making use of the name of Jesus (e.g., Acts 19:11–20 and the disaster that overtook the seven sons of Sceva, who attempted to cast out a demon "by the Jesus whom Paul preaches" RSV), it is not likely the early church created the story in Mark 9, in which Jesus seems untroubled by this exorcist's activities. The authenticity of the story is therefore highly probable.

Just as Jesus' critics could not deny that Jesus was able to cast out evil spirits, so they could not deny that he truly healed people. One thinks of the story in John 9, where the man born blind is healed by Jesus on the Sabbath.

According to the teaching of some, healing was not permitted on the Sabbath, for it constituted work. Jesus was criticized for healing, but his critics were forced to acknowledge that the man who regained his sight really was born blind. [See Figure 10.]

Jesus, Judaism, and the Jewish People

The evidence as a whole shows that Jesus was deeply rooted in Israel's ancient, biblical heritage. Jesus accepted all the major tenets of the Jewish faith. These tenets include the unity and sovereignty of God, the value and sanctity of the Temple of Jerusalem, the authority of the Jewish Scriptures, the election of the people of Israel, and the hope of Israel's redemption.

Jesus, moreover, observed many of the practices associated with Jewish piety in his day: alms, prayer, and fasting (Matt 6:1–18). Jesus fasted in the wilderness during his period of temptation (Mark 1:12–13); he prayed and taught his disciples to pray (Matt 6:7–15; Luke 11:1–13; 22:39–46); he and his disciples gave alms, and he taught others to do likewise (Luke 11:41; 12:33; John 13:29). Jesus presupposed the validity of the Temple, the sacrifices, and Israel's holy days (Matt 5:23–24; Mark 14:14). He read and quoted from the Jewish Scriptures and clearly regarded them as authoritative (Luke 4:16–22; 10:25–28; Mark 10:19; 12:24–34). Apparently he attended synagogue services regularly (Luke 4:16); his style and interpretation of Scripture reflect at many points the style and interpretation that emerged within the synagogue.

Jesus accepted the authority of Torah (i.e., the law of Moses); he did not reject it, as has sometimes been asserted. What Jesus opposed were certain interpretations and applications of the Law. In the so-called "antitheses" of the Sermon on the Mount (i.e., "You have heard it said, but I say to you"; cf. Matt 5:21–48), Jesus does not contradict the commands of Moses; he challenges conventional interpretations and applications of those laws. The antithetical "but I say to you" does not oppose the commandments themselves. Jesus in fact warns his followers that their righteousness had better exceed that of the scribes and Pharisees if they hope to enter the kingdom of God (Matt 5:20).

Jesus loved his people and firmly believed in their future. He warned of judgment, but he was fully convinced that someday God would vindicate and restore his people. Jesus' entire mission was centered on that conviction.

Why Did Jesus Die and Who Killed Him?

Jesus of Nazareth did not die because he quarreled with Pharisees over matters of legal interpretation. He did not die because he taught love, mercy, and forgiveness. Jesus did not die because he associated with "sinners." He did not die because he was a good man. Jesus died because he threatened the political establishment with the prospect of undesired change. His contemporaries foresaw the very real possibility of a serious riot, perhaps even a full-scale rebellion.

The ruling priests took action against Jesus because they feared his preaching and his prophetic criticism of the ruling priesthood might lead to insurrection. If this happened, the ruling priests could be deposed by the Roman governor. An insurrection could lead to a very costly civil war, which is in fact what happened three decades later, in 66–70 CE.

Pontius Pilate, the Roman prefect of Samaria and Judea, agreed that the charges against Jesus were serious. He, like the ruling priests, was committed to avoiding insurrection and so had Jesus put to death by crucifixion, with a placard identifying Jesus as "the King of the Jews" (Mark 15:26 RSV).

It is important to emphasize that although the ruling priests called for Jesus' death, they were only speaking for themselves; they were not speaking for the whole nation. It is probable that the Jews who supported Jesus far outnumbered the elite few who feared him and called for his death. Only a few thousand Jews, who happened to be in Jerusalem for the annual Passover feast, were even aware of Jesus and his condemnation. The Jewish people as a whole were not responsible for the death of Jesus. From a theological perspective, Jesus' death was the will of God and accomplished God's redemptive purposes. Theologically speaking, all of humanity—Jew and gentile alike—was responsible for the death of Jesus.

Works Cited

Allison, Dale C., Jr. 2010. *Constructing Jesus: Memory, Imagination, and History*. Grand Rapids: Baker Academic.

Bockmuehl, Markus N. A. 1994. *This Jesus: Martyr, Lord, Messiah*. Edinburgh: T&T Clark.

———, ed. 2001. *The Cambridge Companion to Jesus*. Cambridge Companions to Religion. Cambridge: Cambridge University Press.

Chilton, Bruce D. 1984. *A Galilean Rabbi and His Bible: Jesus' Use of the Interpreted Scripture of His Time*. GNS 8. Wilmington, DE: Glazier.

Dunn, James D. G. 2003. *Jesus Remembered*. Christianity in the Making 1. Grand Rapids: Eerdmans, 2003.

Meier, John P. 1991–2016. *A Marginal Jew: Rethinking the Historical Jesus*. 5 vols. ABRL. New York: Doubleday.

Meyer, Ben F. 1979. *The Aims of Jesus*. London: SCM.

Sanders, E. P. 1985. *Jesus and Judaism*. Philadelphia: Fortress.

Twelftree, G. H. 1999. *Jesus the Miracle Worker: A Historical and Theological Study*. Downers Grove, IL: InterVarsity Press.

Vermes, Geza. 1973. *Jesus the Jew: A Historian's Reading of the Gospels*. London: Collins.

Wright, N. T. 1996. *Jesus and the Victory of God*. Christian Origins and the Question of God 2. Minneapolis: Fortress.

7.2 Son of Man: Daniel 7

Andreas Stutz

The main designation that Jesus used to refer to himself (in the canonical Gospels) is "Son of man" (see Kmiecik 1997; Müller 1978; Neubauer 1972), which is a reference to Dan 7. While there are many interpretations of this passage (Caragounis 1986, 42–43; Casey 1979; Reynolds 2008), this article will argue that Dan 7:13–14 is messianic, as demonstrated by both its original context and its usage by Jesus in the New Testament.

The Meaning of Daniel 7:13

Daniel 7:13 speaks of an individual who looks like a "son of man" (Aram. *kevar enash*). There is nothing unusual about this phrase, since it corresponds to the Hebrew phrase *ben adam* ("son of man") and simply means "man" (see, e.g., "son of man" in Heb 2:6). Thus, the term "son of man" in Dan 7:13 is not a title, but a description reminiscent of Ezek 1:5, 10, and 26. The description of this figure as one *resembling* a son of man testifies to the fact that although the appearance makes one think of a human being, it is not in fact describing a mere human. Since this individual comes from the heavenly sphere, the most plausible assumption (for now) is that it is a heavenly figure.

This figure receives from God authority, glory, and kingship, so that his kingdom replaces the other kingdoms mentioned in the context. Special attention must be drawn to the description "all nations and people *served* him" (Dan 7:14, author's translation) as the Aramaic word for "serve" (*yiflehun*) can have the connotation of "worship" (see, e.g., Hoffmann 1999, 89). After all, the Aramaic verb *plh* and the corresponding noun *polhan* (described in Dan 3:12, 14, 17, 28; 6:17, 21; Ezra 7:24) simply means *worship*. The Septuagint confirms this observation by reproducing the verb *plh* in Dan 7:14 with the Greek verb *latreuō* ("worship"). This description clearly qualifies the heavenly figure as divine. The kingship of this heavenly figure is described as indestructible. Here the same language is found that describes the kingdom of God in Dan 2:44 and 6:27. Therefore, the figure represents an eternal kingdom.

In Early Judaism and the New Testament

In early Judaism (the first few centuries CE), Dan 7:13–14 was—as far as we can tell from our sources—unequivocally related to the Messiah (see Hoffman 1999). This is true, on the one hand, concerning Hellenistic Judaism (see, e.g., *1 Enoch* 46:1–6; 90:37; *Dial.* 1.32). But it is also true in respect to Rabbinic Judaism. The Babylonian Talmud (*Sanhedrin* 98a) states that if Israel is worthy of the Messiah, he will come with the clouds of heaven (according to Dan 7:13–14); but if they are not worthy, he will come lowly and riding on a donkey (according to Zech 9:9). Strack and Billerbeck, after considering numerous rabbinic passages, come to the following conclusion: "Dan 7:13–14 was never interpreted by the old synagogue as the 'people of the saints' (=Israel, Dan 7:27), but consistently as the Messiah" (Strack and Billerbeck 1986, 1:956; translation mine). However, this does not mean that the term "son of man" became a messianic title.

The term *mashiah* was the usual messianic title, but it was already connected to the expectation of a victorious, ruling individual who would lead the scattered people of Israel back to their homeland and lead the nation to a new place spiritually as well (see article 6.5). By contrast, the term "son of man" in the Second Temple period was not at all a messianic title, which meant that Jesus could fill and shape it himself. Accordingly, Jesus adapted the term ("*the* son of man") in a very balanced way: sixteen times relating to his earthly life, twenty-seven times referring to his suffering, and twenty-six times referring to his glorification (see Caragounis 1986, 146).

While Jesus applied the *term* "Son of Man" from Dan 7:13–14 to the various states of his ministry, he applied the vision reported in Dan 7:13–14 (along with Zech 12:10) exclusively and unambiguously to his return (see Matt 24:30; 26:64; Luke 21:26–27). This observation confirms that Jesus understood himself as the Danielic "Son of Man."

The fact that Dan 7:13–14 speaks of a human *likeness* also supports the biblical claim about the divine sonship of Jesus. Accordingly, in John 5:25–27 there is a conscious connection between the Son of God (v. 25) and the Son of Man (v. 27). In this sense, the term "son of man" actually points to the deity of Jesus (Kim 1983).

Works Cited

Caragounis, Chrys C. 1986. *The Son of Man: Vision and Interpretation.* WUNT 38. Tübingen: Mohr Siebeck.

Casey, Maurice. 1979. *Son of Man: The Interpretation and Influence of Daniel 7.* London: SPCK.

Hoffmann, Heinrich. 1999. *Das Gesetz in der frühjüdischen Apokalyptik.* SUNT 23. Göttingen: Vandenhoeck & Ruprecht.

Kim, Seyoon. 1983. *"The Son of Man" as the Son of God*. WUNT 30. Tübingen: Mohr Siebeck.

Kmiecik, Ulrich. 1997. *Der Menschensohn im Markusevangelium*. Würzburg: Echter.

Müller, Morgens. 1978. *Der Ausdruck "Menschensohn" in den Evangelien: Voraussetzungen und Bedeutung*. ATDan 17. Leiden: Brill.

Neubauer, Fritz. 1972. *Jesus der Menschhensohn: Ein Beitrag zur Klärung der Wege historischer Wahrheitsfindung im Bereich der Evangelien*. AzTh 50 (first series). Stuttgart: Calwer.

Reynolds, Benjamin E. 2008. "The 'One Like a Son of Man' According to the Old Greek of Daniel 7:13–14." *Biblica* 89.1:70–80.

Strack, Herman L., and Paul Billerbeck. 1986. *Kommentar zum Neuen Testament aus Talmud und Midrasch*. Vols. 1–4. 8th ed. Munich: Beck.

7.3 "I Am" Statements

Andreas J. Köstenberger

Jesus' "I am" statements are a distinct feature of John's Gospel. These appear in two main categories. The first category includes seven predicate nominatives (descriptive information about the subject), such as "I am *the light of the world*" (NIV). The second category is comprised of absolute statements in which Jesus identifies himself as "I am."

Specific Statements

"I am the bread of life." The first "I am" saying in 6:35—reiterated in 6:48—forms the "narrative and theological centre of the scene" (Lee 1994, 135–36). It is part of John's narration of one of Jesus' signs, the feeding of the five thousand (6:1–15). As elsewhere, an extended discourse follows, elaborating on the significance of Jesus' actions. In this case, Jesus is revealed as none other than God, the Life-giver. Not only does Jesus miraculously provide bread as God did through Moses during the exodus, he in his very essence *is* the "bread from heaven" that gives life to the world. Earlier, Jesus had staked the astonishing claim that "just as the Father raises the dead and gives them life, so also the Son gives life to whomever he is pleased to give it," adding, "For just as the Father has life in himself, so also he has given to the Son to have life in himself" (5:21, 26). Later "I am" sayings, likewise, involve Jesus' claim to *be*—not just to *have*—life (11:25; 14:6; see also 8:12; 9:5; cf. 1:4–5; Williams 2013, 397). The present "I

am" saying culminates in Jesus' pronouncement that "whoever eats this bread will live forever" (6:58), causing the defection of many who find this claim too hard to stomach (6:60–71).

"I am the light of the world." The second "I am" statement, identifying Jesus as "the light of the world" (8:12)—reiterated in 9:5—is part of Jesus' second teaching cycle at the Feast of Tabernacles (see also Köstenberger 2009, 341–49). In Jesus' day, Tabernacles—also called the Feast of Booths—was observed as a weeklong festival celebrating the Israelites' wilderness journey at the exodus. Every day, priests would march from the pool of Siloam to the Temple in solemn procession and pour out water at the base of the altar. On the seventh day of the festival, the last day proper (Lev 23:34, 41–42), they would perform a special water-pouring and torch-lighting ceremony (*m. Sukkah* 4:1, 9–10). Then, on the eighth day, a sacred assembly was held. It included offering sacrifices, dismantling booths, and repeatedly singing the Hallel (Pss 113–18). The "I am" statement invokes the distinctive Johannine contrast between light and darkness, connecting with (1) the prologue's reference to Jesus as the preexistent Word through whom God created the world (1:3–5); (2) Jesus' fulfillment of Tabernacles symbolism (ch. 7; cf. *m. Sukkah* 5:2–4); (3) the healing of the man born blind (9:4–5); (4) the raising of Lazarus (11:9–10); and (5) the contrast between spiritual life and death in conjunction with Jewish unbelief (12:35–36; cf. vv. 37–50). Moreover, along with the manna (ch. 6) and rivers of living water (ch. 7), the reference to Jesus as "light" in chapter 8 is part of a "wilderness theme," which alludes to God's presence with the Israelites as a pillar of fire. [See Figures 22–23.]

"I am the gate." The third "I am" saying in 10:7—reiterated in 10:9—is given in the context of Jesus' "Good Shepherd" discourse. The lack of transition between chapters 9 and 10 suggests that the Pharisees who are mentioned at the end of chapter 9 (vv. 40–41) are still in view in the opening verses of chapter 10, where Jesus posits a contrast between illegitimate shepherds who "do not enter the sheep pen through the gate" and the legitimate shepherd—Jesus himself—who "enters through the gate" (v. 1). Then, in verse 7, Jesus shifts the metaphor: while in verse 1 the shepherd enters *through* the gate, in verse 7 the shepherd *is* the gate through whom the sheep enter, culminating in Jesus' assertion, "I am the gate; whoever enters through me will be saved, and will go in and out and find pasture" (v. 9). This saying, in turn, anticipates Jesus' later assertion, "I am the way" (14:6), maintaining that Jesus alone provides access to God and to the believing community. There are many rich connections between chapter 10 and (1) Old Testament figures such as Jacob (Gen 28:17: "the gate of heaven"; cf. John 1:51) and Joshua ("go out and come in"; Num 27:16–17), (2) the depiction of God as Israel's shepherd (e.g., Ps 23:1) and of Israel as God's sheep (e.g., Ps 100:3), and (3) Ezekiel's denunciation of the "shepherds of Israel who only take care of themselves" and "do not take care of the flock" (Ezek 34:2–4).

"I am the good shepherd." Closely associated with the third "I am" saying is the fourth such statement, found in 10:11 and 14, by which Jesus identifies himself as the "good shepherd." As mentioned, *"good* shepherd" implies a contrast with Israel's *faithless* shepherds, the religious leaders who pursued self-interest rather than genuinely caring for God's people (Jer 23:1–4; cf. 3:15; Ezek 34; Zech 11:4–17). As the "good shepherd," Jesus stands in an Old Testament trajectory that includes both Yahweh himself (e.g., Gen 48:15; 49:24; Ps 23:1; Isa 40:11; Jer 31:10; Ezek 34:11–31) as well as human "shepherds" such as Moses (Isa 63:11; cf. Ps 77:20) and David or the Davidic Messiah (2 Sam 5:2; Ps 78:70–72; Ezek 37:24; Mic 5:4; cf. Psalms of Solomon 17:40–41; *Exodus Rabbah* 2.2 on Exod 3:1). Verse 14 further develops the saying in verse 11 with regard to Jesus' sacrificial death on behalf of his "sheep"; verse 16 then expands the scope of Jesus' saving and shepherding activity beyond Israel to the gentiles, with the result that there will be "one flock, one shepherd" (v. 16, an allusion to Ezek 34:23; 37:24; cf. John 11:52; Köstenberger 2002).

"I am the resurrection and the life." The fifth "I am" saying, affirming that Jesus is the resurrection and the life (11:25), is given in the context of the raising of Lazarus. Jesus has identified himself as the Life-giver previously in the first "I am" saying (6:35; see discussion above). Again, the pronouncement is made in conjunction with one of Jesus' messianic signs. By this seventh, climactic sign, John shows that Jesus has the authority to give life (cf. 10:15, 17–18). In the context of John's realized eschatology, Martha serves as a representative of conventional Jewish thinking about the end times which divided history into "the present age" and "the age to come" (e.g., 2 Maccabees 7:9; *1 Enoch* 103:1–104:9; *2 Enoch* 66:6–8; Bauckham 1998). John, however, avers that this distinction collapsed when applied to Jesus because in him the future had already arrived—he was going to raise Lazarus *right then*, not only in the age to come (Köstenberger, Stewart, and Makara 2017). The reason he could do so is because he, in his very essence, is the resurrection and the life.

"I am the way and the truth and the life." The sixth "I am" statement, given in the context of the Farewell Discourse, involves Jesus' self-affirmation that he is "the way and the truth and the life" (14:6). "Way," "truth," and "life" frequently occur in conjunction with one another in the Old Testament wisdom literature (e.g., Pss 16:11; 86:11; 119:30; Prov 15:24). The sect at Qumran understood itself to be "the way" or those who had chosen "the way" (1QS 8:12–16; 9:17–20), in likely allusion to Isa 40:3 (cited in the New Testament with reference to John the Baptist; e.g., John 1:23). The early Christians were similarly called followers of "the Way" (Acts 9:2; 19:9, 23; 22:4; 24:14, 22). Jesus' claim of being "the way" asserts that he alone, through his vicarious death on the cross, can restore believers to a right relationship with God. His claim to *be* the truth and the life—not merely to *know* truth and to *have* life—sets him apart and designates

him as the very incarnation of truth and life (1:14, 17; cf. Pilate's question later in the Gospel: "What is truth?"; John 18:38).

"*I am the true vine.*" The seventh and final "I am" statement in John's Gospel is found in 15:1 where Jesus identifies himself as "the true vine" against the backdrop of the Old Testament depiction of Israel as God's vineyard (e.g., Ps 80:8; Isa 5:1–7; 27:2–6; Jer 2:21; Ezek 17:6–8). While God's intention was for Israel to be fruitful, the nation tragically did not live up to God's purpose. By claiming to be "the true vine," Jesus affirmed that he was going to yield the fruit Israel failed to produce. Thus, Jesus here identifies himself as the new and true Israel. This does not mean that the church will replace Israel but rather that God's blessings to his people—in keeping with his promises to Abraham and David—will be mediated through Jesus, the true Israel (cf. 11:24). Jesus' followers, likewise, are to produce and help reap an abundant spiritual harvest (15:8, 16; cf. 4:35–38; Matt 9:37–38).

Absolute Statements

John's Gospel also features several important instances where the phrase "I am" is not complemented by a descriptive phrase indicating what kind of Messiah Jesus is (Williams 2013, 398). Rather, in these instances Jesus simply claims to be "I am." These statements are of crucial importance, since Jesus here consciously invokes the name of God—"I am"—in the Hebrew Scriptures (cf. Exod 3:14–15; Deut 32:39; and frequently in Isa 40–66: e.g., 41:4; 43:10–13, 25; 45:18; 46:4; 48:12; 51:12; 52:6; Ball 1996, 188–95; Williams 2000, 271–73).

At the same time, the phrase "I am" can simply mean, "It is I." In a work such as John's Gospel where *double entendre* is commonplace, there may be instances where both meanings—Jesus appropriating the divine name *and* a simple self-identification—are in play. Below is a list of all major instances of the absolute use of "I am" in John's Gospel grouped according to the likelihood that they involve a divine self-reference, followed by a very brief commentary (italicized; taken from Köstenberger 2013, 247–48; used by publisher's permission):

(1) *Virtually certain:*

    a.   8:58: "Very truly I tell you, before Abraham was born, I am!" *The reaction of Jesus' Jewish opponents—they pick up stones to stone him—makes clear that they took Jesus' statement as involving a claim to deity.*

    b.   18:5–6: "Who is it you want?" "Jesus of Nazareth," they replied. "I am [he]," Jesus said. When Jesus said, "I am [he]," they drew back and fell to the ground. *On one level, this is a simple self-identification: "It is I!" At the same time, the soldiers' response to Jesus' words indicates that they also involved a manifestation of his deity (a theophany; cf., e.g., Gen 17:3; Lev 9:24; Judg 13:20; Ezek 1:28).*

(2) *Highly probable:*

    a.   6:20: "But he said to them, 'It is I; don't be afraid'" (cf. Matt 14:27; Mark 6:50). *Again, on one level this is a mere self-reference. But, as the preceding verse tells us, Jesus was walking on the water when he made this statement, exercising God's power over the elements (cf. Job 9:8; Ps 77:20; Hab 3:15; Williams 2013, 396).*

    b.   8:24, 28: "If you do not believe that I am he, you will indeed die in your sins"; "Then you will know that I am he." *The least that can be said here is that apart from insinuations of deity this would be a somewhat awkward statement, which makes a divine self-reference likely.*

    c.   13:19: "I am telling you now before it happens, so that when it does happen you will believe that I am who I am." *This is another emphatic declaration that appears to involve more than mere self-reference.*

(3) *Possible:*

    a.   4:26: "I, the one speaking to you—I am he" [i.e., the Messiah]. *Possibly the absolute use of "I am" here involves reference to deity. At a minimum, Jesus here affirms that he is the Messiah.*

    b.   8:18: "I am one who testifies for myself; my other witness is the Father, who sent me." *The reference is not dissimilar to 8:24, 28 (see above), so that divine self-reference cannot be ruled out.*

An additional instance of an absolute "I am" statement is found in the Synoptics, where the high priest asks Jesus, "Are you the Christ, the Son of the Blessed?" at his Jewish trial. Jesus' response: "I am, and you will see the Son of Man sitting at the right hand of the Mighty One and coming on the clouds of heaven" (Mark 14:61–62). The high priest promptly tears his robes and charges Jesus with blasphemy, and the entire Sanhedrin concurs and pronounces the death sentence (v. 64; cf. Matt 26:63–66). Jesus' use of "I am" was clearly taken as a use of the divine name and perceived as blasphemy, which prompted this extreme response.

Together with various other indications of Jesus' deity in John's Gospel, his "I am" sayings and absolute "I am" statements impressively underscore the central claim in the Gospel that "Jesus is the Christ, the Son of God," and that those who believe in him "may have life in his name" (John 20:31). In addition, Jesus' use of the divine name points to a claim of deity on par with Yahweh, the Creator and covenant-keeping God of Israel.

Works Cited

Ball, David. 1996. *"I Am" in John's Gospel*. JSNTSup 124. Sheffield: Sheffield Academic.

Bauckham, Richard. 1998. "Life, Death, and the Afterlife in Second Temple Judaism." Pages 80–95 in *Life in the Face of Death: The Resurrection Message of the New Testament*. Edited by Richard N. Longenecker. Grand Rapids: Eerdmans.

Köstenberger, Andreas J. 2002. "Jesus the Good Shepherd Who Will Also Bring Other Sheep (John 10:16): The Old Testament Background of a Familiar Metaphor." *BBR* 12:67–96.

———. 2009. *A Theology of John's Gospel and Letters: The Word, the Christ, the Son of God*. Biblical Theology of the New Testament. Grand Rapids: Zondervan.

———. 2013. *Encountering John: The Gospel in Historical, Literary, and Theological Perspective*. 2nd ed. Encountering Biblical Studies. Grand Rapids: Baker Academic.

Köstenberger, Andreas J., Alexander E. Stewart, and Apollo Makara. 2017. *Jesus and the Future: Understanding What He Taught about the End Times*. Bellingham, WA: Lexham Press.

Lee, Dorothy A. 1994. *The Symbolic Narratives of the Fourth Gospel: The Interplay of Form and Meaning*. JSNTSup 95. Sheffield: JSOT Press.

Williams, Catrin H. 2000. *I Am He: The Interpretation of 'ani hu' in Jewish and Early Christian Literature*. WUNT 2/113. Tübingen: Mohr Siebeck.

———. 2013. "I Am Sayings." *DJG* 396–99.

7.4 Trials and Crucifixion

Andreas J. Köstenberger

Jesus' final week culminated in his trials and death sentence, followed by his crucifixion (for relevant texts and commentary, see Chapman and Schnabel 2015). Based on what we know about how trials were conducted in first-century Palestine, the Gospels provide historically accurate accounts of Jesus' trials (Matt 26:57–27:26; Mark 14:53–15:5; Luke 22:54–23:25; John 18:12–14, 19–24; 18:28–19:16; Bock 2007, 53–56; Cohick 2013, 978–79), narrating two interrogations, a Jewish trial (in two phases) followed by a Roman one (Bammel 1970; Cohick 2013, 972–79).

Informal Hearing before Annas

The Jewish trial started with an informal hearing before Annas the high priest (John 18:12–14, 19–24). Later, the Sanhedrin convened for a more official trial (Matt 26:57–68; Mark 14:53–65), resulting in formal charges. After this, a delegation was sent to Pilate who, as the Roman governor, needed to ratify the capital sentence (Matt 27:1–2; Luke 22:66–71; see below). Also, because no executions could take place on the Sabbath (*b. Sanhedrin* 35b; Dalman 1929, 98–100), little time—less than 24 hours—remained after Jesus' arrest late Thursday evening to put him on trial and to execute him prior to the beginning of Sabbath at sundown the next day. In addition, Roman officials like Pilate worked only until late morning (Sherwin-White 1963, 45), so the case against Jesus needed to be prepared posthaste (Carson 1991, 574; Egger 1997).

John alone records Jesus' appearance before Annas. Apparently, Jesus was first led to Annas due to Annas's abiding status and influence. Annas had served as high priest from 6 CE until 15 CE, having been appointed by Quirinius, Roman prefect and governor of Syria. He was removed by Valerius Gratus (15–26 CE), Pilate's predecessor (Josephus, *Ant.* 18.34). In the years that followed, at least five of Annas's sons served as high priests, as well as his son-in-law, Joseph Caiaphas (*Ant.* 20.197–198; Carson 1991, 580–81). Because the Mosaic legislation stipulated that the high priestly appointment was for life (Num 35:25; cf. *m. Horayot* 3:4; *m. Megillah* 1:9; *m. Makkot* 2:6; *t. Yoma* 1.4), many still viewed Annas as the real high priest (Josephus, *J.W.* 2.243; cf. 4.151–160; *m. Horayot* 3:1–2, 4). The fact that Jesus was queried directly suggests an informal hearing (Carson 1991, 584), because in formal trials a case rested on witness testimony by persons other than the accused (e.g., *m. Sanhedrin* 6:2). The focus on Jesus' teaching and disciples indicates that the leaders' primary concern was theological, notwithstanding the political charges presented to Pilate (cf. John 19:7, 12). The authorities apparently viewed Jesus as a false prophet who lured people away from the pure worship of Yahweh (Luke 23:2; cf. *b. Sanhedrin* 43a)—a capital offense (Deut 13:1–11). Annas, it seems, hoped Jesus might incriminate himself in this regard (Strobel 1980, 85).

Formal Trial before Caiaphas and the Sanhedrin

For the formal trial to proceed, Jesus needed to be brought to Caiaphas—who, as the high priest that year, presided over the Sanhedrin—and to "all the chief priests, the elders and the teachers of the law" making up the Jewish supreme council (Mark 14:53 NIV; Alexander 1988, esp. 46–49; Schürer 1973–1987, 2:199–226). The trial (narrated in Mark 14:53–65, slightly expanded in Matt 26:57–68, and significantly condensed in Luke 22:66–71) begins with the interrogation of witnesses (Matt 26:59–61; Mark 14:56–59; cf. Susanna 44–62; *m. Sanhedrin* 5:1–5; Chapman and Schnabel 2015, 83–86, 92–96). After a prolonged period of inconclusive testimony, some charge Jesus with speaking against the Temple, saying, "We heard him say, 'I will destroy this temple made with human hands and in three days will build another, not made with hands'" (Mark 14:58; cf. Matt 26:59–61). This calls to mind Jesus' statement at the Temple clearing featured in John 2:13–22, "Destroy this temple, and I will raise it again in three days" (v. 19; cf. esp. Mark 15:29 // Matt 27:40; see also Matt 12:6; 24:2 // Mark 13:2). If, as is likely, the Temple clearing recorded in John had taken place over three years earlier, this would help explain the lack of consistency in the witnesses' testimony (Morris 1995, 168).

When challenged by the high priest to *answer* the charges, Jesus remained silent (Matt 26:62–63a; Mark 14:60–61a; cf. Isa 53:7; Moo 1983, 148–51). Then Caiaphas asked Jesus *directly*, "Are you the Messiah, the Son of the Blessed One?" (Mark 14:61b; cf. Matt 26:63b, which adds that the high priest charged Jesus "under oath by the living God"). Jesus answered affirmatively (lifting the "messianic secret" in Mark): "I am," adding, "And you will see the Son of Man sitting at the right hand of the Mighty One and coming on the clouds of heaven" (Mark 14:62 // Matt 26:64). With this, Jesus applied both Dan 7:13–14 and Ps 110:1–2 to himself, lodging two claims. First, he affirmed that the rulers will see him exalted to a place of honor and authority belonging to God alone. While Jewish literature refers to other figures in exalted positions—"the Son of Man" in the Enochic literature (e.g., *1 Enoch* 62:3), Job (*Testament of Job* 33:2–4), Enoch, Seth, Abraham, Isaac, and Jacob (*Testament of Benjamin* 10:5–6)—who received honor from God, Jesus affirmed that he will share in God's eternal rule. Because of his claim to possess what was rightfully God's alone, the leaders regarded Jesus as guilty of blasphemy (cf. Philo, *Dreams* 2.130–131; *Decalogue* 61–64). Second, Jesus' words may have called to mind the language of passages such as *1 Enoch* 62:3–5, according to which the Son of Man is seated on a throne, executing judgment. If so, the Jewish leaders would have likely taken offense at Jesus sitting in judgment over them, believing this violated Exod 22:28 (Bock 2007, 74–85, 107–9, 112–13).

At this, the high priest tears his clothes and exclaims: "Why do we need any more witnesses?" Addressing the assembled members of the Sanhedrin, he asks: "You have heard the blasphemy. What do you think?" (Mark 14:63–64a // Matt 26:65). At this, the council condemns Jesus as worthy to die because of *blasphemy* (Matt 26:66; Mark 14:64b). John's Gospel features a series of occasions throughout Jesus' ministry at which the Jewish leaders charge Jesus with blasphemy (John 5:18; 8:59; 10:31, 33), culminating in their statement before Pilate: "We have a law, and according to that law he must die, because he claimed to be the Son of God" (John 19:7). However, the claim of being God's son need not be blasphemous, but may be legitimately used as an epithet for the anointed king of Israel (2 Sam 7:14; Pss 2:7; 89:26–27) or the Messiah (4Q174 1:10–12; Michel 1978, 3:637). Jewish law required the declaration of God's name for a person to be found guilty of blasphemy (*m. Sanhedrin* 7:5), though most likely the larger culture defined blasphemy more broadly (Bock 2007, 56–57; Collins 2006, 151–65).

Before Pilate

Following his narrative of Jesus' Jewish trial, Mark writes, "Very early in the morning, the chief priests, with the elders, the teachers of the law and the whole Sanhedrin . . . bound Jesus, led him away and handed him over to Pilate" (Mark 15:1; cf. Matt 27:1–2). Some take this as an indication of a second formal Jewish trial, but it is more likely that this simply refers to the formal arraignment of Jesus and the Sanhedrin's ratification to proceed with the next phase of the proceedings against him. Consequently, they hand him over to the Roman governor, who alone can pronounce the "guilty" verdict and impose a capital sentence (cf. Cohick 2013, 973–74). While Pilate fails to find grounds for the charges against Jesus, he eventually yields to the pressure put on him by the Jewish authorities to find Jesus guilty as charged and pronounces the death sentence. With this, Jesus is led away to be crucified (for Pilate's involvement, see Matt 27:2, 11–26; Mark 15:1–15; Luke 23:1–15, including an informal hearing before Herod Antipas in vv. 6–12; John 18:28–19:16).

Crucifixion

Crucifixion (from Latin *crux*, "cross," and *figere*, "attach")—an "executionary suspension of a person on a cross-shaped object" (Chapman 2008, 32; cf. Cook 2014, 2–4)—was a severe form of capital punishment practiced in the ancient world by "Persians, Assyrians, Scythians, Indians, Carthaginians, Celts, Britons and Germans" (Dennis 2013, 173).

The Jewish people in Jesus' day were well acquainted with the practice of crucifixion due to its use by the Romans and even some Hasmonean leaders. As to the latter, Josephus records an instance when Alexander Jannaeus crucified eight hundred Jews, who had rebelled against him, in the center of Jerusalem, and then went on to kill their wives and children as well, watching the events while cavorting with his concubines (*J. W.* 1.97–98; *Ant.* 13.380). The fate of crucifixion was considered so horrible that a group of Jews besieged in Machaerus in 71 CE were willing to surrender to the Romans to prevent the crucifixion of one of their compatriots who had been captured (Josephus, *J.W.* 7.202–203; Chapman 2008, 96). As a deterrent, the Romans erected crosses near major thoroughfares and typically left crucified individuals on the cross until they died (which sometimes took days) and vultures devoured their bodies (Josephus, *J.W.* 5.449–451).

There are no records of crucifixion in the Hebrew Scriptures, though reference is made to the practice of impaling victims, either before or after they died. Some of these texts were later interpreted in terms of crucifixion (e.g., Gen 40:19; Num 25:4; Deut 21:22–23; Est 9:25; Chapman 2008, 97, 101–70). Jews regarded crucifixion with horror (e.g., 4Q169 frags. 3–4 i 6–8: "It is horrible for the one hanged alive from the tree"). Execution on a cross was viewed as equivalent to hanging, so early Christians could refer to Jesus' crucifixion in terms of him being "hanged on a tree" (Acts 5:30; 10:39), and Mosaic law stated that "Anyone who is hung on a pole is under God's curse" (Deut 21:23; cf. Gal 3:13). The syntax of Deut 21:23 is ambiguous and was variously interpreted as referring to one who is cursed by God or one who curses God (i.e., a blasphemer), with the former being the earliest recorded view and the latter being the more common rabbinic view. In either case, it appears that in later times rabbis made a connection between crucifixion and blasphemy and/or being cursed by God based on this passage (*m. Sanhedrin* 6:4–5; 11Q19 64:6–13; Chapman 2008, 121–49, 216–17; Dennis 2013, 174).

The Crucifixion of Jesus

The crucifixion of Jesus took place in either 30 or 33 CE, with the latter date being more likely (the precise date would be April 3, 33 CE; Köstenberger and Taylor 2014; Hoehner and Brown 2013, 137–38). If the Sanhedrin had put Jesus to death, the mode of execution would most likely have been stoning, the penalty specified in the Old Testament for blasphemy (Lev 24:16). In Jesus' day, as mentioned, the Sanhedrin had no power to impose capital punishment (instances of mob lynching or authority breaches are no real exceptions; cf. Josephus, *J.W.* 2.117; *Ant.* 20.197–203), and "capital punishment was the most jealously guarded of all governmental powers" (Sherwin-White 1963, 36; see discussion at 24–47). Romans normally stripped crucified persons naked, though in deference to the Jewish aversion to public nudity Jesus was left with his undergarment.

Culminating with the passion narratives, the crucifixion of Jesus is narrated in all four Gospels at some length, though with remarkable restraint (Matt 27:27–56; Mark 15:16–41; Luke 23:26–49; John 19:16–37). The evangelists, particularly

John, repeatedly draw attention to the fulfillment of Old Testament prophecy in the various details surrounding Jesus' crucifixion, no doubt because Jewish readers would have been sceptical regarding a crucified Messiah (Carson 1991, 612). This includes (see detailed discussion in Köstenberger 2007, 500–506):

(1) The Roman soldiers dividing Jesus' clothes among them and casting lots for his garment (John 19:24; cf. Ps 22:18, a Davidic messianic passage on the righteous sufferer; Carson 1991, 614);

(2) The soldiers giving Jesus vinegar for his thirst (John 19:28; cf. Ps 69:21);

(3) Jesus' cry of dereliction and abandonment (Mark 15:34; cf. Ps 22:1);

(4) The piercing of Jesus' side, eliciting a flow of blood and water (John 19:34; cf. Exod 17:6; Num 20:11; Carson 1991, 624);

(5) Jesus' death as a Passover lamb, involving hyssop (John 19:29), intact bones (John 19:33, 36; cf. Exod 12:46; Num 9:12; Ps 34:20; 1 Cor 5:7; 1 Pet 1:19), and mingled blood (John 19:34; cf. *m. Pesahim* 5.5–8; *m. Ohalot* 3.5); and

(6) People looking at the pierced Jesus (John 19:37; cf. Zech 12:10; Rev 1:7). While the passage in Zechariah originally referred to the piercing of Yahweh (with sorrow), this notion later led to the belief that the Messiah would be pierced and people would look to Yahweh (*b. Sukkah* 52a); similarly, the suffering servant of Isa 53:5, 10 was "pierced for our transgressions" and "crushed" and "caused to suffer."

The Meaning of the Crucifixion

Jesus' death, together with his resurrection, forms the climax in all four Gospels, as the vicarious atonement and penal substitution provided by the Son of God for the sins of the world. Through him, God's wrath on sinners is appeased and believers are provided redemption, reconciled with God, and placed in a right relationship with him (e.g., Mark 10:45; Rom 3:25; 1 John 2:2).

The early Christians believed that Jesus' death was the product of collaboration between the Jewish authorities and the Romans—representing the non-Jewish world—in keeping with biblical prophecy, according to the predetermined sovereign plan of God (Acts 2:23–24; 4:25–26; cf. Ps 2:1–2). But the cross stands as an abiding testimony to God's love for a sinful world in Christ (John 3:16), and Jesus stands ready to forgive both Jews and gentiles, anyone who comes to him in heartfelt repentance and faith. As the dying Jesus prayed on the cross, "Father, forgive them, for they do not know what they are doing" (Luke 23:34).

Works Cited

Alexander, Philip S. 1988. "Jewish Law in the Time of Jesus: Towards a Clarification of the Problem." Pages 44–58 in *Law and Religion: Essays on the Place of the Law in Israel and Early Christianity*. Edited by Barnabas Lindars. Cambridge: Clarke.

Bammel, Ernst, ed. 1970. *The Trial of Jesus: Cambridge Studies in Honour of C. F. D. Moule*. SBT 2/13. London: SCM.

Bock, Darrell L. 2007. "Blasphemy and the Jewish Examination of Jesus." *BBR* 17:53–114.

Carson, D. A. 1991. *The Gospel according to John*. PNTC. Grand Rapids: Eerdmans.

Chapman, David W. 2008. *Ancient Jewish and Christian Perceptions of Crucifixion*. WUNT 2/244. Tübingen: Mohr Siebeck.

Chapman, David W., and Eckhard J. Schnabel. 2015. *The Trial and Crucifixion of Jesus: Texts and Commentary*. WUNT 344. Tübingen: Mohr Siebeck.

Cohick, Lynn H. 2013. "Trial of Jesus." *DJG* 972–79.

Collins, Adela Yarbro. 2006. "The Charge of Blasphemy in Mark 14:65." Pages 149–70 in *The Trial and Death of Jesus: Essays on the Passion Narrative in Mark*. Edited by Gert Van Oyen and Tom Shepherd. Leuven: Peeters.

Cook, John Granger. 2014. *Crucifixion in the Mediterranean World*. WUNT 327. Tübingen: Mohr Siebeck.

Dalman, Gustaf. 1929. *Jesus–Jeshua: Studies in the Gospels*. London: SPCK.

Dennis, J. 2013. "Death of Jesus." *DJG* 172–93.

Egger, Peter. 1997. *Crucifixus sub Pontio Pilato*. NTAbh 32. Münster: Aschendorff.

Hoehner, H. W., and Jeannine K. Brown. 2013. "Chronology." *DJG* 134–38.

Köstenberger, Andreas J. 2007. "John." Pages 415–512 in *Commentary on the New Testament Use of the Old Testament*. Edited by G. K. Beale and D. A. Carson. Grand Rapids: Baker Academic.

Köstenberger, Andreas J., and Justin Taylor. 2014. *The Final Days of Jesus: The Most Important Week of the Most Important Person Who Ever Lived*. Wheaton: Crossway.

Michel, Otto. 1978. "Son." *NIDNTT* 3:636–37.

Moo, Douglas J. 1983. *The Old Testament in the Gospel Passion Narratives*. Sheffield: Almond Press.

Morris, Leon. 1995. *The Gospel according to John*. 2nd ed. NICNT. Grand Rapids: Eerdmans.

Schürer, Emil. 1973–1987. *The History of the Jewish People in the Age of Jesus Christ*. 4 vols. Revised and edited by Geza Vermes, Fergus Millar, and Matthew Black. New York: T&T Clark.

Sherwin-White, A. N. 1963. *Roman Society and Roman Law in the New Testament*. Oxford: Oxford University Press.

Strobel, August. 1980. *Die Stunde der Wahrheit*. WUNT 21. Tübingen: Mohr Siebeck.

7.5 Early Jesus-Devotion

Larry W. Hurtado

Jesus was the focus and main subject of proclamation for the original disciples. This continued to be the case among Jesus-believers who came later. In addition (and in my view even more remarkably), Jesus also featured distinctively in their devotional practices. Indeed, in our earliest extant evidence, the undisputed letters of Paul (ca. 50–65 CE), there is already what may be characterized as a remarkable "dyadic" devotional pattern in place (and even taken for granted) among various circles of the young Christian movement. In this pattern, the risen Jesus was included programmatically along with God as a rightful recipient. So, what connection was there between the proclamation and devotional practices of Jesus-believers in the "post-Easter" period and Jesus' own proclamation and activities (see Hengel 1995, 1–72; Allison 2010, 221–304)?

In my opinion, several forces and factors likely prompted and shaped early post-Easter Jesus-devotion, among them Jesus himself, particularly the impact of his person and actions (see Hurtado 2003, 27–78, 53–64). As I've written previously, "whatever may have been Jesus' intentions . . . , the *effect* of his public activity was very much to polarize a good many of his contemporaries over the question of how to regard him, whether to take a negative or positive stance about him" (55). During his ministry, some individuals became his devoted followers, throwing in their lot with him in his ministry and deferring to him as their master. Others, however, judged him dangerous, both among the Jewish religious authorities and the Roman political regime, and of these some even went so far as to execute him. This clearly reflects a strong polarization over the validity and significance of Jesus' person and activities! It is commonly agreed among scholars that Jesus proclaimed "the kingdom of God." Clearly, however, already during his ministry he himself (not simply his proclamation about the kingdom of God) became the issue that could not be avoided. But can we say more about the connection between Jesus' ministry and subsequent Jesus-devotion?

Before addressing this question, however, I think it important to emphasize that I treat it here as a historical question, not a theological one. Granted, a good many Christians and non-Christians as well assume today that the *theological/ religious* validity of Christian claims about Jesus rest upon whether he himself made equivalent claims during his ministry. So, for some, the theological legitimacy of treating Jesus as sharing divine glory and being worthy of worship rests upon whether he declared himself divine and demanded worship. But this is a fallacy, both theologically and historically. For the early christological claims reflected in the New Testament rest upon convictions about *God's* affirmation of Jesus, demonstrated in raising him from death and exalting him to heavenly glory. In historical terms, it was primarily these convictions about God's actions that fired the post-Easter claims about Jesus' high status and significance, and that also generated the inclusion of the exalted Jesus in the devotional practices of earliest believers. In theological terms as well, the christological claims of earliest believers rested primarily upon claims about God (Hurtado 2010). Indeed, what mattered most to these early believers was not whether Jesus had proclaimed his own glory and demanded reverence, but that God had given Jesus glory and now required him to be reverenced (Acts 2:36; Phil 2:9–11; Heb 1:3–4; 1 Pet 1:21).

Starting with the Basics

But let us return to the historical question of how Jesus' ministry was related to, and contributed to, the subsequent Jesus-devotion that burst forth early in the post-Easter period. We can begin with what is probably the most assured historical datum about Jesus, his crucifixion under Pontius Pilate. Although some have proposed that Jesus' execution should be viewed simply as a serious administrative error, perhaps an overreaction by nervous authorities during the high-tension period of the Passover, such ideas seem somewhat fanciful.

Instead, we must accept that Jesus' execution by the Roman governor means that Jesus was found guilty of a very serious offense against the Roman order. The Gospels accounts have Jesus executed as "King of the Jews" (Matt 27:37; Mark 15:26; Luke 23:38; John 19:19), which corresponds to the charge of sedition, and would account very well for both Jesus' execution and its form, by crucifixion (Hengel 1977). Moreover, "king of the Jews" is best taken as the Roman reflection of a royal-messianic claim. That is, in Jewish terms, Jesus was charged with claiming to be the royal Messiah, the heir of King David. As an alternative, it is equally plausible that Jesus did not directly articulate a messianic claim himself, but that, nevertheless, his ministry generated strong messianic expectation and claims among his followers; and these claims about him may have been what led to his arrest. But even so, at the very least Jesus must not have disassociated himself from these claims when he was arraigned, and so went to his death as a messianic claimant (Dahl 1991, 42–45).

As numerous scholars have observed, all of this accounts best for the subsequent proclamation that Jesus is the Messiah, which seems to have erupted early after Jesus' execution, and as the direct consequence of the experiences that communicated God's resurrection of Jesus from death, such as visions of the risen and exalted Jesus (Hengel 1995). By itself, of course, a resurrection does not signify messiahship. But if Jesus had been put to death as a (false and failed) messiah, then the conviction that God had raised Jesus from death and exalted him to heavenly glory would readily be taken as the divine vindication of Messiah Jesus.

Although often attempted, it is difficult to fathom the specific workings of the historical Jesus' mind, especially when all we have are reports about him written several decades after his ministry. But we can make some basic conclusions. In particular, to underscore the point, we can confidently observe that Jesus was condemned to a horrible death on the charge of being a royal-messianic pretender, a charge that he apparently did not deny, and that his ministry generated both committed followers who saw him as their authoritative leader and individuals in religious and political authority who judged Jesus a sufficient danger to execute him by the most humiliating measure in the Roman arsenal. It is worth noting the contrast with Josephus's account of the treatment of Jesus, son of Ananias, who predicted the divine destruction of the Jerusalem Temple (*J.W.* 6.301–309). He was brought to the governor (Albinus), flayed with scourges and interrogated, and then released. Obviously, Jesus of Nazareth was seen as guilty of something much more serious.

It is also noteworthy that the authorities thought it sufficient to execute only Jesus, and not to round up his followers as well (Fredricksen 2007, 415–19). This is further indication that the person of Jesus was the issue, and that eliminating him was judged both necessary and adequate to deal with the problem he had generated for the authorities. Consequently, the focus on Jesus from the earliest post-Easter proclamation of Jewish believers onward was not something new, because Jesus had already become the polarizing issue during his ministry. And, as we have noted, the early emphasis specifically on Jesus' royal-messianic status, likewise, seems to have had its roots in Jesus' ministry. That is, Jesus likely held, and expressed in his actions, the conviction that he was (or would be designated by God in the future) the Messiah. In the vivid words of Dale Allison (2010, 303–4): "when [Jesus] looked into the future, he saw thrones, including one for himself," and so "We should hold a funeral for the view that Jesus entertained no exalted thoughts about himself."

Another basic matter now widely accepted is that Jesus typically used "the son of man" as his preferred self-referential expression. It is important to note that the Greek form is a particularizing or emphatic construction, "*the* son of man," and that this likely reflects an equivalent Aramaic expression, which also conveys a particularizing/emphatic force in Jesus' setting (Shepherd 2011, 50–60; Owen 2011, 28–49). "Son of man" is, of course, a familiar Semitic way of designating a human. But, as a self-referential term, the *emphatic* singular form of the Greek expression in the Gospels (and its Aramaic equivalent) connotes a particularity, *the* human. Both in Greek and in Aramaic, these emphatic forms are highly unusual, and so it appears that Jesus coined this emphatic form as his characteristic self-designation in various statements to connote a special significance attached to him and his actions (Hurtado 2011). It was not an established title in Jewish tradition. The particularity of "the son of man" accords with the conclusion offered above that Jesus generated messianic expectations arising from his actions and his sayings, including this distinctive self-referential expression.

"High Christology"

Scholars often use the term "high Christology" to designate New Testament claims that Jesus shares with God (in whatever manner) in divine glory and status, and that it is proper, or even necessary, to treat him as a recipient of cultic devotion (worship). These phenomena comprise a transition beyond any typical view of what "Messiah" meant in Second Temple Judaism. The closest analogy is the messianic figure of *1 Enoch* 37–71, who is portrayed as chosen from the creation, and is to be given authority over all the earth. But this passage of *1 Enoch* is a body of dream-vision material about a figure to be revealed at some future point, whereas early Jesus-devotion comprises a real historical development. Also, it is not actually clear that the *1 Enoch* visions project an equivalent cultic devotion onto this mysterious figure.

If we turn again to our earliest evidence for illustrations, Paul's undisputed letters (ca. 50–65 CE), we see several christological terms that seem to have been characteristic of the beliefs of earliest circles of believers. Granted, Paul most frequently refers to Jesus as *Christos* (a curious Greek term which, contrary to the assumptions of many, retains in Paul's usage a messianic connotation), reflecting what may have been the earliest christological claim (Witherington 1993; Novenson 2012). As we have noted, this claim originally was a confident reaffirmation of the messianic hopes about Jesus that were first generated among his followers and reacted to by opponents during his ministry. The messianic claim, above all others, expressed Jesus' relationship to his ancestral people and to biblical hopes for a universal recognition of Israel's God among the nations as well. This is how references to Jesus as Messiah (*Christos*) continued to be meaningful in Paul's gentile mission: Through the gospel about Messiah Jesus, the nations were being brought to the light of the true God (Novenson 2009; Fredricksen 2017).

In addition, although Paul refers to Jesus' divine sonship less frequently, this designation seems to have carried a particularly strong meaning for Paul, as reflected, for example, in his brief description of the cognitive content of the "revelation" that turned him from opponent to avid proponent of the gospel: It was God's revelation of "his Son" (Gal 1:16). Note that in all instances where Paul refers to Jesus as God's Son he uses the definite article, connoting Jesus as *the* Son par excellence. Note also Paul's poignant reference to Jesus as "the Son of God who loved me and gave himself for me" (Gal 2:20 NRSV). In Rom 1:3–4, Paul refers to Jesus as "son of David according to the flesh" and also "designated/

appointed the Son of God in power according to the Spirit of holiness by resurrection from the dead" (author's translation). Given that Paul appears to treat Jesus as God's unique Son prior to his resurrection (e.g., Rom 8:3, 32; Gal 4:4), we should probably see the emphasis in his statement in Romans 1:4 as this: By raising Jesus from the dead, God designated him as his unique Son "*in power*" (*en dynamei*), that is, divinely confirmed and declared, and empowered now to rule (cf. 1 Cor 15:23–28).

This sort of claim about Jesus' divine sonship likewise has a connection to Jesus' ministry. It is widely agreed that Jesus acted in ways that expressed a sense of his special mission and status, and that he emphasized the traditional Jewish notion of God as "Father" to him and also to his followers (Thompson 2000, 56–86). Moreover, given the biblical references to the Davidic king as God's "Son" (e.g., Ps 2:7), God's vindication of Jesus' royal-messianic status would also justify and reinforce the claim that Jesus is God's unique "Son."

But the experiences that confirmed Jesus' resurrection for early believers (such as visions of the glorified/risen Jesus and prophetic oracles declaring God's actions) also conveyed the belief that God had exalted Jesus to heavenly and cosmic-wide rule, and to sharing in divine glory and even the divine name (e.g., 2 Cor 4:3–4; Phil 2:9–11; Heb 1:1–4; 1 Pet 1:21). Moreover, accompanying these beliefs was the conviction that believers were now to reverence the risen/exalted Jesus, and in ways that were unprecedented, producing a dyadic devotional pattern, a constellation of devotional practices in which Jesus was central along with God (Hurtado 1988). So, for example, the initiation ritual was baptism "in/into" Jesus' name. As another example, Paul refers to the church meal as "the Lord's supper," at which the risen Jesus presides. We also have references to the corporate acclamation and invocation of Jesus as a feature of the gathered worship, both in Greek (e.g., 1 Cor 12:3) and in Aramaic (1 Cor 16:22). Indeed, Paul refers to believers "in every place" as those who "call upon the name of the Lord Jesus Christ" (1 Cor 1:2, author's translation). This is a remarkable adaptation of the Old Testament expression for invocation and worship of YHWH (e.g., Gen 4:26; Ps 116:13, 17; Zeph 3:9). All of these (and the other) devotional practices that constitute the dyadic devotional pattern are without analogy or precedent in ancient Jewish tradition.

Although Jesus' followers revered him during his ministry, this dyadic devotional pattern seems to have been a major escalation in which the risen Jesus was given the kinds of reverence that are otherwise restricted to God. Jesus was not worshiped in an equivalent way during his ministry, and did not demand it (Hurtado 2005; against Fletcher-Louis 2015; Loke 2017). Instead, this novel development appears to have erupted quite early and quickly after his crucifixion, in response to profound convictions that God had vindicated and also exalted Jesus to a glorious status, and now required him to be reverenced accordingly. That is, although Jesus' actions and words surely made him central in the minds of his followers, the intense and remarkable level of cultic devotion reflected in our earliest texts was based also on the strong sense of God's acts, and so, on a profound level, was seen as obedience to the one God.

Works Cited

Allison, Dale C., Jr. 2010. *Constructing Jesus: Memory, Imagination and History*. Grand Rapids: Baker Academic.

Dahl, Nils Astrup. 1991. *Jesus the Christ: The Historical Origins of Christological Doctrine*. Edited by Donald H. Juel. Minneapolis: Fortress.

Fletcher-Louis, Crispin. 2015. *Jesus Monotheism*. Vol. 1 of *Christological Origins. The Emerging Consensus and Beyond*. Eugene, OR: Cascade.

Fredricksen, Paula. 2007. "Why Was Jesus Crucified? But His Followers Were Not?" *JSNT* 29:415–19.

———. 2017. *Paul, the Pagan's Apostle*. New Haven: Yale University Press.

Hengel, Martin. 1977. *Crucifixion in the Ancient World and the Folly of the Message of the Cross*. Translated by John Bowden. Philadelphia: Fortress.

———. 1995. "Jesus the Messiah of Israel." Pages 1–72 in *Studies in Early Christology*. Edinburgh: T&T Clark.

Hurtado, Larry W. 1988. *One God, One Lord: Early Christian Devotion and Ancient Jewish Monotheism*. Philadelphia: Fortress.

———. 2003. *Lord Jesus Christ: Devotion to Jesus in Earliest Christianity*. Grand Rapids: Eerdmans.

———. 2005. "Homage to the Historical Jesus and Early Christian Devotion." Pages 134–51 in *How on Earth Did Jesus Become a God? Historical Questions about Earliest Devotion to Jesus*. Grand Rapids: Eerdmans.

———. 2010. *God in New Testament Theology*. Nashville: Abingdon.

———. 2011. "Summary and Concluding Observations." Pages 159–77 in *'Who is this Son of Man?' The Latest Scholarship on a Puzzling Expression of the Historical Jesus*. Edited by Paul L. Owen and Larry W. Hurtado. London: T&T Clark.

Loke, Andrew Ter Ern. 2017. *The Origin of Divine Christology*. SNTSMS 169. Cambridge: Cambridge University Press.

Novenson, Matthew V. 2009. "The Jewish Messiah, the Pauline Christ, and the Gentile Question." *JBL* 128:357–73.

———. 2012. *Christ among the Messiahs: Christ Language in Paul and Messiah Language in Ancient Judaism*. New York: Oxford University Press.

Owen, Paul L. 2011. "Problems with Casey's 'Solution.'" Pages 28–49 in *'Who is this Son of Man?' The Latest Scholarship on a Puzzling Expression of the Historical Jesus*. Edited by Paul L. Owen and Larry W. Hurtado. London: T&T Clark.

Shepherd, David. 2011. "Resolving the 'Son of Man' Problem in Aramaic." Pages 50–60 in *'Who is this Son of Man?' The Latest Scholarship on a Puzzling Expression of the Historical Jesus.* Edited by Paul L. Owen and Larry W. Hurtado. London: T&T Clark.

Thompson, Marianne Meye. 2000. *The Promise of the Father: Jesus and God in the New Testament.* Louisville: Westminster John Knox.

Witherington, Ben. 1993. "Christ." *DPL* 95–100.

CHAPTER 8

The Jewish Teachings of Jesus

8.1 Jesus as Rabbi

Andreas J. Köstenberger

Jesus appointed twelve apostles, all of whom were Jewish: Simon Peter and Andrew, James and John (the sons of Zebedee), Philip and Bartholomew (Nathanael), Thomas and Matthew (Levi), James (son of Alphaeus) and Thaddaeus (Judas son of James), Simon the Zealot and Judas Iscariot (Matt 10:2–4; cf. Mark 3:16–19; Luke 6:14–16; Acts 1:13; Dawson forthcoming; Köstenberger and Köstenberger 2014, 84–90). As first-century Jews, they would have had a variety of messianic expectations in keeping with views current in Jewish parties and sects of their day (Collins 2010; Horbury 1998; 2016; Neusner, Green, and Frerichs 1988). They would have generally regarded gentiles, including Samaritans, as unclean (Acts 10; cf. John 4:9). Some viewed the Romans with contempt (Simon the Zealot), while others were former collaborators of Rome (Matthew the tax collector). The following discussion will center particularly on the relationship between Jesus and his disciples, which was both similar to and distinct from the relationship rabbis and their disciples typically sustained in the first century (Wilkins 2013, 205–7).

The Perception of Jesus as Rabbi by His Contemporaries

Jesus was perceived by his contemporaries primarily as a teacher, as is attested in both the Synoptic Gospels (Riesner 1988; Neusner 1986, 187–97) and the Gospel of John (Köstenberger 1998, from which portions of this essay are adapted, by permission; cf. Evans 1993, 151-68; Chilton 1984). There can be little doubt that the Gospels reflect the common perception among Jesus' Jewish contemporaries that he was a rabbi (Wenthe 2006, 143–74); he was perhaps more than a rabbi—but certainly no less. In fact, other than "Lord/Master," *rabbi* is the only address for Jesus in John's Gospel (John 1:38, 49; 3:2; 4:31; 6:25; 9:2; 11:8; cf. 20:16), and the picture in the other Gospels is much the same (Wenthe 2006, 167–71; see below). While the evangelists, as is well known, also cast Jesus as the "Son of Man," "Son of God," and "Messiah," their accounts make clear that Jesus' contemporaries perceived and addressed him primarily as a religious teacher, a rabbi.

Not only is "rabbi" or "teacher" the customary address for Jesus in the Gospels, the evangelists portray Jesus' relationship with his followers in keeping with first-century Judaism: Jesus assumed the role of teacher, instructing his disciples through word and action, protecting them from harm, and providing for their needs. The disciples assumed the role of faithful followers, performing menial tasks and perpetuating their Master's teaching. The fact that Jesus' contemporaries viewed him primarily as a rabbi does not level distinctions between Jesus and other Jewish rabbis. Rather, Jesus adapted this model in multiple ways and even broke common conventions (Köstenberger 1998; Neudecker 1999, 245–61; Wenthe 2006, 143–74; Wilkins 2013, 205–7). Strikingly, he interpreted messianic prophecy with reference to himself, something no other rabbi of his day would have dared to do.

The term *rabbi*, derived from the Hebrew/Aramaic "my great one," conveyed respect. A saying attributed to Rabbi Eleazar ben Shammua (130–160 CE), student of Rabbi Akiva, reflects this high regard: "Let the fear of your teacher be as the fear of heaven" (*m. Avot* 4:12; Schürer 2014, 2:325; Lohse 1969, 961–62). While Jesus discouraged his disciples from being called rabbis themselves (Matt 23:8), a student in first-century Judaism earned the right to be addressed as *rabbi* after several years of association with his teacher. The use of *rabbi* as an address rather than a title for a Jewish religious teacher is attested for Rabbi Eleazar ben Azariah, who called his teacher Rabbi Yohanan ben Zakkai (d. ca. 80 CE) *rabbi* when visiting him at the occasion of the death of Yohanan's son (*Avot of Rabbi Nathan* 14). Hillel, likewise, was addressed as *rabbi* (*Leviticus Rabbah* 34, 130d). The term *rabbi* is confined to Palestine in the first century CE, underscoring the historicity of the Gospel accounts. [See Figure 24.]

John's Gospel, as mentioned, is particularly noteworthy in featuring Jesus as a rabbi, including eight instances where Jesus is addressed as such (John 1:38, 49; 3:2; 4:31; 6:25; 9:2; 11:8; 20:16). This constitutes over half of the references in all four Gospels combined. John is also unmatched in both the range of individuals referring to Jesus as rabbi and the consistency with which *rabbi* is the chosen address of Jesus. The address is attributed to Jesus' first followers (John 1:38), Nathanael (John 1:49), Nicodemus (John 3:2), his disciples (John 4:31; 9:2; 11:8), the multitudes (John 6:25), and Mary Magdalene (John 20:16) (see detailed discussion of these passages in Köstenberger 1998). John frequently uses the Hebrew/Aramaic term *rabbi* while the Synoptists generally use the Greek equivalent, *didaskalos*. In the first and last instance, John uses *didaskalos* as well as *rabbi* (John 1:38; 20:16).

Matthew, by contrast, seems to avoid reference to Jesus as *rabbi*, perhaps to safeguard his uniqueness as the Jewish Messiah. Of Matthew's four uses of the term, two caution Jesus' disciples against allowing themselves to be addressed as *rabbi* (Matt 23:7–8), and two are found on the lips of the traitor, Judas Is-cariot (Matt 26:25, 49). Mark has three individuals address Jesus as *rabbi*: Peter (9:5; 11:21), a blind man (10:51), and Judas (14:45). Mark also features several instances where Jesus is addressed or referred to as *didaskalos*. Interestingly, Mark thus comes closest to John in reflecting the probable historical address of Jesus as *rabbi* by his contemporaries. Luke does not use the term *rabbi* at all but generally substitutes the Greek word *didaskalos* in deference to his gentile audience (Wenthe 2006, 167–68). He does this, however, without downplaying the significance of Jesus' role as teacher.

Jesus' Relationship with His Followers in the Context of First-Century Jewish Teacher-Disciple Relationships

The Gospels portray Jesus as instructing his followers in several ways: by verbal instruction, by didactic actions such as "mystifying gestures" accompanied by an explanation, and by personal example (Wach 1962, 1–21). In addition to instructing his followers, Jesus also provides for his disciples' other needs and protects them from harm, not least the negative influence of false teaching by others (the following adapts portions of Köstenberger 1998; see also Riesner 1991, 201–8).

Verbal Instruction. Jesus often interpreted the Hebrew Scriptures in a way that transcended common interpretation. His messianic consciousness led him to read the Scriptures with reference to himself, in stark contrast with other contemporary rabbis. Jesus' pronouncements consistently exceeded the wisdom of other religious authorities, and Jesus regularly affirmed his author-ity and interpreted Scripture as pointing to himself (cf., e.g., Matt 8:28–29; 21:23–22:46). When challenged regarding his healing of a man on the Sabbath, he pointed out that even in rabbinic interpretation the prohibition of work on the Sabbath was not absolute: if the eighth day on which a newborn male was to be circumcised fell on a Sabbath, circumcision was to proceed to fulfill the commandment of Lev 12:3 (cf. esp. *m. Shabbat* 19:1–3; Thomas 1991, 173–74). In view of this precedent, Jesus argued, he was justified in healing an entire man on the Sabbath (John 7:21–23; cf. 5:1–18). In fact, he asserted his authority over the Sabbath and declared himself "Lord of the Sabbath" (Matt 12:8 ESV). On another occasion, when his disciples asked about the cause of a man's blindness, Jesus rejected the customary simplistic cause-and-effect explanations of suffering and proceeded to heal the man (John 9:1–7; cf. Evans 1993, 154).

Jesus also used rabbinic style, such as arguments from the lesser to the greater (e.g., Matt 6:25–30; 7:11; 10:28–30; 12:11–12; John 3:12; 5:46; 6:27; 7:23; 10:34–36; cf. *t. Sanhedrin* 7:11). Some of his sayings appear to reflect targumic language and tradition, such as his pronouncement, "Your father Abraham rejoiced that he would see my day" (John 8:56; Reim 1983, 6–7), and his state-ment to Thomas that those are blessed who do not see and yet believe (John 20:29; cf. Evans 1993, 154, 157–64). Jesus' verbal instruction of his disciples and others is clearly consistent with his Jewish environment. His use of the Scriptures, his rabbinic adjudications, his style of argumentation, and even specific language place him squarely within a Jewish rabbinic context. This, of course, does not mean that Jesus merely conformed to the pattern of teaching used by other rabbis of his day. Rather, his teaching was devoted to establishing his messianic claims based on scriptural expectations and to distancing himself from the illegitimate heirs of God's promises to Israel.

Didactic Actions. Jesus' method of teaching was not limited to verbal in-struction. In keeping with contemporary rabbinic practice, it also included the use of "mystifying gestures"—startling actions that demanded an explanation (Gerhardsson 1961, 185). Two major examples of this are Jesus' clearing of the Temple and his footwashing, found in John's Gospel at the beginning and the end of Jesus' ministry.

Jesus' clearing of the Temple (John 2:13–22) is cast as a deliberate action designed to provoke discussion as Jesus presented himself as the fulfillment of the symbolism inherent in the Temple (Evans 1993, 59–60; Reim 1983, 10). When challenging Jesus' authority in response to his startling act of overthrow-ing the tables of the moneychangers, his detractors did not seek evidence of the usual type (Daube 1973, 211); rather, they sought confirmation of Jesus' special divine call as the prophet or Messiah. Indeed, a rabbi's authority ex-tended to both his didactic and prophetic functions and was manifest in both words and deeds. Jesus' miraculous healings and other amazing acts thus may be viewed, at least in part, as serving the purpose of attesting to his authority as a religious teacher. In this instance, however, Jesus did not acquiesce to the Jews' demand for a sign; instead, he elaborated on the significance of the act he had just performed (Köstenberger 1995). At the time, Jesus' explanation of the Temple clearing as a prophetic foreshadowing of the meaning of his death and resurrection remained a mystery, not only to the Pharisees but even to his own disciples; only later would his followers understand (John 2:22; cf. 12:16).

The second "mystifying gesture" performed by Jesus was the footwashing (John 13:1–17). The unfolding of Jesus' last extended time with his disciples follows the rabbinic pattern of "mystifying gesture—question—interpretation" (Daube 1973, 182–83). In a similar vein, Yohanan ben Zakkai (d. 80 CE) sobbed on his death bed, inducing his followers to ask about the cause of his grief, which provided him with the opportunity to explain (*b. Berakhot* 28b; Daube 1973, 167–77). Similarly, Jesus performed the footwashing to teach his disciples about their need to serve one another in love following his earthly departure. Contrary to contemporary custom, Jesus got up, wrapped a towel around his waist, and began to wash the feet of his followers. According to Jewish belief, "All manner of service that a slave must render to his master, the pupil must render to his teacher—except that of taking off his shoe" (*b. Ketubbot* 96a). Only a household slave performed this menial service, and a student engaging in it could be mistaken for such a slave (Aberbach 1967, 5). Jesus' actions in the upper room thus dramatically run counter to contemporary Jewish convention: Jesus the teacher rendered a service to his pupils rather than vice versa, and the specific task performed exceeded even that expected from pupils.

Other Provision and Protection. The role of rabbi also entailed providing for his disciples' various other needs and protecting them from false teaching and other harm. In keeping with this role, Jesus frequently issued warnings to his followers regarding the negative influence of the Jewish religious leaders. These issues come to the fore in Jesus' shepherd allegory (John 10). There, alluding to Ezek 34 and utilizing the familiar motif of God as Israel's shepherd, Jesus identifies the current Jewish leaders as faithless (cf. Zech 11:15–17) in contrast to himself, the "good shepherd." Here the image of shepherd and the role of rabbi merge in that Jesus, the shepherd-teacher, is shown to take great care to nurture a close, trusting relationship with his followers to protect them from any spiritual harm resulting from exposure to false teaching.

Teaching by Example. Jesus also taught by example. He embodied his teaching and expected his followers to emulate his example (Wach 1962, 1–21). As the sent Son of the Father, Jesus modeled dependence, obedience, and faithfulness to his sender (e.g., Mark 14:36; John 4:34; 5:23, 30, 36, 38; etc.). Consequently, Jesus asserted that "the Father loves the Son, and shows him all things that he himself is doing" (John 5:20; cf. 1:18; Matt 11:27; Luke 10:22). Jesus' statement at the footwashing scene illustrates this dynamic: "You call me Teacher and Lord, and you are right, for so I am. If I then, your Lord and the Teacher, have washed your feet, you also ought to wash one another's feet. For I have given you an example, that you also should do just as I have done to you" (John 13:13–15; Riesner 1988, 256–59). Jesus' teaching by example had the desired result that his followers do his works and even "greater ones" than these (John 14:12).

In accordance with contemporary Jewish belief, the presence of a messenger was equivalent to the presence of the sender himself (cf. John 13:20; *m. Berakhot* 5:5: "A person's messenger is [considered] like himself"). This was especially true if the one sent was the son, particularly the firstborn. At the occasion of the disciples' commissioning, Jesus charged his followers to emulate the same characteristics he had displayed during his earthly sojourn as the paradigmatic Sent One: "As the Father has sent me, even so I am sending you" (John 20:21; cf. 9:7; Köstenberger 1998). Jesus the teacher sought to impart the core characteristics of his own disposition toward his mission to his closest followers as part of their preparation for ministry. This transcended even verbal instruction, the use of mystifying gestures, and other methods of teaching.

Works Cited

Aberbach, Moses. 1967. "The Relations between Master and Disciple in the Talmudic Age." Pages 1–24 in *Essays Presented to Chief Rabbi Israel Brodie.* Edited by H. J. Zimmels, J. Rabbinowitz, and L. Finestein. London: Soncino.

Chilton, Bruce. 1984. *A Galilean Rabbi and His Bible: Jesus' Use of the Interpreted Scripture of His Time. GNS* 8. Wilmington, DE: Glazier.

Collins, John J. 2010. *The Scepter and the Star: Messianism in Light of the Dead Sea Scrolls.* 2nd ed. Grand Rapids: Eerdmans.

Daube, David. 1973. *The New Testament and Rabbinic Judaism.* New York: Arno Press.

Dawson, Nancy S. Forthcoming. *Genealogies of the Bible.* Edited by Eugene H. Merrill and Andreas J. Köstenberger. Grand Rapids: Zondervan.

Evans, Craig A. 1993. *Word and Glory: On the Exegetical and Theological Background of John's Prologue.* JSNTSup 89. Sheffield: JSOT Press.

Gerhardsson, Birger. 1961. *Memory and Manuscript: Oral Tradition and Written Transmission in Rabbinic Judaism and Early Christianity.* Lund: Gleerup.

Horbury, William. 1998. *Jewish Messianism and the Cult of Christ.* London: SCM.

———. 2016. *Messianism among Jews and Christians: Biblical and Historical Studies.* 2nd ed. T&T Clark Cornerstones. London: Bloomsbury T&T Clark.

Köstenberger, Andreas J. 1995. "The Seventh Johannine Sign: A Study in John's Christology." *BBR* 5:87–103.

———. 1998. "Jesus as Rabbi in the Fourth Gospel." *BBR* 8:97–128.

Köstenberger, Andreas J., and Margaret E. Köstenberger. 2014. *God's Design for Man and Woman: A Biblical-Theological Survey.* Wheaton, IL: Crossway.

Lohse, Eduard. 1969. "ῥαββί, ῥαββουνί." *TDNT* 6:961–65.

Neudecker, Reinhard. 1999. "Master-Disciple/Disciple-Master Relationship in Rabbinic Judaism and in the Gospels." *Gregorianum* 80:245–61.

Neusner, Jacob. 1986. "Death-Scenes and Farewell Stories: An Aspect of the Master-Disciple Relationship in Mark and in Some Talmudic Tales." *HTR* 79:187–97.

Neusner, Jacob, William S. Green, and Ernest S. Frerichs. 1988. *Judaisms and Their Messiahs at the Turn of the Christian Era.* Cambridge: Cambridge University Press.

Reim, Günter. 1983. "Targum und Johannesevangelium." *BZ* 27:1–13.

Riesner, Rainer. 1988. *Jesus als Lehrer.* 3rd ed. WUNT 2/7. Tübingen: Mohr Siebeck.

———.1991. "Jesus as Preacher and Teacher." Pages 185–210 in *Jesus and the Oral Gospel Tradition.* Edited by Henry Wansborough. JSNTSup 64. Sheffield: JSOT Press.

Schürer, Emil. 2014. *The History of the Jewish People in the Age of Jesus Christ.* Vol 2. Revised and edited by Geza Vermes, Fergus Millar, and Matthew Black. London: Bloomsbury T&T Clark.

Thomas, John Christopher. 1991. "The Fourth Gospel and Rabbinic Judaism." *ZNW* 82:159–82.

Wach, Joachim. 1962. "Master and Disciple: Two Religio-Sociological Studies." *JR* 42:1–21.

Wenthe, Dean O. 2006. "The Social Configuration of the Rabbi-Disciple Relationship: Evidence and Implications for First Century Palestine." Pages 143–74 in *Studies in the Hebrew Bible, Qumran, and the Septuagint: Presented to Eugene Ulrich*. Edited by Peter W. Flint, Emanuel Tov, and James C. Vanderkam. VTSup 101. Leiden: Brill.

Wilkins, M. J. 2013. "Disciples and Discipleship." *DJG* 202–12.

8.2 The Lord's Prayer

Scot McKnight

Ancient Jewish prayer traditions are a great help in understanding the words of Jesus as he taught his followers how to pray.

Prayer in Judaism

Prayer at the time of Jesus begins with the book of Psalms. Understood as the prayers of David, it flows into temple worship but is also capable of just as much spontaneity as one finds in the Christian prayer tradition. Indeed, the prayers of Qumran (e.g., 1Q35), whether they should be read as individual or group prayers, illustrate how spontaneous, personal, and raw Jewish prayer could be. Jewish prayers are marked by time in three ways: a daily rhythm (evening, morning, midday) was enveloped into a weekly rhythm, where the Sabbath was featured, as well as an annual rhythm shaped by the calendar(s) of Judaism (e.g., *1 Enoch* 72–82; *Jubilees* 6:35–37; 4Q317; 4Q319; 4Q320; 4Q321). Prayer then coursed between the structured (set prayers at set times) and the spontaneous. A classic Jewish prayer, with at least origins in the time of Jesus, is called *Shemoneh Esreh* or *Amidah* or *Ha-Tephillah*, and it had eighteen benedictions on which one could hang one's personal, spontaneous prayers (Schürer 1973–1987, 2:454–63; Sanders 2016, 311–47). One may surmise a generalization: the daily prayer practice of the observant Jew included reciting the Shema two or more times (Deut 6:4–9), the Ten Commandments, and the *Ha-Tephillah*. One is reminded of Ps 55:17 and Dan 6:10, where prayers are said three times a day. This was a common Jewish prayer habit. This is confirmed in Matt 6:5 and Acts 3:1 as well as in an early Christian document, *Didache* 8:3.

There are good reasons to think the Lord's Prayer is Jesus' version of what is now called the Kaddish in Judaism. That prayer looked something like this: "May his great name be exalted and holy, in the world that he created in accordance to his will. May God bring the rule of his kingdom during your lifetime and in the lifetime of the entire house of Israel, and may it be soon." At least the first half of the Lord's Prayer evokes this Kaddish.

The Lord's Prayer (Luke 11:1–4; Matt 6:7–13 [14–15]): Lukan and Matthean Contexts

The Lord's Prayer's dual tradition in Matthew and Luke creates two different settings for the prayer. The Lukan setting in Luke 11:1 carries distinct cultural information: "He was praying in a certain place, and after he had finished, one of his disciples said to him, 'Lord, teach us to pray, as John taught his disciples'" (RSV). We are to locate Jesus at a set time (and place), saying set prayers with spontaneous prayers mixed in. His disciples, noticing a pause (perhaps between set prayers), asked Jesus to give them a prayer as John the Baptist had given his disciples a prayer. That is, they asked for a set prayer, which is what the Lord's Prayer is in Luke: a set prayer for disciples of Jesus. Furthermore, Jesus continues with "When*ever* you pray, *recite* this: 'Father . . .'" (author's translation). There is an important distinction between "when" and "when*ever*," and Jesus says the latter. Jesus is giving a set prayer to his disciples to pray every time they pray (personally and corporately) in true Jewish fashion.

Matthew provides two contextual clues for how to understand the Lord's Prayer. First, in Matt 6:5–7 we learn that Jesus taught on prayer to counter the "hypocrites," a term used for a false guide as much as for someone whose practice contradicted one's teaching (Garland 1979, 91–123), and to counter their publicity of their prayers. Jesus' prayer illustrates private prayer (6:6). Second, more connected to the Lord's Prayer is the profusion of prayers one finds in the Greco-Roman world, where it was believed that longer prayers were more likely to be heard by God, and prayers included using "whatever sacred name pleases you" (Catullus). The term Jesus uses here, "their many words," translates the Greek term *battalogeō*, which is sometimes translated "babbling" or "mumbling." The Lord's Prayer, in this context, emphasizes simplicity and brevity. In the Jewish context one might consider that it was designed by Jesus both to be recited constantly and used to evoke one's personal and spontaneous prayers.

Interpreting the Lord's Prayer

Due to the interpretive tradition of the church every term in the Lord's Prayer has a rich history of interpretation, not all of it connected to the context of the Jewish world of Jesus. Prior to speaking to each element of the Lord's Prayer, several differences between Matthew's and Luke's version are worthy of attention (all references are from Luke 11:2–4 and Matt 6:7–13 RSV): (1) Luke has "Father" but Matthew has "Our Father who art in heaven"; (2) Matthew has "Thy will be done, on earth as it is in heaven" while Luke does not have this; (3) Luke has "sins" and Matthew "debts"; (4) Luke does not have Matthew's "but deliver us from evil." Luke also does not have the famous "For Thine is the kingdom, the power . . . ," which was not original to the Gospel of Matthew either.

To call God "Father" is to use the name Jesus used constantly for God in his prayers (e.g., Matt 11:25–26; John 17) and, while it is not unique to Jesus (e.g., Ps 68:5; Jer 31:9, 20), it is his distinct emphasis in addressing God (Jeremias 1967, 11–65). The word "Father" combines the intimacy of the child and the father, the father's love for the child, and the power and authority of the father in the child's home. Hence, even the petitions of the Lord's Prayer that follow yearn for and carry out the lordship of the Father and the kingdom. The sanctification of the Name, which is YHWH (Exod 3:13–15), refers to a name representing a person and that person's character and status. Sanctification of the Name of God (sometimes *ha-Shem*) manifested itself in two ways in the world of Jesus: not using or rarely using the Name (e.g., Matt 23:39) and both obeying God and not disobeying God (which profanes the Name; cf. Lev 18:21; Ezek 36:22; 39:27–28). But the emphasis here is the request for God to act, and this action has to do with ushering in the full kingdom of God.

The second and third petitions ask God to bring the kingdom and his will into realization on earth (Matt 6:10; Luke 11:2). Defining "kingdom" becomes vital to understanding the prayer. Kingdom includes themes like the future, interiority (the inner-self), heaven, the institutional expressions of kingdom (and church), subversion of the world's values and, in their place, God's rule, as well as themes of transformation and utopia (Snyder 1991). Once again, "kingdom" has been captured too often by Christian theology (e.g., church life) and history and has lost its Jewish edge. A kingdom in the Jewish world, made clear by any examination of the term "kingdom" in the Old Testament, Josephus, or the Dead Sea Scrolls, refers to a people governed by a king. There are, in fact, five elements at work when the term kingdom was used in the Jewish world, and each must be given play for Jesus' kingdom theology to make sense in the Galilee or in Judea. First, there must be a king (God, Jesus); the king must rule (and the rule of God in the world of Jesus involved both redemption and governance as Lord); the king must rule over a people (Israel); the kingdom must have a law/ethic; and the king must rule over a people in a land. There is no kingdom without territory (Marshall 1990; McKnight 2014; Pennington 2009; Allison 2013, 164–204).

The fourth petition of the Lord's Prayer, for daily bread, turns the prayer away from what was seen above in the Kaddish, away from God and toward others. As Jesus emphasized that true piety was love of God *and love of others* (Mark 12:28–32), so prayer, especially the Lord's Prayer, yearns for both God's glory and human redemption. No one has finally resolved the meaning of the unusual term *epiousios*, which is translated often as "daily bread" but could mean "needful," "for the current day," "substantial," or possibly "for the coming day." If the latter, it could be a request for the bread of the eschatological kingdom. "Daily bread" is traditional, and probably the most accurate. The term "debts," in the fifth petition, emerges out of Judaism's use of sin and forgiveness in commercial categories (Anderson 2009), and thus is a synonym for Luke's "sins" (Luke 11:4). Noticeably, the prayer for forgiveness is tied to human forgiveness (Matt 6:12b) and there is an added "footnote" of emphasis on this in 6:14–15, a text drawn from Mark 11:25–26. There is, so Jesus teaches, a correlation between one's response to God and one's response to others. The sixth petition, concerning temptation, is covered with an interpretive gloss in Matthew about rescue (seventh petition). While some have understood this as a reference to the final eschaton (the final time of trial and the evil one's onslaught at the end of days; Brown 1968), the traditional view has much in its favor: a request to live each day resisting temptation and experiencing the deliverance of God.

No prayer does more in fewer words in religious history, and no prayer has prompted more spontaneous prayers than reciting the seven petitions of the Lord's Prayer as the branches on which we can hang our personal petitions.

Works Cited

Allison, Dale C., Jr. 2013. *Constructing Jesus: Memory, Imagination, and History.* Grand Rapids: Baker Academic.

Anderson, Gary A. 2009. *Sin: A History.* New Haven: Yale University Press.

Brown, Raymond E. 1968. "The Pater Noster as an Eschatological Prayer." Pages 265–320 in *New Testament Essays.* Garden City: Image.

Catullus: The Poems. 2001. Translated by A. S. Kline. Poetry in Translation. http://www.poetryintranslation.com/PITBR/Latin/Catullus.php#_Toc531846759.

Garland, David E. 1979. *The Intention of Matthew 23.* NovTSup 52. Leiden: Brill.

Jeremias, Joachim. 1967. *The Prayers of Jesus.* London: SCM.

Marshall, I. Howard. 1990. Pages 213–38 in *Jesus the Saviour: Studies in New Testament Theology.* Downers Grove, IL: InterVarsity Press.

McKnight, Scot. 2014. *Kingdom Conspiracy: Returning to the Radical Mission of the Local Church.* Grand Rapids: Brazos.

Pennington, Jonathan T. 2009. *Heaven and Earth in the Gospel of Matthew*. Grand Rapids: Baker Academic.

Sanders, E. P. 2016. *Judaism: Practice and Belief. 63 BCE–66 CE*. Minneapolis: Fortress.

Schürer, Emil. 1973–1987. *The History of the Jewish People in the Age of Jesus Christ (175 B.C.–A.D. 135)*. 4 vols. Revised and edited by Geza Vermes, Fergus Millar, and Martin Goodman. Edinburgh: T&T Clark.

Snyder, Howard A. 1991. *Models of the Kingdom*. Nashville: Abingdon.

8.3 The Sermon on the Mount

Scot McKnight

The Sermon on the Mount, the clearest crystallization of the teachings of Jesus on discipleship, is found in two locations in the Gospels: Matt 4:23–8:1 (usually referred to as Matt 5–7) and Luke 6:17–49. The overlap between the two passages is substantive, leading many scholars today to posit the so-called Q source as the origin for Matthew and Luke, or at least for one of them. What Matthew calls a "mountain" Luke calls a "level place" (Matt 5:1; Luke 6:17 RSV), leading many to suspect Matthew uses "mountain" to highlight parallels between Jesus and Moses (cf. Matt 5:1 with Exod 19:3; 24:12–13; Matt 8:1 with Exod 34:29; also Matt 5:1's "sat down" corresponds to Moses' seat as in Matt 23:2; Eusebius, *Dem. ev.* 3.2; Allison 1993). Christian theology, armed as it has been for centuries against any appreciation of the law of Moses, fails to comprehend the Sermon of its Lord when it fails to see the Mosaic themes of the Sermon (cf. 5:17–48).

Comparing Matthew and Luke

If Matthew and Luke relay the same sermon to their audiences, the differences between the two are worthy of attention: (1) Matthew's Beatitudes are both more numerous and absent of the woes (cf. 5:3–12 with Luke 6:20–26); (2) Matthew's salt and light are absent in Luke's Sermon but present elsewhere in Luke (Matt 5:13–16; Luke 14:34–35); (3) Matthew's extensive collection of "You have heard . . . but I say" in 5:21–48 has echoes in Luke (6:29–30, 27–28, 32–33), but Luke barely echoes Matt 5:17–20 (cf. Luke 16:5–6); (4) the entire section on the spiritual disciplines in Matt 6:1–18 is absent in Luke's Sermon except for the Lord's Prayer (Matt 6:9–15) which finds a parallel in Luke 11:2–4; (5) Matt 6:19–34 has parallels in Luke but not in the Sermon (cf. Luke 12:33–34; 11:34–36; 16:13; 12:22–31); (6) the theme of judging (Matt 7:1–5) is found in

Luke but with additional material (cf. Luke 6:37–38); (7) the famous saying on casting pearls before swine (Matt 7:6) is not found in Luke at all; (8) the answers to prayer section (Matt 7:7–11) is found elsewhere in Luke (11:9–13); (9) the Golden Rule (Matt 7:12) appears in Luke's Sermon (6:31); but (10) the narrow gate saying (Matt 7:13–14) has only an echo in another location in Luke (13:23–24); (11) Matthew's famous test of goodness (7:15–20) has a similar passage at Luke 6:43–45; (12) the "not everyone who says to Me" warning in Matt 7:21–23 has a slight parallel in Luke 6:46 with more at 13:26–27; and (13) Matthew's famous parable of the wise and foolish builders (7:24–27) has a strong parallel in Luke 6:47–49. Both the beginnings and endings of the two Gospel accounts of the Sermon differ significantly (cf. Matt 5:1 and Luke 6:17 as well as Matt 7:28–8:1 with Luke 7:1). These differences reflect the respective forms of the tradition that the evangelists accessed, as well as their respective compositional strategies.

Reading the Sermon in the Context of Moral Theory

It is customary to swallow the teachings of Jesus, crystallized as they are in the Sermon, into one's own moral theory or one's ethics. From the second century on, not least in the days of Aquinas and Luther/Calvin as well as in late modern (i.e., eighteenth and nineteenth century) Europe and North America, ruling moral theories have found a way to use (and abuse) Jesus. Most commonly he is ripped from his Jewish world and made into a European. Hence, the categorical imperative of Immanuel Kant, the virtue ethics of so many of today's ethicists (Pennington 2017), and the utilitarian ethics of thinkers like Bentham and Mill have each found a way to use Jesus to their own theory's advantage (for discussion, Hauerwas and Wells 2006; Allison 1999).

Jesus, however, was not an Aristotelian virtue ethicist with his emphasis on habits and character; nor was Jesus a modern Kantian reducing ethics to bare bones; and neither was he a consequentialist. Jesus was a Jew. Jewish ethics and morality derive not from Moses, from Moses on Mount Sinai, but from God who speaks to Moses from Mount Sinai (Exod 19–24). The passing of the Mosaic Torah through the prophets may well have turned Mosaic legislation in new directions, but Torah remained the will of God for Israel. Even wisdom thinking, which many today have mistakenly connected to little more than creational reasoning, remains firmly attached to Mosaic Torah, even if there is an abundance of practical reasoning in the wisdom tradition (Longman 2017; Kynes 2016). These three streams of the Jewish tradition—law, prophets and wisdom—are the streams in which Jesus swam and it is out of those waters that Jesus emerges in the Galilee to instruct others on the will of God in the Sermon. Hence, it is wisest to avoid swallowing Jesus' ethics into our own theories and instead let him remain the Jew that he was. His ethics then are an ethics from above (from God on Sinai), from beyond (the prophets), and from below (wisdom) (McKnight 2013). But Jesus' ethics are not simply a warming over of the Jewish tradition. Rather, there are at least three moments of newness: Jesus' ethics are messianic in that he becomes central to defining the will of God (Matt 5:17–20, 21–48); Jesus' ethics are ecclesial in the sense that Jesus is summoning his followers into a fellowship (*haberim*, or members) that is family-like and forms a group identity; and Jesus' ethics are pneumatic in his evocation of the presence of the eschatological gift of the Spirit at the end of the age. Eduard Lohse (1991, 70) long ago said, "Jesus' word is not separable from the one who speaks it." Stanley Hauerwas (2006, 61) said, "The sermon, therefore, is not a list of requirements, but rather a description of the life of the people gathered by and around Jesus." While "Spirit" does not show up in the Sermon, few question the centrality of the Spirit to the Jesus traditions and to the power at work in Jesus both for redemption and eschatological transformation (Hawthorne 1991).

Interpretation of the Sermon on the Mount

Neither the introduction (Matt 5:1) nor the conclusion (7:28–8:1), though less clear in the Lukan tradition (6:17; 7:1), can be ignored: Jesus ascends the mountain in Moses-like fashion to reveal the will of God to his disciples and the crowds (Matt 5:1; 7:28; see Allison 1993). As the new Moses, Jesus announces those who are kingdom people and (by implication in Matthew and overt announcement in Luke) those who are not (Luke 6:24–26 has woes on non-kingdom people). The Beatitudes (Matt 5:3–12) are not a list of virtues but a list of people who are "in," or who are kingdom people. The implication of the list then is "Am I a kingdom person or not?" and one has to think that many listening to Jesus, not least his opponents, wanted to know: "Why did you exclude me?"

While the salt and light sayings of Matt 5:13–16 have fashionably been appropriated by many today to teach both evangelism and social action, there are clues in the text to indicate that this was not how Jesus understood his own words: Jesus speaks of salt with respect to "earth" (Greek *gē*; Hebrew *eretz*), which could be translated "land," while he speaks of light with respect to "world" (Greek *kosmos*). That distinguishing of location—land versus world—suggests the salt is action by his disciples among Jews while the light is action by his disciples among gentiles.

The most dramatic moment on the mountain comes in Matt 5:17–20, for there Jesus declares that he is—in his person, in his ministry, in his actions, in his teaching, and thus as well in his death, burial, resurrection, commissioning, and ascension—the fulfillment of the "Law and the Prophets" (5:17). There is some dispute over the meaning of "fulfill." Does it mean that Jesus *observes* the Law and the Prophets completely, that he *teaches* the true meaning of the Law and the Prophets, or that Jesus is the goal and fulfillment of all that God has disclosed in the Law and the Prophets? The last view has gained the consensus and indicates not that the Mosaic Torah has been abolished or superseded but completed and clarified to the fullest extent of divine revelation to humans (Guelich 1982, 138–43). Put differently, the teachings of Jesus are what Moses meant. Each of the six antitheses of 5:21–48 (anger, adultery, divorce, oaths, retaliation, hatred of enemies) illustrates both what "fulfill" means and what surpassing "righteousness" means in 5:20. The term "righteousness" comes from the Hebrew *tsedeq* (Greek *dikaiosynē*) and refers to behaviors that conform to the will of God. Thus, what makes a disciple "righteous" is behavior that conforms to the will of God as taught by Jesus.

This theme of righteousness (5:6, 10, 20) is redirected toward spiritual disciplines in 6:1, though calling alms, prayer, and fasting spiritual disciplines once again turns a Jewish Jesus into a modern Christian. The three acts of obedience in the Jewish world were understood as preeminent acts of the Torah-observant and halakically oriented Jew. In particular, almsgiving was the epitome of observance (cf. Lev 19:9–10; Isa 3:14–15; Amos 8:4–6; Sirach 3:30; *m. Avot* 1:2; see Downs 2016). Jesus makes two points about prayer in the Sermon of Matthew: he discusses both the hypocrisy of finding oneself in the most convenient public space at prayer times (6:5–6) and the need to make words count by avoiding excessive words in prayer. Instead, Jesus wants simple, direct prayers, and the Lord's Prayer illustrates just that (6:7–13, with vv. 14–15 as commentary). Fasting is the most abused action Jesus focuses on here. It has become an instrument to get what people want in the Christian tradition, while in the Jewish tradition fasting was a response to a grievous situation (death, famine, war or threat of war, divine warnings of discipline) in which the fasting person identified with God—the divine pathos (Heschel 1962)—and sometimes (not always!) got what they prayed for (McKnight 2009).

Righteousness takes a subtle turn at 6:19 to focus on the single-mindedness expected of kingdom followers of Jesus. Jesus uses four images to illustrate single-mindedness, all in the theme of possessions: treasures (6:19–21), the sound eye (6:22–23), two masters (6:24), and the providential care of the Father for all creation (6:25–34). For Jews the Bible's teachings on money, possessions, and poverty fluctuate from wealth as a sign of obedience to poverty as a sign of obedience, with nuances and variations between the two poles (Brueggemann 2016; Wheeler 1995). Jesus stands closer to the second pole and advocates for the poor (cf. Luke 4:16–30), and these sayings emerge out of that position. Matthew 6:33 expresses all that 6:19–34 is teaching: seeking above all to possess God's kingdom and righteousness, which here means the will of God connected to following Jesus.

When the reader turns from Matt 6 to 7 the topics shift, the edge of righteousness is lost, and one encounters a hodgepodge of themes and commands.

They are: a command not to judge (7:1–5; this term allows a distinction between moral discernment, which is good, and personal condemnation of others, which is bad); a command against profaning the holy (7:6); a discussion of prayer, intercession, and God's goodness (7:7–11); the golden rule (7:12); and a summons to listen to these words and put them into practice. This final command is found in four separate warnings: the narrow gate (7:13–14), fruit that indicates the quality of the tree (7:15–20), a warning to those who think their charismatic gifts are a sign of entrance into the final kingdom (7:21–23), and the parable of the builders (7:24–27).

The Sermon on the Mount finds its meaning in the context of Matthew's Gospel and the arc of its narrative: at 4:23–25 we read of Jesus going throughout Galilee doing three things: teaching in the synagogues, preaching the kingdom, and healing "every kind of disease and every infirmity" (4:23). At 9:35 we find a similar paragraph where Jesus is said to be teaching, preaching, and healing "every kind of disease and every kind of sickness." This is a literary device of beginning and ending a section with the same lines in order to tie it into a unit. The unit, then, is to be read as a description of the teaching and preaching of Jesus (the Sermon on the Mount), as well as the healing of Jesus (chs. 8–9). It is thus a way to present who Jesus is and what he wants from those who heed his kingdom call. The proper response to the Sermon, then, is one that asks "Who is he?" and answers that question with "He is the Messiah! He is the Lord!" The only proper follow-up to that answer is to surrender one's life to Jesus as Messiah and Lord.

Works Cited

Allison. Dale C., Jr. 1993. *The New Moses: A Matthean Typology*. Minneapolis: Fortress.

———. 1999. *The Sermon on the Mount: Inspiring the Moral Imagination*. Companions to the New Testament. New York: Crossroad.

Brueggemann, Walter. 2016. *Money and Possessions*. Louisville: Westminster John Knox.

Downs, David J. 2016. *Alms: Charity, Reward, and Atonement in Early Christianity*. Waco, TX: Baylor University Press.

Guelich, Robert A. 1982. *The Sermon on the Mount: A Foundation for Understanding*. Waco, TX: Word.

Hauerwas, Stanley. 2006. *Matthew*. Brazos Theological Commentary on the Bible. Grand Rapids: Brazos.

Hauerwas, Stanley, and Samuel Wells, eds. 2006. *The Blackwell Companion to Christian Ethics*. Oxford: Blackwell.

Hawthorne, Gerald. 1991. *The Presence and the Power: The Significance of the Holy Spirit in the Life and Ministry of Jesus*. Waco, TX: Word.

Heschel, Abraham J. 1962. *The Prophets*. 2 vols. New York: Harper & Row.

Kynes, Will. 2016. "The Nineteenth-Century Beginnings of 'Wisdom Literature,' and Its Twenty-First Century End?" Pages 83–108 in *Perspectives on Israelite Wisdom: Proceedings of the Oxford Old Testament Seminar*. Edited by John Jarick. London: Bloomsbury.

Lohse, Eduard. 1991. *Theological Ethics of the New Testament*. Translated by M. E. Boring. Minneapolis: Fortress.

Longman, Tremper, III. 2017. *The Fear of the Lord Is Wisdom: A Theological Introduction to Wisdom in Israel*. Grand Rapids: Baker Academic.

McKnight, Scot. 2009. *Fasting.*The Ancient Practices. Nashville: Nelson.

———. 2013. *The Sermon on the Mount*. Story of God Bible Commentary. Grand Rapids: Zondervan.

Pennington, Jonathan T. 2017. *The Sermon on the Mount and Human Flourishing: A Theological Commentary*. Grand Rapids: Baker Academic.

Wheeler, Sondra Ely. 1995. *Wealth as Peril and Obligation: The New Testament on Possessions*. Grand Rapids: Eerdmans.

8.4 Parables of Jesus

Russell Morton

The parables of Jesus and the later rabbis did not emerge in a vacuum. They reflect the heritage of pre-literary and early literary societies, which used stories both in etiological narratives, which explain why things are the way they are, and to convey moral and religious instruction. Examples include the Homeric epics (the *Illiad* and *Odyssey*), the Aesopic fables, and the Icelandic Sagas. In a similar fashion, Synoptic, Tannaitic, and Amoraitic parables (*meshalim*) are linked to ancient Near Eastern traditions of storytelling, examples of which are found in narratives of the Hebrew Bible.

Terms

Discussion of parables usually begins with an analysis of the Hebrew and Greek words translated "parable." The Hebrew term is *mashal*. In the verbal form, the word refers to a comparison, where one thing is "like" another (Beyse 1998, 65; Westermann 1990). Examples of this usage are found in Job 30:19; Ps 28:1; 49:13, 21; 143:7; Isa 14:10; and Isa 46:5. The last example is the only case where YHWH speaks of his own incomparability, "to whom will you liken and equate me, and compare me and we are alike" (author's translation; Beyse 1998, 65). In ten instances the word means "to speak in proverbs or in parables" (Snodgrass 2008, 39). It can also be used in a negative sense to mean a "byword" (1 Kgs 9:7; 2 Chr 7:20; Job 17:6; Ps 44:14; Jer 24:9; Ezek 14:8; Joel 2:17; Wilson 1997, 1135).

The nominal form of *mashal* usually carries the meaning of "proverb" (see Prov 1:6). While normally associated with wisdom literature, *mashal* can also refer to an oracle, such as those found in the Balaam sequence of Num 23:7, 18; 24:3, 15, 20–21, 23. *Mashal* is also found in proverbial utterances in the prophetic corpus, such as 1 Sam 10:12 ("is Saul also among the prophets") and Ezekiel 18:2 // Jer 31:29 (Beyse 1998, 66). Ezekiel, likewise, provides a particularly rich source for understanding how the term *mashal* was employed in a prophetic context. Of the forty-eight times the root *mashal* occurs in the Hebrew Bible, one third of these are found in Ezekiel (Polk 1983, 573). Interestingly, *mashal* is not used in the Hebrew Bible to refer to extended "narrative parables." Rather, the word *meshal* (pl. *meshalim*) would be used in a later period to describe rabbinic stories.

The Greek word for "parable" is *parabolē*. Originally, it referred to a comparison. Yet, in the LXX, it was the term most commonly use to translate the Hebrew *mashal*. Like *mashal*, *parabolē* took on variety of meanings. It can refer to either a parable as an extended story (Mark 4:2), an aphorism (see Luke 4:23), a proverb, or an apocalyptic "similitude" (see *1 Enoch* 37–71; *4 Ezra* 4:13–18; see Hauck 1967, 744–51).

Parables in the Hebrew Bible

As noted, the term *mashal* is not applied to the stories in the Hebrew Bible that most closely resemble either Jesus' parables recorded in the Synoptic Gospels or the rabbinic *meshalim*. Furthermore, these stories are not found in the wisdom writings of the Hebrew Bible, but in the Former and Latter Prophets. Examples include: (1) Jotham's tale of the trees (Judg 9:7–15); (2) Nathan's judicial tale of the poor man's only lamb (2 Sam 12:1–4); (3) Joash's analogy of the thistle (2 Kgs 14:9); (4) Isaiah's song of the vineyard (Isa 5:1–6); and (5) Ezekiel's story of the vine and the eagles (Ezek 17:3–10). In addition, we may add: (6) Ezek 16:1–35, the allegory of the unfaithful wife; and (7) Ezek 23:1–34, the allegory of Ohola and Oholiabah. These examples represent different forms. Examples 1, 3, and 5 can be considered fables. Example 4 can be classified as an allegorical parable. Example 2 corresponds most in form to the parables found in the Synoptic Gospels (Gerhardson 1988, 345). Examples 6 and 7 are extended metaphors or allegories.

These cases indicate that narrative parables, or *meshalim*, cannot be specified by linguistic indicators alone. Parables are indicated by the comparative function of a narrative (Schipper 2009, 264n1). In the seven examples cited, the stories illuminate specific issues and introduce larger dialogues. In Nathan's story of the poor man and his lamb, the prophet specifically states the point of the judicial narrative is his indictment of David. In Isaiah's song of the vineyard, the prophet applies his analogy to Israel (Isa 5:7; Gerhardson 1988, 348). Likewise, Ezekiel's allegory of the faithless wife (Ezek 16:1–35) introduces his condemnation of Israel in verses 36–63. Similarly, Ezek 23:1–34 provides the introduction of Ezekiel's indictment of Jerusalem in verses 35–49.

Parables in the Synoptic Gospels

Although they are not described as *meshalim*, the extended metaphors or allegories of the Hebrew Bible provide a precedent for conveying ethical proclamations through storytelling. This model would be more fully developed in the ethical, theological, and eschatological messages transmitted via the parables of the Synoptic Gospels and the *Coptic Gospel of Thomas*. This section will focus on the parables of the Synoptic tradition, for while many scholars have held that the *Coptic Gospel of Thomas* represents an independent witness to Jesus (see Jeremias 1963; Crossan 1993; Funk 1993), I agree with others who conclude that *Thomas* is a second-century document, dependent in part upon one or more of the Synoptic Gospels (Meier 2016, 89–188).

There is little debate that Jesus spoke in parables. Scholars, however, do dispute how many of the parables recorded in the Synoptic tradition derive from Jesus. Craig Blomberg, for example, affirms that at their core the parables indisputably represent the teachings of Jesus (Blomberg 2012, 22–23). John Meier, on the other hand, disagrees. Other scholars, including Blomberg, Snodgrass, and Jeremias, assert that virtually no one in the Christian church followed Jesus' example by teaching in parables (see Blomberg 2012, 23). Meier, however, contends that it is absurd to think that Jesus' followers did not follow their master's example. Meier is convinced that only four parables can, with confidence, be attributed to the historical Jesus: the parables of the mustard seed; the evil tenants; the great supper; and the talents/pounds (2016, 48–57, 230–362).

Genre of Gospel Parables

Debate not only arises over how many of the parables recorded in the Synoptic Gospels are authentic to Jesus, but also over what constitutes a parable. Because the word *parabolē* possesses a wide range of meanings, it can be applied to brief proverbs (see Mark 7:16), short comparisons or similitudes (see Matt 13:31–32 // Luke 13:18–19; Matt 13:33 // Luke 13:20–21; Matt 13:44; Mark 4:26–29; Mark 4:30–32), and narrative parables (see Mark 4:3–8; Luke 10:25–37). Proverbial sayings and to a lesser extent similitudes roughly correspond to the wisdom *mashalim* recorded in the Hebrew Bible. Narrative parables reflect a development that is observed in the later rabbinic narrative *meshalim*. The Synoptic Gospels' narrative parables take various forms. Hultgren (2000), for example, has identified seven genres of parables: (1) parables of God's revelation; (2) parables of exemplary behavior; (3) wisdom parables; (4) parables of life before God; (5) parables of the final judgment; (6) allegorical parables; and (7) parables of the kingdom.

Interpretation of Gospel Parables

While Hultgren's classification is only one of many, it reflects the broader debate about how Synoptic parables should be interpreted. One question that has occupied scholars for over a century is whether Jesus' parables were allegories, or at least contained allegorical elements. Until the late nineteenth century, Synoptic parables were generally read as allegories. This view was challenged by Adolf Jülicher (1886–1899), who contended that Jesus' parables were not allegories. Jülicher's conclusion derived from an exhaustive comparison of Synoptic parables with rabbinic *meshalim*. Jülicher decided that allegory was a Greco-Roman phenomenon, foreign to the intellectual world of Judaism. Allegorical elements in parables, such as those found in the parables of the ten maidens (Matt 25:1–13) and the evil tenants (Matt 21:33–46 // Mark 12:1–12 // Luke 20:9–19), or allegorical interpretations of parables (Matt 13:18–33 // Mark 4:13–20 // Luke 8:11–15; see Matt 13:36–43), were the product of the later church. Jülicher's conclusions were adopted by later scholars, such as Dodd (1961) and Jeremias (1963).

This consensus, however, has been challenged. While it is true that patristic interpretations of parables as complex allegories, such as Augustine's explanation of the good Samaritan, missed the mark, this does not mean that parables do not contain allegorical elements. Not every feature of a parable is allegorical, but we can find features with double meanings (Blomberg 2012, 24–25). Furthermore, the fundamental assumption that allegory is foreign to Judaism cannot be maintained in light of the allegories of Ezek 16:1–35; 23:1–34. Meier's (2016, 87) conclusion that "one must come to each Synoptic parable with an open mind rather than a rigid grid" is well founded.

Another necessary consideration for interpreting the Synoptic parables is to determine whether they represent wisdom or prophetic speech. Witherington (1994, 155–83) asserts that parables, similitudes, and aphorisms represent wisdom speech. Crossan (1973) concurs, with the assertion that through his aphorisms, Jesus established a new view of humanity. Jesus' vision of God's commonwealth was constituted by a kingdom of "nobodies" and "undesirables." This new society is established in the present rather than the eschatological future

(Crossan 1993, 266–304). Thus, parables are not to be interpreted as examples of an anticipation of apocalyptic eschatological judgment, but as metaphors (Crossan 1973; see Funk 1983; Scott 1989). Wright (1996, 229–43) also declines to interpret Jesus' parables as pronouncements of apocalyptic judgment, but understands them as a recitation of Israel's paradoxical history. Meier (2016, 37–40) and Gerhardson (1988), on the other hand, recognize that the biblical precedent for narrative parables is found in the prophetic corpus rather than among the wisdom writings, and interpret them as prophetic announcements.

Part of the difficulty in determining whether the Synoptic parables represent wisdom or prophetic speech derives from the term *parabolē* itself. Since a *parabolē* can refer to an allegory, similitude, aphorism, or metaphor, interpreters must be careful not to employ a single rigid paradigm as their interpretive framework. Certain parables, such as the prodigal son, do have allegorical features. The three figures represent three different types of people: The father represents the compassionate God, a figure also found in the prophetic corpus (see Hos 11:1, 8). The younger son represents the repentant sinner. The elder son represents the religious establishment. Yet these three elements also represent a single point: God's patient yearning for Israel's lost to repent. Other parables, such as the evil tenants, may be interpreted eschatologically. On the other hand, short aphorisms such as Mark 7:16 are most likely wisdom sayings, expressing early Christian halakah.

Rabbinic Parables

Rabbinic parables reflect later developments of the storytelling tradition. Few rabbinic parables are attributed to early sages such as Shammai and Hillel, and even these examples may be later tales attributed to earlier teachers. This fact has led Jeremias (1963) to conclude that Jesus invented the parabolic genre, and that his example was adopted by the rabbis. This position is untenable. Teaching in parables reflects a form of instruction popular in Jesus' time. Outside the Synoptic Gospels, these tales were likely not preserved. Furthermore, scholars now recognize that the Synoptic Gospels, particularly Matthew, are not only Christian documents, but also reflect a Jewish milieu. Thus, it is likely that Jesus' use of parables as a tool in popular preaching was not unique (Stern 1991, 187). If parabolic preaching also reflected a prophetic rather than wisdom matrix, we may find a further contributing factor for the dearth of examples of parabolic teaching among Jesus' contemporaries, since the preaching of prophetic figures such as John the Baptist has been only scantily preserved.

Rabbinic parables also emerged out of a very different social setting from Jesus' parables. First, in contrast to the limited period of gospel ministry, rabbinic stories developed over a thousand years, from late antiquity to the late medieval period. Second, in contrast to Jesus' employment of parables in popular preaching, the rabbinic stories were largely exegetical. As exegesis, the *meshalim* employed rabbinic hermeneutical principles, such as *qal wahomer*, *hekeish*, *gezera shavah*, and *gematria* (Stern 1991, 42). Yet, while *meshalim* are exegetical, they display a unique form of exegesis, which can be described as "narrative exegesis." The classic narrative consisted of the following parts, although not necessarily in this order: (1) a prolegomenon, which sometimes includes Scripture reference(s); (2) an introduction, containing a simple statement such as "R. Eleazar said"; (3) the *mashal* itself; (4) the interpretation, or *nimshal*; and (5) prooftext(s) (Stern 1991, 8, 24; see Young 1998, 24–25).

The rabbinic *meshalim* often contain the Jewish community's apologetic responses to its neighbors. The destruction of the Temple in 70 CE was used by both Christians (see Tertullian, *Adv. Jud.* 13) and polytheists as evidence of God's rejection of Israel. One answer to this conclusion was the *mashal* on Lamentations 4:11 (*Lamentations Rabbah* 4.11), where a king decorated a wedding chamber for his son, but destroyed it after the son angered him. The conclusion was that it was better for God to pour out wrath on wood and stones (the Temple), rather than upon Israel.

The above example demonstrates common typological features in *meshalim*. Many featured a king who represents God (see also Matt 18:23; 22:2), a relative who represents Israel, and a comment on God's gracious treatment of Israel. Yet, king *meshalim* are not the only form of rabbinic parables. Other forms include fables or disputes among sages. The common feature of all the forms is that *meshalim* are fictional stories used to make exegetical observations.

The intended audience of rabbinic *meshalim* also differs from the implied hearers of Jesus' parables. Jesus' parables are directed toward the rural laity of first-century Galilee. The *meshalim* often reflect the apologetic concerns and disputes of the rabbinic class. This difference led Jeremias (1963) to conclude that rabbinic parables were inferior to Jesus' parables. A better evaluation is that rabbinic *meshalim* were never intended to compete with Jesus' parables in the popular imagination, and it is inappropriate to judge them as inferior.

Works Cited

Beyse, K. M. 1998. "לשׁמ." *TDOT* 9:64–67.

Blomberg, Craig L. 2012. *Interpreting the Parables*. 2nd ed. Downers Grove, IL: IVP Academic.

Crossan, John Dominic. 1973. *In Parables: The Challenge of the Historical Jesus*. New York: Harper & Row.

———. 1993. *The Historical Jesus: The Life of a Mediterranean Jewish Peasant*. San Francisco: HarperSanFrancisco.

Dodd, C. H. 1961. *The Parables of the Kingdom.* New York: Scribner's Sons.

Funk, Robert. 1983. *Parables as Presence.* Philadelphia: Fortress.

———. 1993. *The Five Gospels: The Search for the Authentic Words of Jesus. New Translation and Commentary.* New York: Macmillan.

Gerhardson, Birger. 1988. "The Narrative Meshalim in the Synoptic Gospels: A Comparison with the Narrative Meshalim in the Old Testament. *NTS* 34:339–63.

Hauck, F. 1967. "παραβολή." *TDNT* 5:744–61.

Hultgren, Arlen. 2000. *The Parables of Jesus: A Commentary.* Grand Rapids: Eerdmans.

Jeremias, Joachim.1963. *The Parables of Jesus.* 2nd ed. New York: Scribner's Sons.

Jülicher, Adolf. 1886–1899. *Gleichnisreden Jesu.* Tübingen: Mohr Siebeck.

Meier, John P. 2016. *Probing the Authenticity of the Parables.* Vol. 5 of *A Marginal Jew: Rethinking the Historical Jesus.* Anchor Yale Bible Reference Library. New Haven: Yale University Press.

Polk, Timothy. 1983. "Paradigms, Parables and Měšalîm: On Reading the Māšāl in Scripture." *CBQ* 45:564–83.

Schipper, Jeremy. 2009. *Parables and Conflict in the Hebrew Bible.* Cambridge: Cambridge University Press.

Scott, Bernhard B. 1989. *Hear Then the Parable.* Minneapolis: Fortress.

Snodgrass, Klyne. 2008. *Tales with Intent: A Comprehensive Guide to the Parables of Jesus.* Grand Rapids: Eerdmans.

Stern, David. 1991. *Parables in Midrash: Narrative and Exegesis in Rabbinic Literature.* Cambridge: Harvard University Press.

Westermann, Claus. 1990. *The Parables of Jesus in Light of the Old Testament.* Translated and edited by Friedemann W. Golka and Alastair H. B. Logan. Minneapolis: Fortress.

Wilson, Gerald. 1997. "לשמ." *NIDOTTE* 2:1134–36.

Witherington, Ben, III. 1994. *Jesu the Sage: The Pilgrimage of Wisdom.* Minneapolis: Fortress.

Wright, N. T. 1996. *Jesus and the Victory of God.* Vol 2. of Christian Origins and the Question of God. Minneapolis: Fortress.

Young, Brad H. 1998. *The Parables: Jewish Tradition and Christian Interpretation.* Peabody, MA: Hendrickson.

PART III: THE TRUNK

CHAPTER 9

The Jewish Disciples

9.1 The Jewish Disciples in the Gospels

Andreas J. Köstenberger

The term customarily used for Jesus' followers in the Gospels is *mathētēs*, which occurs some two hundred times with reference to followers of Jesus in the Gospels. It occurs about seventy-five times in John's Gospel, the first instance being John 2:2 at the wedding in Cana. Linguistically, this expression is closely related to the rabbinic *talmid* (Rengstorf 1967, 442). The fact that the term is found nowhere else in the New Testament outside of the Gospels and the book of Acts indicates that the early church tied the term inextricably to the historical followers of Jesus. This suggests that the term *mathētēs* is part and parcel of the teacher-disciple relationship Jesus sustained with his followers during his earthly ministry (the following adapts portions of Köstenberger 1998b, used by permission; for a typology of rabbi-disciple relationships, see Wenthe 2006, 158–61).

The Disciples' Relationship with Their Teacher

Disciples of a certain rabbi would often follow their teacher wherever he went (*b. Berakhot* 23a, b, 24a, 60a; *b. Shabbat* 12b, 108b, 112a; *b. Eruvin* 30a; *b. Rosh Hashanah* 34b; *y. Hagigah* 2.1; *y. Bava Metzi'a* 2.3; Aberbach 1967, 7). The seriousness of commitment between rabbi and disciples overrode even one's commitment to one's own family (Luke 9:59–62; 14:26; Wenthe 2006, 158; Neudecker 1999, 251–52 cites *Leviticus Rabbah* 19.1 on Job 38:41: "If a man does not become as cruel towards himself, his children and his household as a raven [towards its young], he does not succeed in learning Torah").

In keeping with this practice, John and the other evangelists portray Jesus' disciples as accompanying their teacher at a large variety of occasions. They lived with him (e.g., John 1:39; 3:22). They joined him at a wedding together with his mother and brothers (John 2:1–12). They were the witnesses and beneficiaries of his teaching (e.g., Matt 10:1–42). They accompanied him when he healed the sick (e.g., Mark 5:21–43; Luke 6:17–19; John 9) and fed the multitudes (Mark 6:33–44; 8:1–9). In this way, the disciples' major calling was following Jesus and living in close fellowship with him (Schulz 1962, 137).

One key difference between contemporary rabbinic practice and Jesus was the fact that Jesus chose his disciples (John 15:16), while generally in his day disciples elected to attach themselves to a certain rabbi, as indicated by a statement attributed to Joshua ben Perahyah (ca. 100 BCE): "Provide yourself with a teacher and get yourself a fellow disciple" (*m. Avot* 1:6; cf. 1:16; Riesner 1991, 197; Lohse 1969, 962; Neudecker 1999, 249–51 contends the emphasis is on acquiring *one* teacher rather than multiple ones; cf. Matt 23:8).

Jesus and his followers shared a relationship that allowed his disciples to inquire regarding the significance of their teacher's actions or even to challenge him (e.g., John 13:6–10). During the Last Supper (a Passover meal; see Köstenberger 2011), the disciples repeatedly queried Jesus whenever they failed to grasp the meaning of his teaching (Peter: John 13:36–38; Thomas: John 14:5; Philip: John 14:8; and Judas [not Iscariot]: John 14:22). This cohered with contemporary Jewish practice (*m. Berakhot* 2:6–7; *y. Sotah* 1.4; Aberbach 1967, 20; Neudecker 1999, 252–55). "Students could also argue freely with their teachers during discussions," yet they were to do so "not in a contentious spirit but reverently and with due restraint" (Aberbach 1967, 9). This open interchange did not diminish the disciples' respect for their teacher. Rather, respect grew into love, loyalty, and deep devotion (*m. Avot* 4:12; *Song of Songs Rabbah* 8.7; *b. Berakhot* 5b; *b. Sanhedrin* 101a; Aberbach 1967, 17–18; Neudecker 1999, 257–59).

The relationship of master and disciples was akin to that of parents and children. In fact, at times a student would place his teacher even above his father because his

> father had brought him only into this world, but the master would show him the way to eternal life. . . . The master was truly and really the second father of the disciple, who would shape him for eternity as the father had for this world. The father had given the physical features. The master would sculpt the soul. (Neusner 1975, 95)

While the parent-child relationship was based on nature, the master-disciple relationship was a matter of choice (Daube 1972, 3). Like family members, master and disciples had responsibilities, not just *to* but also *for* one another in the outside world (1972). This identification in the eyes of the world came into sharper focus toward the end of Jesus' ministry when it became clear that his disciples would be held responsible for his teaching (John 15:18–21).

Performing Acts of Service

One of the key characteristics of Jesus' disciples was rendering service to their teacher (Neudecker 1999, 255–56). They were sent to buy bread (John 4:8) and asked to help provide food for the multitudes (Matt 14:16). At the latter occasion, Jesus instructed them to have the people sit down, to distribute the food, and later to gather the leftovers (Luke 9:14–16; John 6:12). In this regard, they conformed to the customary pattern of disciples in that day. Buying food, together with the preparation, cooking, and serving of food, were considered duties of the followers of a rabbi (*y. Shevi'it* 9.9; *y. Berakhot* 8.5; *t. Berakhot* 6.4–5; Aberbach 1967, 6). Notably, as in the case of the footwashing, Jesus' preparation of breakfast for his disciples following his resurrection reversed the common pattern of teacher-disciple relationships in his day (John 21:9–13).

The disciples' duty to care for their master's various needs even transcended his death. In keeping with this, "the disciple Jesus loved" was given the responsibility of caring for Jesus' mother (John 19:26–27) while Joseph of Arimathea and Nicodemus, two secret followers of Jesus from among the Pharisees, assumed responsibility for Jesus' burial, as was customary for disciples. In fact, "The death of a teacher was a major disaster for his students.... It was a matter of course for disciples to attend their master's funeral or even to bury him themselves" (Aberbach 1967, 21; see also Wenthe 2006, 160; cf. *y. Berakhot* 3.1; *y. Mo'ed Qatan* 3.5; *b. Berakhot* 42b; *b. Sanhedrin* 68a). Disciples must honor their deceased teacher by closely adhering to his teaching (*b. Yoma* 28a). The faithful witness borne by "the disciple Jesus loved" to his master's teaching in form of a written Gospel constituted a discharge of this responsibility (John 21:24–25; Köstenberger 1998a, 158–61; Gerhardsson 1961, 330).

Works Cited

Aberbach, Moses. 1967. "The Relations between Master and Disciple in the Talmudic Age." Pages 1–24 in *Essays Presented to Chief Rabbi Israel Brodie*. Edited by H. J. Zimmels, J. Rabbinowitz, and L. Finestein. London: Soncino.

Daube, David. 1972. "Responsibilities of Master and Disciples in the Gospels." *NTS* 19:1–15.

Gerhardsson, Birger. 1961. *Memory and Manuscript: Oral Tradition and Written Transmission in Rabbinic Judaism and Early Christianity*. Lund: Gleerup.

Köstenberger, Andreas J. 1998a. *The Missions of Jesus and the Disciples according to the Fourth Gospel*. Grand Rapids: Eerdmans.

———. 1998b. "Jesus as Rabbi in the Fourth Gospel." *BBR* 8:97–128.

———. 2011. "The Lord's Supper as a Passover Meal." Pages 6–30 in *The Lord's Supper: Remembering and Proclaiming Christ Until He Comes*. Edited by Thomas R. Schreiner and Matthew R. Crawford. NAC Studies in Bible & Theology 10. Nashville: B&H Academic.

Lohse, Eduard. 1969. "ῥαββί, ῥαββουνί." *TDNT* 6:961–65.

Neudecker, Reinhard. 1999. "Master-Disciple/Disciple-Master Relationship in Rabbinic Judaism and in the Gospels." *Gregorianum* 80:245–61.

Neusner, Jacob. 1975. *First-Century Judaism in Crisis*. New York: Abingdon.

Rengstorf, K. H. 1967. "μανθάνω, κτλ." *TDNT* 4:390–461.

Riesner, Rainer.1991. "Jesus as Preacher and Teacher." Pages 185–210 in *Jesus and the Oral Gospel Tradition*. Edited by Henry Wansborough. JSNTSup 64. Sheffield: JSOT Press.

Schulz, Anselm. 1962. *Nachfolgen und Nachahmen. Studien über das Verhältnis der neutestamentlichen Jüngerschaft zur urchristlichen Vorbildethik*. SANT 6. Munich: Kosel.

Wenthe, Dean O. 2006. "The Social Configuration of the Rabbi-Disciple Relationship: Evidence and Implications for First Century Palestine." Pages 143–74 in *Studies in the Hebrew Bible, Qumran, and the Septuagint: Presented to Eugene Ulrich*. Edited by Peter W. Flint, Emanuel Tov, and James C. Vanderkam. VTSup 101. Leiden: Brill.

9.2 The Jewish Disciples in the Book of Acts

Jim R. Sibley

The early church did not need to conduct a careful search for its Jewish roots. It was entirely Jewish! It was born in the Temple precincts, in Solomon's Portico, founded upon faith in Israel's Messiah, fulfilling the prophecies of the ancient Hebrew Scriptures, and empowered by the Holy Spirit, even as the prophet Joel had prophesied. And all of this happened on a Jewish holiday, Pentecost, or as it is known in Hebrew, *Shavuot*, the Feast of Weeks.

In the New Testament, we are given four accounts of the birth and life of Jesus, but only one account of the birth and life of the early assembly of believers in Jesus. Acts gives us a history that is not recorded anywhere else. This book is essential for the Jewish roots of faith in Jesus and for knowledge about the Jewish believers in Jesus in the earliest period of the church. What can the book of Acts tell us about these early Jewish believers in Jesus?

We must first address issues with the book of Acts itself. Skepticism about Lukan authorship and a date for the composition as late as ca. 150 CE characterize more liberal scholarship. That Luke wrote the book is generally accepted by evangelicals, but debate exists regarding the date of its writing. One leading evangelical scholar prefers a date close to 70 CE (Keener 2012, 384), but gives the range of dates most are comfortable with as extending to no later than 90 CE (400). Another argues for a date of composition at 64 CE (Longenecker 1981, 238). Yet another suggests that Acts was written "not long after AD 62" (Schnabel 2012, 28).

However, the real issue is the period covered by this history, not the date of its composition. The last recorded event is Paul's imprisonment in Rome. Acts ends with these words: "And he stayed two full years in his own rented quarters and was welcoming all who came to him, preaching the kingdom of God and teaching concerning the Lord Jesus Christ with all openness, unhindered" (NASB). If Paul was released in the spring of 62 CE, the period under review here is from ca. 30 CE to 62 CE.

Named and Unnamed Individuals

There are approximately forty-nine individuals in Acts who are named and generally identified as having been Jewish (for a summary of what can be known about each, see Bauckham 2007, 81–92; Hvalvik 2007, 154–77). Two other possibilities are worth noting: Luke and Theophilus. Although not named directly, Luke is generally believed to have referred to himself in the so-called "we passages" (16:10–17; 20:5–15; 21:1–18; 27:1–37; 28:1–16). Scholars have traditionally assumed that Luke was a gentile; however, a growing number of New Testament scholars believe he was Jewish (see Allen 2010, 261–319). Theophilus, often assumed to be an otherwise unknown Roman official due to the manner of address ("most excellent," Luke 1:3), may well have been a former Sadducee and high priest. Josephus tells us that the third son of Annas was named Theophilus. He served as high priest from 37–41 CE. Allen (324–41) proposes that he was deposed because of his favorability toward the new faith in Jesus. If this is true, Acts may have been written by a Jewish physician to strengthen the faith of a former high priest.

There are also a number of unnamed individuals and groups that must be included. For example, in the upper room, prior to Pentecost, the apostles are gathered "with the women . . . and with His brothers" (1:14). "The women" likely refers to those who have been introduced in the Gospel of Luke in 8:2–3; 23:49; and 23:55–24:10, who followed Jesus throughout his ministry, were present at his death, and supported him and his apostles out of their personal means. These women, and others who would join them in faith later, function mostly in the background, but throughout Acts they play very significant roles in the early movement of Jesus' disciples. "His brothers" has reference to Jesus' brothers (sons of Joseph and Mary). Mark 6:3 and Matt 13:55–56 say that his brothers were James, Joses (or Joseph), Jude, and Simon. James would later lead the congregation in Jerusalem, and tradition claims that he was succeeded by his brothers. These, along with scores of others, were gathered in the upper room. More would be added in the course of the numerical growth of Jewish disciples.

The Numerical Growth of Jewish Disciples

We know that the group of disciples left the upper room and moved to the Temple, because Acts 2:6 indicates that the multitude came to them, and not vice versa. In other words, the miracle of Pentecost occurred in the same place as the sermon of Peter. It is impossible to imagine multitudes gathering in an upper room. On the other hand, the Temple was the place to be on the day of Pentecost. This is where the multitudes were (Dunn 2009, 180).

Solomon's Portico, although not the Temple building itself, was a part of the Temple complex. It could be referred to as a "house" (v. 1) or a "place" (v. 2), but also as "the temple" (v. 46). It is specifically the place of Peter's next address (3:11–26). As a part of the Temple, it would also be an appropriate place to bring the "first fruits" of the gospel proclamation. Two centuries later, Tertullian insisted (1956, 7): "Our principles come from the Porch of Solomon." He was insisting that Christian faith did not come from pagan sources, but from the very center of the Jewish people, the Temple in Jerusalem. With attention having moved to Solomon's Portico, in the precincts of the Temple, the events of Pentecost and of Peter's sermon gave birth to the Spirit-empowered congregation of Jewish disciples of Jesus. Here, three thousand Jewish pilgrims, mostly from the diaspora, would become disciples of Jesus and be baptized in the huge, public *mikva'ot*, or ritual baths, in the area.

Following the healing of the lame man (3:1–11), who had doubtless become a follower of Jesus, and Peter's second sermon (3:12–26), an additional two thousand were added to the initial harvest. This brought the number to five thousand (4:4). Later in Acts, Paul is told of the "many thousands there [were] among the Jews of those who have believed" (21:20).

Luke reports that "a great many of the priests were becoming obedient to the faith" (6:7). The Sadducean aristocracy had become thoroughly corrupt and was among those held responsible for nailing Jesus "to a cross by the hands of godless men" (2:23). Yet many of the priests had doubtless heard the apostolic testimony at the Temple; they had seen the miraculous displays of supernatural power that authenticated the testimony of the disciples, and they had witnessed their sincerity and faith. Jesus had transferred spiritual authority for the nation from "the chief priests and Pharisees" (Matt 21:45) to the apostles (Matt 21:41) and declared the Temple "desolate" (Matt 23:38). The nation was now under new management; better results were expected! Later, we are told of "some of the sect of the Pharisees who had believed" (15:5). These were the only ones who reportedly brought a defective theology, which was overruled by the apostolic leadership (15:23–29).

The record of this growth in Jerusalem is significant. It is intended to emphasize that faith in Jesus was thoroughly Jewish and that the church began with a large Jewish contingent, in fact, with the remnant of Israel. This remnant was drawn from all segments of the Jewish population. Fiensy (1995, 213) concluded that "nearly all levels of society were represented." If the number of disciples was "many tens of thousands" (Greek *myriades*; 21:20), and the total population of Jerusalem was slightly more than a hundred thousand (Reinhardt 1995, 263), the Jewish disciples of Jesus constituted a very significant proportion. Jervell says it was half of the population (Jervell 1972b, 158). These disciples were drawn from all of the major Jewish groups at the time.

Outside of Jerusalem, the gospel spread throughout Judea and Samaria. It should be noted that sometimes "Judea" is understood as including Galilee. In the New Testament, it means the land of the Jews. For example, in Luke 4, Jesus is in Capernaum (v. 31), but announces his intention to preach in "the other cities also" (v. 43). The next verse (v. 44) says, "So He kept on preaching in the synagogues of Judea." Here, "Judea" includes Capernaum, as well as "the other cities" in Galilee. The brothers of Jesus and perhaps others from Galilee took the gospel there after the persecution which followed the martyrdom of Stephen (8:1).

At the same time, Philip went to Samaria and began to preach the gospel. The result was that "the multitudes with one accord were giving attention to what was said by Philip" (8:6). As these Samaritans came to faith in Jesus, they were moving not only from separation from God to fellowship with him but also from apostasy to orthodoxy. Thus, there is a sense in which there was a partial reunification of the tribes of Israel. In fact, there are reasons to believe that these Samaritans followed the example of Pharisees, Sadducees, priests, Essenes, Zealots, and many of the common people who were joining the earliest disciples of Jesus. It should be noted here that Philip's daughters were also believers, as we see in 21:9.

Prior to the admission of Cornelius, the first gentile believer (11:1; 15:7), the entire movement of Jesus' disciples was Jewish. This included the Ethiopian eunuch (8:26–40). He is often thought to have been a gentile, but the way Luke has constructed his narrative, it is clear that he is presented as Jewish (Jervell 1972a). Some suggest he was a proselyte, but it is also possible that he was born Jewish and had been given his role as the "minister of finance" for the queen of Ethiopia, even as Joseph had held a high position in Egypt.

Following Peter's miraculous deliverance from prison, Luke says that Peter "left and went to another place" (12:17). He returns for the Jerusalem Council (15:7–11), but otherwise is not heard from again in Acts. It is possible that he visited some who had become disciples on the day of Pentecost, establishing congregations in their regions, primarily in Asia Minor (cf. 2:9–11 with 1 Pet 1:1) and ministering in Babylon, one of the largest Jewish population centers of the day (see 1 Pet 5:13).

Even as the number of disciples continued to grow throughout Jerusalem, Judea, and Samaria, the gospel went forth to "the remotest part of the earth"

(1:8). This sphere of growth is narrated primarily with reference to Paul. Surely there were others, like Peter, who took the gospel to the diaspora. Barnabas, John Mark, and Silas accompanied Paul as representatives of Jerusalem. Later, his Jewish companions from the diaspora were Timothy, Aristarchus, and Luke.

Almost every city where Paul preached the gospel had a Jewish population. Perga, Lystra, and Troas may have been the only exceptions. Everywhere Paul went, his practice, based on the conviction he stated in Rom 1:16, was to go "to the Jew first, and also to the Greek." Every time Paul preached to Jewish people, there were at least some who became disciples.

Congregational Life of Jewish Disciples

On Pentecost and for the subsequent period of time, the earliest disciples met in Solomon's Portico, probably at the site of the present Al-Aqsa Mosque. Acts 2:46 says that they met "in the Temple" and also "house to house." Bagatti (1971) presents the archaeological evidence of early worship centers in Jerusalem, Nazareth, and Capernaum. [See Figures 8, 12–13, 19.]

The resurrection took place on Sunday, which was the Feast of First Fruits, so the Feast of Weeks (Pentecost), which was to be seven weeks later, was also on Sunday. Peter's sermon on the day of Pentecost was at 9:00 a.m. (2:15). Initially, the disciples met daily (2:46). Eventually, the pattern emerges of teaching in the synagogues on Saturday for evangelism (13:14, 42, 44; 16:13; 17:2; 18:4) and on Sundays for teaching the disciples (20:7; see also John 20:19, where Jesus appeared to the disciples on Sunday; and Rev 1:10, where it is called "the Lord's Day"). Interestingly, Pharisaic traditions say that Elijah would introduce Messiah on the first day of the week (*b. Eruvin*, 43b).

The authority for the beliefs and practices of the Jewish disciples in Acts were twofold: The Hebrew Scriptures and the authoritative teaching of the apostles. The Scriptures had been fulfilled by Jesus in many specific ways. These were neither contrived nor did they violate the original meaning of the texts. There are roughly the same number of citations from Psalms as from the Torah in Acts, and at least ten books from the Hebrew Scriptures are cited.

With the inauguration of the new covenant, the apostles constituted the spiritual authorities, and the miraculous signs authenticated their message. In addition to the Twelve, the authority of Paul is also emphasized. Having been specifically commissioned by the risen Jesus, and as a Hebrew-speaking Pharisee, brought up in Jerusalem, educated under Gamaliel "strictly according to the law of our fathers, being zealous for God" (22:2–3), and believing in the Messiah, "Paul is the real Pharisee and the true Jew who has the right to serve as the teacher of Israel" (Jervell 1972b, 171).

Jesus formed the essential core of the belief system of the Jewish disciples in Acts. He is Messiah (Greek, *Christos*), and "'Christ' was seen as the chief identity marker of the new sect" (Dunn 2009, 214). As Messiah, he was also the long-awaited prophet like Moses (Deut 18:15, 18–19; Acts 3:22–23; 7:37). He was the Lamb of Isa 53 and the Son of David who was raised from the dead according to prophecy (Acts 2:27–32; Ps 16:8–11). Perhaps under the influence of Pss 2 and 110, Jesus was understood as the Son of God (Dunn 2009, 216). These Jewish disciples are presented from the first (2:33–36) as having believed in the deity of Jesus (Bauckham 1999). They believed that Jesus' death constituted the final and ultimate atonement for sin (2:38; 4:12; 5:30–31; 20:28).

Jesus was the Lord, and this was clearly evident in his resurrection. Dunn (2009, 212–13) says, "The claim that Jesus had been raised from the dead is the central and principal message of the preaching in Acts." Jervell (1972b, 170) adds that "Belief in the resurrection is thus the distinguishing mark of Israel." Jesus' death and resurrection signaled a new age of Israel's final covenant, the "new covenant" of Jer 31:31. His return could be imminent, but they were to wait for it (3:19–21), not in idleness, but in teaching, preaching, and persuading others.

Water baptism (immersion), as a first step of obedience, was practiced by these Jewish disciples from the very first, at Pentecost (2:41). Likewise, observance of the Lord's Supper was evidently a regular feature of worship (e.g., 2:42; 20:7). Polhill (1992, 418), commenting on Paul's preaching in Troas (20:7), says: "At Troas we are given a glimpse into the main elements of an early Christian worship service. It was observed on the first day of the week and consisted of the breaking of bread (the Lord's Supper) and preaching. That the Lord's Supper was accompanied by a larger fellowship meal may be indicated by the reference to their 'eating' in v. 11."

In addition to baptism and the Lord's Supper, prayer was a central practice. These early Jewish disciples "were continually devoting themselves to the apostles' teaching and to fellowship, to the breaking of bread and to prayer" (2:42). These references also bear witness to the centrality of preaching and teaching the Scriptures. While apostles are prominent at the beginning, increasingly elders rise to prominence in Acts. They are first mentioned in 11:30, but become prominent in chapter 15, in 16:4, and in 21:18.

The attitude toward the Mosaic law held by the Jewish disciples in Acts is a matter of some controversy. Luke emphasizes fidelity, if not zeal, toward the law (e.g., 21:20). Some today argue the continuing "obligatory observance of the Torah" for Jewish disciples of Jesus (Brumbach 2012, 52). Yet, it seems that in Acts there is a debate between the Jewish disciples of Jesus and others regarding what it meant to be zealous toward the law.

Laws of purity and the food laws had presented obstacles between Jews and gentiles. These obstacles had been rendered obsolete by Acts 10 (vv. 15, 28, 34), when it was clear not only that Peter could enter the home of Cornelius, but also could stay with him for several days (v. 48), and apparently eat his food as well. Furthermore, the Jewish disciples of Jesus believed that Jesus' death and resurrection had served to atone for sin (3:18–19; 4:12; 5:30–31; 13:38–39), thus rendering any atoning significance of the sacrificial system meaningless. Obviously, what it meant to be zealous for the law was a point of disputation.

Both Peter and Stephen believed that the law spoke of the prophet like Moses, and they believed Jesus was the fulfillment of this prophecy (3:22–23; 7:37–39). Faith in Jesus as the authoritative prophet prophesied in Deuteronomy (18:15, 18–19) was now seen as essential to Torah. Those who did not believe in him were apostate in their relationship to Torah. Those who sought atonement in any other way than through faith in Jesus were lost (4:12).

Zeal for the Torah, then, was understood by the Jewish disciples of Jesus in Acts as zeal for the God of Israel, zeal for the people of Israel, and zeal for the Messiah of Israel. It was to have an internal focus on faith and love. Faith in God's deliverance through Jesus (16:31) and love for God and for one's neighbor (Lev 19:18; Deut 6:5; Matt 22:36–40) defined what it meant to be faithful to Torah. This was the view of Joshua (Josh 22:5), Jesus, and also of James (see Evans 2014, 76, 92). Luke's emphasis on Torah in Acts is to make the point that belief in Jesus and new covenant faith is in perfect alignment with Torah and with the Hebrew Scriptures. It is the true faith of Israel.

Persecution

The apostles were arrested and placed in jail (5:17). Stephen met death by stoning (7:57–60). Subsequent persecution sent disciples all over Judea and Samaria "preaching the Word" (8:4). Herod was mistreating them, and he had James, the son of Zebedee, executed with a sword (12:1–2). Physical beatings and attempted murder became relatively common for Paul (9:29; 13:50; 14:5, 19; 16:22; 18:12; 21:36; 22:22; 23:10, 12–13). Of course, he was also imprisoned in Caesarea for two years (24:27) and later held under house arrest in Rome (28:16, 30). The way the disciples responded to persecution is a model for disciples of Jesus in all generations.

Works Cited

Allen, David L. 2010. *Lukan Authorship of Hebrews*. NAC Studies in Bible & Theology 8. Nashville: B&H Academic.

Bagatti, Bellarmino. 1971. *The Church of the Circumcision: History and Archaeology of the Judeo-Christians*. SBFCMi 2. Jerusalem: Franciscan Printing Press.

Bauckham, Richard. 1999. *God Crucified: Monotheism and Christology in the New Testament*. Grand Rapids: Eerdmans.

———. 2007. "James and the Jerusalem Community." Pages 55–95 in *Jewish Believers in Jesus: The Early Centuries*. Edited by Oskar Skarsaune and Reidar Hvalvik. Peabody, MA: Hendrickson.

Brumbach, Joshua. 2012. "The Role of Torah and Jewish Tradition in the Messianic Jewish Community." Pages 51–64 in *The Borough Park Papers, Symposium III: How Jewish Should the Messianic Jewish Community Be*? Clarksville, MD: Borough Park Symposium.

Dunn, James D. G. 2009. *Beginning from Jerusalem*. Vol. 2 of *Christianity in the Making*. Grand Rapids: Eerdmans.

Evans, Craig A. 2014. *From Jesus to the Church: The First Christian Generation*. Louisville: Westminster John Knox.

Fiensy, David A. 1995. "The Composition of the Jerusalem Church." Pages 213–36 in *The Book of Acts in Its Palestinian Setting*. Vol. 4 of *The Book of Acts in Its First Century Setting*. Edited by Richard Bauckham. Grand Rapids: Eerdmans.

Hvalvik, Reidar. 2007. "Named Jewish Believers Connected with the Pauline Mission." Pages 154–78 in *Jewish Believers in Jesus: The Early Centuries*. Edited by Oskar Skarsaune and Reidar Hvalvik. Peabody, MA: Hendrickson.

Jervell, Jacob. 1972a. "The Lost Sheep of the House of Israel: The Understanding of the Samaritans in Luke-Acts." Pages 113–32 in *Luke and the People of God: A New Look at Luke-Acts*. Minneapolis: Augsburg.

———. 1972b. "Paul: The Teacher of Israel; The Apologetic Speeches of Paul in Acts." Pages 153–83 in *Luke and the People of God: A New Look at Luke-Acts*. Minneapolis: Augsburg.

Keener, Craig S. 2012. *Introduction and 1:1–2:47*. Vol. 1 of *Acts: An Exegetical Commentary*. Grand Rapids: Baker Academic.

Longenecker, Richard N. 1981. *Acts*. The Expositor's Bible Commentary. Grand Rapids: Zondervan.

Polhill, John B. 1992. *Acts*. NAC. Nashville: Broadman & Holman.

Reinhardt, Wolfgang. 1995. "The Population Size of Jerusalem and the Numerical Growth of the Jerusalem Church." Pages 237–65 in *The Book of Acts in Its Palestinian Setting*. Vol. 4 of *The Book of Acts in Its First Century Setting*. Edited by Richard Bauckham. Grand Rapids: Eerdmans.

Schnabel, Eckhard J. 2012. *Acts*. Zondervan Exegetical Commentary on the New Testament. Grand Rapids: Zondervan.

Tertullian. 1956. "Prescription against Heretics." Pages 31–64 in *Early Latin Theology: Selections from Tertullian, Cyprian, Ambrose and Jerome*. LCC. Edited and translated by S. L. Greenslade. Philadelphia: Westminster.

9.3 The Jewishness of the Book of Hebrews

George H. Guthrie

The exact origin of the title "To the Hebrews" for the nineteenth book of the New Testament canon has been lost in the mists of early Christianity. Yet we know that by about 200 CE the title was being used in some quarters. 𝔓46, a papyrus collection of Paul's writings dated to 200 CE, has the oldest extant copy of Hebrews placed just after Romans. The document there carries the title, perhaps given to match the pattern of Paul's letters, bearing the title of the assumed addressees. In his *Miscellanies*, written at about the same time, Clement of Alexandria refers to the "Epistle to the Hebrews," as does Origen in various writings from the first half of the third century CE (Cockerill 2012, 3; Koester 2001, 20–21).

Yet, the title probably stems from the book's contents, rather than a lost salutation or an early memory of the specific audience to whom Hebrews was written. That audience, perhaps, consisted of a mix of those who were Jewish ethnically and gentile God-fearers, but they certainly "had been nurtured spiritually and intellectually in the hellenistic synagogue" (Lane 1991, liv), for the book is profoundly Jewish, especially in the Scriptures to which it appeals, its background of thought, argumentation, theological reflection, and mode of exhortation.

Jewish in Form

Unlike the letters of the New Testament, Hebrews begins with an impressive, highly crafted introduction (at times called a *proem* or *exordium*), rather than an epistolary opening (Guthrie 1994, 118). The author labels the work as a "word of exhortation," an expression that could be used of a synagogue homily (Heb 13:22, author's translation; cf. Acts 13:15); many scholars, in fact, believe that the book provides us with our most complete exemplar of an early Jewish sermon of the hellenistic synagogue context (Gelardini 2011). Characteristics like the exalted introduction, use of a communal "we" in exhorting the audience, the shift back and forth between exposition and exhortation, focus on the Psalms and the Pentateuch in their Greek form, formulae introducing biblical quotations as if they are falling from the lips of God (i.e., "God says," or "the Spirit says"), and the extensive use of exhortation material all point to "sermon" as the genre of the book (Thyen 1955, 106; Lane 1991, lxix–lxxv; Stegner 1988). In addition, Hebrews is replete with rhetorical devices such as strategic comparisons, example lists, rhetorical questions, alliteration, anaphora, antithesis, assonance, and asyndeton, suggesting that the author has reinforced the traditional homily form with a sophisticated use of devices from classical rhetoric (Wills 1984, 277–99; Black 1988, 1–18). Thus, the data and formal elements of the book suggest that the author had a background in both hellenistic, advanced education of the period and the Jewish synagogue.

Jewish Sources of Authority

The author of Hebrews builds his message on two great sources of authority: the Jewish Scriptures and the Christ Event (i.e., Messianic revelation). This becomes clear from the outset, where the author states that God has spoken in the former age through the prophets to the ancestors, but, with the coming of Messiah, he has spoken through that superior Son (Heb 1:1–2a). The author accesses the first of these authorities through the Scriptures and the second through historical witness. The two authorities are read in light of one another. The Scriptures anticipate the Messiah, and the Messiah clarifies the Scriptures, embodying their fulfillment.

As to the textual authority, no other New Testament book stands more thoroughly saturated with the Jewish Scriptures, except perhaps Revelation, which appropriates the Scriptures through allusions rather than direct quotations or reflections on people, events, or institutions. Most scholars agree, moreover, that not only was Hebrews written in a high style of Greek, it also uses a Greek translation of the Hebrew Scriptures. Yet, the author had some freedom to make stylistic changes, for literary purposes, to the form of those Scriptures or to emphasize nuances of the biblical text (Guthrie 2007, 922).

Appropriating the Scriptures, Hebrews utilizes some thirty-seven quotations, around forty allusions, nineteen summaries of Old Testament material, thirteen references where a name or topic occurs apart from a specific context, and at least a dozen or so echoes, or very faint allusions (Guthrie 2007, 919). The author's exposition of Christology draws mostly on the Psalms, which constitute nineteen of the book's quotations and fifteen allusions. The Pentateuch, on the other hand, provides a framework for redemptive history, with nine quotations and some fifteen allusions. The author also accesses a variety of texts from the Prophets, among whom Isaiah holds pride of place, and other texts such as 2 Samuel, Proverbs, and Joshua (Guthrie 2007, 921).

Further, argumentation in the book of Hebrews cannot be understood apart from a grasp of how the author utilizes rabbinic techniques of argumentation. Both the "string of pearls" (i.e., the *haraz*) of 1:5–14 (Bateman 1997) and the breathtaking *exempla* (example list) of Heb 11 were used by the rabbis to marshal a great deal of evidence in support of a particular viewpoint. The former consisted of stringing together Scripture passages, at times by virtue of common language or referents, in order to argue forcefully for a point. Hebrews does this with three pairs of texts that argue for the Son's superiority to the angels (1:5–12), followed by a climactic quotation of Ps 110:1. The Son is superior by virtue of his unique relationship to the Father (1:5; Ps 2:7; 2 Sam 7:14); his different role than that of the angels, who serve and worship him (1:6–7; Deut 32:43; Ps 104:4); and by his role as ruler and creator of the universe (1:8–12; Ps 45:6–7; Ps 102:25–27).

The example list of Heb 11, on the other hand, builds a rhythmic repetition (*anaphora*) of the term *pistei* ("by faith"), with the author mentioning a hero of the faith, the endeavor fueled by faith, and at times the outcome. Example upon example is given, with the message driven home—"faith is the only way to live well for God!" The author also utilizes a midrashic type of exposition in commenting on Ps 95 in Heb 3:7–19. "Midrash" as a method consists of a running commentary on a biblical text, as we find in the latter half of Hebrews' third chapter. He also uses the rabbinic practice of seizing on the meaning of a particular word, as with the emphasis on the term *kainē* ("new"; 8:13) from Jer 31:31–34, quoted at 8:8–12. Yet, the author's favorite method of using the scriptural text is "reinforcement," by which he supports a theological point or enhances a word of exhortation (2:5–8a, 12–13; 3:15; 4:7; 5:5–6; 7:17, 21; 8:5, 7; 10:16–17, 30, 37–38; 12:26; 13:5–6). Normally a quotation is provided just after a proposition or exhortation.

As for Hillel's guidelines for appropriation of the Scriptures, two stand as most vital to the arguments of Hebrews. Verbal analogy involved two texts being interpreted, one in light of the other, based on a common word or words. For instance, the quotations of Ps 2:7 and 2 Sam 7:14 are paired at 1:5 based on the common terms "son" (*huios*), the first person singular pronoun "I" (*egō*), and perhaps the verb of being. Similarly, each of the other two pairs of texts (1:6–12) in the string of pearls are also brought together by verbal analogy, as are Ps 95:7–11 and Gen 2:2 at 3:7–4:10, which share a common reference to God's "rest."

A second of Hillel's guidelines, an *a fortiori* or "argument from lesser to greater," reasoned that if something were true in a less significant situation, it certainly was true in a more significant situation and had greater implications. For example, having marshaled his texts in support of the Son's superiority to the angels in 1:5–14, the author then uses an argument from lesser to greater at 2:1–4. The reasoning goes something like this: *Those who received God's revelation of the word of God under the old covenant and rejected it were punished severely. How much greater punishment is deserved by those who turn away from the word of salvation given through the superior Son!* An *a fortiori* argument can also be found in other warnings such as Heb 10:28–29 and 12:25–27.

Although the Jewish Scriptures and (proto) rabbinic interpretation of those Scriptures form a primary backdrop for the author of Hebrews' discourse, the

Scriptures certainly are understood as being fulfilled in and therefore explicated in light of the coming and ministry of the messiah, through whom God has spoken preeminently (Heb 1:2). Thus, many of the quotations in Hebrews are presented as being about the son, often as words addressed to the son by God the Father (e.g., 1:5–13). For instance, Ps 8:4–6 is presented as fulfilled in the incarnation and exaltation of the Son, the anthropology of that original psalm taken up into the Christology of Hebrews (2:5–9). At 5:6 and throughout Heb 7, Ps 110:4 is presented as a word of solemn oath addressed to the Son, appointing him as priest before God.

Further, not only does God's word speak about the Son, the Son himself speaks revelation. In the argument from lesser to greater at 2:1–4, the author notes that the word of salvation was spoken first through the Lord Jesus and then confirmed by those who heard him, God himself also bearing witness to the veracity of the message by miracles and gifts of the Holy Spirit (2:3–4). Further, Hebrews presents the Messiah Son as a speaker of Scripture, particularly speaking of things he accomplishes through his ministry (e.g., 2:12–13; Ps 22:22; Isa 8:17–18; 10:5–7; Ps 40:6–8).

Jewish Thought and an Apocalyptic Framework

Scholars have tried to understand Hebrews' message against the backdrop of various other branches of first-century Judaism. Until the early 1960s, the dominant theory for Hebrews' background of thought was a form of platonic idealism similar to the Jewish writer Philo, argued, for instance, in Ceslas Spicq's (1953) great French commentary on Hebrews and more recently by James Thompson (1982). Other suggestions have been an association with the thought reflected at Qumran, a form of Gnosticism, or Merkabah Mysticism (Hurst 1990, 7–84). Yet, the majority of scholars now hold that Hebrews best fits a Jewish apocalyptic framework (Barrett 1954; Hurst 1990, 131). That framework holds several beliefs that seem to fit Hebrews' view of reality (Laansma 2008).

For example, like apocalyptic thought, a "heaven and earth" dualism exists in Hebrews, with movement between heaven and earth. For instance, Hebrews uses Ps 110:1 in part to move the discourse from a heavenly vantage point (1:3, 13), to incarnation (Ps 8 in conversation with Ps 110:1 at 2:5–9), back to heaven (8:1–2), where the son, having finished his work of offering, sits down at the right hand of the Father (10:12). Unlike platonic thought but very much in line with apocalyptic, Hebrews also evinces temporal movement from the age prior to the coming of Messiah to "the last days" (i.e., the time initiated with the coming of Messiah and continuing to the present), and anticipates the age to come (10:37–38; 12:25–28). Further, like apocalyptic thought, Hebrews also makes a clear distinction between the faithful people of God and those under the judgment and wrath of God (6:4–8; 10:26–31). Thus, Jewish apocalyptic thought forms the background for Hebrews' message.

At the center of Hebrews' theology is God himself, with the word *theos* ("God") occurring sixty-eight times in Hebrews. Foundationally, as with the creation account in Gen 1:1–2:4, God is a God who speaks (Heb 1:1–2a), and his word is "alive and active" (Heb 4:12). In speaking Scripture, God the Father is joined by God the Son (1:8; Ps 45:6) and God the Spirit (2:12–13; 3:7; 4:3; 10:5–7, 15–18), and at times the Father speaks Scripture to the Son (e.g., 1:5, 8–13; 5:6; 7:17, 21).

As to identity, the Son is God's exalted Messiah, who will be the heir of all things (Heb 1:2b, 5; Ps 2:7). The Scriptures point to the deity of the Son, who joins the Father both in the act of creating the universe (1:2, 10) and in sitting enthroned above it (1:3, 8–9, 13; Ps 110:1; 45:6–7; Bauckham 2009). He upholds all things by his powerful word (1:3). He is also the one who, in accordance with Ps 102:25–27, will wrap up the created order at the end of the age (Heb 1:11–12). The Son manifests God's glory, is the exact representation of his nature (1:3), and is worshiped and served by the angels (1:6–7; Ps 104:4). Thus, Hebrews begins with an exalted view of the Messiah.

Hebrews 2:5–9 effects a transition from this exalted view of the Son by the rabbinic technique of "dispelling confusion," considering Ps 110:1 in light of Ps 8:4–6, both psalms referring to things being submitted under the "feet" of the Son. Yet, Ps 110:1 suggests this submission will be in the future, while Ps 8 presents the submission as an accomplished fact. The author dispels confusion by proclaiming that Ps 8 means that all things have indeed been completely put under the Son's authority (Heb 2:8). Yet, the future orientation of Ps 110:1 means that we as human beings do not yet see all things submitted to him, that consummation of the submission will happen at the end of the age (Heb 2:8).

In his incarnation, the Son identifies with human beings, taking on flesh and blood in order to break the devil's power by dying, thus bringing spiritual freedom to humanity (2:10–16). God has accomplished this program of liberation by the new covenant, which is the basis for a worship system that parallels in numerous ways the old covenant system of relating to God. Thus, as with the old covenant high priests, the Messiah Son is taken from among human beings (Heb 2:17–18) and appointed as high priest (5:4–6; Lev 8–9). He is appointed a superior priest by virtue of the oath of Ps 110:4 (Heb 5:6) and in accordance with the order of Melchizedek (5:10; 7:1–10, 11–14). His superiority in part rests in the fact that he has an indestructible life and thus always lives to make intercession for new covenant people (7:16–25).

This superior high priest has established a new covenant with God (8:7–13; Jer 31:31–34), which means that the old covenant has become outdated (8:13). Part of the new covenant's superiority has to do with the Son's superior offering, which is made with the blood of the Messiah rather than the blood of animals

(9:9–14), is brought right into the presence of God in the heavenly holy of holies rather than an earthly tabernacle (9:11, 23–24; 10:12), and has been made once for all time rather than repeatedly (9:25–28; 10:1–4). Thus, the new covenant sacrifice of the Messiah has done away with sacrifice, having dealt decisively with the problem of sin (10:14–18).

The author's understanding of the identity and work of the Messiah lays the foundation for the exhortatory material in the book. Just like the old covenant law, the word delivered through the Son is binding and must be responded to, or severe punishment will be the result (2:1–4). The hearers must not follow the example of those in the wilderness generation, who lacked trust in God and were disobedient, to their peril (3:7–19). Rather, they should hear the promise of rest, which is a new covenant, Day of Atonement rest (4:1–10), and respond to it in trust, like the great saints of the ages (6:11; 11:1–40), experiencing fruit and salvation (6:7–12). They should endure to the end and receive the promised inheritance of God (6:12; 10:32–39), rather than facing the fiery judgment of God (6:4–8; 10:26–31, 39; 12:5–29). In the meantime, they should live in light of foundational Jewish beliefs (6:1–3), as well as more advanced teaching about the Messiah (6:1–3). They should spur each other on to love and good deeds (3:12–13; 13:1–6), meeting together (10:25) even as they anticipate the day of the Lord (10:25).

The Jewish Context and Purpose of Hebrews

It seems likely, given the message of Hebrews, that the book was written to first-century believers of Jesus, the majority of whom either were Jewish ethnically or had an extensive background in the Hellenistic synagogue. The author was trained in the Jewish Scriptures, skilled in rabbinic argumentation, familiar with the theology of the Hellenistic synagogue, and a practiced preacher in that context. He had a pastoral agenda with the congregation(s) to whom he wrote. It seems the hearers' allegiance to Messiah Jesus had become a stimulus for significant persecution of some kind, and some, perhaps, had been tempted to return to mainline Judaism. The message and challenge for the book's original audience concerned continuing to embrace belief in Jesus as Messiah and the exalted Lord, and standing in association with the church in the face of a hostile world. The author's solution to the waning commitment of some in the congregation(s) involved deepening their understanding of the teachings about Jesus, specifically his identity as Savior and king of the universe and the superiority of his new covenant with its superior offering and basis for relationship with God. The first hearers of Hebrews were called to respond to this "word of exhortation" (13:22) by remaining faithful to God, his Messiah, his church, and the mission carried out on the way to the heavenly Jerusalem.

Works Cited

Barrett, C. K. 1954. "The Eschatology of the Epistle to the Hebrews." Pages 363–93 in *The Background of the New Testament and Its Eschatology*. Edited by W. D. Davies and D. Daube. Cambridge: Cambridge University Press.

Bateman, Herbert W., IV. 1997. *Early Jewish Hermeneutics and Hebrews 1:5–13*. American University Studies, Series 7: Theology and Religion 193. New York: Peter Lang.

Bauckham, Richard. 2009. "The Divinity of Jesus Christ in the Epistle to the Hebrews." Pages 15–36 in *The Epistle to the Hebrews and Christian Theology*. Edited by Richard Bauckham, Daniel R. Driver, Trevor A. Hart, and Nathan MacDonald. Grand Rapids: Eerdmans.

Black, C. Clifton, II. 1988. "The Rhetorical Form of the Hellenistic Jewish and Early Christian Sermon: A Response to Lawrence Wills." *HTR* 81:1–18.

Cockerill, Gareth L. 2012. *The Epistle to the Hebrews*. NICNT. Grand Rapids: Eerdmans.

Gelardini, Gabriella. 2011. "Hebrews, Homiletics, and Liturgical Scripture Interpretation." Pages 121–43 in *Reading the Epistle to the Hebrews: A Resource for Students*. Edited by Eric F. Mason and Kevin B. McCruden. RBS. Atlanta: SBL Press.

Guthrie, George H. 1994. *The Structure of Hebrews: A Text-linguistic Analysis*. NovTSup. Leiden: Brill.

———. 2007. "Hebrews." Pages 919–95 in *Commentary on the New Testament Use on the Old Testament*. Edited by G. K. Beale and D. A. Carson. Grand Rapids: Baker Academic.

Hurst, L. D. 1990. *The Epistle to the Hebrews: Its Background of Thought*. SNTSMS 65. Cambridge: Cambridge University Press.

Koester, Craig R. 2001. *Hebrews: A New Testament Translation with Introduction and Commentary*. AB 36. New York: Doubleday.

Laansma, Jon. 2008. "The Cosmology of Hebrews." Pages 125–43 in *Cosmology and New Testament Theology*. Edited by Jonathan T. Pennington and Sean M. McDonough. London: T&T Clark.

Lane, William L. 1991. *Hebrews*. 2 vols. WBC 47a–47b. Dallas: Word.

Spicq, Ceslas. 1953. *L'Épître aux Hébreux*. 2nd ed. 2 vols. *EBib*. Paris: Gabalda.

Stegner, W. R. 1988. "The Ancient Jewish Synagogue Homily." Pages 51–69 in *Greco-Roman Literature and the New Testament: Selected Forms and Genres*. Edited by David E. Aune. SBLSBS 21. Atlanta: SBL Press.

Thompson, James W. 1982. *The Beginnings of Christian Philosophy*. CBQMS 13. Washington, DC: The Catholic Biblical Association of America.

Thyen, Hartwig. 1955. *Der Stil der Jüdisch-Hellenistischen Homilie*. FRLANT 47. Göttingen: Vandenhoeck & Ruprecht.

Wills, Lawrence. 1984. "The Form of the Sermon in Hellenistic Judaism and Early Christianity." *HTR* 77:277–99.

9.4 Jews and Judaism in the Gospel of John

Craig A. Evans

The Gospel of John is sometimes identified as the most anti-Semitic writing of the New Testament. This is asserted because of the book's pointed criticisms and polemic directed against a group called "the Jews." But does criticism of these people constitute anti-Semitism? Many scholars rightly point out that John can be understood this way only if it is interpreted out of context.

Robert Kysar (1993, 125), a well-respected Johannine scholar, puts his finger on the problem when he observes that John is "often read and understood without reference to its first purpose." Moody Smith (1990, 82), another leading interpreter of John, comments that the contention that John is anti-Semitic "is a misreading of the text and, presumably, of the intention of its author(s)." Alas, it is an all too common misreading, in which it is believed that the "Jews" (or Judeans) who plot against Jesus and his disciples in the first century represent the Jewish people as a whole, and for all generations, who perversely oppose the true faith. The language and meaning of John can only be understood aright when interpreted in its original setting (von Wahlde 1982; Donaldson 2010; Reinhartz 2011; Culpepper and Anderson 2017).

The Meaning of "Jews" (*Ioudaioi*) in the Gospel of John

"Jews" (*Ioudaioi*) are mentioned in the Gospel of John some seventy times (Ashton 1985). Most scholars agree that the majority of occurrences mean Judeans, that is, the Jewish people who live in Judea as opposed to the Samaritans or the Jewish people who live in Galilee. For example, the first time the word occurs is in reference to the Jews who "sent priests and Levites from Jerusalem" to put a question to the John the Baptist (John 1:19, author's translation). John, of course, was Jewish and, according to the Gospel of Luke, was himself of Levitical descent (Luke 1:5, 57–63). We see the same thing when Jesus is in Jerusalem: "The Jews" approach Jesus and ask him a question (John 2:18). Again, "Jews" means Judean Jews.

Sometimes a reference to "the Jews" in the Gospel of John is a way of saying *Jewish*, as in the story of the wedding at Cana of Galilee: "Now there were six stone water pots set there for the Jewish custom of purification" (John 2:6

NASB). The text literally reads, "according to the purification (custom) of the Jews." Here the evangelist is not distinguishing the Jews of Judea from the Jews of Galilee, but is explaining a Jewish custom that all Jews observe to non-Jewish readers. The same applies in the next passage, when the evangelist states that the "Passover of the Jews was at hand" (John 2:13). The slaughter of the Passover lambs may have taken place in Jerusalem, but the reference "of the Jews" is not restricted to the Jewish people who live in Judea. After all, Jews everywhere, in Israel and in the diaspora, celebrated Passover. We see this again in the Gospel of John, when we are told of the "feast of the Jews" (John 5:1; cf. 6:4).

One very important example is somewhat ambiguous. In Sycar, Samaria, a Samaritan woman asks Jesus: "How is it that you, a Jew, ask a drink of me, a woman of Samaria?" (John 4:9 RSV). One assumes that by "Jew" she means all ethnic Jews, whether they are from Galilee, as Jesus and most of his disciples were, or from Judea, like Nicodemus and Joseph of Arimathea, among others. The woman says to Jesus: "Our fathers worshiped on this mountain; and you say that in Jerusalem is the place where people ought to worship" (John 4:26). Here the woman has contrasted Samaria's Mount Gerizim, which was sacred to the Samaritan people, with Judea's Jerusalem (or the Temple Mount, it would have been assumed). Perhaps she is contrasting the Jews of Judea with the people of Samaria. But I think it is more likely that the Samaritan woman lumps together the Jews of Galilee with the Jews of Judea as a single people, over against their Samaritan rivals. After all, both the Jews of Galilee and the Jews of Judea worship God in the Temple in Jerusalem. The Samaritan woman does not think of Jesus as a Galilean Jew; she thinks of him and his followers simply as Jews.

The encounter with the Samaritan woman gives the Jesus of the Gospel of John the opportunity to make a very positive statement regarding the Jewish people: "You worship what you do not know; we worship what we know, for salvation is from the Jews" (John 4:22 RSV). Whatever the precise nuance of this statement might be, it is clearly affirming of the Jewish people and their faith. Salvation comes from the Jewish people (and not simply the Judean Jews, but all Jews). This salvation, moreover, extends to the whole world, including Jews, Samaritans, and gentiles (as affirmed in John 3:16, which speaks of God's love for "the world").

There are negative references to the *Ioudaioi*, which some think are in reference to the Jewish people in general. Careful consideration of the context of each passage, however, suggests that regional and/or party identities are in play. For example, when Jesus heals the man near the Sheep Gate on the Sabbath, "the Jews" criticize the man for carrying the bed on which he had lain (John 5:10). The healed man informs "the Jews" that it was Jesus who healed him (John 5:15). "The Jews" persecute Jesus (5:16) and seek to kill him (5:18). But these *Ioudaioi* are Judean Jews, not Jews in general (e.g., from Galilee or from the diaspora). Other occurrences of *Ioudaioi* should be understood the same way.

"The Jews" murmur at Jesus when he speaks of himself as having come "down from heaven" (6:41) and refers to his flesh as food (6:52). But is *Ioudaioi* here a reference to Jews in general or to Judeans? Jesus is in Galilee, where he has fed the multitude (6:5–14) and then likened himself to bread from heaven (6:25–40). It seems, then, that "the Jews" who murmur are in fact Judeans, in contrast to the local Galileans. There is no criticism of the Jewish people as a whole, only an implied criticism of some Judeans.

The same seems to apply in John 7:1, where we are told that Jesus traveled about in Galilee, not Judea, "because the Jews sought to kill him." Here *Ioudaioi* surely means some Judean Jews, not Jews in general. So also in 7:11. Jesus is in Jerusalem, at a feast (Passover?), and again "the Jews" are looking for him. We are told, moreover, that people are afraid to speak openly about Jesus "for fear of the Jews" (7:13). The evangelist must be speaking of Judeans—as opposed to Galilean Jews and diaspora Jews. The *Ioudaioi* of 7:15 and 7:35 are Judeans, not Jews in general. Otherwise, who are the people who are afraid to speak? Are they not also Jews? The same applies to 8:22 and 8:31. In the latter passage we learn that some Judeans believe in Jesus. *Ioudaioi* would not make sense translated as "Jews" here.

Other *Ioudaioi* do not believe in Jesus, saying, instead, "Do we not rightly say that you are a Samaritan and have a demon?" (8:48; cf. 8:52). Here the Judeans distinguish themselves from Jesus with a racial slur, suggesting that perhaps he really is a possessed Samaritan and, it is implied, not even a Galilean.

The *Ioudaioi* who question the formerly blind man who had been healed by Jesus (John 9:1–34) must be seen as "Judeans," in contrast to the Galilean Jesus. After all, the formerly blind man and his parents, who play important roles in the story, are themselves Jews (and presumably Judeans as well). The evangelist is writing to people who might not realize that there are factional, regional, and even tribal distinctions among the Jewish people. The Jews of Judea are not the same as the Jews of Galilee (and the Samaritans who reside between the Judeans and Galileans represent yet another closely related group).

The *Ioudaioi* of John 10 seem to function the same way as the *Ioudaioi* of John 8–9. They are Judeans whose opinions of Jesus are sharply divided (10:19, 24). Some think Jesus could be the Messiah; others do not. Some are ready to kill Jesus (10:31, 33; 11:8). The Pharisaic party is strongly opposed to Jesus in the latter part of the Gospel of John (7:32, 45, 47, 48; 8:13; 9:13, 15, 16, 40; 11:46, 47, 57; 12:19, 42; 18:3).

When Lazarus dies in Bethany, near Jerusalem, "many of the Jews" come to Martha and Mary to console them (John 11:19, 31, 33, 36, 45). Once again, *Ioudaioi* is best understood as Judeans. Of course those who console them are *Jews*; who else could it be? When Jesus raises Lazarus from the dead, some of the *Ioudaioi* believe in him (11:45), while others report him to the Pharisees (11:46). These *Ioudaioi* are Judeans. They plot to kill Jesus, so "Jesus therefore no longer went about openly among" the *Ioudaioi*, that is, among the Judeans (11:54).

Certain Judeans were the enemies of Jesus and his followers. They were in part identified with the Pharisees, but this does not mean that all Pharisees were enemies of Jesus. These Judean Jews represented a powerful minority that could intimidate and persecute other Jews, such as Jesus, whose teachings and claims they found objectionable and dangerous. But these Judeans, or *Ioudaioi*, were only a minority; they did not represent the whole of the Jewish people (see Boyarin 2002).

The Threat of Expulsion from the Synagogue

Another distinctive feature of Judaism in the Gospel of John is the threat of being cast out of the synagogue for confessing Jesus. There are three passages in which this threat is expressed: John 9:22; 12:42; 16:2. After Jesus heals the blind man on the Sabbath, Pharisees declare that Jesus could not have done such a thing, that he "is not from God, for he does not keep the Sabbath" (9:16). Soon after we are told that "the Jews" (*Ioudaioi*) flat out do not believe the healed man had been blind at all (9:18). Even the parents of the man who had been born blind are reluctant to debate the point with "the Jews," for "the Jews had already agreed" that if anyone should confess him (Jesus) to be the Messiah, he was to be put out of the synagogue (9:22). But again, translating *Ioudaioi* as Jews in this narrative hardly makes sense. Rather, the *Ioudaioi* who persecute the healed blind man represent a distinct group of Judean Jews.

After word spreads that Jesus had restored life to Lazarus, the *Ioudaioi* become interested in Jesus (John 12:9), and "many of the *Ioudaioi* were going away and believing in Jesus" (12:11). For this reason "ruling priests" conspire to murder Lazarus (12:10). We are also told that even many of the rulers believe in Jesus, but because of "fear of the Pharisees they did not confess it, lest they should be put out of the synagogue" (12:42). Here again we see the Pharisees functioning as a subgroup within the *Ioudaioi*. The "rulers" who believed in Jesus were, of course, Judean Jews, but they were not part of the Judean Jews who were opposed to Jesus.

The third passage in John that speaks of expulsion from the synagogue is found in the Farewell Discourse (John 14–17). Jesus warns his disciples, "They will put you out of the synagogues" (16:2). The "they" here is almost certainly the Pharisees or the *Ioudaioi*.

These threats of being removed from the synagogue likely reflect a specific situation in the life of the Johannine community. Expulsion from the synagogue created a crisis for this community of believers in Jesus because of their deep roots in the synagogue and Jewish tradition.

Although the language of the Gospel of John is sometimes misunderstood and regrettably has been used to promote or justify anti-Semitism, the author of this Gospel sees himself and his followers as closely tied to the Jewish people and to Israel's historic faith. The *Ioudaioi* are a distinct subset of mostly Judean Jews, closely tied to Jerusalem and the Temple. It is this group that persecutes Jesus and his followers and it is to this persecution that the author of the Gospel of John responds. It is this group and this group alone that the evangelist criticizes. His criticisms are not directed against the Jewish people as a whole.

Understanding the *Ioudaioi* who are criticized in John as a distinct subset of Judean Jews and not the Jewish people in general makes good sense of the Jewish traditions everywhere present. The Gospel of John is rich with quotations of and allusions to Old Testament Scripture, as well as ideas that reflect early Jewish midrash and targumic tradition—all of it from a very positive point of view.

Works Cited

Ashton, John. 1985. "The Identity and Function of the ΙΟΥΔΑΙΟΙ in the Fourth Gospel." *NovT* 27:40–75.

Boyarin, Daniel. 2002. "The IOUDAIOI in John and the Prehistory of 'Judaism.'" Pages 216–39 in *Pauline Conversations in Context: Essays in Honour of Calvin J. Roetzel*. Edited by Janice Capel Anderson, Philip Sellew, and Claudia Setzer. JSNTSup 221. Sheffield: Sheffield Academic.

Culpepper, R. Alan, and Paul N. Anderson, eds. 2017. *John and Judaism: A Contested Relationship in Context*. RBS 87. Atlanta: SBL Press.

Donaldson, Terry L. 2010. *Jews and Anti-Judaism in the New Testament: Decision Points and Divergent Interpretations*. Waco, TX: Baylor University Press; London: SPCK.

Kysar, Robert. 1993. "Anti-Semitism and the Gospel of John." Pages 113–27 in *Anti-Semitism and Early Christianity: Issues of Polemic and Faith*. Edited by Craig A. Evans and Donald A. Hagner. Minneapolis: Fortress.

Reinhartz, Adele. 2011. "The Gospel according to John." Pages 152–96 in *The Jewish Annotated New Testament*. Edited by Amy-Jill Levine and Mark Zvi Brettler. Oxford: Oxford University Press.

Smith, D. Moody. 1990. "Judaism and the Gospel of John." Pages 76–96 in *Jews and Christians: Exploring the Past, Present, and Future*. Edited by James H. Charlesworth. New York: Crossroad.

Wahlde, Urban C. von. 1982. "The Johannine 'Jews': A Critical Survey." *NTS* 28:33–60.

CHAPTER 10

The Jewish Paul

10.1 Paul's Life

Jason Maston

A single event divides Paul's life into two periods. That event is the revelation of Jesus he experienced. In the pre-conversion/call period, he "advanced in Judaism . . . was far more zealous for the traditions of my ancestors" and "was trying to destroy" the church (Gal 1:13–14 NRSV). In the post-conversion/call period, he identifies himself as a slave of God and the apostle to the gentiles (e.g., Rom 1:1–5; Gal 1:16; Eph 3:2–9). While it is a mistake to trace all of Paul's theology to this event, there is little doubt that it significantly redirected his life from persecutor to proclaimer. The task of this essay is to briefly explain Paul's life by tracing his movement from one who sought to destroy the church to the church's greatest apostle and theologian.

Sources

One of the first matters to address is the sources used to reconstruct Paul's life. The New Testament contains thirteen letters that identify Paul as the author. Most scholars do not consider Paul to be the author of all these letters. The letters are often divided into three categories: the undisputed letters (Romans, 1–2 Corinthians, Galatians, Philippians, 1 Thessalonians, and Philemon), the disputed (Ephesians, Colossians, and 2 Thessalonians), and the deutero-Pauline (the Pastoral Epistles: 1–2 Timothy and Titus). In recent scholarship, however, these divisions have been called into question. Several studies have argued for the authenticity of the three disputed letters (Foster 2012; Campbell 2014), and other scholars have argued for the authenticity of 2 Timothy (Johnson 2001; conservative scholars have maintained that all the Pastorals were composed by Paul [Towner 2006]). Incorporating the later letters, like the Pastorals, provides some more clarity about the final years of Paul's life, but none of the (so-called) disputed letters or the Pastorals provide significant details to assist in reconstructing Paul's life.

The other major source for Paul's life is the Acts of the Apostles. Paul is introduced at the end of the account about Stephen where he is holding the garments of those stoning Stephen (7:58). He reappears in chapter 9 when Luke records Paul's Damascus Road experience, and he makes a brief appearance in 11:25–30. In the latter half of Acts (chs. 13–28), Paul is the main human character. The historical authenticity of Acts has been widely disputed. A strong current in scholarship contends that the account is at best secondary evidence (Campbell 2014, 20–26), if not in flat contradiction to the (authentic) Pauline letters (Phillips 2009).

Disregarding Acts outright seems methodologically precarious, although this is not to claim that Acts and Paul's letters agree at every point. F. F. Bruce (2000, 17) suggests that the difference between Acts and Paul is that of "a man's self-portrait and the portrait painted of him by someone else . . . the Paul of Acts is the historical Paul as he was seen and depicted by a sympathetic and accurate but independent observer." Caution should of course be taken in the use of Acts, as it should with any historical source, including Paul's own claims about himself. Hyper-skepticism, though, is unwarranted (on the use of Acts as a historical source, see, e.g., Riesner 1998; Hengel and Schwemer 1997).

Pre-Christian Life

Paul provides very few details about his upbringing. He notes that he was circumcised on the eighth day and belonged to the tribe of Benjamin (Phil 3:5). According to Acts, Paul bore the name of Israel's first king, Saul, also from the tribe of Benjamin (Acts 7:58; 1 Sam 9:1–2). Paul also indicates that he was a member of the Pharisees, one of the leading Jewish sects during the Second Temple period (Phil 3:5). The defining element in Paul's pre-Christ life is that he was a persecutor of the church. In 1 Tim 1:13, Paul is identified as "formerly a blasphemer, a persecutor, and a man of violence." The sentiment here, whether written by Paul or a later person, captures well the way Paul portrays himself in other places. Out of his zeal (Phil 3:6), he sought to destroy the church (Gal 1:14).

Luke, in the Acts of the Apostles, also knows of Paul as a Pharisee (26:5). According to Luke, Paul was a disciple of Gamaliel, one of the leading rabbis of the first century CE (22:3). Because of Paul's extreme persecution of the church and devotion to the Torah, some scholars contend that Luke is mistaken in his identification of Paul as a follower of Gamaliel, who adopted the views of Hillel, a first century BCE Jewish teacher, which were more "pacifist" (cf. Acts 5:33–39). It is equally plausible, though, that Paul embraced the views of his teacher on most aspects but adopted a more radical position with regard to the claims of the church. Luke also records Paul's persecution of the church, placing him at the killing of Stephen (7:58). After a brief interlude, he reinserts Paul on his way to Damascus to bring back Christians for trial before the Sanhedrin (9:1–18; cf. 22:4–13; 26:9–18). Luke and Paul thus both identify Paul's pre-conversion/call life as one defined primarily by his persecution. It is in this context that both also describe the revelation of Jesus that shifts Paul's life.

Luke adds two other important details. First, he reports that Paul was raised in the city of Tarsus (21:39; 22:3; cf. 26:4). Tarsus was the provincial capital of Cilicia (modern-day Turkey), a free city and well-known as a place of learning (Roetzel 1999, 12–16). This statement, however, is notoriously ambiguous, and it sheds very little light on Paul's upbringing. It is unclear how long Paul was in Tarsus before moving to Jerusalem. The statement also does not make clear what kind of education Paul had while in Tarsus (on Paul's education, see Hock 2016). Given that Paul's letters evidence some awareness of rhetorical practices, some scholars hold that he had received some education in Tarsus. However, in his letters and Acts, Paul expresses more interest in his training as a Pharisee than any education he may have received elsewhere.

Second, Luke indicates that Paul was a Roman citizen (Acts 16:37–38; 22:23–29; 23:27). This is particularly important for Luke's narrative, and he describes Paul using his Roman citizenship to secure his freedom from prison and to gain an audience with Caesar in Rome (25:10–11; cf. 28:19). It is not clear why Paul does not mention his citizenship in his letters, but his silence is no reason to doubt the veracity of Luke's statement. It is important to remember that in his letters Paul writes what is necessary to help the congregations he addresses, not matters of interest to historians.

Conversion/Call

Christ's appearance to Paul on the road to Damascus, as Luke records it, resulted in a complete turnabout for Paul. His view of Christ was changed, as well as his view of the church, which he now identifies as "the church of God" (Gal 1:13). While the significance of this event can be overstated (e.g., Kim 1981), one must not undercut its impact either. This event changed Paul.

Scholars have wrestled with whether to identify this event as a conversion (see below, article 10.2). Proponents of the New Perspective on Paul argue that this event is best understand as a "call" since Paul is commissioned, in the pattern of the prophets, to be the apostle to the gentiles (Stendahl 1985; Dunn 2007). This view captures an important aspect, but is surely wrong in what it denies. It eliminates the way Paul contrasts his previous beliefs with his views after the revelation of Christ (Gal 1:13: "my earlier life in Judaism"). Moreover, as Chester (2003) demonstrates, "calling" language in Paul indicates conversion.

Dating the year of Paul's conversion is complicated by several factors. Most scholars agree that it happened within two to four years of Jesus' crucifixion. While the majority of scholars date Jesus' death to 30 CE, a minority hold that it happened in 33 CE. If we assume the former, then Paul's conversion would have happened sometime between 32–34 CE (see the discussion by Riesner 1998, 3–28).

The "Unknown Years"

The years immediately following Paul's conversion are designated the "unknown years" since the narrative of Acts contains only spotty accounts and, on most reconstructions, none of Paul's letters were written during this time (approximately 32–48/49 CE; on this period see Hengel and Schwemer 1997, which has the subtitle "The Unknown Years"). According to Gal 1:17–2:1 Paul went directly to Arabia and then returned to Damascus. After three years, he visited Jerusalem, where he stayed for fifteen days and met with Cephas/Peter and James. He then went to Syria and Cilicia, and after fourteen years returned to Jerusalem. It is doubtful that Paul spent all fourteen years in Syria and Cilicia. The first missionary journey in Acts should be placed in this period (see below), but this still leaves a gap of over ten years (something like 32–45 CE depending on one's view of other matters).

One of the difficulties in reconstructing this period of Paul's life is determining if the years in Gal 1:17–2:1 are consecutive (3 + 14 = 17) or overlap (for a total of fourteen). Most scholars take the position that the years are consecutive. Additionally, ancient authors often rounded numbers, so both time spans could be off by one (two years instead of three or thirteen instead of fourteen), which complicates the reconstruction even more. (For a concise but more thorough analysis of the chronological question than space permits here, see Alexander 1993.)

Missionary Journeys and Rome

Paul's letters testify to widespread and lengthy missionary activity. He visits a variety of locales in the eastern Mediterranean region. Reconstructing the journeys based solely on the letters is problematic. Paul's letters provide very few historical references, so scholars are forced to rely on other sources to fill in the gaps.

Luke's account in Acts tells of three missionary journeys and a trip to Rome. During the first journey (Acts 13:1–14:28) Paul and Barnabas travel to Cyprus and south Galatia. The journey begins and ends in Antioch, which functions as Paul's home base. This journey occurs sometime in the mid-40s CE. Luke next records the Jerusalem Council, which occurred in 48/49 CE (15:1–29). Paul's second missionary journey begins after the Jerusalem Council (Acts 15:30–18:22). He visits some of the regions where he founded churches during his first missionary journey and then heads toward Macedonia after receiving a vision. His journey takes him around the northern and western coasts of the Aegean Sea as he visits major places like Philippi, Thessalonica, Athens, and Corinth. It is difficult to know when the second journey ends and the third begins. During his third journey, Paul circles through the same regions (Acts 18:23–21:16) strengthening the churches. Acts 21:17–28:30 recounts Paul's arrest in Jerusalem and his long journey to Rome. The narrative ends with Paul under house arrest awaiting a trial before Caesar. This happens in the early 60s CE.

In his letter to the Romans, Paul states that he desires to preach the gospel in Spain (15:28). Whether or not he fulfilled this aim is disputed. Luke ends his account with Paul in Rome under house arrest in the early 60s CE. The later Pauline letters do not indicate whether Paul made it to Spain. The late-first-century author Clement of Rome gives the first indication that Paul did travel to Spain when he writes that Paul "preached in the East and in the West" and "reached the farthest bounds of the West" (*1 Clement* 5:5–6). Clement's comment, however, may simply be a deduction from Paul's wish to preach in Spain (see also the *Acts of Peter* 1:1–3).

An engaging account known as the *Martyrdom of Paul*—a portion of a pseudepigraphical work from the latter half of the second century CE called the *Acts of Paul*—recounts Paul's arrest by Nero. Through a series of dialogues, Nero seeks to persuade Paul to renounce his commitment to Jesus as king, but Paul will not. Nero thus orders Paul to be beheaded. The claim that Paul was beheaded under Nero is passed on through tradition. No source provides a specific date for Paul's execution, but it must have happened in the mid-60s, likely after Nero set Rome ablaze (for the sources on Paul's death, see Tajra 2010). The modern church of St. Paul at Tre Fontane sits on an ancient road, the Ostian Way, at the location where Paul was reportedly beheaded (for this and competing traditions see Bruce 2000, 450–54).

Paul the Letter Writer

While Paul self-identified as an apostle of Jesus Christ, he is probably most re-membered as a letter-writer (see Richards 2004; Porter and Adams 2010; Weima 2016). It is certainly the collection and eventual canonization of his letters that made him the revered figure that he is. According to most reconstructions Paul wrote most of his letters after the Jerusalem Council (48/49 CE). Some place Galatians just before the Council, while others have argued that 1 (and 2) Thessalonians were written as early as 40–42 CE (Campbell 2014, 190–253).

Paul's decision to write letters was pragmatic: it enabled him to communicate with his converts at any time and from any place. Through his letters he was able to accomplish a variety of purposes; for example, to encourage, chide, correct, or clarify. While it is common to claim that Paul's letters functioned as a substitute for his physical presence, this oversimplifies why Paul used letters. It appears, as Margaret Mitchell (1992, 641–43) demonstrates, that Paul used letters and envoys strategically. For example, after a disastrous visit to Corinth, he sends Titus and the "letter of tears" (2 Cor 2:4) to mend the relationship. Paul's physical presence would have caused more damage in this case (2 Cor 1:23–2:9). Letters, then, were not a last resort for Paul. Rather, as Mitchell (643) states, "The evidence indicates that there may have been no fixed hierarchy of presence, but that in each situation Paul chose which of the three—a letter, an envoy, a personal visit (or some combination)—would be most effective."

Paul's life gave way to many stories and traditions. While some of these traditions make him into a larger-than-life character, his real life as reflected in his surviving letters and the Acts of the Apostles testifies to a figure who devoted his life to a single mission, indeed, a single person. Whether from his letters or later traditions, Paul is remembered primarily as the apostle who proclaimed Jesus as Messiah to the world.

Works Cited

Alexander, Loveday C. A. 1993. "Chronology of Paul." *DPL* 115–23.

Bruce, F. F. 2000. *Paul, Apostle of the Heart Set Free*. Repr., Grand Rapids: Eerdmans.

Campbell, Douglas A. 2014. *Framing Paul: An Epistolary Biography*. Grand Rapids: Eerdmans.

Chester, Stephen J. 2003. *Conversion at Corinth: An Exploration of the Understandings of Conversion Held by the Apostle Paul and the Corinthian Christians*. SNTW. London: T&T Clark.

Dunn, James D. G. 2007. *The New Perspective on Paul: Collected Essays*. WUNT 185. Tübingen: Mohr Siebeck.

Foster, Paul. 2012. "Who Wrote 2 Thessalonians? A Fresh Look at an Old Problem." *JSNT* 35:150–75.

Hengel, Martin, and Anna Maria Schwemer. 1997. *Paul between Damascus and Antioch: The Unknown Years*. Translated by John Bowden. London: SCM Press.

Hock, Ronald F. 2016. "Paul and Greco-Roman Education." Pages 230–54 in vol. 1 of *Paul in the Greco-Roman World: A Handbook*. 2nd ed. Edited by J. Paul Sampley. London: Bloomsbury T&T Clark.

Johnson, Luke Timothy. 2001. *The First and Second Letters to Timothy: A New Translation with Introduction and Commentary*. AB. New York: Doubleday.

Kim, Seyoon. 1981. *The Origin of Paul's Gospel*. WUNT 4. Tübingen: Mohr Siebeck.

Mitchell, Margaret M. 1992. "New Testament Envoys in the Context of Greco-Roman Diplomatic and Epistolary Conventions: The Example of Timothy and Titus." *JBL* 111:641–62.

Phillips, Thomas E. 2009. *Paul, His Letters and Acts*. Library of Pauline Studies. Peabody, MA: Hendrickson.

Porter, Stanley E., and Sean A. Adams, eds. 2010. *Paul and the Ancient Letter Form*. Pauline Studies 6. Leiden: Brill.

Richards, E. Randolph. 2004. *Paul and First-Century Letter Writing: Secretaries, Composition and Collection*. Downers Grove, IL: InterVarsity Press.

Riesner, Rainer. 1998. *Paul's Early Period: Chronology, Mission Strategy and Theology*. Grand Rapids: Eerdmans.

Roetzel, Calvin J. 1999. *Paul: The Man and the Myth*. Minneapolis: Fortress.

Stendahl, Krister. 1985. *Paul Among Jews and Gentiles and Other Essays*. Philadelphia: Fortress.

Tajra, Harry W. 2010. *The Martyrdom of St. Paul: Historical and Judicial Context, Traditions, and Legends*. Repr., Eugene, OR: Wipf and Stock.

Towner, Philip H. 2006. *The Letters to Timothy and Titus*. NICNT. Grand Rapids: Eerdmans.

Weima, Jeffrey A. D. 2016. *Paul the Ancient Letter Writer: An Introduction to Epistolary Analysis*. Grand Rapids: Baker Academic.

10.2 Paul in Modern Scholarship

Brian S. Rosner

When Paul arrived at Jerusalem after his second missionary journey in Acts 21:21, he was accused by zealous Jews of teaching "all the Jews who live among the Gentiles to turn away from Moses, telling them not to circumcise their children or live according to our customs" (NIV).

Paul's relationship to Judaism was a bone of contention throughout Paul's career as an apostle of Jesus Christ to the gentiles, and continues to be controversial to this day. Scholarly opinion is divided as to whether Paul the Jew was guilty of the charge of apostasy. Alan F. Segal (1990), for example, said that Paul would have been judged to be a renegade by Jews and Jewish Christians. James D. G. Dunn (1988, 269), on the other hand, believes that "Paul could never have accepted that his apostleship to the Gentiles constituted apostasy from Israel. Quite the contrary, he was apostle to the Gentiles precisely as apostle *for* Israel, apostle *of* Israel." Was Paul *converted* to a new religion on the road to Damascus? Or was he just *called* to a mission to the gentiles by the risen Jesus?

The Case against the Jewishness of Paul

Was the apostle Paul guilty of apostasy? Six lines of evidence suggest that Paul broke decisively from Judaism:

(1) Paul said things a good Jew would never say, such as "circumcision is nothing" (Gal 5:6; 6:15; 1 Cor 7:19) and, with respect to Jewish food laws, "nothing is unclean in itself" (Rom 14:14).

(2) Paul distanced himself from Judaism, writing of his "*previous* way of life in Judaism" (Gal 1:13), and writing off his Jewish heritage as "garbage" (Phil 3:5–8).

(3) Paul rejected the bipartite Jewish division of the world into Jews and gentiles. While reflecting this same division at various points in his letters, including seven times in Romans (1:16; 2:9, 10; 3:9, 29; 9:24; 10:12), at one point Paul adds a third category that takes precedence over traditional Jewish privilege ("Jews, Greeks and *the church of God*" [1 Cor 10:32]; cf. too the juxtaposition of the category of "the called" [1 Cor 1:23–24] over against Jews and gentiles).

(4) Paul was critical of Jews. In one of his earliest letters he wrote: "The Jews, who killed both the Lord Jesus and the prophets, and drove us out; they displease God and oppose everyone by hindering us from speaking to the Gentiles so that they may be saved" (1 Thess 2:14–16).

(5) Paul was opposed by certain Jews. Concerted Jewish opposition to Paul is in fact the norm in the book of Acts, where non-Jewish opposition to Paul occurs only twice (in Philippi and Ephesus). Paul himself reports that he received thirty-nine lashes five times (2 Cor 11:24), a standard synagogue punishment.

(6) Paul seems to have abandoned the pillars of Judaism, "the fundamental symbols of Jewish life" (Acts 21:21; Davies 1982, 7).

This sixth point, perhaps the most comprehensive charge, is worth exploring at greater length. In defining first-century Judaism, scholars sometimes refer to core or defining beliefs. The three that are mentioned most often are Israel's election, the law of Moses, and the Temple (the land and the Shema are also sometimes thrown into the mix). The charge brought against Paul in Acts 21 by Jews in Jerusalem mentions these very three; according to his opponents, Paul was teaching against "our people, our law and this place [i.e., the Jewish Temple]" (Acts 21:28).

Did Paul teach against the pillars of Judaism? The charge seems to stick. With respect to the election of Israel, Paul opposes the notion that the Jews, Abraham's sons, constitute the people of God—"For not all who are descended from Israel are Israel" (Rom 9:6). Paul opposed the law of Moses as not bringing life, but death, and insisted that believers in Christ are not under the law (see below, article 10.3). Although Paul never explicitly rejects the Jewish Temple and its priesthood and sacrifices, he implies as much in his use of cultic imagery to refer to the work of Christ. From one vantage point, the career of the apostle Paul shook the three main pillars of ancient Judaism profoundly.

The Case for the Jewishness of Paul

Defenders of Paul's continuing Jewishness might respond in the following ways: Paul may have said un-Jewish things, but his theology remained fundamentally Jewish. To cite an example, Paul's convictions about the inspiration, sufficiency, and authority of Scripture are the standard Jewish view. The Jewish Scriptures are, to use his language, "holy," "the oracles of God," "the prophetic writings," "written for us" and "for our instruction." Most of these assertions about Scripture can be found in Jewish writings contemporary with Paul.

What may be more surprising is the fact that even when Paul disagrees with his fellow Jews, his views are consonant with Jewish beliefs. Take for example Paul's high Christology, his belief that Jesus has the status of unique Lord, which clearly sets him apart from other Jews. Paul finds Christ's divine identity in Israel's famous Shema from Deut 6, the very definition of monotheism for Israel: "Hear O Israel, the Lord our God, the Lord is one." In 1 Cor 8:4–6 Paul alludes to this foundational Jewish text and confesses that "for us there is but one God, the Father, from whom all things came . . . and there is one Lord, Jesus Christ, through whom all things came and through whom we live." Paul incorporates Christ the Lord into the very definition of the God of Israel.

Similarly, while Paul may have distanced himself from Judaism, Paul's moral teaching was thoroughly Jewish. Inasmuch as Jews may have objected to Paul's preaching of a law-free gospel to gentiles, a consistent mark of his work among gentiles was his traditional Jewish approach to dealing with gentile sins. Jews typically considered gentiles to be three things: sexually immoral, idolatrous, and greedy (see Rosner 2007). The same goes for Paul throughout his letters.

Although many Jews abandoned Paul and accused him of apostasy, Paul believed that God has not abandoned the Jews. His passionate commitment to what he calls "my own people" is clear in Rom 9:3: "For I could wish that I myself were cursed and cut off from Christ for the sake of my people, those of my own race." In Paul's view, "Israel has experienced a hardening in part until the full number of the Gentiles has come in" (Rom 11:25); but he also believed that once this has occurred, "all Israel will be saved" (Rom 11:26). Precisely what Paul meant by "all Israel," and when and how they will be saved, is hotly debated by scholars.

Jews objected to Paul's inclusion of the gentiles in the people of God on an equal basis with Jews without the need for circumcision and keeping the law. However, in Paul's view his preaching to the gentiles fulfilled prophecy found in the Jewish Scriptures. Indeed, key ways in which Paul understands his apostolic vocation make this clear.

Paul's famous conversion on the road to Damascus links his identity to that of an Old Testament prophet. The account in Acts 9 echoes the vivid experiences of Isaiah, Jeremiah, and especially Ezekiel. Paul uses the language of calling to describe his commission, and the Old Testament in Greek also regularly uses the concept of calling to refer to the granting of roles or tasks by God; for example, Abraham is called to be the father of a nation, Cyrus of Persia is called as an agent of providence, and Israel is called to be a light to the gentiles. A key term for Paul's own understanding of his role is the notion of "preaching the gospel," something he says God sent him to do in 1 Cor 1:17. As it turns out, the language of preaching the gospel derives from several texts in Isaiah, where an end-time herald commissioned by God announces his reign of salvation. Isaiah 52:7 (which Paul quotes in Rom 10:15) reads: "How beautiful on the mountains are the feet of those who bring good news, who proclaim peace, who bring good tidings, who proclaim salvation, who say to Zion, 'Your God reigns!'"

In Rom 1:1 and elsewhere Paul introduces himself as "a servant of Christ Jesus." A good case can be made that in saying this he is drawing on the scriptural figure of the servant of the Lord found in Isa 40–55. This servant has a special role with respect to the nations. In the Isa 49 Servant Song (vv. 3 and 6) the Lord says: "You are my servant, Israel, in whom I will display my splendor," and "I will also make you a light for the Gentiles, that my salvation may reach to the ends of the earth."

Finally, in Rom 15:15–16 Paul explains his vocation in priestly terms. Much of his understanding here derives from Old Testament texts like Mal 1:11, which prophesies gentiles bringing temple worship, a prophecy which Paul arguably believed was being fulfilled in his ministry. He saw his role of preaching to the gentiles as divinely commissioned by God, who sent Paul as his prophet, herald, servant, and priest. Far from a departure from Jewish Scriptures, for Paul these roles derived from them.

With respect to the pillars of Judaism, Paul reconfigured them rather than abandoned them. Regarding *election*, Paul identifies believers in Christ as the new people of God, whom he describes in Romans as the elect (8:33), called (1:6–7; 8:28, 30; 9:7, 12, 24–28), beloved (1:7; 9:25), saints (1:7), beloved children of Abraham (4:11–12, 16–17), and the true circumcision (2:28–29). Paul rejects *the law* as law-covenant and legal code, but also reappropriates it as prophecy of the gospel and wisdom for living (see Rosner 2013; and below, 10.3). With respect to *the temple*, Paul identifies the church as the dwelling place of God (e.g., 1 Cor 3:16; 6:19). In Romans Christ is the mercy seat and the sacrifice of atonement (3:21–26), believers offer their bodies as living sacrifices (cf. cultic terminology in 12:1–2), and Paul himself gives "priestly service" (15:17), but not, it must be said, in the Jerusalem Temple.

The New Perspective and Paul's Critique of Judaism

The New Perspective on Paul is at heart a fresh examination of Paul's critique of the Judaism of his day. Specifically, it focuses on the target of Paul's teaching about justification; against whom was justification directed? In the broadest terms, whereas the Reformation understood Paul's doctrine of justification by faith to be his answer to the question of how sinners might find acceptance with a righteous God (by grace and not by works), the New Perspective counters that justification is about how gentiles might be admitted to the people of God (without circumcision, Jewish food laws, and Sabbath observance). In other words, rather than pitting Paul over against the legalism of contemporary Judaism, the New Perspective contends that what Paul found wrong with Judaism was its arrogant ethnocentrism. The biggest names in the movement are E. P. Sanders (1977; etc.); James D. G. Dunn (2008; etc.); and N. T. Wright (1991; etc.); with critiques of varying force from Stephen Westerholm (2004); D. A. Carson, P. T. O'Brien, and Mark A. Seifrid (2001; 2004); Francis Watson (2004); and John Barclay (2015).

The New Perspective typically sees a number of concepts and phrases in Paul's letters in a different light. The grace of God is more about his kindness in the inclusion of the gentiles than the general notion of God's unmerited favor. "Works of law," by which human beings are not justified, are not obedience to the law in general but the Jewish identity markers of circumcision and so on. The boasting that is excluded by justification by faith is not moral achievements in general but the arrogance of Jewish presumption of their secure status before God. The blessing of justification itself is less vertical (a new status before God) than it is horizontal (becoming part of a new people of God).

Without subscribing to every position advocated by the New Perspective—and even its proponents disagree on the details—there is much to learn from the movement. It has given impetus to producing a more thorough and nuanced picture of the Judaism(s) that Paul confronted; and it is true that not all Jews were hopelessly legalistic. Paul's gospel definitely addresses the issue of Jewish presumption and gentile inclusion (see, e.g., Eph 3:6). There is a horizontal dimension to justification, as the second halves of Rom 3 and Eph 2 make clear; God is the God of both Jews and gentiles. And salvation history, God's redemptive activity in history, as N. T. Wright and others insist, should be seen as the backdrop of justification by faith (cf. Gal 3:13–14: "Christ redeemed us from the curse of the law . . . in order that the blessing given to Abraham might come to the Gentiles").

However, the horizontal does not negate the vertical. In other words, the blessing of justification is a new status before God as well as becoming part of a new people of God. And the grace of God, while perhaps best illustrated by gentiles, who were without hope, being included as full members of God's people, also refers to the more general notion of God's generous kindness to the undeserving (see Eph 2:8–9; 2 Tim 1:9).

According to Paul the law is a failed path to life and righteousness because of human transgression, to which God has responded with a tsunami wave of grace. And Paul was not the first to come to this conclusion. Teaching in a range of Old Testament prophetic texts has much in common with Paul's response to the law. To varying degrees Jeremiah (e.g., 31:31–33), Ezekiel (36:22–32) and Daniel (9:9–16a) each lament that the Mosaic covenant and law have failed due to human sinfulness and declare that the time has come, or will come, when people must look to God's mercy and grace apart from the law. For Paul these prophetic hopes came to fruition in Christ, in the new covenant, and in the giving of the Spirit.

The above discussion raises the following question: What sort of Jew was Paul? Was he guilty of apostasy from Judaism? Many answers have been given, and the debate continues. Michael Bird (2016) lists former Jew, transformed Jew, faithful Jew, radical Jew, and anomalous Jew (his own view) as live options in current scholarship. But more importantly, what sort of Jew was Paul according to Paul? He was a Jew who believed that Jesus of Nazareth, Israel's long-awaited Messiah, had called him to the servant, prophetic, and priestly task of heralding the gospel to the nations.

Works Cited

Barclay, John M. G. 2015. *Paul and the Gift*. Grand Rapids: Eerdmans.

Bird, Michael F. 2016. *An Anomalous Jew: Paul Among Jews, Greeks, and Romans*. Grand Rapids: Eerdmans.

Carson, Donald A., Peter T. O'Brien, and Mark A. Seifrid, eds. 2001. *The Complexities of Second Temple Judaism*.Vol. 1 of *Justification and Variegated Nomism*. Tübingen: Mohr Siebeck.

———. 2004. *The Paradoxes of Paul*. Vol. 2 of *Justification and Variegated Nomism*. Tübingen: Mohr Siebeck.

Davies, W. D. 1982. "Paul and the Law: Reflections on Pitfalls in Interpretation." Pages 4–16 in *Paul and Paulinism*. Edited by M. D. Hooker and S. G. Wilson. London: SPCK.

Dunn, James D. G. 1988. *Romans 1–8*. WBC. Dallas: Word.

———. 2008. *The New Perspective on Paul*. Grand Rapids: Eerdmans.

Rosner, Brian S. 2007. *Greed as Idolatry: The Origin and Meaning of a Pauline Metaphor*. Grand Rapids: Eerdmans.

———. 2013. *Paul and the Law: Keeping the Commandments of God*. New Studies in Biblical Theology. Leicester: Inter-Varsity Press.

Sanders, E. P. 1977. *Paul and Palestinian Judaism: A Comparison of Patterns of Religion*. London: SCM.

Segal, Alan F. 1990. *Paul the Convert: The Apostolate and Apostasy of Saul the Pharisee*. New Haven: Yale University Press.

Watson, Francis. 2004. *Paul and the Hermeneutics of Faith*. London: T&T Clark.

Westerholm, Stephen. 2004. *Perspectives Old and New on Paul: The "Lutheran" Paul and His Critics*. Grand Rapids: Eerdmans.

Wright, N. T. 1991. *The Climax of the Covenant: Christ and the Law in Pauline Theology*. Edinburgh: T&T Clark.

10.3 Paul's View of the Law

Brian S. Rosner

"Like the stone steps of an ancient university building, the topic of 'Paul and the Law' has been worn smooth by the passing of generations of scholars." So writes Richard Hays (1996, 151). Along with being much-studied, the subject of Paul's view of the law also raises a host of historical, exegetical and theological issues that no student of the New Testament can safely ignore.

Overview

Historically, consideration of Paul's attitude to the law raises questions about his own Jewish identity and relationship to contemporary Judaism. Does Paul's law-free gospel represent a break from Judaism? How does Paul the Jew relate to Paul the Christian? Was Paul converted to a new religion on the Damascus road? The subject of Paul and the law is a subset of one of the biggest issues in the study of early Christianity; namely, the parting of the ways between the nascent movement and the mother faith.

Exegetically, Paul's teaching about the law, especially in Romans and Galatians, raises a myriad of questions. Is Christ the end of the law or its goal or both? Are Christians no longer under the law's jurisdiction or just its condemnation? Do believers fulfill the law or does Christ do it for them? Is "the law of Christ" the law of Moses reconfigured, a new set of commandments, or something else? Are "works of the law," by which Paul says no human being is justified, the identity markers separating Israel from the nations, or works demanded by the law? Is Paul's opposition to doing the law merely his concern that it marks off Jews from gentiles?

Theologically, the issue of Paul and the law touches on the perennial question of the relationship between the grace of God in the gift of salvation and the demand of God in the call for holy living. Misunderstanding Paul and the law leads to distortions of one or both. From the very beginning, even in Paul's day, his teaching on the law has raised hackles on one of two fronts. Either people think that the free gift of salvation has been compromised, or a solid basis for God's demand for obedience and a holy life has been removed. If justification is not by works of the law, doesn't that lead to license? If you remove the law, isn't the result lawlessness? Don't those without the law end up outlaws? On the other hand, if we are still under the law in some sense, doesn't that compromise the free gift of salvation? Furthermore, Paul's teaching concerning salvation, salvation history, Israel, the church, anthropology, ethics, and eschatology are all inextricably linked to his view of the law.

Three theological traditions in particular have a strong interest in Paul's view of the law. Each tends to focus on an emphasis in Paul's letters that is clearly present, but plays down other aspects of the subject. Broadly speaking, Lutheranism holds that Paul believed that Christ abolished the law and that the law is the counterpoint to the gospel. The primary role of the law is to lead us to despair of any hope of obedience leading to God's acceptance and to drive us to seek God's mercy in Christ. The law is not seen as playing a big role in the Christian life (although Luther himself made effective use of the law in his catechisms). Secondly, the Reformed view agrees that salvation is by grace and not by obeying the law, but also argues that once saved we are under the moral law and must obey it in order to please God. Thirdly, the so-called New Perspective on Paul, which is really a new perspective on Paul's relationship to Judaism, thinks that the problem of the law for Paul is not that salvation is by grace and not works. Instead, the New Perspective believes that Paul's opposition to the law was simply that it was used by Jews to exclude gentiles from the people of God; in other words, Jewish ethnocentrism is the reason Paul opposed the law. There is something to learn from each of these perspectives. In my view, the challenge is holding onto their valid insights in a manner that does justice to the full range of evidence and does not deny the validity of other perspectives.

When investigating Paul and the law it is vital to be clear what we mean by both "Paul" and "the law." With respect to Paul, the extent of his corpus is of course a matter of dispute. While Paul's most sustained discussions of Israel's law and the church's faith are in the undisputed letters, significant evidence in Ephesians (see, e.g., 2:15 and 6:1–2) and the Pastoral Epistles (e.g., 1 Tim

1:8–9), for example, should not be ignored, and sometimes offers support to one interpretation over another of texts in Romans and Galatians. Even those scholars who work with a truncated Pauline corpus should recognize that if the law is a central concern for Paul, the later or pseudo-Pauline epistles provide early reflections of, or on, his views.

What Paul means by "the law" is also disputed. Many take "law" in Paul's letters to mean the divine commands in the Pentateuch which are to be heeded and obeyed. The phrase "the receiving of the law" in Rom 9:4 (NIV) points in this direction. And parts of the Pentateuch readily fit the description of "laws," such as the Decalogue, the Covenant Code (Exod 21–23), and the Holiness Code (Lev 17–26).

However, Paul generally deals with the law as a unity, customarily referring to it as Mosaic "law," not "laws." This means that, in the main, his responses to the law are not to its various parts, however we may wish to divide it, but to the law as a whole. And the five books of Moses contain a lot more than just laws. Narrative dominates Genesis, the first half of Exodus, and most of Numbers. Paul not only introduces "laws" from the Pentateuch (see e.g., "you shall not covet" in Rom 7:7) as "law," but also narrative as "law," as in Gal 4:21 (the story of Hagar and Sarah). Francis Watson (2004, 275) is correct to say that "when Paul speaks of 'the law,' he has in mind the text known as the Law of Moses," that is, the Pentateuch as a whole.

When read as a whole, the law of Moses, along with having a legal character, also evinces wisdom and prophetic elements. John P. Meier (2009, 29) writes with reference to the Old Testament conception of the law of Moses: "The word *torah* has clearly come to mean a written document that comes from God to Israel by the hands of Moses, a scroll in which the foundational stories and ordinances of Israel are woven into a literary whole that retains traits of prophetic and sapiential [wisdom] as well as legal *torah*."

Jewish and Gentile Believers in Relation to the Law

Does Paul distinguish between Jewish and gentile believers in Christ when it comes to how they relate to the law of Moses? The answer is yes and no. There is a sense in which all believers, both Jewish and gentile, are not under the law, and a more limited sense in which Jewish believers may choose to live under the law.

This more limited sense is clearly demonstrated in Rom 14:1–15:6, a passage in which Paul addresses the observance or non-observance of certain laws from the law of Moses in the Roman churches. Two topics are mentioned directly: namely, the restriction of diet (see 14:2, 21) and the observation of certain days in preference to others (14:5). John Barclay (2011, 39) summarizes the consensus of commentators: "In common with many others, I take these verses to refer to

Jewish scruples concerning the consumption of meat considered unclean and the observance of the sabbath and other Jewish feasts or fasts." Whereas "the weak" keep Jewish kosher laws and observe the sabbath, "the strong" do not.

Paul counts himself among the strong (see 15:1) and is convinced that the Christian believer may "eat anything" (14:2); Christians are not under the law (6:14–15; 7:1–6). But while holding his own convictions, as Barclay (2011, 51) notes, "Paul accepts an element of subjectivity in the definition of proper conduct relating to diet and calendar." On such matters, each individual is to act in accordance with their own convictions (14:5–6). As he states in 14:22: "whatever you believe about these things keep between yourself and God." In effect, Paul allows for the expression of Jewish cultural tradition, living under the law's direction but not its dominion. Barclay (54) notes that Paul's response to the issue is echoed by Justin Martyr, in *Dialogue with Trypho* 46–47, who accepts that Jewish Christians may practice circumcision, keep the Sabbath, and observe other Jewish laws, but strongly opposes attempts to persuade gentile Christians to follow suit.

But as it turns out, the bulk of Paul's teaching about the law concerns all believers regardless of their ethnic or religious background. Jews in the ancient world conceived of just two categories of people, setting the people of God off against the rest, namely the gentiles. And at many points Paul's letters reflect a similar classification. However, Paul identifies believers in Christ, from whatever background, as the people of God, effectively dividing the human race into three groups rather than two. This is seen in 1 Cor 10:32, where Paul refers to "the church of God," "Jews," and "Greeks." It is this new grouping, "the church of God," that is Paul's main and undifferentiated focus when it comes to his various interactions with the law.

Paul's Criticism of the Law

The most puzzling feature of Paul's view of the law is the fact that his letters present both criticism and approval of the law. James Dunn (1997, 328–29) writes with reference to Romans and Galatians: "Paul does not hesitate to describe it [the law] as 'holy, just and good' (Rom. 7:12), a very positive gift of God (Rom. 9:4). On the other hand, he clearly speaks of the law as an enslaving power, increasing trespass and used by sin to bring about death (Gal. 4:1–10; Rom. 5:20; 7:5)." Studies of Paul and the law distinguish themselves by whether they face these unmistakable tensions in his letters and how they explain them. Rather than asking which bits of the law Paul retains and which he rejects, it is best to consider *the capacity in which the law is functioning* when Paul speaks positively or negatively about the law (Rosner 2013).

With respect to Paul's negative stance toward the law, Paul repudiates the law *as law-covenant* and replaces it with something else. Believers in Christ are not under the law as a law code (Rom 2:29; 2 Cor 3:6) or as commandments (Rom 7:7–12). They are not imprisoned and guarded under the law, nor are they subject to the law as a disciplinarian (Gal 3:23–25). Those who are under the law are under a curse and under sin (Gal 3:10). Even though the law promises life to those who keep it, it is evident that no one keeps the law (Gal 3:10–14). Consequently, no one receives life through the law (Rom 7:7–12). The law used as law is for the lawless (1 Tim 1:8–9). Christ has abolished the law with its commandments and ordinances (Eph 2:15).

Instead of being under the law of Moses (Rom 6:14, 15; Gal 5:18), Christians are under the law of Christ (Gal 6:2; see also 1 Cor 9:21; living our new lives after his example and under Christ's lordship), the law of faith (Rom 3:27; stressing faith as the new covenant badge of membership), and the law of the Spirit (Rom 8:1; acknowledging the source of the new life). Having died to the law, Christ lives in us and we live by faith in the Son of God (Gal 2:20). Above all else, including righteousness under the law, Christians value knowing Christ Jesus our Lord (Phil 3:8). Christians don't "keep" the law, but "fulfill" the law in Christ and through love (Rom 8:3–4; 13:8–9; Gal 5:13–14; see Rosner 2010; 2013, 83–109).

Paul's Positive Appropriation of the Law

On the positive side, according to Paul, Christians read the law, along with the rest of the Old Testament, as Scripture, written to instruct us "for salvation through faith in Christ Jesus" and as "useful for teaching" us how to conduct our lives (2 Tim 3:14–17). In other words, Christians re-appropriate the Law *as prophecy* of the gospel and *as wisdom* for living (see further Rosner 2013, 135–205).

First, the law was written for Christians and is part of the prophetic writings which disclose the gospel and proclamation of Jesus Christ, which was a mystery kept secret for long ages, and is now made known to the gentiles to bring about the obedience of faith (Rom 1:2; 4:23–24; 16:25–26; Gal 3:6–7). The law is a witness to the gospel (Rom 3:21). When it comes to this gospel, the law is upheld (Rom 3:31) and the word of God has not failed (Rom 9:6). While prophecy is not the law's primary genre, when a composite text of varied genres like the law of Moses is read as part of a larger composite text (the Law and the Prophets) in a new context (after the death and resurrection of Christ), it is not surprising that certain elements take on new significance. A number of studies highlight the law's prophetic elements and dimensions in this new setting (see Moberly 2009; Sailhamer 2009; Watson 2004; Millar 1998; Horbury 2006).

Secondly, the law was written for our instruction and the events it records were also written down to instruct us (1 Cor 10:11; Rom 15:4). In fact, all of the law is useful for moral teaching, for reproof, correction, and for training in righteousness (2 Tim 3:16–17). The seed of the notion of the law as wisdom is planted in Moses' description of the purpose of the law in Deut 4:6: "Observe them carefully, for this will show your wisdom and understanding to the nations, who will hear about all these decrees and say, 'Surely this great nation is a wise and understanding people.'" Ezra, Psalms, and Proverbs contain texts that similarly take the law to be a font of wisdom: the law is described as "the wisdom of your God" (Ezra 7:25); according to Psalm 19:7: "The law of the LORD is perfect, refreshing the soul. The statutes of the LORD are trustworthy, *making wise the simple*" (italics added; cf. 119:98); and Prov 28:7a observes that "those who keep the law are *wise children*" (NRSV; italics added). In many places and on many topics Paul models reading the law as wisdom for living in the sense that he internalizes the law, makes reflective and expansive applications of it, and takes careful notice of its basis in the order of creation and the character of God.

Works Cited

Barclay, John M. G. 2011. *Pauline Churches and Diaspora Jews*. WUNT 275. Tübingen: Mohr Siebeck.

Dunn, James D. G. 1997. *The Theology of Paul the Apostle*. Grand Rapids: Eerdmans.

Hays, Richard B. 1996. "Three Dramatic Roles: The Law in Romans 3–4." Pages 151–65 in *Paul and the Mosaic Law: The Third Durham-Tubingen Research Symposium on Earliest Christianity and Judaism*. WUNT 89. Tübingen: Mohr Siebeck.

Horbury, William. 2006. "Monarchy and Messianism in the Greek Pentateuch." Pages 79–128 in *The Septuagint and Messianism*. Edited by Michael A. Nibb. Leuven: Leuven University Press.

Meier, John P. 2009. *A Marginal Jew: Rethinking the Historical Jesus*. 3 vols. The Anchor Bible Reference Library. New York: Doubleday.

Millar, J. Gary. 1998. *Now Choose Life: Theology and Ethics in Deuteronomy*. New Studies in Biblical Theology. Leicester: Inter-Varsity Press.

Moberly, R. W. L. 2009. *The Theology of the Book of Genesis*. Cambridge: Cambridge University Press.

Rosner, Brian S. 2010. "Paul and the Law: What He Does Not Say." *JSNT* 32:405–19.

———. 2013. *Paul and the Law: Keeping the Commandments of God*. New Studies in Biblical Theology. Leicester: Inter-Varsity Press.

Sailhamer, John H. 2009. *The Meaning of the Pentateuch: Revelation, Composition and Interpretation*. Downers Grove, IL: InterVarsity Press.

Watson, Francis. 2004. *Paul and the Hermeneutics of Faith*. London: T&T Clark.

10.4 Paul's View of Israel and the Nations

Jim R. Sibley

No New Testament author has written so extensively and incisively about Israel and the nations as Paul. His theology of Israel and the nations, therefore, should demand the attention of every student of Scripture. Paul deals with this subject throughout his Epistle to the Romans, as well as in Gal 3–4 and Eph 2. Paul's sermons in the book of Acts must also be taken into consideration. Nevertheless, it is in Rom 9–11, and particularly in chapter 11, that Paul's view of Israel and the nations is expressed most clearly. Throughout Paul's writings, however, it should be noted that he was no innovator, but built upon what had already been revealed in the Hebrew Scriptures.

Humanity's Problem

In Paul's preaching in Acts, he speaks specifically of the nations in two verses. In 17:26, he says that God "made from one man every nation of mankind to live on all the face of the earth, having determined their appointed times and the boundaries of their habitation" (NASB). In Acts 14:16, he says that God permitted the nations to "go their own ways" (i.e., in idolatry) before the coming of Jesus. The first three chapters of Romans are largely occupied with Paul presenting God's devastating charge against all humanity: "They are without excuse" (Rom 1:20)! Not only has sin resulted in alienation from God, but it has merited his wrath (Rom 1:18; 2:5, 8). In Rom 3:23 he says, "For all have sinned and fall short of the glory of God." This condition has existed since the sin of Adam and Eve in the garden of Eden (Rom 5:12–14).

God chose Abraham and his descendants, the people of Israel, in order to begin to solve the problem of sin in the world. God's election of the patriarchs and the creation of the nation of Israel became the vehicle by which God's plan to reverse the curse of evil would reach its final denouement. As Andrew Das (2003, 118) writes, "God's eschatological plan revolves entirely around Israel." Paul indicates that prior to the new covenant, there was "no hope" for those who were "strangers to the covenants of promise" (Eph 2:12). This phrase refers to the Abrahamic covenant, renewed with Isaac and Jacob, as well as to the other covenants God made with Israel.

Paul's view of Israel and the nations is inexplicable apart from an understanding of this "promise of the fathers" (Gen 12:3; 18:18; 22:18; 26:4; 28:14; see also Acts 13:32; 26:6; Rom 15:8; Paul quotes the promise in Gal 3:8). Here, God says that through the descendants of Abraham, Isaac, and Jacob, he will bless all the nations, or families, of the earth. This promise is foundational and formative for Paul's thought regarding Israel and the nations (Sibley 2016, 173). It was because of the lostness of the nations that "Christ has become a servant to the circumcision on behalf of the truth of God to confirm the promises given to the fathers, and for the Gentiles to glorify God for His mercy" (Rom 15:8–9a).

As William J. Dumbrell (1984, 78) says, "By way of Abraham and Israel, God enters into the world of the nations." In other words, the promises made to Abraham and to his descendants were for the ultimate purpose of reaching the nations. If God's saving purposes for the nations are vitally related to his purposes for Israel, the unavoidable conclusion is that in order to understand a theology of the nations, a theology of Israel is essential.

Israel: Chosen in Unbelief

Israel didn't choose to be the chosen people; God did the choosing! Neither was Israel's election based on anything good in Israel. In spite of Abraham's faith (Gen 15:6), in Rom 2:17–29, Paul makes it clear that the majority of Israel has not been faithful, yet God already knew this before he entrusted them "with the oracles of God" (Rom 3:2). In Rom 3:10–18, Paul quotes from several Psalms and from Isaiah to make his case against Israel. They are not made right with God by virtue of being Jewish; otherwise, Paul would not wish that he would be "accursed, separated from Christ for the sake of my brethren, my kinsmen according to the flesh," nor would he pray for their salvation (Rom 9:3; 10:1). Even though they are "enemies" from the standpoint of the gospel, from the standpoint of God's choice they are "beloved for the sake of the fathers; for the gifts and the calling of God are irrevocable" (Rom 11:28–29).

They were chosen, however, not to demonstrate their unworthiness, but to illustrate God's mercy, his faithfulness, and his ability to redeem a sinful people and transform them into all he wants them to be. Israel's sinful record was not intended to be a foil to make the nations feel superior, but a mirror in which they were to see their own sin and alienation from their Creator. God's grace to Israel then truly would be a message of hope for the nations. By overcoming Israel's sin and rebellion, God demonstrates his ability and intention to overcome the sin of the nations. The blessing for the nations is the blessing of reconciliation with their Creator—a blessing which is grounded in the original Edenic blessing of Gen 1:28 (Sailhamer 2009, 32).

Israel's unbelief is explained on the basis of four factors: First, lostness is the universal condition of all people (Rom 3:23). Second, God has always restricted his mercy and compassion to those whom he chooses (Rom 9:6–29). Third, they are culpable, for though they have heard and understood the good news (Rom 10:18–19), they have rejected God's righteousness, which comes by faith, and sought their own righteousness instead, which is based upon performance (Rom 9:30–33; 10:3). The fourth and final reason for Israel's unbelief is the spiritual blindness or hardness that Paul mentions in Rom 9:18, which he deals with more fully in Rom 11:7–10.

God's Faithfulness to Israel

Neither Paul nor Scripture in general gives support to the notion that the Jewish people are merely one of thousands of people groups. Israel is God's uniquely chosen nation, "to whom belongs the adoption as sons and the glory and the covenants and the giving of the Law and the temple service and the promises, whose are the fathers, and from whom is the Christ according to the flesh" (Rom 9:4–5). How can the God of Israel be indifferent to the fate of Israel? In the midst of Israel's unbelief, God still stands with outstretched arms, longing for the day Israel will turn to him (Rom 10:21).

In Rom 11:1 and 11:11, Paul raises two very significant questions: (1) Has God rejected Israel? and (2) Has Israel's unbelief disqualified it as his instrument of salvation for the nations? Some answer these questions in the affirmative, and others add a qualification—Israel has been disqualified, but only temporarily. (Most often this "temporary rejection/disqualification" view is based on Rom 11:15. It is better to understand the "rejection" in v. 15 as Israel's rejection of salvation, rather than God's rejection of Israel (cf. Sibley 2015). How different is the apostle's response to these questions. So tightly connected are God's purposes for Israel and the nations that to say God has rejected Israel would be to say that he has rejected the nations, or at least his plan for blessing the nations. Paul reacts to these questions with, "May it never be!" (Rom 11:1, 11). It is crucially important to understand the reason for this response.

First, to speak of the *God* of Israel neglecting the *people* of Israel would introduce confusion and contradiction into Paul's confession. Second, any other answer would call into question the faithfulness of God. How could God make unconditional promises to Israel, fail to keep them, and still be considered faithful? Finally, some might object that although God is faithful and his intention has always been to fulfill his promises, the sin of Israel has prevented him from doing so. Ronald Clements (1980, 107) states it this way: "The repeated disobedience of Israel made it impossible for God to bring to fruition his election promises to his people." However, Paul understood that any other answer would require one of the following three things to be true about God: he would either be indifferent, faithless, or impotent. There can be no other response than, "May it never be!"

God's Three-Step Plan for Israel and the Nations

Romans 9–11 form the climax of Paul's theological argument. Everything Paul has written in Romans prior to 11:25 is preparatory (Cranfield 2004, 573). Romans 11:25–32 contain Paul's summation—his theology of Israel and the nations. It is followed by a beautiful doxology of praise in 11:33–36 and by the practical application in Rom 12–16. Here, in Rom 11:25–32, we find God's plan for Israel and the nations unfolding in three steps: Israel is hardened; a remnant is being saved while the gospel is going to the nations; and, at the end, Israel will be redeemed. Again, God's plan for the nations is bound up with his plan for Israel. It is almost as if Paul were saying, "For God so loved the nations, that he chose Israel to be his instrument, that both Jew and Gentile might come to the knowledge of His Son."

Paul indicates that the judgment of spiritual hardening, or blindness, pronounced on the majority of Israel in the days of Isaiah has continued to his day (Isa 6:9–10; Rom 11:7–10). Has this blindness disqualified Israel to carry out God's purposes with the nations? He asks, "I say then, they did not stumble so as to fall, did they? May it never be! But by their transgression salvation has come to the Gentiles, to make them jealous" (Rom 11:11). This blindness has caused Israel to "stumble" over the stumbling stone (Rom 9:32), Jesus the Messiah. This stumbling refers to their "rejection" of salvation (Rom 11:15). Through this "transgression" (Rom 11:11) and "failure" (Rom 11:12), salvation has come to the nations (Rom 11:11).

Paul is deeply concerned that Christians from the nations understand that Israel has been affected by a supernaturally imposed impediment, for the very purpose that the nations might be saved (Rom 11:11–13). Rather than to engender a sense of superiority with respect to Israel, this knowledge should lead them to humility (Rom 11:18, 20, 25) and to a concern for Israel's salvation (Rom 9:1–3; 10:1, 14–15). This spiritual hardening is both partial and temporary. It is partial in that it affects only a "part" of Israel. It is temporary in that it will end when the "fullness" of the gentiles have been saved (Rom 11:25; in v. 7, he refers to this "part" as the "rest" of Israel, excluding the remnant).

Rather than abandoning Israel, even temporarily, the God who is still longing for Israel to turn to him is preserving a remnant of the nation (Rom 11:5). Paul writes: "For they are not all Israel who are descended from Israel; neither are they all children because they are Abraham's descendants, but: 'through Isaac your descendants will be named'" (Rom 9:6–7). That is, it is not the children of the flesh who are children of God, but the children of the promise are regarded as descendants (Rom 9:8). In this, Paul is referring to Jewish disciples of Jesus (the remnant), in contrast to unbelieving Jewish people. Those who are truly Jewish do not have mere physical descent from Abraham, but also possess the faith of Abraham. It is this remnant of Jewish believers who carry forward the promises of the nation. It is they who are "the children of promise."

Of this remnant, Paul himself is a part. Though the remnant might be small in number, it is of tremendous significance, for it is the indisputable evidence that God has not rejected Israel and that he will be faithful to fulfill his word to bring "all Israel" to salvation (Rom 11:1–4, 26). For this, believers from the nations should pray and, in view of this outcome, the nations should rejoice and praise God (Rom 10:1; 11:30–36). This will mark the capstone of success for God's plan of redeeming the world from the effects of sin and rebellion.

Implications

The relationship between the blindness of the majority of the people of Israel and God's purposes for Israel among the nations lies near the center of Paul's thought in the Epistle to the Romans. Paul discusses three main implications of this. The first is priority in evangelism and missions. In Rom 1:16, Paul says that he is not ashamed of the gospel, "for it is the power of God for salvation to everyone who believes, to the Jew first and also to the Greek." Even though this is the time of gentile ingathering, nevertheless, a priority is given to the Jewish people in missions and evangelism. This priority is seen in that the word "first" is being used in the sense of "in the first place, above all, especially" (Bauer 2001, 892–93), and also in that the present tense carries the sense of something that is true always and in all places. Yet, along with this Jewish priority is gentile inclusion, "also to the Greek." In Gal 3:8, Paul infers from Gen 12:3 that if the message of salvation were withheld from the nations, it would cease to be the gospel.

The second is provoking Israel to jealousy. In the promise of the fathers, it is clear that God would reach the nations through Israel. But the quotations in Rom 11:19–20 indicate not only that Israel is culpable, but also, surprisingly, that God's plan was always to use the nations to reach Israel! On the one hand, Israel is the vehicle by which salvation goes to the nations, but on the other hand, the nations are to provoke Israel to jealousy (see Bell 1994). Unfortunately, this has not been the case historically (see below, article 12.3).

The third is Israel's full restoration. In his three-step plan, Paul puts the stress on this last element: the national salvation of Israel (Cranfield 2004, 575; see also Wilckens 1980, 255). The remnant, currently being saved, is but the harbinger of a future national salvation. Paul argues that "if their transgression be riches for the world and their failure be riches for the Gentiles, how much more will their fulfillment be" (v. 12). He then answers his own question: It will be "life from the dead" (Rom 11:15 [cf. Ezek 36:22–32], 16).

In Rom 10:21, Paul quotes from Isa 65:2: "But as for Israel He says, 'All the day long I have stretched out My hands to a disobedient and obstinate people.'"

In this passage, the emphasis is not on Israel's disobedience, but on God's grace. Cranfield (2004, 541–42) says, "The quotation points firmly to the fact that the last word is not with Israel's disobedience but with God's mercy and patience."

Works Cited

Bauer, Walter. 2001. *A Greek-English Lexicon of the New Testament and Other Early Christian Literature.* 3rd ed. Edited by Frederick William Danker. Chicago: University of Chicago Press.

Bell, Richard H. 1994. *Provoked to Jealousy: The Origin and Purpose of the Jealousy Motif in Romans 9–11.* WUNT 2/63. Tübingen: Mohr Siebeck.

Clements, Ronald E. 1980. "'A Remnant Chosen by Grace' (Romans 11:5): The Old Testament Background and Origin of the Remnant Concept." Pages 106–21 in *Pauline Studies: Essays Presented to Professor F. F. Bruce on His 70th Birthday.* Edited by Donald A. Hagner and Murray J. Harris. Grand Rapids: Eerdmans.

Cranfield, C. E. B. 2004. *A Critical and Exegetical Commentary on the Epistle to the Romans.* ICC. London: T&T Clark.

Das, A. Andrew. 2003. *Paul and the Jews.* Library of Pauline Studies. Peabody, MA: Hendrickson.

Dumbrell, William J. 1984. *Covenant and Creation.* Nashville: Nelson.

Sailhamer, John H. 2009. *The Meaning of the Pentateuch.* Downers Grove, IL: InterVarsity Press.

Sibley, Jim R. 2015. "Has the Church Put Israel on the Shelf? The Evidence from Romans 11:15." *JETS* 58:571–81.

———. 2016. "Israel and the Gospel of Peter, Paul, and Abraham." *BSac* 173:18–31.

Wilckens, Ulrich. 1980. *Der Brief an die Römer.* Vol. 2. EKKNT. Zürich: Benziger.

CHAPTER 11

The Jewish Message: Resurrection

11.1 Resurrection in the Old Testament

Kevin Chen

Modern biblical scholarship tends not to emphasize the Old Testament witness to the resurrection. One reason for this is the belief that the authors of the Old Testament knew little to nothing about it (Johnston 2002, 227). This belief is sometimes tied to hypotheses regarding when ancient Israelites began to have ideas of a Messiah and other eschatological concepts (Mowinckel 1954, 1, 126), such as the resurrection. These hypotheses in turn often depend on one's views of divine revelation, predictive prophecy, progressive revelation, and/or the meaning of the Old Testament. Certainly, biblical authors who did not know about the resurrection, whether of the Messiah or of the righteous, would not have written about it. Conversely, if authors of Old Testament books did write about the resurrection, then this implies that they knew about the resurrection before the fact. For some scholars, pagan ancient Near Eastern conceptions of resurrection also bear on this question because they serve not only as a point of comparison but as a possible influence on the thought of Old Testament authors (Johnston 2002, 230–37). Another more objective reason for the present lack of emphasis on the Old Testament witness to the resurrection is that it can be hard to find passages that provide clear evidence for it.

Nevertheless, the New Testament implies that to miss the Old Testament witness to the resurrection is to miss part of its essential message. For example, Jesus rebuked the Sadducees' unbelief in the resurrection by citing the Old Testament (Matt 22:23–34; Luke 20:27–40). While on the Emmaus road after his resurrection, Jesus also called two discouraged disciples "foolish and slow of heart to believe in all that the prophets have spoken" (Luke 24:25, author's translation), including his death and resurrection (vv. 26, 46). Likewise, Paul claimed that he preached "nothing but what the prophets and Moses said would happen" (Acts 26:22). By describing his gospel as centering on Christ as "the first to rise from the dead" (v. 23), Paul showed his belief in the Old Testament witness both to the resurrection of the Messiah (Acts 13:30–37; 1 Cor 15:4) and to the resurrection of the righteous (Acts 23:6; 1 Cor 15:20–23, 42–56). Peter also claimed that the Old Testament bears witness to the resurrection of Christ

(Acts 2:24–32). With these things in mind, it behooves students of Scripture to carefully consider the resurrection in the Old Testament.

Interrelated Themes: Eschatological Salvation and Eternal Life

As mentioned above, it can be difficult to find Old Testament passages that bear clear witness to the resurrection. Though there are indeed some (which will be discussed in the next section), a treatment of the resurrection requires more than a mere survey of proof-texts. This is because in the Old Testament resurrection is intertwined with eschatological salvation and eternal life. Eschatological salvation includes victory over death itself. Isaiah 25:8 promises, "He will swallow up death forever," and Hos 13:14 declares, "I will redeem them from the hand of Sheol" (with "Sheol" taken by some scholars as meaning "grave" and by others as meaning "underworld"; see Johnston 2002, 73–75). The result of this salvation and redemption is "life forevermore," as mentioned in Ps 133:3. Similarly, resurrection is intrinsically a defeat of death (Acts 2:24, "God raised him up, loosing the pangs of death, because it was not possible for him to be held by it") and results in eternal life (Rom 6:9, "Christ, having been raised from the dead, will never die again").

When considered in this way, resurrection is indirectly related to the very foundation of the Old Testament, Gen 1–3. Adam and Eve were sentenced to death (Gen 3:19) and lost access to the tree of life and the eternal life it offers (Gen 3:23), but they and all humanity can have hope that a "seed of the woman" will one day crush the serpent's head (Gen 3:15). Though not explicitly stated, the eschatological salvation promised would seem to include not only the defeat of the serpent but also of the sin and death (Wenham 1987, 80) that followed. Gen 1–3 thus hints that a "seed" will win a climactic battle, free humanity from sin and death, and open the way back to the tree of (eternal) life in the garden of Eden.

Through the examples of Enoch and Elijah, who bypassed death altogether (Gen 5:24; 2 Kgs 2:11), all who similarly "walk with God," including those who have already died, are given hope of deliverance from death itself. Passages from the Psalms that speak of people praising the Lord "forever" also seem to assume deliverance from death and eternal life for the righteous (Pss 45:17; 79:13; 84:4). Psalm 89, which is an extended prayer for the Lord to fulfill the Davidic covenant, links its fulfillment to the problem of death for "all the sons of Adam" (vv. 47–48). It is as though David's promised "seed" (2 Sam 7:12) is the "seed of the woman" who will not only rule (Gen 1:26, 28) but also defeat death and bring life to humanity. Psalm 90 also laments the problem of death for "the sons of Adam" (v. 3) but does so at even greater length and with probable reference to Gen 2–3 (Gunkel 1986, 399). Instead of death "in the evening" (v. 6) because of sin and divine wrath (vv. 7–11), the psalmist prays for love and joy "in the morning" (v. 14), a new day of the Lord's "work" and "majesty" (v. 16). This accords with the deliverance from sin and death (v. 15) suggested in Gen 3:15.

Key Passages concerning Resurrection in the Old Testament

Having related resurrection to other biblical-theological themes in the Old Testament, several passages may be considered that more directly bear on this theme. One of the clearer references to the resurrection of the righteous in the Old Testament is Isa 26:19, "Your dead will live, corpses will arise; awake and shout, you who dwell in the dust." The Lord's "dead" contrast with other "dead," who will neither "live" nor "arise" (v. 14). The eschatological emphasis in the surrounding context (Isa 24–27) suggests that resurrection is indeed in view here. Another clearer reference to the resurrection of the righteous in the Old Testament is Dan 12:2, "Many of those who sleep in the dust of the ground will awake, some to everlasting life and some to reproach and to everlasting contempt." In the eschatological context of Dan 12, these who will awake to everlasting life are the Lord's "people, all whose names are found written in the book" (v. 1) and "the wise" (v. 3).

Although sometimes interpreted as merely a metaphor for restoration from exile, the language and imagery used in Ezek 37 is clearly that of resurrection. Dry bones (vv. 1–2) are assembled, clothed with flesh, and given the Spirit so that they "live" and become a mighty army (vv. 3–10). They had been "slain" (v. 9), but the Lord will "open your graves and bring you up from your graves" (vv. 12–13). There is no doubt that this relates to restoration from exile (v. 12, "I will bring you to the land of Israel"; see also vv. 14, 21–22) in answer to the nation's hopelessness (v. 11). At the same time, Israel's reunification (vv. 16–22), holiness (v. 23), and permanent dwelling in the land under the rule of the Messiah ("David") with the Lord's sanctuary in their midst (vv. 24–28) implies that eschatological salvation is also in view. As shown above, this salvation includes victory over death itself (Isa 25:8; Hos 13:14) such that it seems reductionistic to interpret the resurrection themes in Ezek 37 as merely a metaphor for Israel's national restoration. Furthermore, exile and death for Israel are closely related in vv. 11–12 (likewise Deut 4:26–27), just as they were for Adam (Gen 3:19, 22–24) and Jonah (Jonah 2:2, 4). At creation, the Lord had "breathed . . . the breath of life" into the nostrils of the first man so that he became "a living soul" (Gen 2:7), and new creation involves a parallel command to "the Spirit" to come and "breathe" into Israel "so that they will live" (Ezek 37:9). In both passages, human life is brought forth from non-living material, which accords with resurrection.

Several passages relate specifically to the resurrection of the Messiah. The climactic Servant Song in Isa 52:13–53:12 predicts the coming of a servant-king who will be "pierced," "crushed" (53:5), "cut off from the land of the living" (v. 8), and buried with the wicked (v. 9). Although this man has clearly died, the same passage says that he will be highly exalted (Isa 52:13) and receive a great reward (53:12). The suggestion that he will live again after dying is reinforced by plant language in 53:2 ("young plant [*yoneq*]," "root [*shoresh*]") that parallels that used of the Messiah in Isa 11 ("branch [*choter*]," "shoot [*netser*]" in v. 1; "root [*shoresh*]" in v. 10). Since the Messiah will rule forever (Isa 9:7), his death in Isa 53 cannot be the end for him (Heb 7:16). His eternal reign assumes his resurrection from the dead for this purpose.

Another passage that relates to the resurrection of the Messiah is the prophecy of the "Lion of Judah" in Gen 49:8–12, interpreted in light of the Joseph narrative in Gen 37–50. As the aged Jacob blessed his sons and foretold what would happen "in the last days [*beacherit hayamim*]" (Gen 49:1), he described a ruler who would come from the tribe of Judah (v. 10). In saying that "the sons of your father shall bow down to you" (v. 8; see Gen 27:29), Jacob declared not only that this Judahite king would rule over Israel but did so in terms of *Joseph's* initial dreams of sheaves and stars bowing down to him (Gen 37:5–11; Ebach 2007, 572). In other words, "that which was to happen to Joseph, and did happen in the course of the narrative (e.g., 42:6), has been picked up by way of this image and transferred to the future of the house of Judah. That which happened to Joseph is portrayed as a picture of that which would happen to Judah 'in the last days'" (Sailhamer 1992, 235). Furthermore, Joseph's ultimate exaltation takes place in spite of and through his apparent death and descent into Sheol (Gen 37:33–35). Not only was his father Jacob certain that Joseph had died, but years later even his brothers thought he was dead (Gen 44:20). The impossible circumstances that led to Joseph's rule are explained in the narrative as being the work of God (Gen 45:5–9; 50:20). Thus, if Jacob's question in Gen 49:9, "Who will raise him [Hiphil of *qum*]?" is also interpreted in terms of the Joseph narrative (including Jacob's perspective), then it can be taken as an allusion to Joseph's sheaf that "arose [*qum*]" (Gen 37:7) by a work of God despite first "going down" to Sheol (Gen 37:35). When understood in this way, the question in Gen 49:9 suggests that God, in an even greater way, will raise the Messiah from the dead to rule the world (Chen, forthcoming).

Both Peter and Paul cited Psalm 16 to show that the Old Testament foretold the resurrection of the Messiah (see Acts 2:24–32; 13:35–37). Citing Ps 16:8–11, Peter explained that David had died and was buried but spoke as a "prophet" about one of his descendants, the Messiah, who would be raised from the dead (Acts 2:29–32). Having also cited Isa 55:3, Paul cited part of Ps 16:10 ("You will not let your holy one see corruption") and explained that David died and "saw corruption," but Jesus "did not see corruption" (Acts 13:36–37). Peter made even greater use of Ps 16:10 when he emphasized that the Messiah "was not abandoned to Hades, nor did his flesh see corruption" (Acts 2:31). Thus, for both Peter and

Paul, this verse from the Old Testament directly predicts the resurrection of the Messiah. Both men were careful to explain that it exclusively concerns the Messiah and hence should not be applied to David also, who died, was buried, and did see corruption (Acts 2:29; 13:36). [See Figures 25–28.]

The challenge is to understand how Peter and Paul came to their common conclusion. Is not Ps 16:10 more easily understood as David's expression of confidence that the Lord will deliver him from *threats* of death, rather than from death itself (through resurrection)? One promising way forward is to consider Ps 16 as an integrated part of the Psalter. Wilson's (1985) seminal work has stimulated studies of the Psalter as a whole, and some, such as Mitchell (1997), have applied it and derived eschatological results. For Ps 16:10, this approach yields constructive results. The Hebrew phrase "see the pit" in this verse has close parallels with one other passage in the Psalter, Ps 49:9 ("see the pit"). In Ps 49 no one can redeem his brother or pay his ransom to God (v. 7). The cost is too high (v. 8) for him to "live forever and not see the pit" (v. 9). This parallel use of "see the pit" is associated with the common human experience of death, burial, and decay ("their graves [LXX *taphoi*] are their homes forever, their dwelling places for all generations," v. 11), even for the wise (v. 10). Relatedly, Ps 89:48 asks, "Which man will live and not *see death*, and deliver his soul from the hand of Sheol?"

Both Peter and Paul's interpretation of Ps 16:10 accords with the probable meaning of "see corruption/the pit" in Ps 49:9, reinforced by Ps 89:48. David shared the common human experience of death, burial, and decay, and hence was not speaking about himself in Ps 16:10 (see Acts 2:29–31; 13:36–37). The Messiah, to be sure, would still die and be buried (Isa 53:9), but strictly speaking, he would not "see corruption/the pit" nor be "abandon[ed] . . . to Sheol" (Ps 16:10) because his grave would not be his home forever (Ps 49:11). As the first to rise from the dead (Acts 26:23), Jesus secured the resurrection of the righteous (Ps 49:15; Hos 13:14). Thus, the Messiah's "path of life" (Ps 16:11) passed through death (Ps 23:4; John 12:24–25), not around it. On the other side are the satisfying joys of the Lord's presence and eternal pleasures of his right hand (Ps 16:11). The joy of the Lord's presence is mentioned again as part of the inheritance of the same messianic king in Ps 21:6, to whom the Lord accordingly gives eternal life and great glory (vv. 4–5).

Works Cited

Chen, Kevin. Forthcoming. *The Messianic Vision of the Pentateuch*. Downers Grove, IL: InterVarsity Press.

Ebach, Jürgen. 2007. *Genesis 37–50*. HThKAT. Freiburg im Breisgau: Herder.

Gunkel, Hermann. 1986. *Die Psalmen*. 6th ed. Göttingen: Vandenhoeck & Ruprecht.

Johnston, Philip. 2002. *Shades of Sheol: Death and Afterlife in the Old Testament.* Downers Grove, IL: InterVarsity Press.

Mitchell, David. 1997. *The Message of the Psalter: An Eschatological Programme in the Book of Psalms.* Sheffield: Sheffield Academic.

Mowinckel, Sigmund. 1954. *He That Cometh.* Translated by G. W. Anderson. New York: Abingdon.

Sailhamer, John. 1992. *The Pentateuch as Narrative.* Grand Rapids: Zondervan.

Wenham, Gordon. 1987. *Genesis 1–15.* WBC. Waco, TX: Word.

Wilson, Gerald. 1985. *The Editing of the Hebrew Psalter.* Chico, CA: Scholars Press.

11.2 Resurrection in the Second Temple Period

Jason Maston

Ancient views of the human experience after death were wide-ranging. Some held a position of non-existence, others a fully embodied experience (resurrection), and others the idea that the soul/spirit survived beyond death while the body perished in the grave. All three of these ideas can be found in the Jewish literature of the Second Temple period. This brief survey will highlight representative texts from each perspective. While there can be a tendency to assume that most Jews held a belief in resurrection, the evidence actually indicates that resurrection was not a widely held belief. There was no one accepted position, nor is it even clear that one position was held more widely than another.

Non-Existence after Death

Josephus writes that the Sadducees "hold that the soul perishes along with the body" (*Ant.* 18.16; cf. *J.W.* 2.165). This view is also stated in Mark 12:18–27 (and parallels) when the Sadducees attempt to use the law of levirate marriage to disprove resurrection (cf. Acts 23:7–9). Earlier works, such as Sirach, operate without a belief in an afterlife for the individual. Death is part of the divinely established order of the world: "Good is the opposite of evil, and life the opposite of death" (Sirach 33:14); "All living beings become old like a garment, for the decree from of old is, 'You must surely die!'" (14:17). Sirach knows that humans fear death, but he does not view death as problematic (cf. 38:21–23).

It is possible that Sirach 48:11 contains an allusion to resurrection: "Happy are those who saw you and those who sleep in love. For we also shall surely live." This statement, which appears at the end of the praise of Elijah, could refer to resurrection, but it is more likely that it refers to blessing coming to those who were alive when Elijah lived. The affirmation that "we also shall surely live" is not indicating a future resurrection, but is contrasting with those who are dead. This interpretation fits the general tenor of Sirach better. In line with the Old Testament wisdom tradition of Proverbs, Sirach exhorts his readers to honor God in the present. Their reward can come in multiple ways: a pleasant life, obedient children, and even being remembered after their death (41:12–13). In lieu of a doctrine of individual afterlife, this is what Sirach offers (on Sirach see Collins 1978, 179–85; Sanders 2005, 270–73).

"Immortal" Soul

While some held that death was the final end of a human, others took the position that the human spirit or soul would endure after death. For example, *Jubilees* 23:31 reads, "And their bones shall rest in the earth, and their spirits will increase joy." Wisdom of Solomon probably belongs in this perspective as well. The author boldly claims that "God created us for incorruption, and made us in the image of his own eternity" (2:23; cf. 3:14), for God "did not make death" (1:13). The emphasis on reward for the righteous in 3:1–9 could imply resurrection, but the text does not state this explicitly (see the discussions in Collins 1978, 186–92; and Wright 2003, 162–75).

Resurrection

Other texts of this time period do speak strongly and clearly of resurrection. Josephus himself appears to believe in resurrection (*Ag. Ap.* 2.217–218), and he ascribes this position to the Pharisees (*J.W.* 2.163; *Ant.* 18.14). Inscriptions indicate that resurrection was not merely a literary motif, but also a feature of common or popular belief. "This is the grave of dear father Yehudah known as Gurk. May his resting place be with the righteous, his resurrection with the worthy." "Good luck in your resurrection" (both texts cited from Evans 2015, 225, citing respectively Avigad 1976, 241–43 [no. 15] + fig. 115; Schwabe and Lifshitz 1974, 180–81 [no.194] + fig. 20). Other inscriptions state alternative views of the afterlife (Evans 2015), which indicates the diversity of views about the afterlife.

An especially moving, and grotesque, statement about resurrection is found in the account of the martyrdom of the seven brothers and their mother in 2 Maccabees 7. The second, third, and fourth brothers taunt their torturers with claims that God will raise them and even restore to them the body parts that have been cut off. Throughout the whole ordeal, their mother encourages them with these words:

I do not know how you came into being in my womb. It was not I who gave you life and breath, nor I who set in order the elements within each of you. Therefore the Creator of the world, who shaped the beginning of humankind and devised the origin of all things, will in his mercy give life and breath back to you again, since you now forget yourselves for the sake of his laws. (7:22–23)

To her last son, she says, "Accept death, so that in God's mercy I may get you back again along with your brothers" (7:29). These statements demonstrate both a belief in resurrection and how it can be used to encourage obedience, even in the face of such horrendous conditions. (Interestingly, 4 Maccabees 8:3–13:1 alters the account of the seven brothers by removing any references to resurrection.)

2 Baruch also reflects on the resurrection, addressing particularly the question of the nature of the resurrected body: "Will they, perhaps, take again this present form, and will they put on the chained members which are in evil and by which evils are accomplished?" (*2 Baruch* 49:3; cf. 1 Cor 15:35). He is particularly concerned because a restoration of the present body in the afterlife is the restoration of a body involved in evil. The answer is that when the earth returns the dead there will be no "changing anything in their form. But as it has received them so it will give them back. And as I have delivered them to it so it will raise them" (50:2). The living will in fact be able to recognize those who have been raised (50:4). Yet, later in the text it says that the resurrected righteous shall "be changed . . . into the splendor of angels . . . and they will be like the angels and be equal to the stars. And they shall be changed into any shape which they wish" (51:5, 10). The text may imply a two-stage resurrection in which the human is raised with the same body and then that body is changed into something like angels and stars. Alternatively, the author may draw the connections with angels and stars not because he thinks humans will become these, but because they are the most glorious things he knows. He is trying to describe the resurrection of the dead as glorious, and angels and stars provide him with imagery to help accomplish that task (for discussion see Henze 2013, 453–55).

This text from *2 Baruch* brings up an important issue regarding ancient Jewish views of the afterlife and particularly resurrection, namely, the role of Scripture. Scripture serves not only to provide a vocabulary for statements about resurrection, but it also seems that the authors are drawn to resurrection because of the illocutionary force of the texts (cf. Chester 2001). *2 Baruch's* reference to the resurrected looking like stars comes from Dan 12:3. *1 Enoch* 104.2 is a similar statement: "you shall shine like the lights of heaven" (cf. vv. 4, 6). Shining like the stars or the angelic host is also found in some Dead Sea Scrolls (see below). Ezekiel's vision of the resurrection of the dry bones is another important text (Ezek 37:1–14; Levenson 2006, 156–65). While this text in its original context likely points to a restoration of the nation, in later hands it is interpreted as a grand vision of the resurrection of righteous individuals. 4Q385 and 4Q386 recast Ezekiel's vision as a statement about individual resurrection.

The Dead Sea Scrolls

These last two texts raise the problematic issue of whether the Dead Sea Scrolls generally describe resurrection or not. Scholars are divided on the matter (for overviews see Davies 2000; Lichtenberger 2001; for classic statements against, see Kuhn 1966; Nickelsburg 2006; the most extensive argument for is Puech 1993). There are a few texts, such as the Ezekiel texts and 4Q521, which indicate that resurrection was part of the eschatological ideas of the community. The evidence among other scrolls, however, is quite limited.

Key texts like 1QS (*Rule of the Community*), CD (*Damascus Document*), and 1QM (*War Scroll*) provide little clear evidence for belief in resurrection. Moreover, some scrolls depict the postmortem existence for the elect as a fellowship with the angels. For example, 1QS 11:5–8 reads "To those whom God has selected he has given them as everlasting possession; and he has given them to inheritance in the lot of the holy ones. He unites their assembly to the sons of the heavens in order (to form) the council of the community. . . ." Oftentimes connections are made with Daniel's statement that the elect will become like stars (Dan 12:3), which is understood as the elect becoming like the angelic host. For some scholars, this indicates that the scrolls do not refer to (bodily) resurrection but an afterlife that mirrors the existence of the angels (for this reading of the scrolls, see Collins 1997, 110–29; 2009).

The *Hodayot* (1QH[a]) provide the clearest potential statements in favor of resurrection. An important text is 19:13–17. The statement consists of five clauses, and the middle one reads "so that a corpse infesting maggot might be raised up from the dust to the council of [your] t[ruth]" (line 15). The statement has a resurrection ring to it. However, the surrounding clauses point to present realties, so it is difficult to judge this one alone as a statement about a future resurrection (Kuhn 1966, 82–85; contrast Brooke 2006). The hymnists may be utilizing resurrection language to describe one's entrance into the community (Nickelsburg 2006, 192–93). Nevertheless, one should probably not eliminate all future anticipation. More important than any single individual phrase is the combination of Gen 2:7 and Ezek 37:1–14 across the *Hodayot*, which points to an expectation of the redemption of the present human body not only in the present but also in the future (cf. Maston 2016).

The Dead Sea Scrolls offer little explicit evidence for resurrection. Often, the authors utilize eschatological language to describe the present situation of the community. This fits their general concern with the present situation. There are, though, subtle hints that the authors expect something more with life after death.

One should note also what Josephus writes about the Essenes:

> For it is a fixed belief of theirs that bodies are corruptible and their constituent matter impermanent, but that souls are immortal and imperishable . . . but when once they [i.e., the souls] are released from the bonds of the flesh, then, as though liberated from a long servitude, they rejoice and are borne aloft. (*J.W.* 2.154)

Josephus has certainly crafted his statement about the Essenes to match Greek views with which his readers would have been familiar. Even granting this literary license, scholars debate whether he is providing an accurate statement, is ignorant of Essene views, or is deliberating misleading readers (see Klawans 2012, 223–28). Several issues complicate the matter. First, writing about 200 CE, Hippolytus states that the Essenes hold a doctrine of resurrection: "They confess that the flesh will rise again and it will be immortal, in the same manner as the soul is already immortal" (*Haer.* 9.27.1). While the two texts note similarities with Greek views, their fundamental statements contradict each other. It is quite possible, though, that Hippolytus has added a reference to resurrection in an attempt to "Christianize" his source. Second, it is widely believed that the Essenes should be associated with the Dead Sea Scrolls. For many scholars, the Dead Sea Scrolls articulate a view of resurrection. If this is the case, then Josephus must be incorrect. Yet, whether the Dead Sea Scrolls do present a belief in resurrection is far from clear, as discussed above. Other issues could be noted, but the point is that the uncertainties over the accuracy of Josephus's statement highlight the ambiguous nature of much of the ancient literature on resurrection.

Works Cited

Avigad, Nahman. 1976. *Beth She'arim: The Excavations 1953–1958.* Vol. 3, *Catacombs 12–23.* New Brunswick, NJ: Rutgers University Press.

Brooke, George J. 2006. "The Structure of 1QH^a XII 5–XIII 4 and the Meaning of Resurrection." Pages 15–33 in *From 4QMMT to Resurrection: Melanges Qumraniens En Hommage À Émile Puech.* Edited by Florentino García Martínez, Annette Steudeland, and Eibert Tigchelaar. STDJ 61. Leiden: Brill.

Chester, Andrew. 2001. "Resurrection and Transformation." Pages 47–77 in *Auferstehung-Resurrection.* Edited by Friedrich Avemarie and Hermann Lichtenberger. WUNT 135. Tübingen: Mohr Siebeck.

Collins, John J. 1978. "The Root of Immortality: Death in the Context of Jewish Wisdom." *HTR* 71:177–92.

———. 1997. *Apocalypticism in the Dead Sea Scrolls. The Literature of the Dead Sea Scrolls.* New York: Routledge.

———. 2009. "The Angelic Life." Pages 291–310 in *Metamorphoses: Resurrection, Body and Transformative Practices in Early Christianity.* Edited by Turid Karlsen Seim and Jorunn Økland. Ekstasis 1. Berlin: de Gruyter.

Davies, Philip R. 2000. "Death, Resurrection, and the Life after Death in the Qumran Scrolls." Pages 189–211 in *Death, Life-after-Death, Resurrection and the World-to-Come in the Judaisms of Antiquity.* Edited by Alan J. Avery-Peck and Jacob Neusner. SJLA 4. Leiden: Brill.

Evans, Craig A. 2015. *Jesus and the Remains of His Day: Studies in Jesus and the Evidence of Material Culture.* Peabody, MA: Hendrickson.

Henze, Matthias. 2013. "'Then the Messiah Will Begin to Be Revealed.' Resurrection and the Apocalyptic Drama in 1 Corinthians 15 and Second Baruch 29–30, 49–51." Pages 441–62 in *Anthropologie Und Ethik Im Frühjudentum Und Im Neuen Testament.* Edited by Matthias Konradt and Esther Schläpfer. Tübingen: Mohr Siebeck.

Klawans, Jonathan. 2012. *Josephus and the Theologies of Ancient Judaism.* Oxford: Oxford University Press.

Kuhn, Heinz-Wolfgang. 1966. *Enderwartung Und Gegenwärtiges Heil: Untersuchungen Zu Den Gemeindeliedern von Qumran Mit Einem Anhang Über Eschatologie Und Gegenwart in Der Verkündigung Jesu.* SUNT 4. Göttingen: Vandenhoeck & Ruprecht.

Levenson, Jon Douglas. 2006. *Resurrection and the Restoration of Israel: The Ultimate Victory of the God of Life.* New Haven: Yale University Press.

Lichtenberger, Hermann. 2001. "Auferstehung in den Qumranfunden." Pages 79–91 in *Auferstehung-Resurrection.* Edited by Friedrich Avemarie and Hermann Lichtenberger. WUNT 135. Tübingen: Mohr Siebeck.

Maston, Jason. 2016. "Anthropological Crisis and Solution in the *Hodayot* and 1 Corinthians 15." *NTS* 62:533–48.

Nickelsburg, George W. E. 2006. *Resurrection, Immortality, and Eternal Life in Intertestamental Judaism and Early Christianity.* 2nd ed. HTS 56. Cambridge: Harvard University Press.

Puech, Émile. 1993. *La Croyance des Esséniens en la Vie Future: Immortalité, Resurrection, Vie Éternelle?* Paris: Librairie Lecoffre.

Sanders, Jack T. 2005. "Wisdom, Theodicy, Death, and the Evolution of Intellectual Traditions." *JSJ* 36:263–77.

Schwabe, Moshe, and Baruch Lifshitz. 1974. *Beth She'arim.* Vol. 2, *The Greek Inscriptions.* New Brunswick, NJ: Rutgers University Press.

Wright, N. T. 2003. *The Resurrection of the Son of God.* Minneapolis: Fortress.

11.3 Resurrection in Paul's Theology

Paul T. Sloan

"How do some among you say that there is no resurrection of the dead?" (1 Cor 15:12 NASB).

Paul puts this question to the befuddled Corinthians, who apparently deny the future resurrection of God's people. In principle, Paul argues, their denial of a future resurrection entails the denial that even Christ was raised from the dead, which if true would nullify the gospel the apostles preach. Consequently, Paul proceeds to explain the significance of Jesus' resurrection, the timing of the future resurrection, and the types of bodies that constitute the resurrected state, all of which undergird and reinforce his moral exhortations. Though we will examine other passages as well, 1 Cor 15 succinctly addresses some of the multifaceted features of "resurrection" this essay will expound: (1) the significance of Jesus' resurrection; (2) the timing of, and the types of bodies given in, the future resurrection; and (3) "resurrection" as a metaphor for renewed, Messiah-shaped human behavior.

The Resurrection of Jesus

In Rom 1:1, Paul declares that he has been set apart to proclaim God's gospel. Scholars debate whether 1:3's phrase "concerning his son" modifies "the Gospel" (Moo 1996, 44; Kirk 2008, 44) or "the holy scriptures" (Hays 1989, 85). The former reading would signify that the gospel Paul proclaims is "about God's son," while the latter would indicate that the gospel he preaches was pre-announced in the Scriptures "that pertain to his son." In either case, the gospel is pre-announced in Israel's Scriptures, and evidently relates to God's son, Jesus. Paul's statement in 1:9 that he serves God in "the gospel of His son" may tip the scales in favor of the former. The significance of this conclusion is that 1:3 proceeds by providing features of the gospel he proclaims, namely, that God's son, Jesus, "was born of a descendant of David according to the flesh, who was declared the Son of God with power by the resurrection from the dead, according to the Spirit of holiness" (1:3–4). Constant debate engages the extent to which 1:3–4 is a pre-Pauline tradition (see Jewett 2007, 97–108, for bibliography and detailed engagement with the arguments). If so, Paul is embedding a creedal formula written by others that was apparently circulated among teachers and believing communities. However, for present purposes, it is enough to concede that whether Paul authored these lines or not, he uses them presently because they communicate what he wants to communicate.

The meaning of the terms "seed of David" and "Son of God" too have been debated at length. Nathan Johnson (2017, 468–76) recently examined several biblical and extrabiblical texts that use comparable terminology and concluded that "seed of David" and "son of God" are consistently paired, and consistently refer to the promised Davidic king (see also Wright 2002, 416; for God's "son" in reference to Israel's king, see 2 Sam 7:12–14; Ps 2). The formulation in Rom 1:3–4 likely depends on 2 Sam 7:12–14, in which God promises David that he would "raise up" David's seed after him, and that descendant would be God's son and the king of Israel. Romans 15:12 corroborates this reading, as it states that the "root of Jesse" who "rises" will "rule the nations." Thus, the resurrected son of David will be installed as the universal king. Accordingly, Paul states that Jesus was appointed "son of God in power" (likely referring to his enthronement) by virtue of his resurrection from the dead.

Another angle of Jesus' resurrection is worth mentioning. Evidently, it is his resurrection that vindicated his life and death as Israel's Messiah (Wright 2002, 417). Romans 4:25 demonstrates a comparable logic. There Paul says: "[Jesus] was delivered up because of our transgressions, and was raised because of our justification." Paul seems to be saying that Jesus' death effected "our justification," and his resurrection was evidence of God's acceptance of, or vindication of, Jesus' death on "our" behalf (so Kirk 2008, 74–81). This reading is corroborated by Paul's earlier statement in Rom 3:24–25, in which he declares that people are "justified . . . freely through the redemption which is in Messiah Jesus, whom God put forth . . . in his blood . . ." Here Paul is able to refer to Jesus' shed blood as the basis for "justification"; comparably, in Rom 4:25, Jesus' being "handed over" effected "our justification," and the evidence that God accepted Jesus' self-giving is his vindicating resurrection (see also 1 Cor 15:17).

A final, vital feature to note is the timing of Jesus' resurrection relative to that of God's people. I will reserve the question of the nature of Jesus' resurrected body for the discussion below on the nature of the bodies given at the future resurrection. Among Jews who believed in the resurrection, the hope was for a single resurrection of God's people in the future; however, an innovation of early Christianity, also evident in Paul's letters, is the belief that God resurrected one person before the rest. Paul teaches God's bodily resurrection of Jesus as a one-off, past event that itself anticipates and shapes the future resurrection of the rest of God's people. Or, as Paul states: "Christ, the first fruits, after that those who are Christ's at his coming" (1 Cor 15:23). The unexpected resurrection of a single human before the future, general resurrection created for Paul a sense of living within a transformed space and time. In light of Jesus' death and resurrection, Paul claims that "the end of the ages" has fallen upon his generation (1 Cor 10:11). Consequently, those who are of the Messiah are no longer bound—either by social obligation or mental and spiritual enslavement—to obey the authorities that formerly governed God's world, such as the Mosaic law (Gal 4:1–9; Rom 14:1–23), the power of sin (Rom 6:1–23), or even certain otherwise-acceptable cultural and anthropological norms, such as marrying (1 Cor 7:29–31). Because certain Jewish eschatologies considered the general resurrection a pivotal point in world history, often accompanied by the final judgment and a transformed mode of existence (see 11.2), Jesus' *past* resurrection is evidence for Paul that God has *begun* his climactic act of restoration, but not yet completed it. Accordingly, life in the present is transformed in the shadow of Jesus' past resurrection, and lived in the peeking dawn of the future resurrection assured to those who belong to the resurrected and reigning Messiah.

The General Resurrection: When and What Kind of Body?

Subsequent generations can thank the confusion in Corinth for Paul's lengthy discourse on the timing of the general resurrection and the type of bodies consistent with that resurrection. Though 1 Cor 15 is rightly regarded as the most thorough Pauline discussion of such matters, other letters address comparable questions (Rom 8:11; 2 Cor 4:13–5:10; Phil 3:20–21; Col 3:1–4; 1 Thess 4:13–18). Regarding the timing of the resurrection, Paul consistently teaches that "the rest" will be raised from the dead when Jesus returns (1 Cor 15:23; Phil 3:20–21; 1 Thess 4:13–18). Addressing the Thessalonians' concern that those who have died before Jesus' return have irrevocably perished, Paul tells them: "For if we believe that Jesus died and rose again, even so God will bring with him those who have fallen asleep in Jesus" (1 Thess 4:14). In 1 Cor 15:23 he states: "But each in his own order: Christ the first fruits, after that those who are Christ's at his coming." Thus he claims that those who have already died will be resurrected when Jesus returns. Those who have not yet died will be "transformed" at his return, "in the twinkling of an eye" (1 Cor 15:51–52). Or as he says in Phil 3:20–21: Jesus, whom we await from heaven, will return and "will transform the body of our humble state into conformity with the body of his glory, by the exertion of the power that he has even to subject all things to himself." In other words, the Spirit—the power of God by which Jesus subjects the parodic principalities and authorities, and by which he himself was raised—will also transform the bodies of those who are alive when he returns (see also Rom 8:11; 1 Cor 15:20–28, 51–52). But the question remains, what kind of body? Paul responds with characteristic boldness.

> You fool! That which you sow does not come to life unless it dies. And that which you sow, you do not sow the body which is to be, but a bare grain, perhaps of wheat or of something else. But God gives it a body just as He wished, and to each of the seeds a body of its own. (1 Cor 15:36–38)

This and the ensuing passage have rightly engendered fruitful debate. Paul ultimately answers in 1 Cor 15:44, saying that God's people will receive "a

spiritual body" (*sōma pneumatikon*), one that is "immortal" and "imperishable."
The Platonic echoes of "a spiritual body" easily conjure the image of an ethereal,
immaterial body. But that is probably not what Paul has in mind. Here he is
emphasizing that the body given by God in the resurrection will be *energized*
by the Spirit, not *composed* of spirit. An appropriate analogy might be a "steam
boat" (so also Wright 2003, 352). The latter phrase does not denote a wispy boat
composed of steam, but a boat powered, or energized, by steam. Comparably,
by "spiritual body" Paul does not envisage a body composed of spirit, but one
finally powered by God's Spirit (contra Engberg-Pedersen 2010, 28–30). Wright
(2003, 283) points out that "the Greek forms ending in -*nos* refer to *the material
of which something is composed*, while the forms ending in -*kos* are either ethical
or functional, and refer to *the sphere within which it belongs* or *the power which
animates it*" (see also Moulton 1908–1976, 2:378, cited in Wright 2003, 351n120).

Paul's usage supports this conclusion. For example, in 1 Cor 3:1, due to the
jealous divisions among the believers, Paul tells them they are "fleshly" rather than
"spiritual" (*pneumatikois*). Here he is not comparing their bodily composition,
but the power that animates their person and consequent behavior. Similarly,
in Gal 5:16–17, Paul contradistinguishes the "spirit" and the "flesh," exhorting
the muddled Galatians to be led by the Spirit rather than tempted by the flesh.
Once more, he is not exhorting them to be composed of ethereal spirit rather
than skin; he is exhorting them to submit to the power of the Spirit rather than
that of the inimical flesh. Consequently, he is able to direct his address in Gal
6:1 to those who are "spiritual" (*hoi pneumatikoi*), that is, to those capable due
to the direction of the Spirit to gently restore one caught in sin. Numerous
additional examples demonstrate comparable usage (Rom 1:11; 7:14; 1 Cor
2:13–15; 10:3–4; 12:1; 14:1; Eph 1:3; 5:19; Col 1:9; 3:16).

Thus the problem Paul envisages with the current body is not that it is physical
as opposed to ethereal, but that it is subject to death and decay. The solution to this
problem therefore is not to receive an ethereal body, but a physical one that is not
subject to death and decay; or, in Paul's language: "This perishable must put on
the imperishable, and this mortal must put on immortality" (1 Cor 15:53; see also
2 Cor 5:1–4). His statement that "flesh and blood" cannot inherit God's kingdom
should be understood as a functional parallel to his statements about "mortal"
and "perishable" bodies. In other words, by "flesh and blood" he does not mean
mere physicality or the status of embodiment; he is referring to "flesh and blood"
in its state of subjection to death and decay (see, e.g., Jeremias 1956, 153; Maston
2016, 13). Thus the resurrection body will be physical, energized by God's Spirit,
and not subject to death and decay. These conclusions allow us to say something
about the nature of Jesus' resurrected body. Paul relates the Corinthians' denial
of the future resurrection with a consequent denial of Jesus' resurrection. If denying the future resurrection entails denying Jesus' resurrection, then presumably
Paul's description of the future resurrection bodies entails a description of what

he thinks occurred to Jesus. Therefore, his exposition of the future resurrection describes what has already happened to Jesus; consequently, Jesus' resurrection body was physical, fully energized by the Spirit, and immortal (cf. Moffitt 2011).

Resurrection as Metaphor

Paul uses the language of resurrection not just to denote Jesus' past bodily resurrection or the future one of God's people. He also uses it to exhort renewed human behavior in the present. The person who has been joined to Christ has joined Christ in his death and burial (Rom 6:3–4), *so that* "as Christ was raised from the dead . . . we too might walk in newness of life" (Rom 6:4). Jesus "died to sin" and now, in his resurrected state, he "lives to God" (Rom 6:10). In the same way, because believers have joined themselves to Christ's death, they should consider themselves "dead to sin but alive to God in Christ Jesus" (Rom 6:11). On that basis, they should not let sin have mastery over them, but should instead serve God (Rom 6:12), and present themselves to God "as those alive from the dead" and their members as "instruments of righteousness to God" (Rom 6:13).

Not only does he use such language to describe and exhort present behavior, but he also uses the expectation of a future resurrection to reinforce present obedience. His logic seems to depend on some continuity between the present and future realities. The fact that believers' embodied state will be renewed and energized by the Spirit means that what they do with their bodies in the present is very important. This idea that the future resurrection should affect current behavior is quite clear from several of Paul's statements in 1 Cor 15: "If the dead are not raised at all . . . then why are we in danger every hour?" (15:29–30). "If the dead are not raised, let us eat and drink, for tomorrow we die. Do not be deceived: 'Bad company corrupts good morals.' Become sober-minded as you ought, and stop sinning" (15:32–34). "Therefore, my beloved brethren, be steadfast, immovable, always abounding in the work of the Lord, knowing that your toil is not in vain in the Lord" (15:58). The assumption underlying these conclusions seems to be that the resurrected state, despite its certain discontinuities vis-à-vis "immortality" and "imperishability," will contain some degree of continuity with the present body, such that Paul warns them to "stop sinning" and "be steadfast" in view of the future resurrection.

Though this essay is particularly focused on the topic of the resurrection, a brief statement integrating resurrection with the renewed creation is appropriate. The climactic statements in Rom 8:18–23 provide us a fleeting glimpse of Paul's vision for the future, consisting not of ethereal bodies occupying heavenly abodes, but of the whole creation liberated from its curse with renewed, resurrected humans at its helm. Previously in Romans Paul had already alluded to the future, expected reality, describing those who are united with the Messiah as those who would "reign in life through the Messiah, Jesus" (Rom 5:17). Romans 8:18–23, in conjunction with 1 Cor 15:23–28, expands this statement to reveal a panoramic snapshot of Paul's vision, namely, the renewed, resurrected humanity reigning over the liberated creation under the Lordship of Jesus and the Kingship of God. In the present, those "in Christ" are empowered by the Spirit that raised Jesus from the dead to live as those "alive from the dead" in anticipation of the future resurrection, after which, with resurrected bodies empowered by the Spirit, they will reign through the Messiah over the renewed creation.

Works Cited

Engberg-Pedersen, Troels. 2010. *Cosmology and Self in the Apostle Paul: The Material Spirit*. Oxford: Oxford University Press.

Hays, Richard B. 1989. *Echoes of Scripture in the Letters of Paul*. New Haven: Yale University Press.

Jeremias, Joachim. 1956. "'Flesh and Blood Cannot Inherit the Kingdom of God.'" *NTS* 2:151–59.

Jewett, Robert. 2007. *Romans*. Hermeneia. Minneapolis: Fortress.

Johnson, Nathan C. 2017. "Romans 1:3–4: Beyond Antithetical Parallelism." *JBL* 136:467–90.

Kirk, J. R. Daniel. 2008. *Unlocking Romans: Resurrection and the Justification of God*. Grand Rapids: Eerdmans.

Maston, Jason. 2016. "Anthropological Crisis and Solution in the *Hodayot* and 1 Corinthians 15." *NTS* 62:1–16.

Moffitt, David M. 2011. *Atonement and the Logic of Resurrection in the Epistle to the Hebrews*. NovTSup 141. Leiden: Brill.

Moo, Douglas. 1996. *The Epistle to the Romans*. NICNT. Grand Rapids: Eerdmans.

Moulton, James Hope. 1908–1976. *A Grammar of New Testament Greek*. Edinburgh: T&T Clark.

Wright, N. T. 2002. *Romans*. NIB 10. Nashville: Abingdon.

———. 2003. *The Resurrection of the Son of God*. Vol. 3 of *Christian Origins and the Question of God*. Minneapolis: Fortress.

11.4 Jewish Perspectives on the Resurrection of Jesus

David Mishkin

The resurrection of Jesus has a prominent place in the narrative of the Gospels, it is the message of proclamation in the book of Acts, the foundation to Paul's theology, and it is mentioned or alluded to throughout the remainder of the New Testament. It is both a historical and a theological subject. Jewish interaction with this issue has varied throughout history yet it provides a unique perspective to the discussion.

Early Opinions

The resurrection was first proclaimed by Jewish followers of Jesus but the belief of the remainder of the Jewish community at the time is not as clear. According to the Gospel of Matthew (28:12–15), the Jewish leaders devised a story saying that the disciples stole the body. This passage was alluded to in the second century by Justin Martyr (*Dial.* 108) and the non-canonical *Gospel of Peter* (8.29).

There are two early Jewish works which comment on the resurrection of Jesus. There is a famous passage in the Talmud (*Gittin* 56b, 57a) that speaks of a man named Onkelos who wants to convert to Judaism. He raises several people from the dead to learn about the fate of those who act or speak against Judaism. These include the Roman Emperor Titus, Balaam, and the "sinners of Israel." This third designation is commonly understood to be a reference to Jesus, disguised because of later censorship (Steinsaltz 2000, 244; Visotzky 2011). There are two polemical aspects to this story. On one hand it acknowledges that Jesus was raised from the dead temporarily (as opposed to permanently). Also, the text is clear to say that this was done by "incantation" and therefore by a force other than the one true God. The main point seems to be that Jesus was ultimately *not* raised from the dead as is the Christian claim.

The other early work is called *Toledot Yeshu*, which is a polemical version of the life of Jesus. The oldest extant copy is an Aramaic source from the tenth century, although fragments appear much earlier and some have suggested that it originates as early as the third century (Schäfer et al. 2011, 3). The basic narrative states that after Jesus died a gardener took the body down from the cross because he did not want a curse upon the land (based on Deut 21:23). He then reburied the body. Jesus' disciples came and believed that he rose from the dead.

The Jewish-Christian debate in the Middle Ages revolved around theological concerns, with very little interest in the actual life of Jesus. The resurrection was a non-issue, hidden behind more pressing theological concerns such as the Trinity and the Messiahship of Jesus (McMichael 2009).The first direct Jewish comment on the resurrection after the Middle Ages was by Baruch Spinoza in the seventeenth century. He was already expelled from the Jewish community, and his polemic was that of a skeptic responding to the possibility of miracles. Spinoza (1955, 304) believed that "the resurrection of Christ from the dead was in reality spiritual, and that to the faithful alone, according to their understanding."

Modern Views

Jewish writers began to address the issue more formally in the nineteenth century, as the wider field of New Testament scholars were immersed in the quest for the historical Jesus. Heinrich Graetz briefly approached the resurrection in his multivolume work, *History of the Jews*. The disciples were devastated by the crucifixion, he acknowledged, but ultimately turned to Isa 53 to make sense of their Messiah's death (Graetz 1974, 166). A short time after this, Paul began to persecute the disciples. But, as he noticed how many gentiles were attracted to the new movement, Paul concluded that it was now time for them to recognize the God of Israel and that they would not need to be burdened with keeping the law. This led to Paul's belief that "Jesus had made himself manifest to him" by rising from the dead (226).

In 1909, the liberal British scholar Claude Montefiore wrote a massive commentary on the Synoptic Gospels. He was sympathetic toward Jesus and was quite nuanced in his approach to the resurrection. He first acknowledged that the disciples had some type of encounter with the risen Jesus. He believed in God and did not necessarily deny the possibility of supernatural intervention, yet he concluded that it is "our scientific duty to do without miracles when we can" (Montefiore 1909, 384). He also discussed the empty tomb and he rejected the alternative theories of his day. These included the following: that the body was stolen, that it was buried and then reburied, and that Mary Magdalene went to the tomb and had a vision that grew into the empty tomb story. He said that accounting for the empty tomb is "not quite easy." He therefore ended with the following: "It is better to assume that the body of Jesus remained where it was placed without disturbance or miracle" (385).

Joseph Klausner was the first major author to write about Jesus in Hebrew. He believed that Joseph of Aramithea buried Jesus but then felt guilty about using a family tomb. Joseph therefore "secretly removed the body at the close of Sabbath and buried it in an unknown grave" (Klausner 1927, 357). The disciples then found an empty tomb, which led to them having visions. Klausner revisited this issue in his book on Paul. This work, written a few years later, had a decidedly more negative tone. The disciples had visions, he wrote, because they were "enthusiastic to the point of madness and credulous to the point of blindness" (1943, 256). The reason he gives for Paul's belief is highly speculative. Klausner wondered if Paul might have been a witness to the crucifixion. This, along with being a spectator at the stoning of Stephen (Acts 7:58), might have triggered "an involved psychological process" that resulted in Paul's vision on the road to Damascus (316).

If Klausner's view is fanciful history, Hugh Schonfield took the discussion to a whole new level a few decades later. In 1965 he wrote the bestselling book *The Passover Plot*. According to this view, Jesus went to Jerusalem expecting to be captured, found guilty, and crucified, but not killed. A drug would be given to him while he was on the cross that would cause a coma and the appearance of death. "Two things, however, were indispensable to the success of a rescue operation. The first was to administer a drug to Jesus on the cross to give the impression of premature death, and the second was to obtain the speedy delivery of the body to Joseph" (Schonfield 1965, 66). Jesus was taken out of the tomb on Saturday night, and had told his disciples just before he died that he would rise from the dead. The next morning Mary Magdalene and others would find an empty tomb. They would also see visions of Jesus, and for this Schonfield offers two possibilities. Either they saw someone else and mistook him for Jesus, or the man they saw was a medium who enabled Jesus to speak from beyond the grave (179).

A significant work in the ongoing Jewish discussion about Jesus was written by David Flusser in the late 1960s. It was simply called *Jesus*, and was originally written in German. This work famously ends with Jesus on the cross and Flusser's (1969) final words, "and Jesus died." The first Jewish scholar to write a complete book on the resurrection of Jesus, about a decade later, was Pinchas Lapide. His opinion was unique, as he was an Orthodox Jew who concluded that the best historical explanation is that Jesus actually did rise from the dead. One of his key points was the transformation of the disciples. They had been frightened, "they denied their master and then failed him miserably." Yet they became something quite different, to which he comments: "no vision or hallucination is sufficient to explain such a revolutionary transformation" (Lapide 1984, 125). In spite of this, Lapide ultimately concluded that Jesus was not the messiah for the Jewish people. Almost two decades later, Reform Rabbi Dan Cohn-Sherbok wrote an article on the resurrection of Jesus. He did not comment on the empty tomb or Paul's experience, and he was not convinced that the disciples had "some experience with the living Jesus." If they did, he reasoned, "It is after all possible, indeed likely, that those who encountered Jesus after his crucifixion had nothing more than a subjective psychological experience" (Cohn-Sherbok 1996, 197).

In the Twenty-First Century

There has been a new interest in the resurrection of Jesus among Jewish scholars in our current century, and even polemical works have become more sophisticated (Alter 2015). Two Jewish scholars who provided rigorous discussions will be addressed here. The first is Alan F. Segal, who taught at Columbia University. His working assumption on this issue was that historians are not able to verify a supernatural event (2006, 136–37); therefore, he was not attempting to argue for or against the historicity of the resurrection. Nevertheless, he did comment extensively on the main pieces of evidence that are traditionally part of the debate (see Mishkin 2017, 169–76). One is the disciples' belief that Jesus had been resurrected. Segal's view is very much in line with the canonical narrative: "the original experience of the risen Christ must have been visionary appearances after death and that they must have started, as tradition has it, on the first day after the Sabbath, Easter Sunday" (Segal 2004, 448). The cause of the disciples' belief is debated and Segal concludes the following: "It must have come from the historical experience of the events of Jesus' life, not the other way around. The early Christian community, after they experienced these events, found the Scriptures that explained the meaning of the events" (428). He did not attempt to explain what type of event might have been the catalyst for belief in the resurrection.

Segal also wrote a whole book on Paul, called *Paul the Convert*. He again interacted with a wealth of information from religious studies, history, and the social sciences. Much of the book deals with "converts" and conversion in general, focusing on what happens to those who join a new movement. His discussion of what happened to Paul is, again, consistent with the canonical narrative: "Paul is not converted by Jesus' teachings, but rather by an experience, a revelation of Christ, which radically reorients his life. Initially a religious persecutor of Christians, he becomes a principal Christian evangelist" (1990, 3). The reason for this turnaround is of little interest to him, but he did offer the following: "Paul may have decided to become a Christian for the reason that Luke suggests," he writes, "or the experience itself may be lost forever since Paul himself does not tell us how it took place" (38).

The second major work comes from Geza Vermes, who was head of the Jewish studies department at Oxford for several decades. In 2008 he became the second Jewish writer (after Lapide) to produce a scholarly book on the resurrection. Vermes focuses largely on the empty tomb and the appearances to the disciples and the women. In an earlier work he boldly affirmed the historicity of the empty tomb. "When every argument is considered and weighed," he wrote, "the only conclusion acceptable to the historian [is that] the women who set out to pay their last respects to Jesus found to their consternation, not a body, but an empty tomb" (1973, 41). Returning to his 2008 book, his affirmation was positive but slightly less dogmatic. He questioned aspects of the narrative because of discrepancies between the evangelists, but he nevertheless affirmed that the empty tomb was "clearly an early tradition" (2008, 142). He also acknowledged that the disciples believed that they had some type of encounter with the risen Jesus.

Vermes then proposes and interacts with six potential alternative explanations to the canonical narrative. In the end, none of them "stand up to stringent scrutiny" (2008, 149). The reader is left somewhat hanging regarding Vermes's belief. In his view, the evidence is not overwhelming but the counterargument is nonexistent. What might have happened to the disciples is explained briefly and somewhat circuitously in the final chapter. The empty tomb seems to be the catalyst for the disciples' transformation from timidity to boldness. Vermes does not explain how belief in Jesus' resurrection might have emerged in the context of Second Temple Judaism. In fact, earlier in the book he referred to the disciples' unique belief as one which "altered the vista and changed the perspective" of contemporary thought (66). Vermes's estimation of the impact of this belief should have been brought in again during his later discussion, as it raises relevant questions. For example, how and why would a psychological experience lead to a belief that was antithetical to existing paradigms, and why would other Jews who were not originally committed to Jesus come to embrace the resurrection as well? Vermes does say, however, that the disciples went on to became "ecstatic spiritual warriors" who preached, taught, and healed with "charismatic potency." This new vigor was both the result of their belief and the catalyst for understanding it: "The reality of the charisma opened the apostles' eyes to the mystery of the resurrection" (150).

Works Cited

Alter, Michael J. 2015. *The Resurrection: A Critical Inquiry*. Bloomington, IN: Xlibris.

Cohn-Sherbok, Dan. 1996. "The Resurrection of Jesus: a Jewish View." Pages 184–200 in *Resurrection Reconsidered*. Edited by Gavin D'Costa. Oxford: Oneworld.

Flusser, David. 1969. *Jesus*. Translated by R. Walls. New York: Herder.

Graetz, Heinrich. 1974. *The History of the Jews*. Vol. 2. Philadelphia: Jewish Publication Society of America.

Klausner, Joseph. 1927. *Jesus of Nazareth: His Life, Times and Teaching*. Translated by Herbert Danby. London: Allen and Unwin.

———. 1943. *From Jesus to Paul*. Translated by William F. Stinespring. New York: Macmillan.

Lapide, Pinchas. 1984. *The Resurrection of Jesus: A Jewish Perspective*. London: SPCK.

McMichael, Stephen J. 2009. "The Resurrection of Jesus and Human Beings in Medieval Christian and Jewish Theology and Polemical Literature." *Studies in Christian-Jewish Relations* 4:1–18.

Mishkin, David. 2017. *Jewish Scholarship on the Resurrection of Jesus*. Eugene, OR: Pickwick.

Montefiore, Claude. 1909. *The Synoptic Gospels*. Vol. 1. London: Macmillan.

Schäfer, Peter, Michael Mearson, and Yaacov Deutsch, eds. 2011. *Toledot Yeshu ("The Life Story of Jesus"): A Princeton Conference*. Tübingen: Mohr Siebeck.

Schonfield, Hugh. 1965. *The Passover Plot*. London: Hutchinson.

Segal, Alan F. 1990. *Paul the Convert: The Apostolate and Apostleship of Saul the Pharisee*. New Haven: Yale University Press.

———. 2004. *Life after Death*. New York: Random House.

———. 2006. "The Resurrection: Faith or History?" Pages 121–38 in *The Resurrection of Jesus: John Dominic Crossan and N. T. Wright in Dialogue*. Edited by Robert B. Stewart. Minneapolis: Fortress.

Spinoza, Benedict de. 1955. *On the Improvement of the Understanding/The Ethics/Correspondence*. Translated by R. H. M. Elwes. Mineola, NY: Dover Publications.

Steinsaltz, Adin. 2000. *Talmud Bavli* (Babylonian Talmud). Hebrew ed. *Gittin*. Jerusalem: Israel Institute for Talmudic Publications.

Vermes, Geza. 1973. *Jesus the Jew: A Historian's Reading of the Gospels*. London: Collins.

———. 2008. *The Resurrection of Jesus: History and Myth*. London: Penguin Books.

Visotzky, Burton. 2011. "Jesus in Rabbinic Tradition." Pages 580–81 in *Jewish Annotated New Testament*. Edited by Amy-Jill Levine and Marc Zvi Brettler. Oxford: Oxford University Press.

PART IV: THE BRANCHES

CHAPTER 12

The Parting of the Ways

12.1 Early Judaism

David Mishkin

The word "rabbi" is commonly used to mean "teacher" (see John 1:38) although it stems from the Aramaic for "my great one" or "master." Jewish teachers in the first century CE commonly had disciples (*talmidim*) who would become part of their lives in almost every way. Jesus was called rabbi numerous times in the Gospels (Matt 26:25, 49; Mark 9:5; 11:21; 14:45; John 1:49; 3:2; 4:31; 6:25; 9:2; 11:8) and the designation was used of John the Baptist at least once (John 3:26). The term would take on a more formal and institutional meaning in the years following the destruction of the Second Temple. This history must be pieced together based on the later rabbinic literature itself, which was written over the course of several centuries. What would become known as Rabbinic Judaism would emerge from a combination of factors.

Historical Origins

Hillel and Shammai were prominent sages in the early years of the first century. Their respective teachings developed into rival camps among the Pharisees, known as the School of Hillel and the School of Shammai. Their opinions and rulings are still widely discussed in Orthodox Jewish circles, and today virtually every city in Israel has streets named after each of them. Hillel's rulings were the more liberal and, to use today's language, more inclusive. His views became the dominant ones in Judaism. Originally from Babylonia, his later life was spent in Jerusalem and he is famous for his methods of exegesis. Some of these were known in Greek thought and include arguing from a minor point to a major one, inference by analogy, intertextual comparisons, and perhaps most importantly allowing for the possibility that texts may be interpreted in more than one way (Daube 1949; Telushkin 2010). A famous story illustrates the difference between Hillel and Shammai. A gentile came to Shammai to ask about Judaism. The inquirer said he would convert to Judaism if Shammai could explain the whole Torah while he (the gentile) stood on one foot. Shammai threw him out. Hillel, by contrast, accepted the challenge and said: "What is hateful to you, do not to your neighbor: that is the whole Torah, while the rest is commentary thereof; go and learn it" (*Shabbat* 31a). These words are reminiscent of the words of Jesus in the New Testament (Matt 7:12; Luke 6:31), the difference being that the words of Jesus are in the positive as opposed to the negative, and his version is a direct citation of Lev 19:18.

Hillel is also important for setting up a dynasty among both his family and those who would come to study with him. His grandson was Gamaliel, who was probably the teacher of the apostle Paul (Acts 22:3; see also 26:4; Gal 1:14). Gamaliel was the father of Simon ben Gamaliel and the grandfather of Gamaliel II, who is mentioned in the book of Acts (5:34) as the one who suggested waiting to see what might develop with the new movement of Jesus' followers. Hillel's youngest disciple apart from family members would become the most important figure in the transition from first-century Pharisaism to the development of post 70 CE Judaism. His name was Yohanan ben Zakkai. After studying for a time with Hillel, ben Zakkai went to Galilee, where his own disciple, Hanina ben Dosa, would become famous as a healer and worker of miracles (Avery-Peck 2006). Eventually ben Zakkai returned to Jerusalem. His various influences and experiences continued to shape his beliefs (Neusner 1974).

There are many stories about ben Zakkai, most written about four hundred years after his death (Josephus, writing at the end of the first century, does not mention him at all). Chief among the episodes is his escape from Jerusalem during the First Jewish Revolt (66–70 CE). When the Roman army was attacking, ben Zakkai was smuggled out of the city in a coffin. On the way he met the Roman general Vespasian and prophesied that Vespasian would become emperor of Rome (*Gittin* 56 a, b). The city of Yavneh (also spelled *Jamnia*, from the Greek) became the home for a new school of discipleship and was the birthplace—both literally and figuratively—of Rabbinic Judaism. Details about the school, its participants, and its rulings are lacking, but we know that they were concerned about how Judaism would continue after the destruction of the Temple. The Pharisaic form of Judaism became dominant. The Sadducees (for the most part) had served as priests in the Temple and were therefore no longer relevant. Theological and cultural boundaries needed to be determined anew to address the contemporary situation. This process would take the better part of several centuries.

The other Jewish group to remain after 70 CE was the followers of Jesus. The fourth-century church historian Eusebius of Caesarea wrote that the Jewish followers of Jesus received "an oracle" which caused them to flee from Jerusalem before the war. He said that they went to Pella (Eusebius, *Hist. eccl.* 3.5.3), the area designated as the Decapolis in the New Testament and which is part of modern Jordan. This furthered the split between the majority of Jews living in Jerusalem and those who believed in Jesus. One famous piece of liturgy in the synagogue was (and is) known as both the *Amidah* ("standing") and the *Eighteen Benedictions*. At some point at the end of the first century, an additional "blessing" was added to this prayer. It is known as the *Birkat HaMinim* or "the blessing of the heretics." There has been much debate over the identity of the *minim* (or sectarians) in question. Later versions of this prayer clearly use the word *Notzrim* ("Christians") as part of the escalating rivalry between these two groups. But, to what extent the original wording of this prayer included Jewish followers of Jesus is much debated (Langer 2012).

After another revolt in the years 115–117 CE, the next major event in the "parting of the ways" between the two burgeoning communities was the Second Jewish Revolt (Mor 2016; Schäfer 2003). This was the final battle between the remaining Jews in Jerusalem and Rome in the years 132–135 CE. Notable in this war was the proclamation by Rabbi Akiva that a certain man was the messiah. Akiva gave him the name Bar Kokhba, or "Son of the Star," based on the messianic prophecy in Num 24:17. According to Justin Martyr (*1 Apol.* 31.6), the Jewish followers of Jesus were still living among the larger Jewish community in Jerusalem and did not want to fight under someone they believed to be a false messiah. This was another factor in the split between the two groups (Cohen 2014). The defeat by the Romans quelled the general interest in any messiah on the part of those who were not disciples of Jesus, and it also launched the Jewish diaspora throughout Europe and the rest of the world.

Theological Origins: The Oral Law

The primary source for virtually all of Jewish history in the early centuries CE comes from the Talmud. The first major section of the Talmud is called the *Mishnah* (from the word for "repetition") which was produced in approximately the year 200. Judah Ha Nasi (Judah the Prince) compiled the existing traditions from previous generations. [See Figure 24.] Judah himself is designated simply by the title "Rabbi" throughout rabbinic literature. The Mishnah is a compilation of legal rulings, disputes, exhortations, and discussions of temple rituals. The rabbis who are recorded are known as *Tannaim* (repeaters) and are comprised mostly of those from immediately after 70 CE up until the time of Judah himself. Few voices from before 70 CE are mentioned, with Hillel and Shimmai being the notable exceptions. The Mishnah assumes from the outset that the student is working with a teacher who is thoroughly immersed and conversant in the rabbinic world. It opens with a discussion about what time of day the Shema (Deut 6:4) should be recited. The process of debate itself, which includes argumentation, criticism, reason, and logic, is the goal more than securing definite answers. Study itself is a means of sanctification in the rabbinic system (Neusner 1989).

A key objective of the Mishnah is to establish the authority of the rabbis. This is done in the concept of the oral law. The New Testament acknowledges the existence of laws and customs apart from those in the Tanakh. These laws are not necessarily wrong or bad; the problem comes when they are applied in a manner that goes against God's written word (see Matt 15:3–6; Mark 7:6–13). The Mishnah is the earliest document to directly state that such laws had divine authority. This is affirmed in perhaps the most famous verse of the Mishnah, *Avot* 1:1, which says:

> Moses received the law from Sinai and committed it to Joshua, and Joshua to the elders, and the elders to the Prophets; and the Prophets committed it to the men of the Great Assembly. They said three things: Be deliberate in judgement, raise up many disciples, and make a fence around the law.

The verses immediately following this passage trace the continuity of rabbinic authority through Hillel and Shimmai, ben Zakkai, and eventually to "Rabbi" (Judah HaNasi). It is not clear which "law" is being referred to in this verse. Jewish tradition would later claim that it refers to the entirety of the Tanakh as well as the whole Talmud. This view remains strong and foundational in the most traditional Orthodox Jewish communities, although it is not without its critics (see the discussion in Brown 2010, 4–94). Some have wondered, for example, why a series of laws handed down for many generations are discussed almost exclusively by rabbis who lived in the early centuries of the Common Era. The answer usually given is that the *principles* were handed down and that when it was finally written the names of the most recent authorities were used. The length of time between Moses and the Mishnah (approximately fourteen hundred years by the traditional measurement) also raises questions. This is especially significant when it is remembered that in the Tanakh, the written law itself was often not followed and at one point it was actually lost (2 Kgs 22:8–13). Most importantly, many references to obeying the law throughout the Tanakh specifically mention the law being written or read (see Deut 17:18–20; 27:1–8; 28:58; Josh 8:35; 1 Kgs 14:6, etc). For these and other reasons, most Jewish scholars and even some practicing Orthodox Jews see the oral law as a symbolic reference to rabbinic authority in general rather than an explanation of literal transmission from Sinai (Schiffman 1991, 179–81).

The Mishnah sets forth the beliefs that would become normative and undisputed within Judaism. A new vocabulary emerged, with concepts such as the *olam haba* ("the world to come"). One famous verse (*Sanhedrin* 10:1) begins with the following words: "All Israelites have a share in the world to come." The same verse also provides clarification. Those who will not have a place in the world to come include those who deny that the Torah speaks of a resurrection of the dead, those who say that the Law is not "from heaven," and those who oppose rabbinical teaching. Topics are not arranged in a systematic way, although modern compilations of rabbinic thought and beliefs are available (Urbach 1987). About a century after the compilation of the Mishnah, a similar but smaller collection of rulings and decisions was produced as well, called the *Tosefta* ("additions"). This too is part of the Talmud.

The second major part of the Talmud, or oral law, is the *Gemara* ("completion"). There are two versions of the *Gemara*, each one commenting on the Mishnah. The first one to be produced was compiled in Jerusalem and is known as the *Yerushalmi*. This was completed perhaps near 400 CE. The second *Gemara* was produced by the sages in Babylon perhaps around the year 500. It is known as the *Bavli*. Whereas the sages of the land of Israel were called "rabbi," the sages in the Babylonian period are known as "*Rav*." The former title would again become normative in the Middle Ages and today the two are used interchangeably. Each Talmud is encyclopedic in length. Scholars often refer to the two main sections of Talmud as the Mishnah and the Talmud (even though the second major part is technically called the *Gemara*). The Babylonian Talmud is generally considered the more authoritative one. Both Talmuds include corrections, explanations, exegesis, stories, and didactic material. The Mishnah may be read on its own, but it can only be formally studied through the lens of the rest of the Talmud. One difference between the two is the amount of space dedicated to temple regulations. The Mishnah was compiled about a century after the destruction of the Temple and it includes material by sages who wrote from within the land of Israel. The sages that are cited in the Babylonian Talmud wrote in exile and therefore had different concerns.

The *Gemara* continues to uphold the preeminence of the rabbis. In another famous passage (*Bava Metzi'a* 59b), Rabbi Eleazer and Rabbi Joshua were disputing a specific point of law. Eleazer offered supernatural evidence to confirm his position. A voice from heaven (*bat kol*, literally "daughter of a voice") cried out that Joshua should listen to Eleazer since his opinions were correct. Joshua protested, "It is not in heaven." The concluding commentary explains: "the Torah had already been given at Mount Sinai; we pay no attention to a Heavenly Voice, because Thou has long since written in the Torah at Mount Sinai, *After the majority must one incline*." In other words, although the heavenly voice was correct in this case, it is the process of rabbinic discourse—over and above even a voice from heaven—that ultimately settles all issues.

Jesus, the Temple, and Atonement

Rabbinic references to Jesus are rare (Schäfer 2009). There are also brief references to Jewish followers of Jesus. Ironically, these appear more frequently in the later writings, when the Jewish followers of Jesus were no longer a threat (Alexander

2007). One key difference between Rabbinic Judaism and the followers of Jesus was their respective beliefs about atonement in light of the destruction of the Second Temple. This is an extremely important issue throughout the New Testament, although a minor one in rabbinic literature. Some modern scholars have questioned how relevant the destruction of the Temple actually was for Judaism (Schwartz and Weiss 2011; Gurtner 2013), but given the numerous references to temple regulations in the Mishnah, and certainly in the law of Moses itself, it is an issue that deserves to be examined.

The Talmud offers extremely few direct comments about atonement. For example, a scholar approached Yohanan ben Zakkai and proclaimed that on the basis of a man's Torah study, charity, and burying (his) children, "all his sins are forgiven him." Yohanan affirmed at least the first two points, saying that "By mercy and truth iniquity is expiated" (*Berakhot* 5a). Elsewhere, Yohanan says succinctly: "Exile atones for everything" (*Sanhedrin* 37b). In another discussion (*Menahot* 110a), there is a comment on Lev 7:37, which is a passage about sacrificial regulations. This passage, it is declared, "teaches that whosoever occupies himself with the study of the Torah is as though he were offering a burnt-offering, a meal-offering, a sin-offering, and a guilt-offering" (for the connection between blood and atonement, see 5.1). There is also an interesting passage about Yohanan ben Zakkai on his death bed, when he was visited by his disciples (*Berakhot* 28b). They saw that he began to weep and asked him why. Yohanan responded that if he were to be brought before an imperfect, earthly king he would weep. But now, he was faced with meeting "the supreme King of Kings." He says: "there are two ways before me, one leading to Paradise and the other to Gehinnom, and I do not know by which I shall be taken, shall I not weep?"

The completion of the Talmud(s) solidified the authority of the rabbis and the worldview of Judaism in the diaspora just in time to enter the European Middle Ages. It is here that Judaism became a Western (or at least Westernized) religion. The great medieval rabbis, such as Rashi (Rabbi Shlomo ben Itzak), RaMBaM (Maimonides), and RaDaK (David Kimchi), among many others, continued to provide commentaries—oral law—on the Tanakh and the Talmud. The tradition continues today.

Works Cited

Alexander, Philip S. 2007. "Jewish Believers in Jesus in Early Rabbinic Literature." Pages 659–709 in *Jewish Believers in Jesus, The Early Centuries*. Edited by Oskar Skarsaune and Reidar Hvalvik. Peabody, MA: Hendrickson.

Avery-Peck, Alan J. 2006. "The Galilean Charismatic and Rabbinic Piety: The Holy Man in Rabbinic Literature." Pages 149–65 in *The Historical Jesus in Context*.

Edited by Amy-Jill Levine, Dale C. Allison Jr., and Jon Dominick Crossan. Princeton Readings in Religions. Princeton: Princeton University Press.

Brown, Michael L. 2010. *Traditional Jewish Objections*. Vol. 5 of *Answering Jewish Objections to Jesus*. San Francisco: Purple Pomegranate Productions.

Cohen, Shaye. 2014. *From the Maccabees to the Mishnah*. 3rd ed. Louisville: Westminster John Knox.

Danby, Herbert, ed. 2012. *The Mishnah: Translated from the Hebrew with Introduction and Brief Explanatory Notes*. Peabody, MA: Hendrickson.

Daube, David. 1949. "Rabbinic Methods of Interpretation and Hellenistic Rhetoric." *HUCA* 22:239–64.

Epstein, Isidore, ed. 1948. *Soncino Talmud*. 30 vols. London: Soncino.

Gurtner, Daniel M. 2013. *This World and the World to Come: Soteriology in Early Judaism*. London: Bloomsbury T&T Clark.

Langer, Ruth. 2012. *Cursing the Christians? A History of the Birkat Haminim*. Oxford: Oxford University Press.

Mor, Menahem. 2016. *The Second Jewish Revolt: The Bar Kockba War 132–135 CE*. Leiden: Brill.

Neusner, Jacob. 1974. *First Century Judaism in Crises: Yohanan ben Zakkai and the Renaissance of Torah*. Nashville: Abingdon.

———. 1989. *Invitation to the Talmud*. New York: Harper Collins.

Schäfer, Peter. 2003. *The Bar Kochba War Reconsidered: New Perspectives on the Second Jewish Revolt Against Rome*. Tübingen: Mohr Siebeck.

———. 2009. *Jesus in the Talmud*. Princeton: Princeton University Press.

Schiffman, Lawrence. 1991. *From Text to Tradition: A History of Second Temple and Rabbinic Judaism*. New York: Ktav.

Schwartz, Daniel R., and Zeev Weiss, eds. 2011. *Was 70 CE a Watershed in Jewish History? On Jews and Judaism Before and After the Destruction of the Second Temple*. Leiden: Brill.

Telushkin, Joseph. 2010. *Hillel: If Not Now, When?* New York: Bravo Press.

Urbach, Eliezer. 1987. *The Sages: The World and Wisdom of the Rabbis of the Talmud*. Cambridge: Harvard University Press.

12.2 Early Christianity

Jason Maston

As the Acts of the Apostles narrates the expansion of "the Way" (cf. 9:2; 24:14) in its initial years, it repeatedly highlights conflicts between non-Jesus-following Jews and Jesus-following Jews. Acts itself does not describe a hard division between "the Way" and Judaism. In fact, one of the descriptors for Christianity was "the sect of the Nazarenes" (24:5; cf. 24:14; 28:22). The word "sect" is the same that Josephus used to distinguish the different Jewish groups at this time (*J.W.* 2.119–166; *Ant.* 18.11–15), and this may suggest that the author of Acts viewed "Christianity" as one group among many that formed Judaism (so Dunn 2015, 600). Nevertheless, Acts testifies to rising tensions between "the Christians" (cf. Acts 11:26; 26:28) and other Jews.

At the outset it is important to remember that while Christianity and Judaism are today independent religions, this was not always the case. Christianity arose out of Judaism. The parting of ways that was firmly underway in the second century represented an attempt by Christians to explain and justify their existence. Moreover, even a cursory survey of the texts shows that the parting of the ways between Judaism and Christianity is very complex (cf. the discussions in Dunn 1999; 2006; Becker and Reed 2007). There was no single event that caused the split nor was the split universal and consistent. Relationships among individual Christians and Jews were remarkably diverse. While the literature moved toward a position of clearer distinction, this did not always translate into clear differences on the ground. My aim in this essay is to highlight key features in the parting of the ways *from the early Christian perspective.* A comprehensive account of the issues and of the texts is not possible here, so the following discussion is necessarily selective.

The Appropriation of the Scriptures

Despite the attempts of Marcion to divorce Christianity from its roots in Israel's Scriptures, the earliest Christian communities embraced these texts as foundational to their religious beliefs and practices. Across the writings of the New Testament, one finds consistent engagement with the Scriptures, and indeed a wrestling with the texts as the authors sought to correlate the Scriptures with God's activity in Jesus (see, e.g., Hays 1989; 2016). This engagement became a source of division. Paul himself uses the Scriptures as part of his arguments for the difference between Christians and those who worshiped in the synagogues (see the discussions throughout Watson 2007). In the second century Scripture is handled in a variety of ways: some use it as a weapon to attack Judaism, while others employ it as common ground to clarify the relationship between Judaism and emerging Christianity.

Written in the second century before the second Jewish revolt (132–135 CE), the *Epistle of Barnabas* argues in a variety of ways for the distinction between "us"—the Christians—and "them"—the Jews (although note that neither "Jew" nor "Christian" is used in *Barnabas*). The author contends that the Jews have failed to keep the law, not least in the fact that they interpreted God's words and instructions literally (9.4–6; 10.9). Ultimately, Israel has been rejected from the covenant because they sinned by worshiping the golden calf (4.6–8; 14.1–4; cf. Exod 32). The patriarchs become witnesses to God's covenant with "us" rather than "them" (*Barn.* 13).

Barnabas's appropriation of Scripture as a witness against Israel and for the Christian community undergirds his concern to demonstrate a clear break between the two communities. For all the arguments against Judaism, though, the author is unwilling to separate entirely from the history of Israel. Indeed, the Scriptures are essential to the community that he is developing. It is "through the prophets" that the "Master" has spoken (*Barn.* 1:7; cf. 5:3). It is "the prophets" who "prophesied about" Jesus (*Barn.* 5:6). The Scriptures "foreshadow" Christ's suffering (*Barn.* 12) and the rite of baptism (*Barn.* 11). Even the number of men circumcised by Abraham testifies to Jesus and his cross (*Barn.* 9:7–9).

Whether Barnabas is responding to an internal or external threat is debated. What is clear is that while he does not see the two communities of Jews and Christians as co-existing, he does not contend for a Christianity utterly separated from its Jewish roots. God loved the Jews (*Barn.* 5:8), and he has rejected them because they disqualified themselves. The emerging Christian community is presented as the true heir of the divine promises, and this argument is developed by means of the Scriptures (cf. Nicklas 2014, 73–74; Dunn 2015, 658).

Whereas *Barnabas* uses the Scriptures to minimize the Jewish community, Justin Martyr, writing about 160 CE, presents a softer view. While for Justin the communities are distinguishable, there is nevertheless a dialogue to be held primarily about the meaning of Scripture. Justin seeks to persuade his Jewish interlocutor, Trypho, by means of interpretation and reason. While it is doubtful that the dialogue represents an actual encounter, the exchange probably reflects lines of discussion that did occur between Jews and Christians.

At the core of the *Dialogue* is a discussion about the correct meaning of the Scriptures. Justin uses the Scriptures to establish, among other things, that the Jews are hard-hearted, that the crucifixion of Christ was prophesied, and the divinity of Christ. Justin's *Dialogue* also highlights the textual traditions that differed between the Christian and Jewish communities. While Justin and Trypho agree on the authority of the Greek text (the so-called Septuagint), Justin contends that the Jews have removed or changed words and thus altered the meaning of the text (*Dial.* 68.6–8; chs. 72–73). Particularly crucial to Justin is the meaning and text of Isa 7:14 (*Dial.* 43.3–8; 66.2–4; cf. Hengel 2004, 29–31). For Trypho the text speaks of a "young woman" (*Dial.* 67.1; 71.3), while Justin insists that the correct text speaks of a "virgin." Moreover, according to Justin, the Jews interpret the prophecy in a purely historical manner as a reference to Hezekiah (*Dial.* 77). Justin argues instead that the text speaks only of "our Christ" (*Dial.* 68; 74; 84).

Justin's employment of the Greek text evidences the church's general reliance on the Greek over the Hebrew. The church in the East and West continued to rely on the Greek text until it was replaced with the Latin in the Western church.

Few attempts were made to claim the Hebrew text as Christian Scripture prior to the Reformation, although Origen famously incorporated the Hebrew into his *Hexapla* (Eusebius, *Hist. eccl.* 6.16; Jerome, *Vir. ill.* 54; Jobes and Silva 2015, 39–43). Jerome spent much of his life in Palestine and learned Hebrew from Jewish rabbis. His use of the Hebrew text as the base text for parts of his Latin translation brought various levels of criticism (Augustine, *Letters* 28.2; 71.2–4; 82.5). Additionally, the creation of several Greek translations (Aquila, Theodotion, Symmachus) in Jewish circles may have been attempts to in part counter the Christian adoption of the Greek text (Jobes and Silva 2015, 24–30). The different approaches to Scripture, including both the base text and its correct meaning, evidence one clear distinguishing feature between the Christians and Jews.

Religious Practices

One important way to distinguish religious groups is by their practices. Early in the development of Christianity, the Jewish distinctives of circumcision and food laws were debated, primarily as a consequence of Paul's mission to the gentiles (cf. Mark 7; Acts 15; Galatians). Also, the Christians began to worship on Sunday, the Lord's Day, in recognition of Jesus' resurrection (Acts 20:7; 1 Cor 16:20; Rev 1:10). As the Christians strove to define themselves more clearly in the following centuries, the proper way to practice the faith became an issue.

One clear dividing line is fasting. In the second century, fasting in the Jewish community was done on Monday and Thursday (*b. Ta'anit* 10a). This practice probably extends back into the first century (cf. Luke 18:12). The *Didache* (possibly late first century) asserts that the Christians must fast on Wednesday and Friday (8:1). The bi-weekly fasting is accepted as a proper religious practice, but it must not be done on the same day as "the hypocrites." The significance of fasting as a dividing and distinguishing marker is indicated by its presence in other texts (e.g., *Barn.* 3; *Didascalia Apostolorum* 21). Similarly, prayer is required, but the form of prayer must align with the prayer taught by Jesus, not "the hypocrites" (*Did.* 8:2; cf. Matt 6:9–13). The instruction to pray three times a day (*Did.* 8:3) may reflect and be in opposition to the Jewish practice of reciting the Shema (Deut 6:4) three times a day.

Trypho criticizes Justin because the Christians have abandoned the law and its distinctive practices, such as circumcision, food laws, and the keeping of various feasts (*Dial.* 10). Justin retorts that these practices were temporal and when properly understood refer to spiritual realities. The practices were temporal in that they were not there at the beginning but were introduced at various points in Israel's history (*Dial.* 19–23). Noah and Abraham did not keep the Sabbath, and Noah was not circumcised (*Dial.* 46). Thus, for Justin, these practices cannot be the means to righteousness. Moreover, in Christ these practices came to an end. Justin argues also that true circumcision is not that done in the flesh but is rather a spiritual circumcision (*Dial.* 24; cf. *Barn.* 9:4). For Justin this proves that the Jewish practice is unnecessary. Justin witnesses here to an ongoing debate that originates in Jewish circles about the meaning of circumcision. While Justin, perhaps following Paul (cf. Rom 2:29; Col 2:12), claims that spiritual circumcision negates the need for physical circumcision, other Jews did not understand the two as opposing (cf. Philo, *Spec. Laws* 1.1–11).

One point of sharp division between Christianity and Judaism was their attitude toward the Temple and its practices (see esp. Bauckham 2008, 175–92). Barnabas, perhaps following the Epistle to the Hebrews, contends that the literal sacrifices had no value (*Barn.* 2:4–10; cf. chs. 7–8). While the Gospel of John employs the feasts to develop its Christology, John Chrysostom levels many critiques of the Jewish feasts and worship practices in his homilies *Against the Jews*. In *Barn.* 16:1–4, the author considers the destruction of the Temple to be the fulfillment of prophecy and ridicules attempts to rebuild the Temple (Horbury 1999, 334; 2016, 320; for an alternative interpretation see Tomson 2014, 361–62). According to Justin Martyr, during the second revolt Christians were persecuted by direct order from Bar Kokhba (*1 Apol.* 31.5–6; cf. Eusebius, *Chron.* Hadrian Year 17; Evans 2000, 22).

For Ignatius (early second century) "it is utterly absurd to profess Jesus Christ and to practice Judaism" (*Magn.* 10:1). In particular this means Sabbath keeping has been replaced by "living according to the Lord's Day" (*Magn.* 9:1; cf. *Barn.* 15). While the target of Ignatius's critique is unclear (is it ethnic Jews or gentile Christians?), the force of his statements should not be overlooked: Judaism and Christianity are distinct entities. In the *Epistle to Diognetus* (possibly mid-second century to early third century) one reads that Christians do not observe the "superstition of the Jews" (1:1). Christians are distinguished by their worship (*Diogn.* 3:1). The Jews make offerings to God as if he is in need of something (*Diogn.* 3:3–5). Moreover, their distinctive practices of Sabbath, circumcision and special days are considered "ridiculous" (*Diogn.* 4:1–6).

These critiques of Jewish practices raise the question of whether a person, particularly a Jew, could believe Jesus is the Messiah and continue to live by the law. Trypho posed this exact question to Justin (*Dial.* 47.1). Justin answers in the affirmative, but with qualifications: those who live by the law must not compel gentiles to observe the law. In his following remarks Justin identifies those who continue to observe the law as doing so because they are "weak-minded" (*Dial.* 47.2). Nevertheless, he will allow their practices. At the same time, though, he mentions a group who has believed in Jesus as the Christ but holds a deficient Christology in which Jesus is merely a man. This group is often identified as the Ebionites, a group of Jews who identified with Christianity (on the Ebionites see Skarsaune 2007; Carleton Paget 2010, 325–79). Jews who held to the belief that Jesus was the Messiah and observed the law sat between the emerging distinctions between Judaism and Christianity. They did not fit into the clean categories that religious authorities like to have. Indeed, their continued practice of Jewish customs, particularly devotion to circumcision and the law, placed them in a precarious position. It seems that neither main group knew exactly what to do with them (on Jewish believers see Skarsaune and Hvalvik 2007).

Jesus as the Messiah

Perhaps the most significant factor that led to the parting between Judaism and Christianity is the person of Jesus (cf. Evans 2000; Bird 2010). I noted above Justin Martyr's concern with the correct reading of Isa 7:14. At stake for Justin is that the text speaks about the Christ, not another historical figure, and that he is divine. Additionally, Justin's *Dialogue* evidences the difficulty that arose with affirming that the Messiah had been crucified. While Trypho finds it bizarre to affirm that the Messiah would suffer, even more abhorrent is the idea that the Messiah would be crucified (89.1; 90.1). Moreover, when Christians began to worship Jesus alongside God, this would have struck most Jews as blasphemous (cf. Hurtado 1999).

The canonical Gospels' claim that Jesus is the long-awaited Messiah raises the question of when the parting between Judaism and the "Way" began. To be sure, nothing in the Gospels suggests that Jesus intended to start a new religion. On the contrary, the Gospels indicate that he saw himself, or was at least re-membered as, fulfilling God's promises to Israel, albeit in new and unexpected ways (cf. Hagner 2012). Nevertheless, while John's Gospel may extend the conflict between Jesus and "the Jews" to greater depths, the Synoptic Gospels indicate a severe conflict between Jesus and the Jewish leaders (e.g., Mark 10:2–9; 12:13–40 and parallels). This conflict between Jesus and the Jewish leaders is probably best viewed from the perspective of internal debates within Judaism as various groups rivaled each other for leadership. But one sees here already the beginnings of the parting of the ways, a parting that is probably already part of the Evangelists' perspectives. As soon as the first Christians announced that the crucified Jesus was God's anointed one and made him an object of worship, the Way was on a path to distinction from Judaism.

Works Cited

Bauckham, Richard. 2008. *The Jewish World around the New Testament*. WUNT 233. Tübingen: Mohr Siebeck.

Becker, Adam H., and Annette Yoshiko Reed, eds. 2007. *The Ways That Never Parted: Jews and Christians in Late Antiquity and the Early Middle Ages*. Minneapolis: Fortress.

Bird, Michael F. 2010. "Jesus and the 'Partings of the Ways.'" Pages 1183–1215 in vol. 2 of *Handbook for the Study of the Historical Jesus*. Edited by Tom Holmén and Stanley E. Porter. Leiden: Brill.

Carleton Paget, James. 2010. *Jews, Christians and Jewish Christians in Antiquity*. WUNT 251. Tübingen: Mohr Siebeck.

Dunn, James D. G. 2006. *The Parting of the Ways: Between Christianity and Judaism and Their Significance for the Character of Christianity*. Rev. ed. London: SCM.

———. 2015. *Neither Jew nor Greek*. Vol. 3 of *Christianity in the Making*. Grand Rapids: Eerdmans.

———, ed. 1999. *Jews and Christians: The Parting of the Ways, A.D. 70 to 135*. Grand Rapids: Eerdmans.

Evans, Craig A. 2000. "Root Causes of the Jewish-Christian Rift from Jesus to Justin." Pages 21–35 in *Christian-Jewish Relations Through the Centuries*. Edited by Stanley E. Porter and Brook W. Pearson. JSNTSup 192. Sheffield: Sheffield Academic.

Hagner, Donald A. 2012. "Another Look at 'The Parting of the Ways.'" Pages 381–427 in *Earliest Christian History: History, Literature, and Theology. Essays from the Tyndale Fellowship in Honor of Martin Hengel*. Edited by Michael F. Bird and Jason Maston. WUNT 2/320. Tübingen: Mohr Siebeck.

Hays, Richard B. 1989. *Echoes of Scripture in the Letters of Paul*. New Haven: Yale University Press.

———. 2016. *Echoes of Scripture in the Gospels*. Waco, TX: Baylor University Press.

Hengel, Martin. 2004. *The Septuagint as Christian Scripture*. London: T&T Clark.

Horbury, William. 1999. "Jewish-Christian Relations in Barnabas and Justin Martyr." Pages 315–45 in *Jews and Christians: The Parting of the Ways, A.D. 70 to 135*. Edited by James D. G. Dunn. Grand Rapids: Eerdmans.

———. 2016. "Messianism among Jews and Christians in the Second Century." Pages 311–24 in *Messianism among Jews and Christians: Biblical and Historical Studies*. 2nd ed. London: Bloomsbury T&T Clark, 2016.

Hurtado, Larry W. 1999. "Pre-70 CE Jewish Opposition to Christ-Devotion." *JTS* 50.1:35–58.

Jobes, Karen H., and Moisés Silva. 2015. *Invitation to the Septuagint*. 2nd ed. Grand Rapids: Baker Academic.

Nicklas, Tobias. 2014. *Jews and Christians? Second-Century "Christian" Perspectives on the "Parting of the Ways."* Tübingen: Mohr Siebeck.

Skarsaune, Oskar. 2007. "The Ebionites." Pages 419–62 in *Jewish Believers in Jesus: The Early Centuries*. Edited by Oskar Skarsaune and Reidar Hvalvik. Peabody, MA: Hendrickson.

Skarsaune, Oskar, and Reidar Hvalvik, eds. 2007. *Jewish Believers in Jesus: The Early Centuries*. Peabody, MA: Hendrickson.

Tomson, Peter J. 2014. "The Didache, Matthew, and Barnabas as Sources for Early Second Century Jewish and Christian History." Pages 348–82 in *Jews and Christians in the First and Second Centuries: How to Write Their History.* Edited by Peter J. Tomson and Joshua J. Schwartz. CRINT 13. Leiden: Brill.

Watson, Francis. 2007. *Paul, Judaism, and the Gentiles: Beyond the New Perspective.* Rev. ed. Grand Rapids: Eerdmans.

12.3 The Middle Ages

Ray Pritz

In 313 CE the Edict of Milan proclaimed that Christianity was a religion to be tolerated, and by 325 CE Christianity had become the official religion of the Roman Empire. It is here, under Constantine, that Jewish-Christian relations took its most dramatic turn. Previously, the two rival groups were both persecuted minorities under Rome, debating theological issues amongst themselves. Now, Christianity represented a purely non-Jewish movement which was aligned with the mightiest empire in the world.

The Merger of Christianity and Rome

Almost overnight the church moved from persecuted to persecuting. It was time to settle accounts with heretics, pagans, and Jews. Constantine quickly became involved in church affairs, and he was in turn influenced by Christian leaders and thinkers. As early as 315 CE, imperial legislation was passed prohibiting Jews from committing violence against any Jew who had believed in Jesus. The penalty for doing so was death by burning at the stake. The law also made it a crime for a person to convert to Judaism (Parkes 1977, 379–81, 386–88, lists imperial legislation and canon law regarding the Jews).

This early round of legislation after the church was officially recognized by the empire would set the tone for the Middle Ages. Laws were frequently passed regarding Jews; their general tenor was to legislate conditions that would ensure widening legal separation between Christians and Jews. The legislation also aimed to make the lot of Jews increasingly difficult. Jews lost an earlier exemption from serving in the *decurionate*, which meant they must pay heavy taxes. They were forbidden from owning Christian slaves and then from owning slaves at all, a serious economic blow. A Christian who became a Jew forfeited his property to the state. Marriage between Jews and Christians was forbidden, and a Jew who married a Christian woman was put to death. By the end of the church's first century in power, Jews were forbidden to build synagogues.

Before Constantine, Christian leaders had rarely been able to gather to discuss doctrine and church order. One of the earliest of these councils was in Elvira, Spain, in the year 300. Among the canons coming out of Elvira were a number dealing with relations between Christians and Jews. Church members were forbidden to marry Jews, and one canon explicitly forbade committing adultery with Jewish women. Christians were not to have their fields blessed by rabbis, and they were not allowed to join with Jews in celebrating any Jewish feasts.

Subsequent councils during the following century would rule against Christians accepting from Jews unleavened bread or indeed any gift related to a Jewish feast. Christians were required by canon law to work on Saturday, and they were not allowed to take oil to Jews on the Sabbath or to help Jews in any way on the Jewish day of rest. In fact, it was forbidden to enter a synagogue for any reason.

It is clear from a series of eight sermons preached by John Chrysostom in Antioch between 386 and 388 that many of his flock were fraternizing with Jews; Chrysostom condemned them in the strongest terms. This went well beyond a religious rivalry and is arguably the beginning of the church's demonization of the Jews as a people.

Another major round of legislation was enacted at the Fourth Lateran Council in 1215. It was decreed that Jews (along with Muslims) needed to wear distinguishing clothing so that Christians would not unintentionally mix socially with them. In many cities throughout Europe, Jews were confined to ghettos. It is significant that both the imperial legislation and the council canons were enacted repeatedly over the centuries, because there is no need to continue forbidding something that is not happening or is not likely to happen. This legislation is a clear indication that in many places there were positive relations between Christians and their Jewish neighbors (Skarsaune 1994).

Explaining the Survival of the Jewish People

The very presence of the Jewish community was a theological problem for the "doctors" of the church. If God had used the nation of Israel to bring the Messiah, then why, after the final atonement has been accomplished, does the nation continue to exist? Not only has God's purpose been fulfilled but, according to the theologians, the Jews were guilty of killing the Son of God and should be annihilated by God's wrath. Two answers were given to the conundrum. They were developed by several thinkers, but they were given their definitive formulation in the early fifth century by Augustine.

The first answer used libraries as an analogy. The ancient world had few libraries and these were usually public archives of official records or private collections of manuscripts. The latter were created by wealthy men for their own pleasure. Usually, an educated slave was responsible for maintaining the library and reading from its books to his master. While the early church had both the Old and the New Testament in Greek, learned men were aware that the Old Testament was originally in Hebrew. However, after the disappearance (or rejection) of the Jewish Christians, there was almost no one who could actually read Hebrew. Two exceptions were Origen and Jerome, both of whom had employed rabbis to teach them.

According to the doctrine of the "slave librarian," the Old Testament in its original language might be lost without Jews. God had preserved the Jews to carry and maintain the books for the church. It was generally considered in the ancient world that the older a religion was, the more likely it was to be true. In debates of Christians with the pagans, Christianity was frequently mocked and dismissed as a recent innovation. Because the Christian Scriptures included the Bible of Jesus and the apostles, Christians appealed to the age of the Old Testament revelation, going back to the very beginning of the world. In answer to the objection that this was the book of the Jews, Christian polemicists claimed that they were now the heirs of God's revelation. The mantle of truth had passed from the nation of Israel to the "third nation," the believers in Jesus. The church fathers argued that the very existence of the Jews was living proof of the truth of the ancient Scriptures.

The second answer was an appeal to Scripture. God had kept the descendants of the patriarchs alive as evidence that the Old Testament revealed divine truth; they were the physical descendants of the biblical characters, living testimony to the historicity of the biblical record. As early as Hippolytus in the third century, proof was brought from Ps 59 and elsewhere that God would not let the Jews disappear (v. 11 RSV, "slay them not"). Hippolytus also argued, however, that Jews would live in poverty and shame because of their sins, and most especially the sin of rejecting Jesus. Indeed, their sorry state was also seen as proof of the truth of Christian doctrine. The pagans knew that the Christians were in conflict with the Jews. Based on the spurious argument "if my enemy falls, that is proof that I am right," Christian thinkers pointed to Jewish poverty as evidence of divine approval of Christianity (this argument was only used, of course, after the church itself had emerged from poverty and persecution). By the time the doctrine was developed, the church was in a position to influence the conditions in which the Jews existed. While the doctrine of the "witness people" insisted that Jews were not to be killed, it was completely justified to take every opportunity to make their lot as difficult as possible.

Disputations, Jewish Converts

While the church generally sought separation from Judaism, it did not seek to exclude Jews. Throughout church history there have been Jews who believed that Jesus was the Messiah (Skarsaune and Hvalvik 2007). Ironically, some of the horrific actions done by the church against Jews were motivated by a desire to bring them into the church. One of the greatest bishops of Rome, Pope Gregory I (590–604), demonstrates this dichotomy. It was reported to him that some were attempting to convert Jews by force. In a letter to two bishops in southern France he strongly rejected such an approach. He allowed that the would-be evangelists had good intentions, but if people did not come to faith of their free will, he said, nothing good would come of it. Citing 2 Pet 2, he said that it would be worse for them than if they had never believed. It was, in fact, never official church policy to force Jews to convert to the Christian faith. Gregory's own desire to see Jews come to faith led him to approve nonviolent methods that were questionable on other grounds, however. For example, if a Jew who was paying rent to live on church lands came to faith and was baptized, his rent was to be reduced; this, Gregory hoped, would encourage other Jews to come to faith.

As early as the ninth century, Christian authorities attempted to evangelize Jews by forcing them to hear the preaching of the gospel. This became an official church program near the end of the thirteenth century, when Pope Nicholas II promulgated the policy of requiring Jews to hear Christian sermons several times a year. These sermons generally were delivered by a local priest in the synagogue. Attendance was mandatory. Ears were inspected for cotton, and attendants moved through the captive audience checking that no one was sleeping. Before the fateful day, the rabbis would often prepare their flock for what they would hear, and in the weeks following the Christian sermon their own weekly sermons were dedicated to countering what the men had been forced to hear.

Here we find another conundrum: at this time Christians were writing extremely negative things about Jews, attacks on their very humanity. And yet, the church continued striving to bring those very same Jews into the fold. And if Jews did come into the church (by choice or by force), they were treated the same as if they had been born into Christian families. Jews' sub-humanity lasted only as long as they adhered to the Jewish faith.

There had been public debates between believers in Jesus and Jews who did not believe in him as early as the book of Acts. Several such debates have been preserved from the second century, the best known being Justin Martyr's *Dialogue with Trypho, a Jew*. Such discussions, most of them informal, were held throughout the first millennium of church history, although few have been preserved in writing. In 1010 the bishop of Limoge instructed Christian scholars to enter into talks with the Jews in his city in order to persuade them to accept baptism. After a debate lasting a month, a few Jews "converted," some killed themselves or were killed, and most fled the city.

The thirteenth and fourteenth centuries saw the initiation of several organized formal debates between Jewish and Christian scholars, usually in the presence of church and/or secular hierarchy. One of them lasted almost two years. Once again, the underlying motive of the church and the Christian kings who sponsored the debates was to convince Jews of the truth of Christianity and that Jesus was the Messiah. The Talmud was usually very much in the foreground in these debates. At times, it was attacked by the Christians, who saw it as an obstacle to Jews coming to faith in Jesus. After one of the debates, many copies of the Talmud were burned publicly. Conversely, in some debates the Christian polemicists attempted to use the Talmud to prove that Jesus was the Messiah. The most well-documented disputation was in Barcelona in 1263, between Rabbi Moses ben Nachman (the "Ramban") and Pablo Christiani.

Many of the disputations were initiated by Jews who had converted to Christianity. Some of them were quite ignorant of the religion into which they had been born, but others were trained well enough in Jewish tradition and doctrine that they were able to conduct a credible debate with leading rabbis in their generation. We meet figures like Nicholas Donin, Pablo Christiani (obviously his baptismal name), Joshua ha-Lorqi, Johannes Pfefferkorn, and many more, all born Jews who converted to Christianity. In one strange case in the sixteenth century there was a public written debate over the Talmud, which was attacked by the Jewish convert Pfefferkorn and defended by the gentile Christian scholar Johannes Reuchlin. The motives of these converted Jews varied. Some had already been marginalized by the Jewish community due to misconduct; only afterward did they get baptized and seek revenge. Others, however, seem to have held a sincere faith in Jesus and initiated actions which they felt would convince other Jews to join them.

Crusades, Ritual Murder, and the Spanish Inquisition

Beginning early in the second millennium, there were a series of Crusades launched in an attempt to recapture Jerusalem. The stated purpose was a holy war against Islam, and the first Crusade officially began in 1095. On the way to the "holy land" from Europe, Christians killed many Jews as infidels in the midst of their fervor. The second Crusade, which had full authorization from the pope, began in 1146. Once again, European Jews were targeted by crusaders making their way to the holy land. This persecution of the Jews was strongly opposed by Bernard of Clairvaux. It was never official doctrine that the Jewish community should be harmed, but thousands of Jews perished at the hands of the crusaders. In 1320, for example, the so-called "Shepherds' Campaign" in the south of France was aimed exclusively against the Jews.

A new form of accusation and persecution against the Jews began in Norwich, England, in 1144. A Christian young man was found dead shortly before Easter. The Jewish community was blamed and rumors began that the Jews had a yearly ritual around Passover where they slaughtered a Christian and used the blood for making matzo (unleavened bread) for Passover. This accusation was known as the "blood libel" and slightly altered versions (known collectively as "ritual murder") were reported throughout Europe. It was partly based on the words from Matt 27:25 ("His blood be on us and our children"). On a similar note, rumors began that Jews stole communion bread from churches in order to pierce Jesus once again (since the bread was considered to be the actual body of Christ). This was known as "desecration of the host." Countless thousands of Jews were killed as a result of these accusations.

In Spain during the fifteenth century there was a unique situation, as Jews had at one time experienced an era of peace and prosperity under Islam (beginning in the eighth or ninth centuries). Now, under Christianity, Jews who freely converted were known as *conversos*. They were members of the church, but their Jewish background was ever present (the idea of identifying as a Jewish believer in Jesus was not an option). There were also others (called *moranos*, literally, "pigs") who converted outwardly, yet continued to practice Judaism. At this time, the church was in the process of examining enemies and traitors from among those who were professing to be Christians. A number of smaller such examinations had already begun in various locations, culminating in the Spanish Inquisition under the leadership of Ferdinand and Isabella. All the *conversos* were specifically in danger, receiving torture and/or death whether or not they repented of their Jewish practices. The remainder of the Jewish community was in jeopardy as well. Torquemada became the grand inquisitor, slaughtering thousands of people and burning thousands of copies of the Hebrew Bible. On March 31, 1492, Ferdinand and Isabella signed the order to expel the Jews from Spain, the largest single expulsion in Jewish history.

Martin Luther and Protestantism

By the sixteenth century, the separation between church and synagogue had long been a reality. The church still sought ways to bring Jews to faith in Jesus, but far too often those efforts resulted in violence against Jews. In many cases there was only the persecution without the evangelistic motive. In some countries, Christian sovereigns decided that the separation was incomplete as long as Judaism was active in their realms. The Jews were expelled from England in 1290, and from France in 1306. In the following century Jews were expelled from Spain, Portugal, Lithuania, and Sicily.

The church underwent a theological upheaval early in the sixteenth century with the rebellion of Martin Luther and the rise of the Protestant Reformation. Luther was the product of a time when Europe was just beginning to come out of what would later be called the Dark Ages. He was subject to all the prejudices and anti-Jewish doctrines that had developed over centuries in the church, a fact reflected even in his writings before 1517. Even so, there was potential for something different, something better.

A central tenet of Luther's stance was that Scripture must be the sole authority. It was Luther's hope that this return to the Bible would be attractive to Jews. Soon after he was excommunicated, Luther met with two Jews, and one of them came to faith in Jesus. Luther was encouraged. In 1521, he wrote a treatise entitled *That Jesus Christ Was Born a Jew*. It was an attack on the Catholic hierarchy, and it was quite positive toward Jews. However, the flood of Jews to "justification by faith" never materialized, and Luther became increasingly bitter. Over the next twenty-five years he wrote and spoke more and more against the Jews, most notably in *On the Jews and their Lies* in 1543. In this book he equated Jews with the devil, advocated stealing and burning Jewish books, and even suggested physical violence. These ideas were later adopted by Hitler, who used Luther's prominence to help justify his own actions. Much that is positive in Jewish-Christian relations has happened in the last five hundred years, but deep wounds remain to be healed (see Harvey 2017).

Works Cited

Harvey, Richard. 2017. *Luther and the Jews: Putting Right the Lies*. Eugene, OR: Cascade.

Parkes, James William. 1977. *The Conflict of the Church and the Synagogue: A Study in the Origins of Antisemitism*. New York: Atheneum.

Skarsaune, Oskar. 1994. "The Neglected Story of Christian Philo-Semitism in Antiquity and the Early Middle Ages." *Mishkan* 21.2:40–51.

Skarsaune, Oskar, and Reidar Hvalvik. 2007. *Jewish Believers in Jesus: The Early Centuries*. Peabody, MA: Hendrickson.

CHAPTER 13

The Mending of the Ways

13.1 Jewish Believers in Jesus in Modern Israel

Erez Soref

Any discussion of the Jewish people in history and theology must include the contemporary period and the land of Israel. Jesus factors into this discussion as well.

Return to the Land and New Possibilities

The re-emergence of the modern state of Israel is an unparalleled phenomenon. It is the culmination of two extraordinary factors coming together, both of which are prefigured in Scripture. The first factor is the very survival of the Jewish people under seemingly impossible odds. Historians search in vain for another group who has been uprooted from their land (for more than a generation or two) and has not only survived, but returned to their original land after constant persecution (not to mention resurrecting a dead language). Jeremiah 31:36–37 records God's promise of survival for the Jewish people:

> "If this fixed order departs from me," declares the Lord, "then the offspring of Israel also will cease from being a nation before Me forever." Thus says the Lord, "If the heavens above can be measured and the foundations of the earth searched out below, then I will cast off all the offspring of Israel for all they have done," declares the Lord. (NASB)

The second factor is the issue of the land itself, which is an integral part of the Abrahamic covenant (Gen 12:1; 15:18). According to the Torah, there would be consequences (exile) for disobedience on the part of the people of Israel (Lev 18:24–30; 20:22–26; Deut 4:25–27). The Torah also states that even while the people were in exile, God would not forget his promise or break his covenant with them (Lev 26:44–46). Later, in the days of the prophets, God reiterated the promise of a return to the land (Jer 29:14; 30:3; Ezek 11:17; 36:24; Zech 10:8–12). The New Testament has less to say about the land promise, likely because the ministry of Jesus happened while Jews were in the land and there was no need to make an issue of it. Nevertheless, Jesus did speak of a time when Jerusalem would be captured by "the Gentiles until the times of the Gentiles are fulfilled" (Luke 21:24), presuming that someone other than gentiles would then inhabit the land. Paul also acknowledged that the covenants (plural) belong (present tense) to the Jewish people (Rom 9:4).

The return to the land created many new opportunities and challenges. The Zionist pioneers in the early twentieth century were creating a new paradigm of what it means to be a Jew—no longer in the diaspora in someone else's land. A number of poets and writers at the time began to look to Jesus as a model of, in the words of one contemporary Israeli author, a "pre-exilic Jew" (Stahl 2012, 11). Most of these authors were unaware of the reality of Jewish believers in Jesus, and they were not interested in Christianity. But Jesus was an intriguing figure. A survey was done among Israelis (in Hebrew) in 1979 regarding their view of Jesus. The results were summarized in four main categories. The first was called a "sea of tears," which reflected a desire for factual information about Jesus while keeping the person of Jesus at a distance. The next two categories saw Jesus through the lens of the Holocaust—one acknowledging him as a fellow (Jewish) sufferer, the other as intimately related to those who had persecuted the Jews. The final category was an attitude of acceptance that Jesus was a Jew. The author concluded: "But, on the whole we are dealing with the Jewish recovery of Jesus, of bringing him home" (Lapide 1979, 7–8).

Roots of the Messianic Movement in Israel

Following the awakening in eschatological interest in Europe in the eighteenth and nineteenth centuries, various groups of Jewish followers of Jesus appeared in England, Germany, Romania, Hungary, Poland, and more (Nerel 1996, 24–32; Stanfield 1995, 1–3). The nineteenth century through WWI is considered by some as the "Golden Age" of Jewish evangelism, with estimates of some two hundred thousand Jews coming to faith in Jesus, more than 650 missionaries sent to share the gospel with Jewish people, and more than 213 agencies focusing on Jewish evangelism (Perlman and Harley 1986, 15–24).

Notably, in 1841 England and Prussia agreed to establish a Protestant bishop in Jerusalem. Michael Solomon Alexander, a Jewish believer in Jesus who was formerly rabbi of Norwich and Plymouth and who later served as professor of Hebrew at King's College London, was named the first Anglican bishop of Jerusalem (Cohn-Sherbok 2000, 15). It is significant that there was a rekindling of interest in the Jewish people and the land of Israel by major Protestant churches, but even more significant that a *Jewish* believer in Jesus was appointed as the main Protestant figure in Jerusalem. To many, no doubt,

this was a step toward reestablishing the original Jewish church in Jerusalem—
a theme that has resonated from the time of bishop Alexander even through
the current Messianic Jewish movement in Israel today (see Soref 2018, from
which portions of this article are taken, by permission). When the British
mandate took over the land of Israel after WWI, the Anglican Church continued its positive attitude toward Jewish believers in Jesus in Israel. Until the
end of the British mandate, following the League of Nations (UN) Resolution
181(II), known as the United Nations Partition Plan for Palestine, Messianic
Jews met regularly—both openly and in secret—and attempted to define what
Israeli Messianic Judaism was. National and regional committees began to
form, and the focus was the restoration of the New Testament Jewish church
in Israel, independently and separately from the patronage of the Protestant
churches. This attempt by Jewish followers of Jesus to define themselves vis-
à-vis the Protestant church parallels similar developments in the Jewish world
in Europe, where advocates of the Jewish enlightenment broke away from
traditional Jewish identity to embrace a secular Jewish identity and European
education in contrast to a strictly religious Jewish education. Alongside the
Jewish enlightenment, the Jewish "emancipation" in various parts of Europe—
seeking equal rights for the Jewish community—necessitated new definitions
for religion, society, and nationhood for the Jewish people (Stanfield 1995,
26–27). As such, new frames of thought and practice, both religious and
secular, emerged in the Jewish world, with independent Messianic Judaism
as part of it. The main national and regional activities of the Messianic Jews
under the British mandate included annual conferences and publications
(Nerel 1996, 82–101).

"Operation Grace" was a significant event in Messianic Jewish history in
Israel. It took place in the few months between the November 1947 UN Partition
Plan announcement and the self-declaration of the State of Israel in May of 1948.
The purpose of this operation was the evacuation of the Messianic Jews from
Israel to the UK under the auspices of the Anglican Church. The reason for it
was the belief that the Jewish people living in Israel, including the Messianic
Jews, would be slaughtered by the outraged Arab countries in the ensuing war.
And in the unlikely event that the Jewish people won the war, it was assumed
that the Messianic Jews, who were already treated with suspicion by the Jewish people because of their ties to the British, would find themselves without a
status in the new Jewish nation. Most Messianic Jews, therefore, left Israel with
"Operation Grace"; their numbers are estimated everywhere from several dozen
to several hundred (Nerel 1996, 114–23).

The few Messianic Jewish families that remained (under thirty people total) in
Israel were scornfully accused by the Jewish community of once again betraying
their people and running away to save themselves in a time of peril for all Jews,
alluding especially to the Bar Kokhba rebellion of 132–135 CE. The Messianic

Jews of that early rebellion, believing in Jesus as Messiah, refused to participate in a rebellion led by Bar Kokhba, a false messiah, and fled to Transjordan (Justin Martyr, *1 Apol.* 31.6). As a result, the community of Jewish believers in Jesus was relatively unharmed by the Romans, while the Jewish rebels were brutally crushed. In many ways, this event marked a climax of the tensions in the Jewish world toward the Messianic Jews, which began at the end of the Second Temple period and set the tone for the relationship that persists until today. Bolstered by hundreds of years of ill treatment and persecution of the Jewish people by the traditional churches—mostly Catholic—the Jewish mindset toward Jews who declare faith in Jesus is extremely negative, since they are viewed as betrayers of their people and their faith. All this surfaced in a dramatic fashion following "Operation Grace," and at some level continues to this day.

Indeed, the Messianic Jews who remained in Israel following "Operation Grace" were also critical of those who fled. "In any case, there is no doubt that 'Operation Grace' is burned in the collective memory of the Messianic Jewish community in Israel as a very traumatic event in their history in Modern Israel" (Nerel 1996, 122). Directly following the establishment of the State of Israel, the few remaining Messianic Jews attempted to define themselves independently of the foreign Christian mission agencies. The main emphasis, both theologically and practically, was on the reestablishment of the ancient Jerusalem Messianic Jewish community mentioned in the book of Acts.

An important event took place in 1957, when a group of Messianic Jews applied to register a nonprofit association called the "Israeli Messianic Community—Jerusalem Assembly." The application letter was based on the proclamation of independence of the State of Israel, and quoted part of it: "[The State of Israel] will ensure complete equality of social and political rights to all its inhabitants irrespective of religion, race or sex; it will guarantee freedom of religion, conscience, language, education and culture."

In light of these foundational statements of the new State of Israel, the letter further stated: "We are a community of Messianic Jews who believe in Jesus the Messiah who has come and who will come again as the Almighty promised, as mentioned in the Torah, the Prophets and the Writings; We have not changed our religion nor our faith, since the Messiah Himself [said], 'I have not come to abolish the law but to fulfill it'" (Nerel 1996, 172). On February 25, 1958, the superintendent of Jerusalem, on behalf of the State of Israel, approved the request to establish the nonprofit. This is significant because it was the first occurrence of a formal recognition of Messianic Jews by the modern State of Israel. The "Jerusalem Assembly" viewed itself as a national center for Messianic Jews and began to publish a journal called *The Torch: The Journal of the Israeli Messianic Assembly which Is the Renewal of the Ancient Original Assembly/Congregation.* Practically, however, the Jerusalem Israeli Messianic Assembly operated locally in Jerusalem only (171–83).

The retaking of Jerusalem in June of 1967 (the Six-Day War) captured the attention of evangelicals worldwide and provoked significant eschatological interest. This contributed to the growth and development of the Messianic community in Israel and served as a catalyst for Messianic Jews living in the diaspora to move to Israel (Cohn-Sherbok 2000, 63–66). The immigration of Messianic Jews from around the world to Israel has continued for several decades now, and has contributed to the expansion of the Messianic Jewish community in Israel. A couple of scholarly endeavors to describe the Messianic Jewish community in Israel were conducted in the late eighties (Sibley 1989), and again in the late nineties (Kjær-Hansen and Skøjtt 1999). It is fascinating to see the ongoing, longitudinal effort to create and define an independent Messianic Jewish identity while enduring ongoing rejection—an effort that carries over to this day, as we will see.

Research and Growth

In 1989, Jim Sibley documented the recent progress of Messianic Jews in Israel. This included the establishment of a national gathering of Messianic Jewish leaders starting in 1981, uniting some two-thirds of the community's leaders, as well as general attempts to raise the profile of the Messianic Jewish community in Israel during the seventies and eighties. He further estimated that at the time of his writing, some thirty Messianic Jewish congregations existed in Israel. He commented on the gradual indigenization of the Messianic Jewish congregations, as is evident by the use of Hebrew as the main language, and the music chosen for worship—original songs in Hebrew, as opposed to translated hymns, which were common in previous decades (1989, 31–32).

The Messianic Jewish community's need and desire for biblical and theological training was expressed clearly, but as reported, very few possibilities were available for local believers at that time. Also evident in this period were attempts by the Messianic Jewish community to use legal professionals in the clarification and application of the religious freedoms offered by the State of Israel. This is an obvious corollary of the 1957 precedent (Sibley 1989, 34).The overall picture in the late eighties, then, was of a small and young community that was taking steps toward establishing and defining itself in an environment that was somewhat oppressive and resistant.

Kai Kjær-Hansen and Bodil Skøjtt, Danish Protestants, conducted a series of interviews with leaders of Messianic Jewish congregations in Israel a decade later. They published their findings in 1999, in a book titled *Facts and Myths about the Messianic Congregations in Israel.* At that time, Kjær-Hansen and Skøjtt reported eighty-one Messianic Jewish congregations in Israel. The total size of the Messianic community in this report was estimated at five thousand, including children (30 percent). The common model of leadership was reportedly a single pastor/elder; some 70 percent of the leaders were Jewish, and only 18 percent of the leaders were born in Israel. Very few leaders reported having any biblical-theological training (Kjær-Hansen and Skøjtt 1999, 24). A later study confirmed this trend (Soref 2008, 2, 4–5). An overall theme of the Messianic Jewish community revealed in Kjær-Hansen and Skøjtt's study is a tendency to "become more Jewish" in both personal and congregational life and expression, a repetition and progression of Sibley's findings a decade prior. Kjær-Hansen and Skøjtt also commented on the commonality of the Messianic Jewish community's experience of persecution by so-called "anti-missionary" organizations. They put it this way: "Harassment and opposition seem to be part and parcel of what it means to be a Jewish believer in Jesus in Israel. The hostility which they face includes posters publicly exposing individuals or groups, unreliable or tendentious newspaper articles on congregations and members, threat of and actual loss of jobs, damage to property, death threats, interruption of meetings or attempts to prevent them from taking place, graffiti, arson, and so forth" (Soref 2008, 25).

The Messianic Jewish community in the 1990s experienced further expansion in numbers, as well as progression in the formative process of creating an independent Israeli Messianic Jewish identity. To date, there has not been any additional study published regarding the growth and development of the Messianic Jewish identity in Israel. Much has happened in the last two decades in the Messianic Jewish community in Israel. In 2017, Erez Soref and Keren Silver conducted a survey via a web-based questionnaire, with detailed statistics regarding the congregations and demographics about the leadership and members. In an unofficial guide to the Messianic congregations in Israel by a reputable agency requesting to remain anonymous (also in 2017), there are more than three hundred Messianic congregations in Israel today. The total number of individual Messianic Jews in Israel is estimated at thirty thousand.

This growth has been noticed among both insiders and outsiders of the movement. One orthodox Jewish writer who lives in Israel wrote the following about Jewish believers in Jesus: "The movement has also proved itself over time, there are now many second and even third-generation Messianic Jews coming of age in those communities. This is also the case in Israel, where Messianic Jewish congregations have been growing significantly in size and—even in a Jewish country—there is no major city lacking a Messianic Jewish congregation" (Shapiro 2012, 14).

Works Cited

Cohn-Sherbok, Dan. 2000. *Messianic Judaism*. London: Black.

Kjær-Hansen, Kai, and Bodil F. Skøjtt. 1999. *Facts and Myths about the Messianic Congregations in Israel*. Jerusalem: United Christian Council in Israel in cooperation with the Caspari Center.

Lapide, Pinchas. 1979. *Israelis, Jews and Jesus*. Translated by Peter Heinegg. Garden City, NY: Doubleday.

Nerel, G. 1996. "Messianic Jews in Eretz-Israel (1917–1967): Trends and Changes in Shaping Self Identity" [Hebrew]. PhD diss., Hebrew University.

Perlman, S., and C. D. Harley. 1986. *World Evangelization* 13, no. 43. Lausanne: Lausanne Committee for World Evangelization.

Shapiro, Faydra. 2011. "Jesus for Jews: The Unique Problem of Messianic Judaism." *Marburg Journal of Religion* 16:1–16.

Sibley, Jim R. 1989. "Trends in Jewish Evangelism in Israel." *Mishkan* 10:24–37.

Soref, Erez. 2008. "Report Summary for ICB's National Leader's Survey, March–April 2008." Pages 2, 4–5 in an unpublished manuscript for re-accreditation of Israel College of the Bible, October 1. Pdf.

————. 2018. "The Messianic Jewish Movement in Modern Israel." Pages 137–150 in *Israel, the Church, and the Middle East: A Biblical Response to the Current Conflict*. Edited by Darrell Bock and Mitch Glaser. Nashville: Kregel.

Stahl, Neta. 2012. *Other and Brother: Jesus in the 20th-Century Jewish Literary Landscape*. Oxford: Oxford University Press.

Stanfield, I. 1995. "Messianic Jews in the 19th Century and the Establishment of the 'Hebrew-Christian Alliance' in England, 1866–1871." MA diss., Hebrew University.

13.2 Jewish and Arab Believers in Jesus in Modern Israel

Erez Soref and Thomas Damianos

This article is written by two native born Israelis, one Jewish and one Arab. They are also both committed followers of Jesus as the Messiah. The discussion of the facts, figures, and anecdotes below is rooted in the following words of the apostle Paul.

> For even as the body is one and yet has many members, and all the members of the body, though they are many, are one body, so also is Christ. For by one Spirit we were all baptized into one body, whether Jews or Greeks, whether slaves or free, and we were all made to drink of one Spirit. (1 Cor 12:12–13 NASB)

The body of Messiah in Israel would be disabled without the Arabs. When Jewish and Arab believers in the Messiah worship God together while at the same time respecting each other's heritage, traditions, and identity, each community learns more about God from one another. Jewish believers have an amazing heritage in the faith of their forefathers, but do not have well-established traditions as they worship the Messiah within that framework, while many times Christian Arabs have very rich and meaningful Christian traditions that are as old as the church itself. Messianic Jews and Evangelical Arabs need one another to enjoy a fuller experience of the greatness of our God as expressed in our various faith traditions. In the Messiah, we love each other, complement each other, and we need each other; Arabs need Jews and Jews need Arabs. We cannot be separated and remain healthy. We belong to the same body.

Our unity should be an outgrowth of our commitment to Jesus and his commands, as he prayed: "That they may all be one" (John 17:21). It is a very powerful testimony to Jesus' true identity when Jewish people and Arab people share the gospel together. Ministry to the Jews and Arabs in Israel is at its best when we raise a united, coordinated voice, and God's blessing flows in abundance when we are able to stand as one in Jesus.

We are very blessed at Israel College of the Bible that about a third of our students are Evangelical Arabs, and two-thirds are Messianic Jews. We worship, serve, and study together, and our media work is taking the gospel to both Jews and Arabs in Israel and beyond. We are now also sending mission trips overseas to different countries to share the gospel in words and in deeds—Jew and Arab serving together, side by side. In one country a team of our staff and students hosted a huge Shabbat dinner, with the Jewish traditions and songs, and an Arab student gave his testimony of salvation and personal transformation. In another country, our students were able to bring the gospel from Zion to Muslims in Europe—in the Arabic language. The Jewish and Arab team was the embodiment of the "One New Man" that Paul writes about in Eph 2, and gave a powerful presentation to a group of German college students about the difference that Jesus can make, as they stood together, united in the gospel of peace.

It would be false, however, to paint a picture of unblemished harmony. Both Messianic Jews and Evangelical Arabs in Israel represent a small, and typically marginalized, part of their larger communities. As a result, they must deal with pressures concerning identity, both as members of their respective people groups and of the body of Messiah as a whole. Members of the Messianic community are considered traitors by the larger Israeli Jewish community because of their faith in Jesus. Arab Evangelicals are also often considered traitors by the traditional churches, and as infidels by the Muslim community. Both feel compelled to challenge their communities with the gospel, but at the same time have a very strong sense of belonging to their own people, despite the rejection they encounter. By coming together, Messianic Jews and Evangelical Arabs risk further rejection by providing "evidence" that they are traitors, fraternizing with the "enemy"! So how can positive interaction take place between Jewish and Arab believers in such a difficult environment?

Two research projects have been carried out with believing Arabs and Jews to survey attitudes towards one another. The first project (Ajaj 2014) was conducted by an Evangelical Arab and personal friend, Azar Ajaj. It was an open-ended, semi-structural interview with Arab Evangelical leaders in Israel. The second was a survey undertaken by Israel College of the Bible in 2014 among a representative group of Israeli Messianic leaders (Soref and Postell 2014). Participants in both studies clearly indicated that fellowship between Jewish and Arab followers of Messiah is extremely important, both for themselves and for the body of Messiah. Among the Messianic Jewish participants, 100 percent indicated that they are interested in deepening their fellowship with the Evangelical Arabs; of those, 75 percent indicated they are "very interested" in deepening the relationship. A significant majority (over 75 percent) of Messianic believers reported that they have hosted Arab believers in their home, indicating a deeper level of relationship than merely superficial acquaintance. Evangelical Arabs also intimated similar sentiments of recognizing the importance of fellowship with Jewish believers. Both Messianic Jews and Evangelical Arabs clearly state that they recognize the importance of, and have desire for, joint meetings and forums, but less than one third of participants indicated their experience of such events had been positive. History and the contemporary reality have been harsh for both peoples and the wounds are very deep, but the desire for connection is real nonetheless.

That Arabs experience discrimination in Israel is without question, and it is important for Jewish believers to be aware of the difficult reality experienced by our Arab brothers and sisters. Eighty-two percent of Messianic respondents recognized that there is discrimination in Israel toward Arab citizens, but there is more that needs to be understood and acknowledged about the experience of born-again Arabs in Israel. In the Ajaj study, Evangelical Arab leaders emphasized the unique challenges they face. They referred to their situation as being "a minority within a minority within a minority": Arabs are an ethnic minority in the state of Israel (21 percent of the population, just over 1.6 million); of that minority, Christians are a tiny group among the majority Muslim Arab community (just under 129,000, approximately 2 percent); and an even smaller minority of those Christians are Evangelicals (the larger Christian community being nominally Catholic, Orthodox, and so forth). The number of Evangelical Arabs in Israel is estimated to be between three and five thousand: approximately 3 percent of Israel's already small Arab Christian minority.

Participants of the survey among Messianic Jewish leaders were asked "To what degree are you aware of the unique challenges Evangelical Arabs go through in Israel because of their faith?" Nineteen percent were not aware of this at all, while 25 percent reported being aware to a lesser degree, and 56 percent to a greater degree (no one reported that they were "very much" aware; population statistics taken from Israel's Central Bureau of Statistics). We can sum this up by saying that Messianic Jews possess only partial awareness of the unique challenges faced by Evangelical Arabs. While there is agreement that there are at least three thousand Evangelical Arabs in Israel, the numbers vary depending on who is included; for example, children, Muslim or Druze background believers, only those in Evangelical churches or including others who worship elsewhere, and so on. The highest number seemed to be five thousand.

Both the Evangelical Arab and Messianic Jewish communities operate at the fringes of Israeli society, as those who have identified themselves as followers of Jesus the Messiah. Strong feelings of belonging to each of our heritages, coupled with a desire to share the gospel with our own peoples, tend to result in separate, politically oriented theologies. The city of Jerusalem represents a huge, insurmountable divide as religious feelings and emotions have skyrocketed, and both communities are making great efforts to recruit world media, and Evangelicalism, to their respective sides. Evangelicals worldwide—scholars, clergy, and laypeople alike—devote much time, energy, and emotion to portraying the situation and grievances experienced by one side or the other. These attempts to capture the allegiance of the larger Evangelical community have resulted in a distinctly non-Evangelical approach that spends far more time delegitimizing the other side than fostering a passion among Evangelicals to evangelize Jews and Arabs, for whose sake God's Son shed his blood.

Often, the dynamics between Messianic Jews and Christian Arabs are characterized by suspicion and competition. For Messianic Jews, there is celebration of our national revival in the land of our fathers, and at the same time, apprehension toward, or even ignorance about, the Evangelical Arabs. Many times, military service results in an emotional block regarding Arabs. The "Arabs," after all, were our enemies when we were in the military. For Evangelical Arabs, who come from an ancient Christian tradition, the attitude is often, "Who are those Jews anyway? We are the true and faithful Christians who have been in this land for centuries!" Interestingly enough, both communities of faith tend to think that Western Christianity largely prefers the other. Sibling rivalry is not abnormal, but it usually subsides with maturity.

As the studies have found, forums arranged to bring Jewish and Arab believers together have not been received very positively by either side. Attempts to sit face to face with the aim of reconciliation have oftentimes been underwhelming. However, we have seen that something wonderful happens when our focus is not on reconciliation between Jewish and Arab believers, but on building God's kingdom and preaching the Gospel—something we can passionately agree on. Rather than facing one another from opposite sides, we instead face outward together in the same direction, toward the same goal, and work shoulder to shoulder. In this manner, relationships are built and become strong as we walk, learn, and grow together. God has been working among a growing minority of Messianic Jews and Evangelical Arabs who worship him together, and who recognize their redemptive-historical interdependency. By focusing on building God's kingdom, our work and walk become more united.

We have deliberately worked toward this since 2007, seeking to ensure that Arab students felt that they had a place and a voice in our college as equally valuable disciples and laborers in God's kingdom. The unusual mixture of believers from different backgrounds that continues contentedly from year to year was also remarked upon by Linga Christian Services, an Arab media group committed to spreading the gospel and sharing the voice of the Arab Christians in the Holy Land. Their report on a graduation ceremony at which many Arab believers received certificates and qualifications informed readers that "The graduation ceremony stood out especially with the different identities of graduates—Arabic, Jewish, British, German, American nationalities—all united by the love of the Lord Jesus" (Linga 2010). They noted the emphasis we have on the message of the gospel and on training leaders, both Jewish and Arab, for ministry in Israel and around the world, and also the blessing ICB enjoys of having both Jewish and Arab believers in unique fellowship based on the word of God, love, and respect. They recognized that our goal is to bring the good news of Messiah to our Arab and Jewish peoples in the land, a goal that we enthusiastically share.

In 2014 we opened the first cohort of an MA program in pastoral ministry for senior pastors in Israel. This is intended for those who are in the trenches, giving out a great deal, but don't have a place where they can receive. Senior pastors can come to study with us at Israel College of the Bible for one year, not only to get training for what they do, but also to receive encouragement, unity, and fellowship with other pastors in various walks of life. The program was open to Messianic Jewish and Evangelical Arab pastors, and to the best of our knowledge, a group like that studying together in a formal academic setting for a whole year with a high level of commitment had never occurred.

The result was even more wonderful than we could have imagined. There were twenty-four pastors—twelve Jewish and twelve Arab—who had come not with the intent of reconciliation, but with the desire to be the best pastor that they could be, in order to better serve their congregation and their area. Each one was there to learn, to serve, and to build God's kingdom. Each one was passionate about the spread of the gospel, the winning of new believers, and the spiritual growth of their flock. It just so happened that half were Jewish and half were Arab.

Here are some words from the pastors as they reflected on their year together, remembering their initial thoughts about the prospect of studying with pastors from "the other side":

> "My first impression was this is going to be great, but it's not going to be easy. . . . I felt that we are fulfilling a prophecy and it's going to be very special, and also challenging—two cultures coming together."

"It's unique because I've never experienced something like that. . . . [I]t's really it's like heaven on earth . . . like half Arab, half Jewish, studying together."

"I didn't know what to expect being with a group of Messianic and Arab. I thought . . . maybe arguing, maybe clashing."

"Who are these people? Are they really believers? Do they believe in the Messiah? Believe in Jesus? What will I share with them? And how do they accept me as an Arab pastor? And how do I accept them as, you know, Jewish pastors? There were a lot of questions in my mind—How they pray, how they worship, how they teach the word of God. Is it the same as us?"

"All the Arab pastors that have been there for me were new creatures. Totally new! I didn't know them before. . . . But when you put all our guys together, listen, we had fun. Sometimes the teachers had problems to calm us down and to be serious."

"We're going through many conflicts and war and the tension that was between Jews and Arabs was very high, so when Jews and Arabs come to-gether to study God's word, one of the challenges is to come to a deep unity."

"It was a divine appointment. What happened in this class is an historical event. Especially as ministers, as pastors, as the leaders, all the unity of the leaders can move and mobilize and transform the whole of Israel."

The personal friendships that were built during that intensive year of study continue to this day, and Jewish and Arab pastors meet together, invite one another to speak to their congregations, and are putting into practice what they have learned along the way. The following year another intake of Jewish and Arab pastors followed, and each year we have both Jewish and Arab undergraduates studying a variety of programs with us, as well as a staff team comprised of both Jews and Arabs. Great friendships are formed over time, rooted in the unity of our gospel focus, and those friendships make it possible to discuss the difficult issues within the context of love, trust, and deep personal relationship. We do not take this fellowship for granted.

Unity in Messiah among Messianic Jews and Evangelical Arabs has a weighty missiological effect upon a war-torn land. There is something very special and "not of this world" when an Arab speaks to a Jewish person about the love of God in the Messiah Jesus, and vice versa. There are stories of Jewish Israelis who have come to faith through Evangelical Arabs, and likewise, stories of Arabs who have discovered the unconditional love of God through the witness of a Jewish follower of Jesus. Sadly, the recent Evangelical preoccupation with politics over evangelization has not only created a growing divide among Evangelicals outside of Israel, but also among Messianic Jews and Evangelical Arabs within Israel. With this divide comes a stunted witness of the supernatural love that has the power to bring us together again into Abraham's family. Jewish and Arab followers of Jesus need one another (now more than ever) to accomplish the missiological task of proclaiming the gospel of God's supernatural love in Israel and throughout the Middle East.

As Messianic Jews and Evangelical Arabs, our challenge is to stay theologically focused on the good news of Messiah Jesus and the Great Commission. We complement one another missiologically, each community able to testify to the other about the love of God in a manner that goes way beyond one's ethnocentric love for his or her own people group. When we recognize Jesus as head and take our orders from him, we can recognize each other as equally important—and necessary—parts of one body that is working not for our own gain, but for God's great plan of redemption, laid out before time began.

Works Cited

Ajaj, Azar. 2014. E-mail message to author on March 25.

Central Bureau of Statistics. August 2014. http://www.cbs.gov.il/publications14/yarhon0814/pdf/b1.pdf.

Linga: Christian Service from the Holy Land. 2010. "Israel College of the Bible (ICB) Graduation Ceremony 2010." Last modified July 2, 2010. https://en.linga.org/christian-news-in-the-holy-land/article-325.html.

Soref, Erez, and Seth Postell. 2014. "The Relationship between Jewish and Arab Believers in Israel: The Current Situation and Hope for the Future." Paper presented at the Borough Park Symposium, New York, November 19.

Index of Modern Authors

Aberbach, Moses, 182, 203–5
Adams, Sean A., 230
Adler, Yonatan, 119, 121
Ahitov, Shmuel, 91
Ajaj, Azar, 303
Alexander, Loveday C. A., 229
Alexander, Michael Solomon, 296
Alexander, Philip S., 166, 279
Alexander, T. Desmond, 14
Allen, David L., 207
Allen, Leslie C., 61
Allison, Dale C., 152, 171, 173, 187–90
Alter, Michael J., 269
Anderson, A. A., 23
Anderson, Gary A., 187
Anderson, Paul N., 221
Ashton, John, 221
Attridge, Harold W., 109
Averbeck, Richard E., 96, 100
Aviam, Mordechai, 119
Avigad, Nahman, 256
Avioz, Michael, 25

Bagatti, Bellarmino, 210
Ball, David, 162
Bammel, Ernst, 165
Barclay, John, 236, 240–41
BarNavi, Eli, 90
Barrett, C. K., 65, 217
Bateman, Herbert W., 143, 215
Bauckham, Richard, 3, 161, 207, 211, 218, 285
Bauer, Walter, 248
Baumgarten, Albert, 134
Beale, G. K., 65
Beasley-Murray, George R., 149
Becker, Adam H., 282
Belkin, Ahuva, 90–91
Bell, Richard H., 248
Bergen, Robert D., 23
Betz, Hans Dieter, 107, 145, 147

Beyse, K. M., 193–94
Bickerman, Elias J., 143
Billerbeck, Paul, 147, 158
Bird, Michael, 237, 286
Black, C. Clifton, 215
Blenkinsopp, Joseph, 54
Block, Daniel I., 24, 42, 44, 51, 56
Blomberg, Craig L., 128, 195–96
Bock, Darrell, 76, 164, 166–67
Bockmuehl, Markus N. A., 151–52
Boda, Mark J., 56
Borsch, Fredrick, 146
Bowker, John, 123
Boyarin, Daniel, 4, 224
Brettler, Marc, 3
Bright, John, 29
Brooke, George J., 258
Brown, Jeannine K., 168
Brown, Michael L., 96, 278
Bruce, F. F., 141, 227, 230
Brueggemann, Walter, 22, 40, 191
Brumbach, Joshua, 211
Bryan, Steven M., 109
Bultmann, Rudolph, 1–2
Burridge, Richard A., 1
Buth, Randall, 131

Calvin, John, 50
Campbell, Douglas, 226, 230
Caragounis, Chrys C., 157–58
Carroll, James, 4
Carson, D. A., 65, 75, 165, 169
Casey, Maurice, 157
Chancey, Mark, 121
Chanikuzhy, Jacob, 107, 109
Chapman, David W., 164, 166–68
Charlesworth, James H., 1, 120, 123, 133
Chen, Kevin, 253
Chester, Andrew, 257
Chester, Stephen J., 228
Chilton, Bruce, 131, 139, 152, 178

Christensen, Duane L., 31
Churgin, Pinkhos, 145
Clements, Ronald, 246
Cocceius, Johannes, 21
Cockerill, Gareth L., 214
Cohen, Jeremy, 4
Cohen, Shaye, 277
Cohick, Lynn H., 164–65, 167
Cohn-Sherbok, Dan, 4, 269, 299
Cole, Robert L., 46, 60
Collins, Adela Yarbro, 107, 167
Collins, John J., 133, 178, 256, 258
Coloe, Mary, 110
Cook, Edward M., 131
Cook, John Granger, 167
Cook, P. M., 40, 43
Craigie, Peter C., 62
Cranfield, C. E. B., 247–49
Crossan, John Dominic, 195–97
Crutchfield, John, 60
Culpepper, R. Alan, 221

Dahl, Nils Astrup, 172
Dalman, Gustaf, 165
Dan, Yosef, 76
Darby, Michael R., 4
Dark, Kenneth, 119, 121
Das, Andrew, 244
Daube, David, 181, 204, 275
Davies, Philip R., 258
Davies, W. D., 233
Delitzch, Franz, 63
Dennis, J., 167–68
DeTroyer, Kristin, 133
Dodd, C. H., 196
Donaldson, Terrence L., 44, 221
Downs, David J., 191
Dumbrell, William J., 43, 245
Dunn, James D. G., 4, 152, 208, 211, 228, 232, 236, 241, 282–83

Ebach, Jürgen, 253
Edersheim, Alfred, 87
Egger, Peter, 165
Eichrodt, Walter, 29–30
Engberg-Pederson, Troels, 264
Eppstein, Victor, 109
Evans, Craig A., 1, 109, 116, 120, 145, 178, 180–81, 211, 256, 285–86

Fabry, H. J., 101
Fee, Gordon, 134
Fiensy, David A., 209
Fitzmyer, Joseph A., 56, 65
Fletcher-Louis, Crispin, 175
Flusser, David, 2, 90, 134, 269
Foerster, Gideon, 119
Foster, Paul, 226
France, R. T., 71
Fredricksen, Paula, 173–74
Frerichs, Ernest S., 178
Fretheim, Terrence, 106
Fruchtenbaum, Arnold G., 72
Funk, Robert, 195, 197

Garland, David E., 185
Geiger, Abraham, 2
Gelardini, Gabriella, 214
Gentry, Peter J., 14, 19
Gerhardsson, Birger, 181, 194–95, 205
Ginsburg, Harold Louis, 61
Goldingay, John, 47
Goranson, Stephen Kraft, 118
Graetz, Heinrich, 268
Green, E. Michael, 132
Green, Joel B., 140
Green, William S., 178
Greenspoon, Leonard, 134
Grisante, Michael, 26
Grogan, Geoffrey, 30
Gruber, Mayer I., 61
Grundmann, Walter, 2
Guelich, Robert A., 191
Gurtner, Daniel M., 280
Guthrie, George H., 110, 214–15

Hafemann, Scott, 19, 21
Haggai, Shmuel, 145
Hagner, Donald, 2, 31, 286
Hamilton, Victor P., 9
Hanson, Anthony Tyrrell, 65
Harley, C. D., 296
Harris, Robert A., 61
Harris, W. Hall, 50
Harrison, Everett F., 31
Harris-Shapiro, Carol, 4
Hartley, John E., 86–87
Harvey, Richard, 294
Hauck, F., 194

Hauerwas, Stanley, 189–90
Hawthorne, Gerald, 190
Hay, John, 135
Hays, J. Daniel, 106
Hays, Richard B., 66, 238, 261, 282
Helman, Anat, 90
Hengel, Martin, 171–72, 227–28, 283
Henze, Matthias, 257
Heschel, Abraham J., 191
Heschel, Susannah, 1
Hevlin, Rina, 93
Hillers, Delbert R., 25, 29
Hoade, Eugene, 119
Hock, Ronalf F., 228
Hoehner, Harold W., 168
Hoffmann, Heinrich, 157
Homolka, Walter, 2
Horbury, William, 178, 242
Hubbard, Robert L., 104
Hugenberger, Gordon P., 54
Hulst, A. R., 41
Hultgren, Arlen, 196
Hurst, L. D., 217
Hurtado, Larry W., 171–74, 286
Hvalvik, Reider, 4, 207, 286

Jacob, Walter, 2
Jacovici, Simcha, 120
Janowski, B., 96
Jeremias, Joachim, 186, 195–98, 264
Jervell, Jacob, 129, 209–11
Jewett, Robert, 261
Jobes, Karen H., 284
Johnson, Jeffrey D., 3
Johnson, Nathan, 262
Johnston, Philip, 250–51
Jones, F. Stanley, 4
Juel, Donald, 107
Jülicher, Adolf, 196

Kaiser, Walter C., 10, 22, 24
Keener, Craig S., 107–8, 206
Kelly, Brian E., 59
Keown, Gerald L., 29
Kidner, Derek, 46, 62
Kim, Seyoon, 158, 228
Kirk, J. R. Daniel, 261–62
Kjær-Hansen, Kai, 299–300
Klausner, Joseph, 2, 268

Klawans, Jonathan, 259
Kline, Meredith, 21
Kline, Ralph, 47
Kmiecik, Ulrich, 157
Knight, George A. F., 35
Knoppers, Gary N., 25
Koester, Craig R., 214
Konradt, Mattias, 127
Köstenberger, Andreas J., 160–62,
    168–69, 178–80, 182, 204–5
Kraus, Hans-Joachim, 46
Kuhn, Heinz-Wolfgang, 258
Kynes, Will, 189
Kysar, Robert, 221

Laansma, Jon, 217
Lane, William L., 214
Lang, B., 96
Langer, Ruth, 277
Lapide, Pinchas, 269, 296
Lee, Brian J., 21
Lee, Dorothy A., 159
Levenson, Jon D., 24
Levine, Amy-Jill, 3
Levine, Baruch A., 96
Levine, Lee I., 77, 139–40
Lichtenberger, Hermann, 258
Lieu, Judith, 109
Lifshitz, Baruch, 256
Lindars, Barnabas, 65
Lohse, Eduard, 141, 179, 190, 204
Loke, Andrew Ter Ern, 175
Longenecker, Richard N., 65, 206
Longman, Tremper III, 60, 189

Maass, F., 96, 100
Magee, M. D., 129
Maier, Johann, 147
Makara, Apollo, 161
Marshall, I. Howard, 187
Mason, Steve, 124
Maston, Jason, 258, 264
McCollough, C. Thomas, 119
McConville, J. G., 35
McKnight, Scot, 187, 190–91
McMichael, Stephen J., 267
McRay, John, 120
Meier, John P., 152, 195–97, 240
Meltzer, Yoram, 93

Mendenhall, George E., 20–21, 24
Mendes-Flor, Paul, 2
Merrill, Eugene H., 9, 11
Meyer, Ben F., 152
Meyer, Michael A., 2
Michel, Otto, 167
Milgrom, Jacob, 99
Millar, J. Gary, 242
Miller, Stephen, 47
Millgram, Abraham E., 72
Mishkin, David, 270
Mitchell, David C., 46, 60, 254
Mitchell, Margaret M., 231
Moberly, R. W. L., 242
Moffitt, David M., 265
Montefiore, Claude, 2, 268
Moo, Douglas J., 166, 261
Moore, George Foot, 87
Mor, Menahem, 277
Morris, Leon, 166
Moulton, James Hope, 264
Mowinkel, Sigmund, 60, 250
Mueller, Ulrich B., 104
Müller, Karlheinz, 141–42
Müller, Morgens, 157
Murphy, Frederick J., 133
Murphy-O'Connor, Jerome, 118, 120, 134
Mykytiuk, Lawrence, 117

Nerel, Gershon, 296–98
Netzer, Ehud, 117
Neubauer, Fritz, 157
Neudecker, Reinhard, 179, 203–4
Neusner, Jacob, 123, 178, 204, 276–77
Nickelsburg, George W. E., 133, 146, 258
Nicklas, Tobias, 283
Niehaus, Jeffrey, 14
Notley, R. Steven, 118–19
Novenson, Matthew V., 174

O'Brian, Peter T., 236
Operhansli-Widmer, Gabrielle, 145, 149
Ory, J., 119
Oswalt, John, 40

Paget, Carleton, 285
Parkes, James William, 288
Patterson, Todd L., 34

Patzia, Arthur G., 51
Pellegrino, Charles, 120
Pennington, Jonathan T., 187, 189
Perlman, Susan, 296
Peters, M. K. H., 131
Petrotta, Anthony J., 51
Phillips, Thomas E., 227
Pines, S., 136
Pixner, Bargil, 118, 128
Polhil, John B., 211
Polk, Timothy, 194
Porter, Stanley E., 230
Postell, Seth D., 35, 303
Prawer, Joshua, 91
Pritz, Ray, 4, 129
Puech, Emile, 258
Pummer, Reinhard, 129

Rabinowitz, Louis I., 138–39
Rad, Gerhard von, 22, 31
Radl, W., 101
Rainey, Anson, 118–19
Raphell, Yoel, 91
Reed, Annette Yoshiko, 282
Reeg, Gottfried, 139
Regev, Moti, 91
Reim, Günther, 181
Reimarus, Samuel, 1
Reinhartz, Adele, 221
Reinharz, Jehuda, 2
Renan, Ernst, 1
Rengstorf, K. H., 203
Reynolds, Benjamin E., 157
Richards, E. Randolph, 230
Riesner, Rainer, 140, 145, 147, 178, 180, 182, 204, 227
Ritmeyer, Leen, 116
Robinson, Richard A., 73
Roetzel, Calvin J., 228
Rose, Wolter H., 58
Rosner, Brian S., 234, 236, 241–42
Ross, Alan P., 11
Rosseau, John J., 120
Rydelnik, Michael, 56, 63

Safrai, Shmuel, 83, 93, 141–43
Sailhamer, John H., 14, 21, 28, 52, 242, 245, 251
Saldarini, Anthony J., 123

Sanders, E. P., 21, 109, 152, 184, 236
Sanders, Jack T., 256
Sarna, Nahum M., 61
Sawyer, J. F. A., 101
Schachter, Lifsa Block, 106
Schäfer, Peter, 148, 267, 277, 279
Schiffman, Lawrence H., 146–48, 278
Schipper, Jeremy, 194
Schlatter, Adolf, 149
Schnabel, Eckhard J., 164, 166, 206
Schonfield, Hugh, 268
Schreiner, Thomas, 21
Schubert, Kurt, 147
Schulz, Anselm, 203
Schürer, Emil, 133, 141, 146, 166, 179, 184
Schwabe, Moshe, 256
Schwartz, Daniel R., 3, 280
Schweitzer, Albert, 1
Schwemer, Ana Maria, 227–28
Scott, Bernhard B., 197
Scott, J. Julius, Jr., 3, 123
Segal, Alan F., 232, 269–70
Seifrid, Mark A., 236
Seybold, Klaus, 104
Shapiro, Faydra, 300
Sherwin-White, A. N., 165, 168
Shires, Henry M., 65
Sibley, Jim R., 245–46, 299
Silva, Moises, 284
Silver, Keren, 300
Skarsaune, Oskar, 4, 285–86, 289, 291
Skøjtt, Bodil F., 299–300
Smith, D. Moody, 65, 131, 221
Snodgrass, Klyne, 194
Snyder, Howard A., 186
Sobel, B. Z., 4
Sokman, Rahel, 91
Soref, Erez, 300, 303
Spicq, Ceslas, 217
Stahl, Neta, 296
Stanfield, Yohanan, 37, 296–97
Stapleton, Andrew J., 145
Stegner, W. R., 214
Stein, Siegfried, 77
Steinman, Andrew E., 26
Steinsaltz, Adin, 267
Stendahl, Krister, 228
Sterling, G. E., 135
Stern, David, 197–98

Stern, M., 83
Stewart, Alexander E., 161
Stone, Michael E., 133, 146
Strack, Hermann L., 147, 158
Strauss, David Friedrich, 1
Strobel, August, 165

Tajra, Harry W., 230
Talmon, Shemaryahu, 133
Tate, Marvin, 46, 61
Taylor, John B., 30
Taylor, Justin, 168
Telushkin, Joseph, 275
Thompson, James W., 217
Thyan, Hartwig, 214
Todd, James, 14
Tov, Emanuel, 134
Towner, Philip H., 226
Tsedaka, Benyamin, 129
Tsevat, Matitiahu, 25
Twelftree, Graham H., 154

Urbach, Eliezer, 279

VanderKam, James, 133
VanGemeren, Willem, 62, 83–84
Vermes, Geza, 2, 151, 270
Visotzky, Burton, 267
Vlach, Michael J., 10

Wach, Joachim, 180, 182
Wahlde, Urban C. von, 221
Walker, Peter, 120
Waltke, Bruce K., 26, 48, 62, 148
Walton, John H., 106
Watson, Francis, 236, 240, 242, 282
Weinfeld, Moshe, 25, 82
Weingreen, J., 138–39
Weiss, Zeev, 280
Welhausen, Julius, 21
Wells, Samuel, 189
Wellum, Stephen J., 14, 19
Wenham, Gordon, 251
Wenthe, Dean O., 178–80, 203, 205
Westerholm, Stephen, 236
Westerman, Claus, 193
Wheeler, Sondra Ely, 191
Wilckens, Ulrich, 248
Wilkins, M. J., 178–79

Williams, Catrin H., 159, 162–63
Williamson, H. G. M., 59, 65
Williamson, Paul R., 14
Wills, Lawrence, 215
Wilson, Gerald H., 45, 60, 194, 254
Wilson, Marvin R., 3
Wise, M. O., 107
Witherington, Ben, III, 2, 174

Wright, D. P., 98
Wright, N. T., 152, 197, 236–37, 256, 262, 264

Yamauchi, Edwin, 139
Young, Brad H., 198
Yu, Charles, 148
Yuval, Israel, 4

Index of Ancient Sources

OLD TESTAMENT

Genesis
1–11   15, 51, 53
1–3   251
1:1–2:4   218
1:1–2:3   51
1   38
1:1   38
1:2   38
1:22   13, 15, 52
1:26–28   9
1:26   9, 251
1:27   45
1:28   9, 13, 15, 51–53, 245, 251
1:31   9
2–3   251
2   9, 15
2:1–3   72
2:2   216
2:3   15, 52
2:4–11:26   15
2:7   9, 252, 258
2:10–15   51
2:10–14   13, 15, 53
2:15   106
2:16   51
2:17   10
2:18   15
2:21–24   15
2:25   9
3   12, 15, 72
3:6   14
3:7   10
3:8–10   10
3:8   9, 87
3:11–12   10
3:14   15, 52
3:15   10, 13, 15, 34, 50, 52–53, 251–52
3:16–19   10
3:17   15, 52

3:19   251–52
3:21   10
3:22–24   252
3:23–24   15
3:23   251
3:24   10
4–11   11
4:11   15, 52
4:25   13, 15
4:26   175
5   11
5:2   52
5:24   11, 251
5:29   15, 34, 52
6–8   11
6:5–6   34
6:5   35, 51
6:11–12   38
6:14   39
8:21–9:17   11
8:21   35, 51
9:1   13, 52–53
9:6   45
9:8–17   15, 25
9:20–25   11
9:25–27   34
9:25   15, 52
9:26   13, 15
10   34
11   11
11:1   34
12–50   13
12–15   13–14
12:1–3   11, 15, 25, 34, 40, 53, 55
12:1   14, 295
12:2–3   14, 52
12:2   23, 45–46
12:3   28, 35, 244, 248
12:7   15
15   11, 13–14, 16, 19
15:1–20   53
15:1–5   13
15:2–3   13

15:3–5   13
15:5   13
15:6–18   13
15:6   13, 16, 20, 70, 245
15:7–21   13
15:7   13, 16, 19
15:8   13
15:9–17   16
15:9   14
15:13–14   13
15:13   19
15:16   13, 19
15:18–21   19
15:18   13, 15, 53, 295
16   14, 16
16:3   14
17   13–14, 16
17:1   106
17:3   163
17:6   23, 25
17:9–14   14
17:10–14   19
17:16   23, 25
17:20   13
18:18–19   10
18:18   35, 45, 52, 244
22   75
22:7–8   76
22:16–18   34
22:17   46, 53
22:18   10, 35, 45, 52
24:60   46, 53
26:4   35, 244
26:5   21
27:29   253
28:3–4   53
28:3   13
28:14   35, 244
28:17   160
32:21   96
35:11–13   53
35:11   23
37–50   253
37:5–11   253

37:7   253
37:33–35   253
37:35   253
38:9   38
40:18   168
42:6   253
44:20   253
45:5–9   253
48:15   161
49:1   253
49:8–12   253
49:8–10   53
49:8   253
49:9   253
49:10   23, 25, 45, 50, 145,
   148, 253
49:11   53
49:24   161
50:20   253

Exodus
1–15   34
1:7   53
2:24   14, 19
3:1   161
3:6–9   19
3:12   19
3:13–15   186
3:14–15   162
3:15–17   19
6:2–8   19
7:8–8:15   35
9:16   35
11:33   120
12   75
12:11   75
12:12   47, 102
12:18–20   78
12:39   78
12:46   76, 169
14:13   102
14:30   102
15   102
15:2   102
15:3–4   102
15:7–12   102
15:17   106–7
15:26   21
16   72
17:6   169
17:8–13   34
19–24   189
19:1–2   17
19:3   54, 188

19:4–6   12
19:4–5   40
19:5–6   28
19:5   18, 20, 21
19:6   31, 45
19:8   18, 54
19:9   13, 18
19:10–11   18
19:16–19   18
19:23–24   54
20:1–17   18–19
20:2   19, 75
20:8–11   72
20:18–21   18
20:18   54
20:19   18
20:22–23:33   18, 20
21–23   41, 240
22:28   166
23:14–17   80
23:16–17   87
23:20   68
23:21–22   18, 21
23:32   18, 41
23:33   41
24   69
24:1–18   68
24:3   18
24:4–8   18
24:4   19
24:6–8   20
24:7   18–19
24:8   97
24:9   68
24:12–15   18
24:12–13   188
24:12   18, 68
24:13   69
24:15–16   69
24:16   68–69
24:17   69
25–31   18
25:8–9   85
25:8   106
25:9   106
25:10–22   18
25:16   18
25:17–22   97
26:1   106
26:7   106
26:9   106
26:11–14   106
28:29–30   97
28:36   99

29:36   96
30:10   96
30:12   96
30:13   106
30:24   106
31:16   18
31:18   18, 54
32   14, 21, 52, 283
32:1–6   18
32:5   38
32:7   38, 67
32:13   19
32:28   82
32:30   39, 98
32:31–32   99
33:1   19
33:5   85
34   14
34:1   18
34:22–23   87
34:28–29   18
34:29–30   69
34:29   188
34:30   69
35:1–3   73
36:1   106
36:3–4   106
36:6   106
40:34–38   85

Leviticus
1–7   21, 85
4–5   85
4:3   145
4:20   97
4:26   97
4:31   97
5:5   100
5:11–13   97
7:37   76, 280
8–9   218
9:24   163
10   52
10:1–3   18
10:10–11   96
12:3   19, 180
14:1–8   85
14:48–53   85
15:31   85
16   85, 100
16:1–2   84
16:2–3   98
16:6   98
16:7–10   85

16:8   98
16:13   84
16:15–19   85
16:16   85, 98, 99
16:19   96
16:20–22   85
16:21   98, 99
16:29   85
16:32–33   85
17–26   240
17:7   18
17:11   96
18:21   186
18:24–30   295
19:9–10   191
19:18   212, 276
19:22   97
20:3   85
20:22–26   295
23   72, 74, 83, 89
23:4–14   74
23:10–11   79
23:10   79, 81
23:15–16   80
23:17   79, 81
23:18–20   81
23:23–25   83
23:24   83
23:26–32   84
23:29–30   84–85
23:34   160
23:36   87
23:39   86
23:41–43   87
23:41–42   160
24:10–12   18
24:16   168
25   73
25:1–11   98
25:1–10   73
26   19, 73
26:3–13   12
26:3–12   28
26:4–12   30
26:11–12   87, 110
26:14–45   12
26:14–41   51
26:42–45   11
26:42   14, 19
26:44–46   295
26:44–45   29

Numbers
3:7–8   106

3:20   146
4:15   106
5:7   100
7:1   67
8   99
8:9   99
8:10–12   99
8:19   99
8:25–26   106
9:12   169
10   84
10:2–3   84
10:2   84
10:5–6   84
10:9   84
10:10   84
10:11–13   18
13–14   52
14:11   13, 16
14:22–23   45
14:24   45
15:22–36   85
15:25   97
16:46   99
19:13   85
19:20   85
20:11   169
20:12   13, 16
21:21–35   34
22–24   34–35
23:7   194
23:18   194
24:3   194
24:7–9   53
24:7–8   67
24:8   45, 67
24:9   52
24:14   53
24:15   194
24:17–19   53
24:17   23, 45, 50, 145–48,
   277
24:20–21   194
24:23   194
25   99
25:1–3   35
25:4   168
25:11   99
25:13   99
27:16–17   160
29:1–6   83
29:1   84
32:11   19
35:25   165

35:28   99
35:31–34   85
35:33   99

Deuteronomy
1:5   19
4:3   19
4:5–7   40
4:6   243
4:9–13   18
4:10–12   18
4:13   18–19
4:23   18
4:25–30   12
4:25–28   28
4:25–27   295
4:25–26   51
4:26–27   252
4:27   47
4:30   19, 54
4:33   18
4:36   18
5:2–3   18
5:2   20
5:4–22   18
5:4   18
5:6–22   19
5:6   19
5:12–15   72
5:22   18
5:23–31   18
5:23–28   19
6   234
6:4–9   184
6:4–7   124
6:4–5   19
6:4   277
6:5   212
7:1–6   35
9:8–21   19
9:10   18
10:1–5   18
10:8   18
10:16   29
12–26   19
12:29–31   41
13:1–11   165
13:6–11   41
16:9   81
16:13–15   87
16:14–15   86
17   25
17:18–20   278
18:15–19   19, 147, 149

18:15   51, 53, 54, 69, 211–12
18:18–19   211–12
18:19   126
21:1–8   100
21:8   98, 100
21:22–23   168
21:23   168, 267
26:16–19   40
27–28   19
27:1–8   278
27:15–26   15
28:15–68   51
28:16–20   15
28:58   278
29:4   19
30   54
30:1–14   19
30:1–9   12
30:1   28, 51, 54
30:2–10   54
30:5   15
30:6–9   29
30:6   17, 19, 54
30:11–14   54
30:11   54
30:12–13   50
30:12   54
30:14   31
30:15–20   35
30:16   15
31–34   51
31   35
31:7   67
31:10–13   86
31:15–18   106
31:16–22   19
31:16–21   28, 51
31:17–18   29
31:19   31
31:21   35, 51
31:24–26   19
31:28–29   53
31:29   19, 28
31:35–36   29
32   35, 38–39, 52
32:1–43   19
32:1   36
32:3–4   36
32:5   36, 38
32:8–9   36
32:10   38
32:11   38
32:18   36
32:26–27   36

32:28–29   36
32:32–34   36
32:35   36
32:36   37
32:37–38   37
32:39–43   37
32:39   36, 162
32:40–42   37
32:43   36, 37, 52, 100, 216
33   52
33:1–29   19
33:1   15
33:7   53
33:11   15
33:13   15
33:16–17   15
33:20   15
33:24   15
33:26–29   52
33:28   15
34   54
34:1–2   15
34:4   15
34:6   54
34:10–12   19
34:10   53, 54

Joshua
22:5   212
24:5   75
24:17   18

Judges
2:1   18, 75
2:2   18
2:20   18
8:35   278
9:7–15   194
13:20   163
15:18   102

Ruth
1:1–4   48
4:18–22   48, 59

1 Samuel
1:22   69
2:1–10   69
2:20   69
2:26   69
3:19   69
4:1   117
9:1–2   227
10:12   194

10:18   75
12:5   145
13:13–14   24
13:14   106
16:7   106
29:1   117

2 Samuel
5   23
5:2   161
5:11   23
6   23
6:6–7   106
6:12–19   23
6:20–23   23
7   22–24, 26, 59
7:1–3   23
7:4–17   23
7:5   23
7:6   75
7:8–16   46, 148
7:8–9   23
7:9–16   69
7:9   23, 46
7:10–14   107
7:10–11   23
7:10   23
7:11–16   12
7:11   23
7:12–16   56
7:12–14   262
7:12–13   23
7:12   251
7:13   23
7:14   24, 25, 167, 216
7:15–16   24
7:15   24
7:16   24
7:18–29   24
7:19   24
7:24   24
7:25   24
8:17   126
12:1–4   194
15:24   126
21:3   99
22:51   145
23:1   56
23:2–7   56
23:5   23, 148

1 Kings
4:4   126
8   100

8:1–2   87
8:2   86
8:10–11   88
8:16   75
8:17–18   106
8:29–30   97
9:4–9   56
9:7   194
10:1–10   46
10:14–11:11   106
10:23–25   46
11:1–13   56
11:14–40   46
12:4   46
12:32   12
14:6   278

2 Kings
2:11   251
12:10   126
13:23   14
14:9   194
17   56
18–19   56
18:12   18
18:18   126
22–23   56
22:8–13   278
22:8–10   126
25   56
25:8–12   106

1 Chronicles
1:1   48
1:5–16   48
16:7–36   48
16:8   48
16:16   14
16:20   48
16:22   145
16:23–24   48
16:26   48
16:28   48
16:30   48
16:31   48
16:35   48
17   59
17:11–14   48, 56
17:14   10, 12
22:8   106
22:10   56
23:32   106
28:7   56

2 Chronicles
5:14   12
6   100
6:20–21   97
6:32–33   48
7:12   97
7:14   97, 124
7:20   194
13:5   23
17   22
20:6   48
21:7   59
30:18   100
36:22–23   48
36:23   48

Ezra
3:1–4   87
7:6   124
7:10   124
7:24   157
7:25   243
9:5–15   124

Nehemiah
3:37   96
8:1–8   124
8:8   131
8:14–18   87
8:18   87

Esther
2:7   90
5:13   90
6:1   89
6:10   90
9:22   90
9:24–26   89
9:25   168

Job
9:8   163
17:6   194
30:19   193
38:41   203

Psalms
1–2   46, 60
2   23, 26, 46, 57, 59–60, 62,
    145, 211, 262
2:1–5   146
2:1–2   46, 169
2:1   46, 62
2:2   59, 62

2:3–6   46
2:7–9   62
2:7   46, 167, 175, 216, 218
2:8   46
2:9–12   46
2:9   146
2:12   47, 62
3:7   102
3:8   102
6:1–2   98
8   9, 60, 218
8:1   51
8:4–6   217–18
8:8   51
14:1–3   47
16   60, 62, 253–54
16:7–11   63
16:8–11   62, 211, 253
16:10–11   46
16:10   62, 253–54
16:11   105, 161, 254
17:15   105
18   59, 102
18:2   102
18:27   102
18:35   102
18:46   102
18:50   102
19:7   243
20   59–60
21   59–60
21:1   102
21:4–5   254
21:4   46
21:5   102
21:6   254
22   60, 63
22:1   169
22:2   63
22:12–19   63
22:17   63
22:18   63, 169
22:22   217
22:27   47
23:1   160–61
23:4   254
24:1   9, 67
25:5   102
27:1   102
27:9   102
28:1   193
28:9   102
34:20   169
35:13   85

36:9   105
38:22   102
40   60
40:6–8   217
41:1–4   98
42–72   46
42:5   102
42:11   102
43:5   102
44:14   194
45   59, 62
45:6–7   216
45:6   218
45:17   251
49   254
49:7   254
49:8   254
49:9   254
49:10   254
49:11   254
49:13   193
49:15   254
49:21   193
51:14   103
51:17–19   97
53:1–3   47
55:17   185
59   290
60:5   102
60:11   102
61   59
62:1–2   102
62:6–7   102
65:4   100
65:5   103
67:3–4   47
68:5   186
69   61
69:9   61, 108
69:20   102
69:21   169
70:4   102
71:15   102
72   46, 59
72:1   46
72:8   46
72:9   46
72:11   46
72:12–13   46
72:17   46
74   103
74:12–23   103
74:12   104
74:13–15   104

74:16–17   104
74:18–23   104
77:20   161, 163
78:38   100
78:60   106
78:70–72   161
79:9   100
79:10   47
79:13   251
80:8   162
81:10   75
84:4   251
85:9   102
86:9   47
86:11   161
88:1   102
89   23, 27, 59–60, 251
89:1–4   27
89:4–5   27
89:4   23
89:11   9
89:22–23   27
89:25   27
89:26–27   167
89:27   27
89:38–51   27
89:47–48   251
89:48   254
90   251
90:3   47, 251
90:6   251
90:7–11   252
90:14   252
90:15   252
91:16   103, 252
95   103, 216
95:1   103
95:3–5   103
95:7–11   216
96:1–6   103
97   60
98:1–3   103
100:3   160
101   59
102   60
102:25–27   216, 218
103:3   98
104:4   216, 218
105:9   14
106:30–31   70
107:13   102
107:19   102
108:6   102
108:12   102

110   12, 26, 59–60, 62–63,
    211
110:1–2   166
110:1   63, 216–18
110:4   58, 63, 217
110:5–7   63
113–118   77, 88, 160
115:15–16   9
116:13   175
116:17   175
118   60
118:14–15   102
118:21   102
118:22–23   60
118:25–26   88
119:30   161
119:155   102
132   27, 59–60
132:10   27
132:11   27
132:12   27
132:16   103
133:3   251
140:6   102
143:7   193
144   59
146:3   102

Proverbs
1:6   194
12:28   105
15:24   161
16:6   100
16:14   96
28:7   243

Isaiah
1   51
1:4   45
1:9–10   41
1:13–16   43
1:24   45
1:27   45
2:1–4   44, 55, 57
2:5–8   41
2:11   43
2:12   43
2:17   43
3:9   41
3:14–15   191
4:2–4   45
5   66
5:1–7   66, 162
5:1–6   194

5:7   195
6:7   96, 100
6:9–10   247
6:10   68
6:22–26   43
7–11   58
7:14   57–58, 283, 286
8:17–18   217
9   26
9:1–7   12
9:1–2   58
9:1   118
9:5–6   23, 26
9:6–7   12, 57–58
9:7   45
10   43
10:3   43
10:5–34   57
10:5–19   43
10:5–7   217
10:5   43
10:7   40
11   23, 26, 30, 253
11:1–16   55, 57
11:1–10   10, 12
11:1–6   145, 148
11:1–5   26
11:1   56, 58, 146, 151, 253
11:4   58
11:6–8   146
11:6   26
11:9   57
11:10   44, 253
11:11–12   148
12:3   88
13–23   40, 43
14:10   193
16:6   43
19:21   44
19:23   44
24–27   43, 252
25:8   251–52
26:14   252
26:18   104
26:19   65, 252
27:2–6   162
27:9   100
27:19   31
28:18   96
30–31   41
32   30
32:15–18   30
33:24   98
34–35   43

34:2   45
35   104
35:1–10   104
35:5–6   65
36–38   41
36:6–9   41
36:18–20   47
39   41
40–66   44, 162
40–55   53, 54, 235
40–53   58
40:3   68, 129, 161
40:9   152
40:11   161
41:1   43
41:4   162
41:5–7   43
41:8–9   11, 58
42:1–7   58
42:1–4   54
42:4   44
42:6   44, 58
42:19   58
43:10–13   162
43:10   58
43:11–12   104
43:11   104
43:25   104, 162
44:3–5   30
44:21   58
45:1   145
45:4   58
45:12   45
45:18   162
45:20   104
45:22   44
46:4   162
46:5   193
46:7   104
47:11   96
47:13   104
48:12   162
48:20   58
49   235
49:1–7   58
49:1–6   54
49:3–9   12
49:3   235
49:4–6   58
49:6   44, 58, 235
50:4–9   54
50:6–7   58
50:10   58
51:12   162

52:6   162
52:7   152, 235
52:13–53:12   12, 54, 58, 149, 252
52:13   58, 253
52:14   58
52:15   58
53   145, 211, 253, 268
53:1   68
53:4–6   58, 98
53:5   169, 253
53:7   166
53:8   253
53:9   253–54
53:10–12   58
53:12   253
54:10   29, 169
55   26
55:3   23, 28–29, 253
55:4–5   26, 44
56:7   44, 48, 108
58:3   85
58:10   85
59   30
59:1–18   30
59:1   104
59:16–20   12
59:16–19   31
59:16   31, 104
59:17–20   12
59:20–21   30–32
59:20   31
59:21   31
60–61   31
60:1–22   57
60:1–3   12, 31
60:3–11   31
60:9   44
60:10   44
60:20   12
61:1–2   153
61:1   65
61:4   44
61:6–9   12, 31
61:8–9   29
63:1   104
63:5   104
63:9   104
63:11   161
65–66   51
65:2   248
66:19   41
66:20   44

Jeremiah
1:5   41
2:6   75
2:18   42
2:21   162
3:12–18   57
3:15   161
3:16–18   57
3:16   106
4:2   45
4:4   29
7:11   108
7:21–23   21
7:22–23   21
7:22   21
7:23   21
8:8   126
8:20   104
9:25–26   29
10:7   40
11:7–8   29
11:10   18
14:19   104
18:23   96, 100
23:1–6   57
23:1–4   161
23:5–6   12, 26, 57–58
24:5–7   57
24:7   31
24:9   194
27   42
27:3   42
27:9–10   42
27:14   42
27:16–17   42
29:7   42
29:14   295
30:1–24   57
30:3   295
30:9   26
31   69
31:1–14   29, 86
31:9   186
31:10   161
31:20   186
31:29   194
31:31–34   18, 28–29, 86,
   216, 218
31:31–33   237
31:31   211
31:32   21
31:33–34   12, 29, 31, 86
31:35–37   94
31:36–37   295

32:37–41   30
32:40   28
33   26
33:2–16   57
33:14–26   23, 26
33:14–16   57
33:15–16   58
34:18–19   16
46–51   40, 43
48   43
48:26   43
48:29–30   43
48:48   43
51:34–36   43

Lamentations
1:3   48
1:10   48
1:21–22   48
4:11   198
4:21–22   48

Ezekiel
1:5   157
1:10   157
1:26   157
1:28   163
5:5   42
5:8   42
5:11   85
8:9   42
8:14   42
10–11   88
10:18   106
11:16   139
11:17–20   30
11:17   295
14:8   194
16:1–35   194–96
16:26   42
16:28   42
16:29   42
16:60–63   30
16:60   28
17:3–10   194
17:6–8   162
17:11–21   42
18:2   194
18:4   47
20:8   42
20:25   21
23   42
23:1–34   194–96
23:35–49   195

24–32   40, 43
31:34   30
34   161
34:2–4   160
34:11–31   161
34:23–31   57
34:23–24   23, 56
34:23   161
34:24–27   30
34:25   28
36   30
36:16–19   30
36:17   85
36:20–21   30
36:22–32   237
36:22–23   30
36:22   186
36:24–27   12
36:24   30, 295
36:25   30
36:26–27   30
36:27–31   12
36:27   30
36:28–30   30
36:35   30
37   26, 252
37:1–14   258
37:1–4   257
37:1–2   252
37:3–10   252
37:9   252
37:11–12   252
37:11   252
37:12–13   252
37:12   252
37:14–26   30
37:14–21   252
37:15–27   57
37:16–22   252
37:22   26
37:23   252
37:24–28   252
37:24–25   23, 56
37:24   161
37:25   26
37:26   30, 106
37:27   110
37:28   57
38–39   43
39:23–24   89
39:27–28   186
40–48   57, 107
40:46   126
43:1–9   88

43:10–11   57
43:18–27   57
43:20   97
43:26   97
45:15   97
45:17   97
45:20   97

Daniel
1:1–2   47
1:2   47
1:8   42
2   47, 145
2:1–11   47
2:12–18   47
2:19   47
2:21   47
2:34–35   48
2:44–45   48
2:44   157
2:47   47
3   42, 48
3:6   47
3:12   157
3:14   157
3:17   157
3:28   157
4   48
4:17   40
4:30–33   43
4:37   43
5   48
6   42
6:3   48
6:4–9   48
6:7   47
6:10   185
6:12–15   48
6:14   48
6:16   48
6:17   157
6:18–20   48
6:21   157
6:23   48
6:27   157
7   59, 145, 157
7:3–7   47
7:8   43
7:11   43
7:13–15   73
7:13–14   58, 147, 158, 166
7:13   157
7:14   157
7:27   158

9   145
9:9–16   237
9:15   75
9:24–27   56
9:24   97, 146
9:26   145, 149
10:13   47
11:33–35   47
12   252
12:1   252
12:2–3   105
12:2   252
12:3   252, 257–58

Hosea
1:2   42
2:2   148
3:5   23, 56–57, 148
7:8   42
7:11   42
11:1   66–67, 197
11:8   197
13:10   104
13:14   251–52, 254

Joel
2:12–17   84
2:15–27   84
2:17   194
2:27–3:1   32
2:32   105
3   43

Amos
1–2   43
1:3–5   43
1:6–8   43
1:9–10   43
1:11–12   43
2:10   75
8:4–6   191
9:11–12   44, 46
9:11   23, 147

Jonah
2:2   252
2:4   252
3:5–9   86

Micah
4:1–4   57
4:1–3   44
5:1   148
5:4   161

6:4   75
6:8   124

Nahum
3:1–3   43

Habakkuk
2:4–20   43
3:15   163

Zephaniah
3:9   175

Haggai
2:9   106
2:21–23   57

Zechariah
2:4–5   87–88
2:10–11   88
2:10   87
2:11   45
3   86
3:3–5   86
3:9–10   86
6:9–16   147
6:11–13   12
6:12–15   58
6:12–13   106
8:11–13   12
8:20–23   12
9–14   43
9:9   58, 158
9:10   45
10:8–12   295
11:4–17   161
11:15–17   182
12:10–13:6   12
12:10–13:1   58
12:10   145, 149, 158, 169
14   57, 87
14:9   87
14:16   87
14:20   109

Malachi
1:11   235
3:1–6   58
3:1   68
4:5   149

NEW TESTAMENT

Matthew

1:1 23, 67
1:17 67
1:22 66
1:23 58
2:4-5 148
2:4 127
2:13-15 66
2:15 66
2:17 66
2:20-21 4
2:23 58, 66
3:2 31
3:7 125
3:11-12 31
4:1-11 118
4:13-16 58
4:14 66
4:15 118
4:18 118
4:23-8:1 188
4:23-25 192
4:23 153, 192
5-7 188
5 118
5:1 188-90
5:3-12 188, 190
5:6 191
5:10 191
5:13-16 188, 190
5:17-48 188
5:17-20 188, 190
5:17 50, 190
5:20 125, 155, 191
5:21-48 155, 188, 190-91
5:23-24 155
6 191
6:1-18 155, 188
6:1 191
6:5-7 185
6:5-6 191
6:5 185
6:6 185
6:7-15 155
6:7-13 185-86, 191
6:9-13 153
6:10 186
6:12 187
6:14-15 185, 187, 191
6:19-34 188, 191
6:19-21 191
6:22-23 191

6:24 191
6:25-34 191
6:25-30 180
6:33 191
7 191
7:1-5 188, 192
7:6 189, 192
7:7-11 189, 192
7:11 180
7:12 189, 192, 276
7:13-14 189, 192
7:15-20 189, 192
7:21-23 189, 192
7:24-27 189, 192
7:28-8:1 189-90
7:28 190
8-9 192
8:1 188
8:16-17 98
8:17 66
8:19 129
8:28-29 180
9:27 148
9:35 192
9:37-38 162
10:1-42 203
10:2-4 178
10:17-18 139
10:28-30 180
11:3 65
11:4-5 65
11:16-19 125
11:25-26 186
11:27 182
11:28-29 73
12:4 107
12:6 166
12:8 73, 180
12:11-12 180
12:17 66
12:21 142
12:33-36 124
12:38-39 148
12:38 125
13:14 66
13:18-33 196
13:31-32 195
13:33 195
13:35 66
13:36-43 196
13:44 195
13:55-56 207
14:16 204
14:27 163

15:1-6 125
15:3-6 278
15:7-20 124
15:22 148
15:29 118
16 118
16:1 125
16:6 125
16:11-12 125
16:21-23 145
16:21 126, 127, 141
17:2 69
17:22-23 145
18:23 198
20:18 127
20:30 148
21:4 66
21:12-13 108
21:13 143
21:15 127
21:23-46 125, 180
21:23 127, 143
21:33-46 196
21:41 208
21:42 61
21:43 127
21:45 125, 127, 208
22:2 198
22:23 250
22:36-40 212
22:41-45 63
23 124, 126
23:2 125, 188
23:7-8 180
23:8 179, 204
23:13-15 125
23:13 125-26
23:16-22 107
23:34 139
23:38 208
23:39 186
24:1 108
24:2 166
24:15 108
24:30 158
25:1-13 196
26:3 126
26:25 180, 275
26:28 31
26:36 117
26:47 143
26:49 180, 275
26:55 143
26:57-27:26 164

26:57–68   165–66
26:59–61   166
26:60–63   141
26:61   109
26:62–63   166
26:63–66   163
26:63   166
26:64   158, 166
26:65   166
26:66   166
27:1–2   165, 167
27:2   167
27:9   66
27:11–26   167
27:11   145
27:25   293
27:27–56   168
27:29   145
27:33   117
27:37   172
27:40   109, 166
27:41   141
27:46   63
27:62   125
28:12–15   267
28:19   44

Mark
1:2–3   68
1:12–13   118, 155
1:15   152
1:16   118
1:27   154
1:39   153
2:1–12   98
2:12   154
2:16   125
2:27   73
2:28   73
3:7   118
3:16–19   178
4:2   194
4:3–8   195
4:12   68
4:13–20   196
4:26–29   195
4:30–32   195
5:21–43   203
6:1–6   153
6:3   207
6:33–44   203
6:50   163
7   284
7:1–17   125

7:6–13   278
7:6–7   68
7:10   68
7:16   197
7:31   118
8:1–9   203
8:18   68
8:31–33   149
9   118, 154
9:2–8   68
9:2   68
9:3   69
9:4   68
9:5   180, 275
9:6   69
9:7   69
9:38–40   154
10:2–9   286
10:19   155
10:45   169
10:51   180
11:11   108
11:15–17   108
11:15–16   108
11:17   68, 108
11:21   180, 275
11:25–26   187
12:1–12   196
12:1–9   66
12:10–11   61
12:12   66
12:13–40   286
12:18–27   255
12:24–34   155
12:28–32   187
12:35–37   63
12:35   143
12:41–44   143
13:2–3   108
13:2   166
13:14   108
14:13   129
14:14   155
14:22–25   69
14:32   117
14:36   182
14:45   180, 275
14:53–15:5   164
14:53–65   165–66
14:53   166
14:56–61   141
14:56–59   166
14:57–58   109
14:58   166

14:60–61   166
14:61–62   163
14:61   166
14:62–64   73
14:62   166
14:63–64   166
14:64   163, 166
15:1–15   167
15:1   167
15:7   128
15:9   145
15:12   145
15:16–41   168
15:22   117
15:24   68
15:26   156, 172
15:29–30   109
15:29   68, 166
15:33–39   69
15:34   63, 169
15:36   68

Luke
1:3   207
1:5   143, 221
1:32–33   69
1:32   23
1:46–55   69
1:57–63   221
1:71–75   11
1:80   69
2:4   151
2:22–24   107
2:22   69
2:34   69
2:36–38   69
2:37   143
2:40   69
2:41   151
2:46   127, 143
2:49   107
2:52   69
3:23   152
4   209
4:1–13   118
4:15   153
4:16–30   153, 191
4:16–22   155
4:16–19   139
4:16   140, 155
4:18–19   140
4:20   140
4:21   153
4:22   153

4:23–30 153
4:23 194
4:31 209
4:43 209
4:44 209
5:1 117
6:4 107
6:5 73
6:14–16 178
6:15 128
6:17–49 188
6:17–19 203
6:17 188–90
6:20–26 188
6:24–26 190
6:27–28 188
6:29–30 188
6:31 189, 276
6:32–33 188
6:37–38 189
6:43–45 189
6:46 189
6:47–49 189
7:1 189–90
7:22 65
7:36–50 101
7:50 101
8:2–3 207
8:11–15 196
8:26–39 101
8:36 101
8:48 101
8:49 101
8:50 101
9:10 117
9:14–16 205
9:29 69
9:59–62 203
10:22 182
10:25–37 195
10:25–28 155
11:1–13 155
11:1–4 185
11:1 185
11:2–4 153, 186, 188
11:2 186
11:4 187
11:9–13 189
11:15 154
11:20 154
11:34–36 188
11:41 155
12:22–31 188
12:33–34 188

12:33 155
13:18–19 195
13:20–21 195
13:23–24 189
13:26–27 189
14:26 203
14:34–35 188
15:2 125
16:5–6 188
16:13 188
18:12 284
19:45–46 108
20:9–19 196
20:17 61
20:27–40 250
20:41–44 63
21:5–6 108
21:24 296
21:26–27 158
22:19 79
22:20 31–32
22:39–46 155
22:54–23:25 164
22:66–71 165–66
23:1–15 167
23:2 165
23:6–12 167
23:26–49 168
23:34 169
23:37 145
23:38 172
23:49 207
23:55–24:10 207
24 50
24:25 250
24:26 250
24:27 50
24:44 50
24:46 250
24:47 44

John
1 135
1:1 76
1:3–5 160
1:4–5 159
1:14 87, 109, 162
1:17 18, 162
1:18 182
1:19 221
1:21 149
1:22 147
1:23 68, 161
1:29 75

1:38 178–79, 275
1:39 203
1:45 50
1:49 178–79, 275
1:51 160
2:1–12 203
2:2 203
2:6 221
2:13–22 166, 181
2:13–17 61
2:13 222
2:14–17 108
2:17 68, 108
2:18–22 109
2:18–19 109
2:18 221
2:19 166
2:21–22 109
2:22 181
3:1–20 129
3:2 178–79, 275
3:12 180
3:16 169, 222
3:22 203
3:26 275
4:8 204
4:9 178, 222
4:20 129
4:22 222
4:26 94, 163
4:31 178–79, 275
4:34 182
4:35–38 162
5:1–18 180
5:1 222
5:2 117
5:10 222
5:15 222
5:16 222
5:18 167, 222
5:20 182
5:21 159
5:23 182
5:25–27 158
5:25 158
5:26 159
5:27 158
5:30 182
5:36 182
5:38 182
5:39 125
5:45–47 126
5:45 50
5:46 50, 180

6   160
6:1–15   159
6:1   118
6:4   222
6:5–14   223
6:12   205
6:14   149
6:20   163
6:25–40   223
6:25   178–79, 275
6:27   180
6:30   148
6:31   68
6:35   159, 161
6:41   223
6:45   68
6:48   159
6:52   223
6:58   160
6:60–71   160
7   160
7:1   86, 223
7:11   223
7:13   223
7:15   223
7:19   18
7:21–23   180
7:23   180
7:32   223
7:35   223
7:37–39   88
7:37–38   94
7:38   68
7:40–41   147
7:41–42   148
7:42   68
7:45   223
7:47   223
7:48   223
7:50–51   129
7:52   125
8–9   223
8   160
8:3   125
8:12   94, 159–60
8:13   223
8:17   68
8:18   163
8:22   223
8:24   163
8:28   163
8:31   223
8:48   223
8:52   223

8:58   162
8:59   167
9   154, 160, 203
9:1–34   223
9:1–7   180
9:2   178–79, 275
9:4–5   160
9:5   94, 159–60
9:7   182
9:13   223
9:15   223
9:16   223–24
9:18   224
9:22   224
9:40–41   160
9:40   223
10   160, 182, 223
10:1   160
10:7   160
10:9   160
10:11   161
10:14   161
10:15   161
10:16   161
10:17–18   161
10:19   223
10:22   94
10:23   117
10:24   94, 223
10:30   94
10:31   167, 223
10:33   167, 223
10:34–36   180
10:34   68
11:8   178–79, 223, 275
11:9–10   160
11:19   223
11:24   162
11:25   159, 161
11:31   223
11:33   223
11:36   223
11:45   223
11:46   223
11:47   223
11:52   161
11:54   223
11:57   223
12:9   224
12:10   224
12:11   224
12:14   68
12:16   181
12:19   223

12:24–25   254
12:35–36   160
12:37–50   160
12:37   68
12:38   68
12:39–40   68
12:42   223–24
13:1–17   181
13:6–10   204
13:13   182
13:18   68
13:19   163
13:20   182
13:29   155
13:36–38   204
14–17   224
14   110
14:1–3   110
14:5   204
14:6   159–61
14:8   204
14:12   182
14:16–17   32
14:22   204
14:26   32
15:1   162
15:8   162
15:16   162, 204
15:18–21   204
15:25   68
16:2   224
17   186
17:1   68
17:21   302
18:3   223
18:5–6   162
18:12–14   164–65
18:19–24   164–65
18:28–19:16   164, 167
18:31   141
18:38   162
19:7   165, 167
19:12   165
19:16–37   168
19:17   117
19:19   145, 172
19:24   68, 169
19:26–27   205
19:28   68, 169
19:29   169
19:33   169
19:34   169
19:36   68, 76, 169
19:37   68, 169

19:39   129
20:16   178–79
20:19   210
20:21   182
20:29   181
20:31   164
21:2   118
21:9–13   205
21:24–25   205

Acts
1:6–11   32
1:6   31
1:8   210
1:9–11   32
1:13   128, 178
1:14   207
2   62, 82
2:1–4   82
2:1   208
2:2   208
2:6   208
2:9–11   209
2:15–21   32
2:15   210
2:21   105
2:23–24   169
2:23   208
2:24–32   251, 253
2:24   251
2:25–31   56
2:25–28   60
2:27–32   211
2:29–32   253
2:29–31   254
2:29   82, 254
2:30–31   60
2:31   253
2:32–33   32
2:33–36   211
2:33   20
2:34–35   60, 63
2:36   172, 172
2:38   32, 211
2:41   82, 211
2:42   211
2:46   208, 210
2:47   105
3:1–11   208
3:1   143, 185
3:2   117
3:11–26   208
3:11   117, 142
3:12–26   208

3:18–19   212
3:19–26   32
3:19–21   211
3:22–23   211–12
3:22   149
3:25   14
4:1   126–27
4:4   208
4:12   211–12
4:23   127
4:25–26   169
5:12   142
5:17   127, 212
5:21   140
5:24   127, 143
5:26   143
5:30–31   211–12
5:30   168
5:33–39   227
5:34–40   125
5:34–39   145
5:34   276
6:7   129, 208
7:37–39   212
7:37   149, 211
7:57–60   212
7:58   227, 268
8:1   209
8:4–8   129
8:4   212
8:6   209
8:25   129
8:26–40   209
9   235
9:1–18   227
9:1–2   141
9:2   129, 161, 281
9:15   44
9:29   212
10   178
10:15   211
10:28   211
10:34–35   44
10:34   211
10:39   168
10:43   44
10:48   212
11:1   209
11:25–30   227
11:26   129, 282
11:30   211
12   135
12:1–2   212
12:17   209

13–28   227
13:1–14:28   229
13:14–15   139
13:14   138, 210
13:15   214
13:27   140
13:30–37   250
13:32   244
13:35–37   253
13:36–37   253–54
13:36   254
13:38–39   212
13:42   210
13:43   138
13:44   210
13:50   212
14:5   212
14:16   244
14:19   212
14:22   32
15   4, 211, 284
15:1–29   229
15:5   129, 208
15:7–11   209
15:7   209
15:11   105
15:15   44
15:21   139
15:23–29   208
15:30–18:22   229
16:4   211
16:10–17   207
16:13   210
16:22   212
16:30–31   105
16:31   212
16:37–38   228
17:2   140, 210
17:26   244
18:4   210
18:12   212
18:23–21:16   230
19:9   129, 161
19:11–20   154
19:23   129, 161
20:5–15   207
20:7   74, 210–11, 284
20:11   211
20:38   211
21:1–18   207
21:9   209
21:17–28:30   230
21:18   211
21:20   208, 211

21:21   232–33
21:36   212
21:37–38   145
21:39   228
22:2–3   210
22:3   227–28, 276
22:4–13   227
22:4   161
22:19   139
22:22   212
22:23–29   228
23:1–10   127
23:6   125, 250
23:7–9   255
23:10   212
23:12–13   212
23:27   228
23:31   117
24:5   129, 282
24:14   50, 129, 161, 281–82
24:15   125
24:21   125
24:22   129, 161
24:27   212
25   136
25:10–11   228
26   136
26:4   228, 276
26:5   129, 227
26:6   244
26:9–18   227
26:22   50, 250
26:23   250
26:28   282
27:1–37   207
27:9   86
28:1–16   207
28:16   212
28:19   228
28:22   282
28:23   50
28:30   212
28:31   207

Romans

1:1–5   226
1:1   235, 261
1:2   242
1:3–4   174, 261–62
1:3   23, 261
1:6–7   235
1:7   235
1:9   261
1:11   264

1:16   210, 233, 248
1:18   244
1:20   244
2:5   244
2:8   244
2:9   233
2:10   233
2:17–29   245
2:27–29   17
2:28–29   235
2:29   242, 285
3   236
3:2   245
3:9   233
3:10–18   245
3:21–26   236
3:21   17, 242
3:23   244–45
3:24–25   262
3:25   169
3:27   242
3:29   233
3:31   242
4   70
4:1–5   16
4:2–3   19
4:11–12   235
4:13–14   20
4:15   20
4:16–17   235
4:23–24   242
4:25   262
5:9–10   105
5:12–14   244
5:17   266
5:20   21, 241
6:1–23   263
6:4   265
6:10   265
6:11   265
6:12   265
6:13   265
6:14–15   241
6:14   242
6:15   242
7–8   32
7:1–6   241
7:5   241
7:6   17
7:7–12   242
7:7   240
7:12   241
7:14   264
8:1–15   20

8:1   242
8:3–4   242
8:3   175
8:11   263
8:18–23   265–66
8:23   32
8:28   235
8:30   235
8:32   175
8:33   235
9–11   244, 247
9:1–3   247
9:3   234, 245
9:4–5   246
9:4   240–41, 296
9:6–29   245
9:6–7   247
9:6   234, 242
9:7   235
9:8   247
9:12   235
9:18   246
9:24–28   235
9:24   233
9:25   235
9:30–33   246
9:32   247
10:1–3   124
10:1   245, 247–48
10:3   246
10:4   50
10:6–8   50
10:12   233
10:14–15   247
10:15   235
10:18–19   246
10:21   246, 248
11   244
11:1–4   248
11:1   246
11:5   247
11:7–10   246–47
11:7   247
11:11–13   247
11:11   246–47
11:12   247–48
11:15   246–47
11:18   247
11:19–20   248
11:20   247
11:21–31   78
11:25–32   247
11:25–29   86
11:25   234, 247

11:26–27 31
11:26 235, 248
11:28–29 11, 15–16, 245
11:30–36 248
11:33–36 247
12–16 247
12:1–2 236
13:8–9 242
13:11–12 32
14:1–15:6 240
14:1–23 263
14:2 240–41
14:5–6 241
14:5 240
14:14 233
14:21 240
14:22 241
15:1 241
15:4 242
15:8–9 245
15:8 244
15:12 262
15:15–16 235
15:17 236
15:28 230
16:25–26 242

1 Corinthians
1:2 175
1:17 235
1:18 105
1:23–24 233
1:23 145
2:13–15 264
3 109
3:1 264
3:10–15 110
3:16–17 110
3:16 236
4:18 78
5:5 101
5:6–8 78
5:7 169
6:19 110, 236
7:19 233
7:29–31 263
8:1 78
8:4–6 234
9:21 242
10:3–4 264
10:11 242, 262
10:32 233, 241
11:25 32
12:1 264

12:3 175
12:12–13 301
13:12 32
14:1 264
15 263, 265
15:2 105
15:4 250
15:12 261
15:17 262
15:20–28 263
15:20–23 250
15:20 79
15:23–28 175, 266
15:23 262–63
15:29–30 265
15:32–34 265
15:33 264
15:35 257
15:36–38 263
15:42–56 250
15:43–53 32
15:44 263
15:51–52 263
15:58 265
16:20 284
16:22 175

2 Corinthians
1:23–2:9 231
2:4 231
3:6–7 17
3:6 32, 242
3:14–15 17
4:3–4 175
4:13–5:10 263
5:1–4 264
6:14–18 110
6:16 110
11:24 233

Galatians
1:13–14 226
1:13 228, 233
1:14 125, 227, 276
1:16 174, 226
1:17–2:1 229
2–3 70
2:12 70
2:16 70
2:20 174, 242
3–5 32
3–4 244
3 19
3:2 20

3:6–7 242
3:6 16, 19
3:8 20, 244, 248
3:10–14 242
3:10–12 20
3:10 242
3:13–14 20, 237
3:13 168
3:14–15 17
3:16 16, 20
3:17 20
3:18 20
3:19–20 18
3:19 21
3:23–25 242
4:1–10 241
4:1–9 263
4:4 175
4:21 240
4:24 17, 20
5:4 17
5:6 233
5:13–14 242
5:16–17 264
5:18 242
6:2 242
6:15 233

Ephesians
1:3 264
2 236, 244, 302
2:5–8 105
2:8–9 237
2:12 244
2:15 239, 242
2:19–22 110
2:21 110
3:2–9 226
3:6 236
5:19 264
6:1–2 239

Philippians
2:9–11 172, 175
3:5–8 233
3:5 227
3:6 227
3:8 242
3:10–11 125
3:20–21 32, 263

Colossians
1:9 264
2:12 285

3:1–4   263
3:4   32
3:16   264

1 Thessalonians
1:9–10   32
2:14–16   233
4:13–18   263
4:14   263

1 Timothy
1:8–9   239–40
1:8   242
1:9   105
1:13   227

2 Timothy
1:9   237
1:10   105
3:14–17   242
3:16–17   243
3:16   17

Hebrews
1:1–4   175
1:1–2   215, 218
1:2   217–18
1:3–4   172
1:3   217–18
1:5–14   215–16
1:5–13   217
1:5–12   216
1:5   216, 218
1:6–12   216
1:6–7   216, 218
1:8–13   218
1:8–9   218
1:8   218
1:10   218
1:11–12   218
1:13   63, 217–18
2:1–4   216–17, 219
2:3–4   217
2:5–9   217–18
2:5–8   216
2:6   157
2:8   218
2:10–16   218
2:12–13   216–18
2:17–18   218
2:27–4:1   32
3:2–6   70
3:5   50
3:7–4:10   216

3:7–19   219
3:7–9   216
3:7   218
3:12–13   219
3:15   216
4   72
4:1–10   219
4:3   218
4:7   216
4:12   218
5:4–6   218
5:5–6   216
5:6   217–18
5:10   218
6:1–3   219
6:4–8   219
6:4–5   32
6:7–12   219
6:11   219
6:12   219
7–10   60
7   217
7:1–28   70
7:1–10   218
7:11–28   127
7:11–14   218
7:16–25   218
7:16   253
7:17   216, 218
7:21   216, 218
7:22   32
8–10   32
8:1–9:28   70
8:1–2   217
8:4–7   17
8:5   135, 216
8:6–13   18
8:6–10   32
8:7–13   17, 218
8:7   216
8:8–12   216
8:13   17, 32, 216, 218
9–10   86
9:9–14   219
9:11   219
9:15   32
9:18–20   18
9:23–24   219
9:25–28   219
10:1–4   219
10:1   135
10:5–7   218
10:12   217, 219
10:14–18   219

10:15–18   218
10:16–17   216
10:16   32
10:25   219
10:26–31   219
10:28–29   216
10:29   32
10:30   216
10:32–39   219
10:37–38   216–17
10:39   219
11   215–16
11:1–40   219
11:26   50
12:5–29   219
12:24   32
12:25–28   217
12:25–27   216
12:26   216
13:1–6   219
13:5–6   216
13:20   32
13:22   214, 219

James
2:2–3   140
5:14–16   98
5:14   140

1 Peter
1:10–12   57
1:19   169
1:20   76
1:21   172, 175
2   110
2:4–8   110
5:13   209

2 Peter
2   291

1 John
2:2   99, 169
4:10   99

Jude
9   132
15   132

Revelation
1:7   169
1:10   210, 284
5:5   23
11   149

13:8   76
21:3   88
21:24   47
21:26   47
22:2   47
22:16   23

OLD TESTAMENT APOCRYPHA AND PSEUDEPIGRAPHA

2 Baruch
49:3   257
50:2   257
50:4   257
51:5   257
51:10   257

1 Enoch
1:9   132
37–71   146, 174, 194
46:1–6 158
48:2   146
48:6   146
52:2   147
62   147
62:3–5 166
62:3   166
69:26–29 147
72–82   184
89:73   107
90:28–29 107
90:37   158
103:1–104:9 161
104:2   257
104:4   257
104:6   257

2 Enoch
66:6–8 161

4 Ezra
4:13–18 194
13:3   146

Jubilees
1:17   107
1:27   107
6:35–37 184
23:31   256

1 Maccabees
4:36–49 93
4:46   147
14:41   147

2 Maccabees
1:9   93
1:18–36 87
1:18   93
2:5–7   143
2:8   69
2:12   93
7   256
7:9   161
7:22–23 257
7:29   257
10:6–8 87

4 Maccabees
8:3–13:1 257

Psalms of Solomon
2:2–3   107
17   146
17:1–3 146
17:21   146
17:22   107
17:23–24 146
17:23   146
17:26–28 146
17:27   146
17:30   107
17:35–36 146
17:36   146
17:37   146
17:40–41 161
17:40   146

Sibylline Oracles
3:652–795 146
3:652   146
3:653   146
3:661–679 146
3:702   146
3:785–795 146

Sirach
3:30   191
14:17   255
33:14   255
36:19–20 107
38:21–23 255
41:12–13 256
48:11   255

Susanna
44–62   166

Testament of Benjamin
9:2   107, 146–47
10:5–6 166

Testament of Job
33:24   166

Testament of Judah
22:1–3 146
24   146

Testament of Levi
15:1   107

Testament of Moses
6:8–9   107

Testament of Reuben
6:7–12 146

Tobit
14:5   107

Wisdom of Solomon
1:13   256
2:23   256
3:1–9   256
3:14   256

DEAD SEA SCROLLS

CD
1:18   125
6:10–11 147
7:13–20 147
7:19–20 147
12:23–13:1 147
14:19   147
19:10–11 147
20:1   147

1QH
19:13–17 258
19:15   258

1QS
8:12–16 161
9:10–11 147
9:17–20 161
11:5–8 258

4Q169
frags. 3–4 i 1–8   125
frags. 3–4 i 6–8   168

4Q174
1:2–7   107
1:10–12   167

4Q246
1:1–2:9   69

4Q266
frag. 3 iv 9   147
frag. 18 iii 12   147

4Q285
frag. 5   148

4Q394
frags. 3–7 i 7–8   70

4Q398
frags. 14–17 ii 7   70

4Q399
frag. 1 ii 4   70

4Q500
frag. 1   66

4Q521
frag. 2 ii 1–12   65

11Q13
ii   70

11Q19
64:6–13   168

PHILO

Decalogue
61–64   166

Dreams
2.130–131   166

Good Person
75   147

Special Laws
1.1–11   285

JOSEPHUS

Against Apion
2.175   139
2.217–218   256

Jewish Antiquities
12.325   93
13.380   167
13.830   125
14.91   141
14.174   141
14.191   141
14.235   139
15.6   141
15.380   116, 142
15.413   116
15.420   116
18.11–15   282
18.14   125, 256
18.16   255
18.20   147
18.34   165
20.97–99   145
20.97   147
20.169–170   147
20.188   147
20.197–203   168
20.197–198   165
20.199–203   127
20.219   116, 142

Jewish War
1.97–98   167
1.169–170   141
1.401   142
2.117   168
2.119–166   282
2.154   259
2.162–163   125
2.163   256
2.165   255
2.243   165
2.261–263   145, 147
4.151–160   165
5.449–451   168
6.124–127   141
6.267   108
6.300–305   141
6.301–309   173
6.312   145
6.422–426   143
7.202–203   168

The Life
62   142
309–310   142

GRECO-ROMAN WRITERS

Catullus

Carmen
34   185

Suetonius

Vespasian
4.5   145

Tacitus

Histories
5.13   145

RABBINIC LITERATURE

Mishnah

Avot
1:1   125, 278
1:2   191
1:6   204
1:16   204
4:12   179, 204

Berakhot
2:6–7   204
5:5   182

Horayot
3:1–2   165
3:4   165

Makkot
2:6   99, 165

Megillah
1:9   165

Niddah
4:2   127

Parah
3:3   127
3:7   127

Pesahim
5:5–8   169

Sanhedrin
1:6   141
2:4   141
5:1–5   166
6:2   165
6:4–5   168
7:5   167
10:1   278

Shabbat
7:2   74
19:1–3   180

Sheqalim
8:5   143

Sotah
3:4   125
7:7   82

Sukkah
4:1   160
4:9–5:1   88
4:9–10   160
5:1   88
5:2–4   160

Yadayim
4:6   125

Yoma
7:1   143
8:1   86

Tosefta

Arakhin
2.6   117

Berakhot
6.4–5   205

Sanhedrin
7.1   143

Yoma
1.4   165

Talmud Bavli

Avodah Zarah
6a   90
8a   90

Bava Batra
4a   108, 143

Bava Metzi'a
59b   279

Berakhot
5a   280
5b   204
23a   203
23b   203
24a   203
28b   181, 280
34b   67
42b   205
60a   203

Eruvin
30a   203
43b   210

Gittin
56a   276
56b   267, 276
57a   267

Ketubbot
96a   182
105a   139

Makkot
11b   99

Megillah
7b   90
29a   139

Menahot
110a   280

Mo'ed Qatan
28a   100

Nazir
32b   145, 149

Pesahim
57a   127
106a   143
119b–120a   78

Rosh Hashanah
31a   142
34b   203

Sanhedrin
35b   165
37b   280
43a   165
64b   91
68a   205
98a   158
98b   149

99a   148
101a   204

Shabbat
12b   203
15a   142
21b   93
31a   276
88b   82
108b   203
112a   203

Sotah
22b   125

Sukkah
52a   149, 169
55a   88

Ta'anit
10a   284

Yoma
28a   205
85b   73

Minor (Talmudic) Tractates

Avot of Rabbi Nathan
14   179

Talmud Yerushalmi

Bava Metzi'a
2.3   203

Berakhot
3.1   205
8.5   205

Hagigah
2.1   203

Ketubbot
13.1   139

Megillah
3.1   139

Mo'ed Qatan
3.5   205

Shevi'it
9.9   205

Sotah
1.4   204

Yoma
2.1   100

Midrash (early)

Sifre Deuteronomy
§305   67

Midrash (late)

Exodus Rabbah
2.2   161
35.4   100
43.9   67

Leviticus Rabbah
10.6   99
19.1   203
20.12   100

Numbers Rabbah
12.4   67
34.3   179

Deuteronomy Rabbah
5.7   67

Lamentations Rabbah
4.11   198

Song of Songs Rabbah
8.7   204

Midrash Psalms
24.3   67

Midrash Tanhuma
Kedoshim
10   105

Pesiqta of Rab Kahana
26.16   100

Pesiqta Rabbati
26.1–2   67

Maimonides

Mishneh Torah
Repentance (*Teshuvah*)
1:3   97
3:3–4   84

Rashi
On Gen 32:21   96
On Lev 17:11   97

Targumic Literature

Fragment Targum
Genesis
49:10   148

Numbers
24:17   148

Targum Neofiti
Genesis
49:10   148
Numbers
24:17   148

Tragum Onqelos
Genesis
49:10   148
Numbers
24:17   148

Targum Pseudo-Jonathan
Genesis
49:10   148
Exodus
24:17   69
Numbers
24:17   148

Targum Jonathan (Prophets)
Isaiah
11:1–6   148
11:11–12   148
28:18   96
40:9   152
47:11   96
52:7   152
53   149
Hosea
2:2   148
3:5   148
Micah
5:1   148
Zechariah
12:10   149

Jewish Prayers
Kaddish   153

CHRISTIAN LITERATURE

Acts of Peter
1:1–3   230

Augustine

Letters
28.2   284
71.2–4   284
82.5   284

1 Clement
5:5–6   230

Didache
8:1   284
8:2   284
8:3   185, 284

Didascalia Apostolorum
21   284

Epistle of Barnabas
1:7   283
2:4–10   285
3   284
4:6–8   283
5:3   283
5:6   283
5:8   283
7–8   285
9:4–6   282
9:4   285
9:7–9   283
10:9   282
11   283
13   283
14:1–4   283
15   285
16:1–4   285

Epistle to Diognetus
1:1   285
3:1   285
3:3–5   285
4:1–6   285

Eusebius

Chronicle
Hadrian Year 17   285

Demonstration of the Gospel
3.2   188

Ecclesiastical History
3.5.3   276
6.16   284

Gospel of Peter
8.29   267

Hippolytus

Refutation of All Heresies
9.27.1   259

Ignatius

Magnesians
9:1   285
10:1   285

Jerome

De viris illustribus
54   284

John Chrysostom

Against the Jews
285

Justin Martyr

First Apology
31.5–6   285
31.6   277, 298

Dialogue with Trypho
1.32   158
10   284
19–23   284
24   285
43.3–8   283
46–47   241
46   284

47.1   285
47.2   285
66.2–4   283
67.1   283
68   283
68.6–8   283
71.3   283
72–73   283
74   283
77   283
84   283
89.1   286
90.1   286
108   267

Tertullian

Against the Jews
13   198

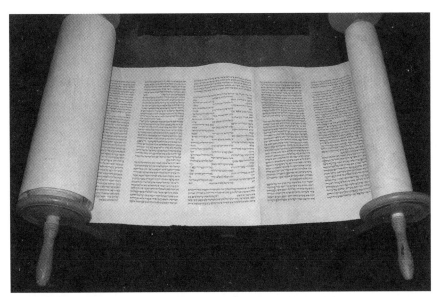

Figure 1: Torah Scroll. A sixteenth-century Torah Scroll from Yemen. Photo © The Dunham Bible Museum of Houston Baptist University and is used by permission.

Figure 2: Exodus Scroll. A damaged Hebrew scroll of Exodus recovered from the Ben Ezra Cairo Synagogue genizah (twelfth century). Photo © The Dunham Bible Museum of Houston Baptist University and is used by permission.

Figure 3: Ancient Ceramic Inscribed Tablet. In the Ancient Near East important records were impressed on clay tablets, which were then baked and turned into ceramic. The cuneiform tablet pictured here contains records, written in Sumerian, of food given to or received from various individuals. The tablet is very old, dating to 2500–2350 BCE, a time well before the great patriarch Abraham. Photo © The Dunham Bible Museum of Houston Baptist University and is used by permission.

Figure 4: Western Wall. Men praying at the Western Wall (or "Wailing Wall").

Figure 5: Shiloh Excavation. Ongoing archaeological work at Shiloh, led by Scott Stripling, may have uncovered the location of the tabernacle storerooms used in the eleventh century BCE. Photo © Scott Stripling and is used by permission.

Figure 6: Mount of Olives. The Temple Mount, with the Dome of the Rock, as seen from the Mount of Olives. Photo © Lee McDonald and is used by permission.

Figure 7: Temple Steps. Partly restored, these steps at the south end of the Temple Mount date back to the time of Jesus and his disciples.

Figure 8: Magdala Synagogue. The ruins of first-century Magdala, the village of Mary Magdalene, were only recently discovered. They contain a synagogue with mosaic floors and a decorated stone, whose symbols were meant to recall the Temple in Jerusalem.

Figure 9: Western Wall and Temple Mount. The Western Wall (or "Wailing Wall"). Men pray on the left side, women on the right. Photo © Eitan Bar and is used by permission.

Figure 10: Pool of Siloam. In 2004 the Pool of Siloam, mentioned in John 9:7, was located south of the Temple Mount by archaeologist Eli Shukron.

Figure 11: Scythopolis. One of the several Hellenistic (Greek) cities of the Decapolis (lit., "Ten Cities"), most of which were located on the east side of the Jordan River. Located on the west side of the river, Scythopolis occupies the site of ancient Beth Shean. Archaeologists are reconstructing Scythopolis and excavating the nearby tell.

Figure 12: Chorazin Synagogue. The fourth-century synagogue of Chorazin; the remains of the first-century synagogue can no longer be located.

Figure 13: Capernaum Synagogue. The remains of this fourth-century synagogue at Capernaum, on the northwest shore of the Sea of Galilee, probably rest on the foundation of the synagogue that stood in the time of Jesus and his disciples.

Figure 14: Capernaum Synagogue Interior. Inside the fourth-century synagogue at Capernaum.

Figure 15: Gamala Miqveh. This miqveh, or ritual bathing pool, is adjacent to the synagogue at Gamala.

Figure 16: Magdala Miqvoth. Across the street from the synagogue at Magdala are several miqvoth, or stepped ritual baths, as depicted here. These miqvoth were fed by natural springs.

Figure 17: Divided Miqveh Steps. A number of miqvoth, or ritual baths, are located near the Temple Mount. Some of them have dividers that help separate those who descend from those who ascend after immersing themselves. This miqveh is located near the southwest corner of the Temple Mount. Photo © Lee McDonald and is used by permission.

Figure 18: Seat of Moses. Inside the fourth-century synagogue of Chorazin is a replica of the "seat of Moses," on which the rabbi or teacher sat. The original seat, also made of volcanic basalt, is in the Israel Museum in Jerusalem.

Figure 19: Gamala Synagogue. The remains of the first-century synagogue at Gamala, in the Golan Heights, destroyed by the Romans in 67 CE. The interior pillars and bench seating around the walls are typical of early synagogues.

Figure 20: Qumran Ruins. The ruins of Qumran, near some of the caves where the famous Dead Sea Scrolls were found in the 1940s and 1950s. The compound at Qumran, which was occupied from about 120 BCE to its destruction by the Romans in either 68 or 73 CE, may have housed about one hundred men. Photo © Lee McDonald and is used by permission.

Figure 21: Cave 4. Qumran's Cave 4, close to the ruins, contained some six hundred scrolls, including Scripture, apocrypha and pseudepigrapha, commentaries on Scripture, works on prayer and worship, and a number of other works.

Figure 22: Decorated Oil Lamp. Thousands of ancient oil lamps have been recovered in Israel. Many, like the one pictured here, are decorated. Black soot can still be seen on most of these ceramic lamps. Photo © The Dunham Bible Museum of Houston Baptist University and is used by permission.

Figure 23: Oil Lamp. Not all lamps are decorated. Many, like the one pictured here, are plain. It would have been understood that the young women in Jesus' parable of the wise and foolish maidens (Matt 25:1–13) held lamps like these. Photo © The Dunham Bible Museum of Houston Baptist University and is used by permission.

Figure 24: Tomb at Beth Shearim. The Galilean city of Beth Shearim contains dozens of tombs dating from the second to fifth centuries, including what might be the tomb of Rabbi Judah the Prince (pictured here), who oversaw the editing and completion of the Mishnah, an early and important assemblage of Jewish oral law that interpreted and extended the Law of Moses.

Figure 25: Kidron Valley. The Kidron Valley, which separates the Mount of Olives and the Temple Mount, is adorned with several monumental tombs, such as the Tomb of Absalom.

Figure 26: Ossuaries. Several ossuaries, or bone boxes, such as these at Dominus Flevit, can be seen in tombs on the Mount of Olives.

Figure 27: Herod Family Tomb. Perhaps the tomb of the family of Herod the Great. One will note the large round stone that served as the door.

Figure 28: Turya Tomb. There are several rock tombs near the village of Nazareth, where Jesus grew up. This tomb is in the village of Turya. Inside are niches, which in some cases still contain human bones.